MINORITY REPORT

Mennonite Identities in Imperial Russia and Soviet Ukraine Reconsidered, 1789–1945

Minority Report

Mennonite Identities in Imperial Russia and Soviet Ukraine Reconsidered, 1789–1945

EDITED BY LEONARD G. FRIESEN

UNIVERSITY OF TORONTO PRESS
Toronto Buffalo London

Toronto Buffalo London
www.utorontopress.com

ISBN 978-1-4875-0194-5

Tsarist and Soviet Mennonite Studies

Library and Archives Canada Cataloguing in Publication

Minority report
Minority report : Mennonite identities in imperial Russia and Soviet Ukraine reconsidered, 1789–1945 / edited by Leonard G. Friesen.

(Tsarist and Soviet Mennonite studies)
Includes bibliographical references and index.
ISBN 978-1-4875-0194-5 (cloth)

1. Mennonites – Soviet Union – History. 2. Ukrainians – Soviet Union – History. I. Friesen, Leonard George, 1956–, editor II. Title. III. Series: Tsarist and Soviet Mennonite studies

DK34.M39M56 2018 289.7'47 C2017-904296-3

University of Toronto Press acknowledges the financial assistance to its publishing program of the Canada Council for the Arts and the Ontario Arts Council, an agency of the Government of Ontario.

Canada Council for the Arts
Conseil des Arts du Canada

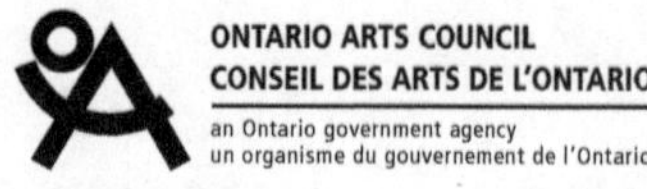

Funded by the Government of Canada
Financé par le gouvernement du Canada
Canada

To Harvey Dyck

Contents

Acknowledgments ix

A Note on Transliteration and Nomenclature xi

Introduction 3
LEONARD G. FRIESEN

Part One: Overviews: New Approaches to Mennonite History

1 "Land of Opportunity, Sites of Devastation": Notes on the History of the Borozenko Daughter Colony 25
SVETLANA BOBYLEVA

2 Afforestation as Performance Art: Johann Cornies' Aesthetics of Civilization 61
JOHN R. STAPLES

Part Two: Imperial Mennonite Isolationism Revisited

3 Mennonite Schools and the Russian Empire: The Transformation of Church-State Relations in Education, 1789–1917 85
IRINA (JANZEN) CHERKAZIANOVA

4 A Foreign Faith but of What Sort? The Mennonite Church and the Russian Empire, 1789–1917 110
OKSANA BEZNOSOVA

5 Mennonite Entrepreneurs and Russian Nationalists in the Russian Empire, 1830–1917 142
NATALIYA VENGER

Part Three: Mennonite Identities in Diaspora

6 Mennonite Identities in a New Land: Abraham A. Friesen and the Russian Mennonite Migration of the 1920s 181
JOHN B. TOEWS

Part Four: Mennonite Identities in the Soviet Cauldron

7 Collectivizing the *Mutter Ansiedlungen*: The Role of Mennonites in Organizing Kolkhozy in the Khortytsia and Molochansk German National Districts in Ukraine in the Late 1920s and Early 1930s 211
COLIN P. NEUFELDT

8 Kulak, Christian, and German: Ukrainian Mennonite Identities in a Time of Famine, 1932–1935 260
ALEXANDER BEZNOSOV

9 Caught between Two Poles: Ukrainian Mennonites and the Trauma of the Second World War 287
VIKTOR K. KLETS

Appendix: Dnipropetrovsk State University, Khortitsa '99, *and the Renaissance of Public (Mennonite) History in Ukraine* 319
LEONARD G. FRIESEN

List of Contributors 333

Index 335

Acknowledgments

I have been privileged to work on this manuscript with a cohort of fine historians from Russia, Ukraine, the United States, and Canada. I wish in particular to thank John Staples and Nataliya Venger for their wise counsel and steadfast encouragement throughout this project. Richard Ratzlaff, Acquisitions Editor extraordinaire, warrants special mention for his strong support from the outset, and for being gently but steadfastly demanding as the manuscript went through various revisions. I thank him and the many others at the press who helped prepare *Minority Report* for publication. In the end, it is all the stronger for their efforts, and all of contributors are honoured to have this collection published by the University of Toronto Press.

Jane Buckingham provided a first translation for versions of several chapters that were originally submitted in the Russian language, and I thank her. I, however, take full responsibility for the final shape of all translations, especially given the manner in which I worked with the respective historians on how best to communicate their findings to English-language readers. Chapters 1, 3–5, 8, and 9 were all submitted in Russian and subsequently translated.

Thanks also to Serhii Plokhy. The Appendix of this volume lays out the vital role that he played in cultivating the rigorous academic engagement of Ukraine's minorities by Ukrainian historians. What must be said about Serhii however, is that as prodigious as his scholarship has been, even it is no match for the warmth of his personality and the generosity of his person.

I first came across Harvey Dyck's name when I read a beautifully evocative article he had written for *Mennonite Life*. I was finishing my fourth undergraduate year of study at the time and had set my sights on graduate studies in Russian history. I eventually chose the University of Toronto for that next chapter – or rather it accepted me into its ranks in the fall of 1980. Harvey was the first academic to welcome me there, and he later served as my doctoral *nauchnii rukovoditel'*. I learned a great deal about the art of teaching from Harvey in addition to what he taught me about research and writing, though his influence in time extended well beyond merely academic achievements. Even so, nothing quite prepared me for the way that colleagues and "ordinary citizens" in Ukraine spoke about him during my visit to Dnipropetrovsk and Zaporizhzhia in 2011. He was, quite simply, highly esteemed in their memories. I could say more, but to do so would take away from the work itself and its concluding Appendix. In short, then, and on behalf of all contributors, this work is dedicated to you, Harvey, for a life well lived and a job well done.

A Note on Transliteration and Nomenclature

Questions of translation and transliteration bedevil any work written in English that uses Ukrainian, Russian, English, and German language sources; especially one that is focused on a corner of the world known over the years as New Russia, southern Ukraine, Ukraine, and simply Russland. What is the best way to proceed in a setting where Dutch, Low German, High German, Ukrainian, and Russian have all played a role and where there are also forms that could best be described as "common practice" in English, such as "Alexander" over the more accurate "Aleksandr"? The following will inform this publication. In general, place names will follow the Russian forms for the imperial era and the Ukrainian form after 1917. This means that the mother Mennonite settlement will switch from Khortitsa to Khortytsia in 1917; Ekaterinoslav will become Katerynoslav, and so on. Some names (for example Alexander and Nicholas) will follow norms of common usage in English. I have also opted for the Russian transliteration of Molochna and Khortitsa over the Germanized versions of Molotschna and Chortitsa favoured by Mennonite memoirists, and Mennonites themselves. Even so, there will inevitably be an eclectic nature to such matters and I fear that some politicized sensitivities may be strained. I ask the reader's forbearance. Indeed, this very complexity reflects the richly diverse and dynamic socio-political and cultural milieu into which "Russian" Mennonites entered southern Ukraine in 1789 and after.

It has been a particular challenge to know how to refer to the university in Ukraine which generated many of the chapters in this collection. Its short form in the 1990s and earlier could best be translated as "Dnipropetrovsk State University." In 2000 it was renamed "Dnipropetrovsk National University," and as this publication moved to press it was anticipated that the name would soon change to "Dnipro National University" (the city of Dnipropetrovsk was officially renamed Dnipro in May, 2016). I have attempted to be historically accurate in all instances, and not to anticipate future likelihoods.

MINORITY REPORT

Introduction

LEONARD G. FRIESEN

This volume offers a bold and timely reassessment of Mennonites in Imperial Russia and the former Soviet Ukraine. It significantly enriches our understanding of minority relations in the history of the Black Sea littoral, an area of long-standing interest to Russia, while providing important insight into the history of Ukraine as a contemporary state. The historians included here debate how Mennonites interacted with the larger world around them, how those relations changed over time, and how those interactions in turn influenced Mennonites' self-perception and representation. As the contributors themselves acknowledge, both Mennonites and non-Mennonites began to debate these very issues as the first Mennonite colonists settled on the banks of the Dnipro River in 1789. Perhaps not surprisingly, opinions varied dramatically from the start. Some maintained that Mennonites were a pilgrim people remarkably unengaged with the larger society. Others declared that these Mennonites, themselves Dutch and German Christians who had emerged out of the Reformation as religious pacifists, were an integral part of that larger Slavic world despite their relatively discrete settlements.

The revolutionary upheavals of 1917 and after intensified the importance of this discussion. Many now concluded that Mennonites were largely responsible for the bloody fate that befell them given their hostility or indifference to, and isolation from, the world beyond their villages and estates, that they got what they deserved in the brutal civil war that followed.[1] One gets an early hint of this perspective in Abraham Friesen's ruminations, as described by John Toews in chapter 6 of this study. By 1921, Friesen had already concluded that Mennonites had focused too much on secondary matters in the imperial era, those ethno-cultural characteristics, such as their Germanness, which he believed only alienated them from the Russian state and people. At the same time, Mennonites had refused to recognize how their settlement in the Black Sea lands had displaced indigenous peoples. Abraham Friesen was therefore not surprised that Mennonites had been singled out in the horrors that unfolded after 1917.

With conclusions so briskly reached and judgments so sternly rendered, it is no wonder that the vital nineteenth-century debate about Mennonite identity and societal (dis)engagement ended abruptly in the cauldron of 1917. Ironically, contemporary Mennonite claims of Mennonite culpability in their revolutionary undoing mirrored those that Slavs had made of themselves centuries earlier when they concluded that the Mongol invasion of Kievan Rus after 1223 had also happened for their sins.[2] A similar historiographical consensus in the West now overwhelmed debate in the Mennonite case, one that Soviet historians happily reinforced with a class-based analysis that, for them, also culminated logically in the Mennonites' inevitable and revolutionary displacement. If the imperial era was about anything when it came to the Mennonites' "cognitive map,"[3] it appeared to have been about their wealth, privilege, and cultural isolationism, and the rather justifiable price they paid as a result.

Mennonite historians – both lay and professional – approached the Soviet era in similarly stark terms, only here Mennonites portrayed themselves as uniformly victimized by a monolithic Soviet state.[4] In this unremittingly bleak narrative the larger Soviet society faded away entirely after the horrors of revolution and civil war. Even as the Soviet state shifted from Stalin's time to Khrushchev's and on to Brezhnev's, it was always deemed external to the Mennonite world, and always hostile to it. No wonder the dominant historiographical discourse of the Soviet era became one of emigration as the story was overwhelmingly told as one of Mennonite escape and trans-settlement, all through the eyes of those who had "made it" to the West. Few bothered to critically examine Mennonite engagement with the Soviet state and its citizens.[5] Even fewer bothered to equip themselves linguistically to have the option of such engagement or to consider more nuanced understandings. Many Cold War-era Soviet and Russian historians further reinforced themes near and dear to Mennonite memoirists. This occurred as the broader historical community underscored the inevitability of the 1917 Russian revolution in light of gross inequities beforehand, the monolithic nature of the Soviet state, and the prison-like conditions under which most Soviet citizens were said to live. From that vantage point, how could Mennonites not have been responsible for the fate that inevitably befell them in 1917, and for their own dramatic undoing? And how could they have been anything other than victims of a totalitarian regime in the period thereafter in which Soviet society itself all but disappeared, including its distinctly Ukrainian, religious, or ethnic dimensions? In short, Mennonite identities from start to finish were neatly reduced to three which unfolded one after the other: first as perpetrators of economic injustice and cultural insensitivity; then as hapless victims of a totalitarian regime; and finally as international refugees or, in the words of a popular Mennonite hymn from that era, "Wehrlos und Verlassen" (*Defenceless and Abandoned*).

Taken on their own, these are powerful images and monikers. In the language of contemporary scholars, they point to important vehicles for "identity formation" or "identity markers" among Mennonites. In their simplest forms, these terms refer to the complex means by which we perceive who we are, and how we map out our relationship to imagined or real "conditions of existence."[6] Such a conception is vast enough to stretch from Charles Taylor's *Sources of the Self* and its exploration of individual identities and the quest for the modern authentic self, to "spatial perceptions" that include our relationships to our homes, nations, or the world beyond time and space itself.[7] Identity formation embraces the broadest definitions of culture associated with Clifford Geertz's "thick" culture. More recently, scholars such as Catherine Brace have paid particular attention to how the natural world has shaped our understandings of identity. Brace reminds us at the outset that landscapes are not passive, nor are we in our engagement and re-engagement with them.[8] Sergei Zhuk and Nataliya Venger have both argued persuasively that such an epistemological approach allows for a reconsideration of Ukrainian history, one that takes seriously the diversity of identities within and between the host of ethnicities and faiths found there. None of this is to say that the triptych-like depiction of Mennonites as perpetrators, victims, and refugees is off the mark when it comes to Mennonite identity formation.[9] It follows that a re-engagement of Mennonite historical identities is warranted in light of these new scholarly approaches and perspectives, and that that re-engagement will necessarily reshape how we understand the lands and polities in which they lived.

The ever-changing present can itself provide fresh opportunities for historians to reconsider the past. Nowhere has this been more evident than in the sea-change in Imperial Russian, Ukrainian, and Soviet historiography since the USSR's collapse in 1991. It is remarkable how dramatically historians have rewritten almost all aspects of Russian and Soviet Cold War-era history over the past several decades. Few now maintain in any serious way that the Bolshevik revolution of 1917 was inevitable. More persuasive is Wayne Dowler's conclusion that civil society was alive and well in Russia by 1913 as fears of revolutionary unrest receded, and as the empire's future looked bright.[10] Historians who engage the Russian revolution of 1917, such as Joshua Sanborn in his study of the militarization of the Russian nation, focus less on discontinuities than on the continuity that linked the later imperial and early Soviet periods.[11] If historians now hesitate to depict 1917 as a dramatic watershed, we see an even more remarkable and provocative transformation in how the Soviet era is now understood. To give a few examples, studies by Page Herrlinger on Russian Orthodoxy in the late imperial era and Heather J. Coleman's study of the Russian Baptists from 1905 to 1929 challenge positivist understandings that Imperial Russian and early Soviet society became less religious as it became more urban.[12] Tracy McDonald's study of the Soviet countryside during the 1920s questions the ease with which we previously identified the Soviet state as a discrete, alien, and totalitarian behemoth that overwhelmed peasant society. For McDonald, the arm of the Soviet state in the countryside was often indistinguishable from other village institutions, in part because the same peasants often sat on both Soviet and village committees. McDonald's work links directly with Stephen Kotkin's now classic depiction of Magnitogorsk, and of how both centre and periphery shaped Stalinism as a civilization. Kotkin also demonstrates the degree to which Soviet citizens learned to "speak Bolshevik" so as to realize whatever gains they could and thereby exercise a modicum of control over the process. Terry Martin has unraveled the many threads that comprised Soviet policy to its myriad ethnic minorities, from Ukrainians to Tatars and beyond, and has offered new insights into Ukraine's terror-famine of 1933. Last, Jochen Hellbeck has gone one step further with his contention that many Soviet citizens worked hard to internalize the progressive worldview proclaimed by Soviet authorities in the 1930s. He concludes that countless Soviet citizens wanted to "speak Bolshevik" in Stalin's time.[13]

As Martin's study suggests, historiographical shifts have been no less evident in Ukraine, where historian Serhii Plokhy stands out. Plokhy's prodigious scholarship has dealt with richly diverse topics in

Ukrainian history, from the vital role played by Ukrainian Cossacks in the formation of contemporary Ukrainian identities to the role played by Ukraine in the collapse of the Soviet Union itself.[14] Two of his works deserve comment for the purposes of this volume: in *The Origins of the Slavic Nations*,[15] Plokhy challenges those who argue that the earliest Slavic history is best understood in unified terms that culminated in only three distinct identities: those of modern Russia, Ukraine, and Belarus. Instead, Plokhy points to multiple trajectories as evidenced by the title's emphasis on Slavic nations, and even then he is at great pains to distinguish Russia's historical development from that of modern-day Ukraine and Belarus.[16] In particular, Plokhy contrasts a more monolithic approach to Slavic identity that developed over many centuries in Russia from one that was ethnically and culturally diverse within modern-day Ukraine. For Plokhy, it was the Mongol influence on Moscow's identity formation that was pivotal because it led Russians to formulate their identity over time as imperial in design. By contrast, identity formation in Ukraine was always less cohesive, less exclusive, and more given to localized identities.[17] A similar, celebrative approach to Ukraine's ethnic diversity is evident in Paul Robert Magocsi's *A History of Ukraine*. Magocsi makes plain his appreciation for Ukraine's considerable ethnic and cultural diversity with the added subtitle *The Land and Its Peoples* in the recent second edition.[18] In the preface to his first edition, Magocsi wrote of his intent to

> give judicious treatment of the many other peoples who developed within the borders of Ukraine, including Greeks, Crimean Tatars, Poles, Russians, Germans, Jews, Mennonites, and Romanians. Only through an understanding of all of their cultures can one hope to gain an adequate introduction to Ukrainian history. In other words, this book is not simply a history of ethnic Ukrainians, but a survey of a wide variety of developments that have taken place during the past two and a half millennia among all peoples living on territory encompassed by the boundaries of the contemporary state of Ukraine.[19]

Plokhy continued to develop this same argument of Ukraine's relative uniqueness in *Ukraine and Russia: Representations of the Past*.[20] "Where does Russian history end and Ukrainian history begin?" he asks at the start of his introduction. Plokhy skilfully interrogates the historiographical debate on this question as it emerged after the collapse of the Soviet Union, Ukraine's sudden independence, and its urgent need to understand itself historically. Nor has Plokhy limited his investigation to top-down approaches on the origins of modern Ukraine. In the chapter entitled "People's History," for example, Plokhy attempts nothing less than to write "the history of the transformation of cultural and national identities in southern Ukraine."[21] The region was, in Plokhy's words, "a bone of contention between two national projects" in the second half of the nineteenth century: one that was "Great Russian" in scope and another that was "the Ukrainian project."[22] Contemporary observers were not always able to distinguish between the two given the coexistence of Russian and Ukrainian peasant villages in a region where some villages themselves were divided into Russian and Ukrainian halves.[23] Based upon his investigation of southern Ukrainian peasant accounts from the First World War, Plokhy concludes that by 1914 regional and even more localized identities had superseded ethnic divisions within Ukraine. This allowed peasants to maintain a strong regional identity while coincidentally continuing to regard the Imperial Russian state as motherland (*rodina*).[24] Though the revolutionary upheavals that unfolded after 1917 deeply politicized Ukrainian and Russian (Moscow-based) identities, Plokhy suggests that the peasants of southern Ukraine retained a staunchly village-centred identity that was simultaneously distinctly regional in scope. In the end, Plokhy concludes that it was this ability to combine aspects of Ukrainian and Russian cultural identity that gave southern Ukrainians a unique cultural identity, one that endured throughout and beyond the collapse of the Soviet Union.[25]

Plokhy's scholarly outpouring on Ukrainian history has coincided with that of a generation of Ukrainian scholars who emerged in the aftermath of the Soviet Union's collapse in 1991; nor should this surprise, as the grand Soviet narrative thereafter gave way to scholarly interest in the nationally and regionally particular. As will be clear from the appendix to this volume, Plokhy's role in this scholarly shift was vital, especially during his years at Dnipropetrovsk State University when he mentored a generation of young scholars whose findings comprise the bulk of this present study. These historians were themselves part of a historiographical shift as unprecedented scholarly access to regional archives allowed for focused regional histories that were freed from erstwhile ideological constraints. Among these new avenues of historical inquiry, for our purposes, there was a pronounced increase in the scholarly investigation of minorities, including Germans and Mennonites.[26] Irina (Janzen) Cherkazianova has contrasted the proliferation of such scholarship after 1990 with the relatively minuscule number of doctoral investigations of the Soviet Union's Germans and Mennonites that had been undertaken from the 1920s to the 1980s.[27]

The post-Soviet interest in Mennonite history initially went in two distinct directions: on the one hand, German scholar Detlef Brandes produced a pioneering work on the "German colonists" of New Russia and Bessarabia in 1993, followed by his student Dmytro Myeshkov's study of the Black Sea Germans, published in 2008.[28] Both scholars placed Mennonites within a larger Germanic world that itself had been regionally situated within the Black Sea lands of southern Ukraine. And though both used Russian archives, Myeshkov's investigation of regional archives found in Crimea, Odessa, Kherson, and Dnipropetrovsk revealed how an independent Ukraine had made regional archival collections more accessible. A similar approach whereby Mennonites were included in a pan-Germanic approach can be seen in Tiuliuliukin's recent study of Germans in the Siberian region of Orenburg.[29] Other scholars, by contrast, have eschewed pan-Germanic approaches and focused instead on Mennonites as a discrete entity with their own distinct cultural map. Interestingly, these studies have also tended to be regionally focused, as in a recent academic conference held on Mennonites in Siberia. Similarly, T.P. Nazarova has investigated how the international Mennonite community responded to the famine of 1921 in the trans-Volga and into Siberia.[30] Yet the connection with Siberia's Germans has not been entirely absent when historians focus on the Mennonites' distinct identity. For example, the collection of articles on Mennonites in Siberia contained in the 2012 issue of the *Journal of Mennonite Studies* was from a Germans of Siberia: History and Culture Conference held at F.M. Dostoevsky Omsk State University in June of 2010. Papers dedicated to Mennonite history comprised one of the conference's four main sub-sections, this one entitled "History and Culture of Mennonites: Issues in the Study of Ethno-Confessional Groups."[31]

The recent scholarship has raised as many questions as it has answers. For example, Petr Wiebe's contribution to the 2010 conference focused exclusively on Mennonites in his survey of Mennonites in Siberia from the late nineteenth to the early twentieth centuries. Germans only appear at the very end, and suddenly, as if the distinction between Mennonites and Germans was somehow obliterated in the Stalinist cauldron of collectivization and industrialization.[32] Does this mean that Wiebe sees Mennonites as distinct from Soviet Germans? Likely not, as Wiebe's rich scholarship has often dealt with Mennonite history in the context of Soviet German history. Yet even here questions arise. For example, in his larger study of "The German Colonies of Siberia," Wiebe identifies three distinct groups of Germans: Lutherans, Catholics, and Mennonites. But almost immediately he declares that Mennonites were a special case because they originated in the Netherlands in the sixteenth century under the lead of Menno Simons. Somewhat later he declares that they lived in the environs of Danzig in Prussia, by which time they had attracted followers from the Netherlands and North-West Germany. Wiebe tells us that Mennonites were distinguished from the other colonists (including, presumably, German colonists) by their religion, way of life, language, and level of cultural and economic sophistication.[33] Wiebe's own introduction, at the very least, raises questions about the Germanness of these predominantly Dutch sectarians, yet what is striking is how his entire manuscript thereafter does not interrogate the means by which these Mennonites became inseparably German along the way. Was that their evaluation and if so, when and why? Was it also or only the state's (imperial and/or Soviet) evaluation, and either way, upon what basis was their Germanness determined and how did those evaluations change over time? We are not told, though the absence of any reference to Mennonites in either the book's title or its conclusion suggests that the transformation is complete.

Several of the chapters found in this study interrogate the complexities of cultural belonging and identity that are glossed over in Wiebe's study. Taken together, they suggest that Mennonites do appear to become Germanic over the course of the nineteenth and early twentieth century, but never in a way that erased all cultural markers with non-acculturated Germans. Moreover, ethnicity was only one of many fluid identity-markers that Mennonites, their non-Mennonite neighbours, imperial and Soviet officials, and even invading armies used in the attempt to understand who these followers of Menno Simons actually were. At the same time, the conclusions reached in this study are similar to those raised by Faith Hillis in her strong investigation of south-west Ukraine in the imperial era. For Hillis, this region – known as Little Russia – was never merely the breeding ground for anti-Russian Ukrainian nationalists. It played a vital role as a laboratory after the rise of Polish nationalism where Russian nationalists could articulate a vision of the empire's Russianness that was most compelling on the empire's borderlands. Hillis concludes that Russian and Ukrainian nationalists both competed across the region by 1905 as both opponents and proponents of the regime flourished.[34] If all that was true for south-west Ukraine, how much more did it apply to the Black Sea littoral, a region known both as southern Ukraine and New Russia? This question is especially timely given the deadly contestation of this region by both Ukraine and Russia in the first decades of the twenty-first century. Several conclusions follow in the chapters that follow. For one, although Plokhy suggests that it is Ukraine's very historic diversity that is a mark of its statecraft, it seems equally clear that Mennonites were not engaged with any Ukrainian polity for much of their history. St Petersburg mattered ultimately in their civil deliberations in the imperial era, as did Moscow after 1918. Sadly, the Mennonite voice in today's geopolitical debate can only be conjectured given that few remained in the Black Sea steppe after the turmoil of the 1930s and 1940s.

One other historian's body of work deserves special comment given the overwhelming focus of this volume on Mennonites in southern Ukraine. Sergei Zhuk, also formerly a historian at Dnipropetrovsk State University, has written widely on the pivotal role southern Ukraine played in challenging Imperial Russian notions of cultural identity in the late nineteenth century. This happened when large numbers of Russian and Ukrainian peasants abandoned Orthodoxy in favour of "Stundism" – one of the largest Protestant sects found in the empire. By 1900, worried governors in the south had warned St Petersburg that up to three-quarters of their peasants had abandoned Orthodoxy for Stundism.[35] Even if fears of such dramatic sectarian growth cannot be fully substantiated, there is enough here to warrant Zhuk's claims that nothing less than Russia's "Lost Reformation" unfolded in southern Ukraine during the nineteenth century.[36] It happened there, Zhuk argues, because the southern Ukrainian provinces were remarkably diverse, and "filled with such various cultural groups as Ukrainian Cossacks, Ukrainian and Russian peasants, German colonists, Mennonites, Jews, and non-Orthodox peasant sectarians," which made possible numerous cross-cultural encounters.[37]

Zhuk's investigations and conclusions open up several important areas of inquiry while raising questions about both Ukraine's and Mennonite identify formation in the nineteenth century and beyond. His successful linkage of Germans and Mennonites with peasant sectarians challenges previous narratives about Mennonite cultural isolationism. Zhuk opens new doors of inquiry when he links colonist piety and their missionizing impulse to peasant religious protestations against Orthodoxy. His conclusions account for why Imperial bureaucrats became increasingly intolerant of Mennonites and Germans in the decades before 1914 in a way that buttresses recent work by Paul Werth on the limits of religious freedom in Imperial Russia, and Nicholas Breyfogle's study of Orthodox religious sectarians and the colonization of the southern Caucasus region.[38]

In sum, historians have utterly re-thought and re-written our understanding of late Imperial Russian, Ukrainian, and Soviet history, and every one of these studies raises probing questions about how we understand the Mennonite experience on the Black Sea littoral. How, for example, can one still depict Mennonites as responsible for the fate that inevitably befell them in Imperial Russia if the collapse of the empire as late as 1913 is no longer deemed inevitable? What new Mennonite identities might we now discover for the imperial era, and what questions might they raise for the history of southern Ukraine as a whole? Might an investigation of Mennonite history provide us with new insights into the distinctive nature of (south) Ukrainian or Imperial Russia history, or even of the Soviet period? Indeed, how are we to regard Mennonite relations with the Soviet state in light of McDonald's findings? Might we finally be able to expand the Mennonite narrative in the Soviet era beyond that of victimization, while still accepting the harsh reality that tens of thousands of Mennonites perished in a "path of thorns" during the Stalinist era?[39] Without denying a single death, is it possible that some Mennonites also learned how to "speak Bolshevik"? Were there others who were drawn to socialism even as they may have been disaffected with the Mennonite church? And have Mennonite scholars adequately mined the vast source materials now available in Russian and Ukrainian archives to even engage in these questions?

Fortunately, there are clear indications that our understanding of Mennonite identities throughout this entire history has begun to shift. We see it in the careful archival work that John Staples has undertaken, by which we are now able to interrogate how Molochna Mennonites understood themselves in relation to their Tatar, Russian, and Ukrainian neighbours of the great steppe regions of southern Ukraine. It is worth noting that more than a decade ago John Staples had already called for an end to a Mennonite history whose tone was primarily moralistic and condemnatory. As he previously concluded: "Mennonites were neither isolated from surrounding populations, nor simply paternalistic benefactors to backward neighbours."[40] In a similar vein, English historian David Moon has used new insights and perspectives to place the Mennonite experience at the centre of developments that unfolded in Imperial Russia's grasslands, not at its periphery.[41] Aileen Friesen has demonstrated how important the records of Imperial Russia's Ministry of Spiritual Affairs are for those who want to understand Mennonite relations in Siberia with state and society in 1900.[42] Last, Colin Neufeldt has begun to make similar inroads for the Soviet era with his use of newly available sources and perspectives to argue that Mennonites were agents of the state as much as they were its victims.[43]

If moralistic and stereotypic depictions are no longer tenable, it is in large part because of the methodical work that contemporary Russian and Ukrainian scholars have undertaken in conjunction with path-breaking scholars in the West. The story of how this very rich scholarship emerged in Ukraine especially over the last years of the twentieth century is itself worth telling. It is included here as an appendix to the main body of work, and concerns a remarkable moment in time when senior Canadian historian Harvey L. Dyck encountered a nascent Ukrainian scholarly community that had begun to explore the religio-ethnic diversities of its own heartland. The story of that dramatic encounter is included here because – without it – neither this volume nor the rich diversity of perspectives included within it would have been possible.

This volume, then, is a celebration of a scholarly community on the Mennonite experience that now stretches from East to West and the new insights it has been able to realize. Taken as a whole, it challenges a previous historiography that has relied heavily on Cold War perspectives and overwhelmingly in-house sources, a world where memoirists have often led the way. Unfortunately, many who had previously reconstructed the Mennonite narrative from solely Germanic sources have themselves been unable to engage with Russian and Ukrainian scholars – including those found here – whose works have been unavailable in English. For that reason alone the present volume makes accessible a particular scholarship that really does inform the whole of our historical understanding. It brings to light unprecedented approaches, interpretations, and sources, and it does so in conversation with correspondingly strong scholars from the West.

We begin with two dramatically different works that provide the reader with fresh approaches to Mennonite history, starting with Svetlana Bobyleva's micro-history of the Borozenko daughter colony, founded in 1865–6. Bobyleva's prose is reflective from the start as she intimately connects the history of this settlement with events that unfolded in the larger empire. This senior Ukrainian historian is the most inclined to bring the region itself into the Mennonite story and as a part of their identity. In that sense alone her work suggests something of David Moon's recent environmental history of Imperial Russia.[44] There are rich insights in this chapter from the interview projects of Mennonites and Ukrainians alike that the Ukrainian-German Institute of Dnipropetrovsk State University has undertaken to such strong effect.[45] Through Bobyleva's careful mining of a wide range of sources we get a particularly nuanced understanding of how Mennonites shifted from ethnically homogenous villages in the Imperial era to Soviet realities when Germans, Ukrainians, and others came to reside there. What is perhaps most remarkable about her study is how she interrogates Mennonite identities during the greatest of traumas, from the First World War and revolution to collectivization and the Second World War, especially in light of the recent historiography on Nestor Makhno. By taking us from the imperial era to the events associated with High Stalinism, Bobyleva's work anticipates the works that follow.

John Staples's study is more narrowly focused in two ways, yet its import is no less significant. Staples has chosen to investigate a single life, that of the Mennonite servitor Johann Cornies, and then only for a decade or two of his life. But such a twofold focus allows Staples to interrogate a long-held truism of imperial Russian Mennonite history since James Urry expounded it in the late 1980s:[46] that Cornies was deemed the lynchpin by which Mennonites "modernized" in the course of the nineteenth century, a trend by which they melded into coincidental trends across Europe.[47] It was a world where, after Cornies, Mennonite ministers mattered less than mayors, and Mennonite politics and economics always trumped Mennonite faith. John Staples invites us to reconsider this positivist interpretation of Mennonite history. In particular, he suggests that Cornies was less a secularizer than he was a pietist. As such, he remained an explicitly Christian voice of reform. The issue for Staples is less about a conflict between the religious and the secular (in which the latter is seen as triumphant after the mid-nineteenth century) than it is between competing forms of religiosity within a modernizing empire. If correct, Staples's case study is consistent with more recent historiography on the persistence of religious faith and identities well into the twentieth century. His work, at the very least, leads directly to the new approaches that follow it, Beznosova's above all.

We see the impact of new approaches from a new generation of Russian and Ukrainian scholars in the three chapters that follow, all of which provide broad thematic and conceptual overviews of the Imperial Russian Mennonite experience. First in this cycle, Irina (Janzen) Cherkazianova critically engages Mennonite education and state educational policy in the

Imperial period in chapter 3 with an eye on the larger issue of church-state relations. In chapter 4, Oksana Beznosova investigates Mennonite church life as seen through the eyes of Tsarist officials from 1789 to 1917; Nataliya Venger's overview of Mennonite entrepreneurship for much of the same period follows in chapter 5. All three of these chapters demonstrate that Mennonites were not isolated from the larger workings of the empire even when contemporaries may have imagined that they were. All three scholars also challenge the classical bifurcation of Mennonite history into the Imperial good and the Soviet bad through their careful analysis of the late Imperial era. There are also important differences in how each depicts the making of the Mennonite identity in the imperial era. Cherkazianova and Beznosova pay careful attention to how increased religious divisions among Mennonites after 1850 led to the politicization of Mennonite society. Mennonite civil officials brought cohesiveness to Mennonite society in late Imperial Russia then, in a way that coincided with the famed colonist reforms introduced by St Petersburg in the 1870s. At the same time, Cherkazianova believes that the effect of anti-colonist legislation on Mennonites may have been exaggerated by previous historians. She points to archival records that suggest that few of these measures were ever enforced because provincial authorities knew that Mennonites were deeply loyal to the empire. Alone among present scholars, Cherkazianova identifies Mennonites as a "little homeland" by 1900, by their own reckoning at least, whereas Venger explores how both peasants and officials perceived Mennonite exclusiveness at the point of settlement.

Venger argues that Mennonites were actively and profitably involved in munitions productions during the First World War, without censure from their own communities. Venger points to increased socio-economic assimilation, which contrasts directly with Beznosova's claim that Russian officials were wary of the strong Mennonite commitment to pacifism during the First World War. Officials feared the Mennonites' anti-war position more than they did any sense of Mennonites as Germans, in part because of the example that Mennonites set for other would-be pacifists among Orthodox sectarians (for which she uses the recent work by Albert W. Wardin Jr on Mennonites, Baptists, and Ukrainians sectarianism).[48] Both Venger and Beznosova agree that Mennonites became more cohesive in the face of increasingly punitive legislation levelled against them by Tsarist officials after 1900, even as they point to a cohesiveness heading in very different directions.

Chapter 6, by John Toews, might appear out of place in a volume focused on southern Ukraine. Moreover, one would normally expect such an essay to be placed at the end so that the volume could end as expected, with the Mennonites somewhere else. The topic and placement of this important essay are, however, deliberate, in this case study of Mennonite identities in transition. John Toews looks at Abraham Friesen, an almost forgotten Mennonite leader who began his days in Imperial Russia but ended them in the western Canadian province of Saskatchewan. Toews demonstrates how Mennonites in the aftermath of catastrophic revolution and civil war continued to create and recreate their world and identities, even as they relentlessly reflected on the shattered worlds they had left behind. The chapter's placement also reminds us that the Mennonite story in southern Ukraine need not be told primarily through the lives of those who left in the 1920s, as thousands continued to hope for the best in what was then Soviet Ukraine.

The next two chapters are part of a piece. Both pertain to the period of Stalinist collectivization that shook the very foundations of Ukrainian society and erupted in a famine that left millions dead. So many questions arise from this episode alone: What can be said about the Mennonite experience of collectivization? Did some Mennonites serve the state as agents of Stalinist change – resulting in the death of countless other Mennonites – because they believed in the cause, or did they seek state positions in order to mitigate the state's power at the local level? And once famine hit, what can be said about the Mennonite experience of the famine as opposed to that of their Ukrainian neighbours? Thus, in chapter 7, Colin Neufeldt considers the role played by Mennonites in the Stalinist collectivization of the late 1920s and early 1930s. He demonstrates how not all Mennonites were victims of the murderous Stalinist regime, even if most certainly were, a rather mixed conclusion that, surprisingly, recent memoir literature has confirmed.[49] And Alexander Beznosov in chapter 8 presents a broad overview of Ukraine's Germans and Mennonites "in the grip of famine," from 1932 to 1935. His study is particularly valuable in demonstrating how Mennonite identities as kulaks shifted to national associations with Germany and Germanness being paramount, all within a year or two of Hitler's rise to power. We see from Beznosov's study how the purges emerged as naturally (and brutally) as they did, and how closely they were linked to collectivization. Neufeldt, it must be said, gives one hope, along with Staples, that Russian and Ukrainian scholars may yet find North American scholars who are able to work with a broad range of sources and perspectives to understand the whole of Mennonite history.

Our final chapter, written by historian Viktor Klets, is a thoughtful reflection of Mennonites in southern Ukraine during the Second World War. It serves as an appropriate endpoint for this volume because his chapter marks the chronological limit of our study. The Mennonite voice in Soviet Ukraine all but disappeared after 1945. But just as important, Klets's contribution encapsulates the difficulties attached to those who see a simplistic assessment of Mennonite identities in the Soviet era. To cite one instance from his work, there is no question that many Mennonites were loyal to the occupying German army during the Nazi occupation, just as it is equally clear that many other Mennonites were loyal servitors of the Soviet state before that. Klets goes further, and suggests that most Mennonites hedged their bets during the German occupation, unsure as they were of the outcome. Regardless of their own vacillating identities as seen from within, there is also evidence to suggest that Mennonites were caught between two poles during the occupation. Soviet officials had good reason to categorize Mennonites as Germans after 1917 and to view them with appropriate suspicion. Yet, ironically, Klets suggests that Mennonites were never quite German enough for the Nazi occupiers; there was always something alien about them. Caught between two vast states, Mennonites during the war were left with the most ambiguous of identity markers, but it was the one that fit best after more than a century and a half on the Black Sea littoral. In a way they had become as German as many officials had claimed, even as they had also been sovietized, though to say even that much is only to scratch the surface.

We begin with Svetlana Bobyleva and the Mennonites of the Borozenko daughter colony.

NOTES

1 For a recent portrayal of Mennonites as those who treated their peasant servants brutally, getting what they deserved in the end, see Doug Klassen, "Clean or Unclean? (What can we learn from Peter's vision?)," *Canadian Mennonite* 20, no. 1 (2015), http://www.canadianmennonite.org/stories/clean-or-unclean.

2 Serge A. Zenkovsky, ed., *Medieval Russia's Epics, Chronicles, and Tales*, 2nd ed. (New York: E.P. Dutton, 1974), 194ff.

3 "Cognitive mapping" refers to the diverse "cognitive or mental abilities that enable us to collect, organize, store, recall, and manipulate information about

the spatial environment." See Roger M. Downs and David Stea, *Maps in Minds: Reflections on Cognitive Mapping* (New York: Harper & Row, 1977), 6.

4 For portrayals of Mennonites and the Soviet state as mutually exclusive and hostile entities, see James Urry, *Mennonites, Politics, and Peoplehood: Europe – Russia – Canada, 1525–1980* (Winnipeg: University of Manitoba Press, 1980), 158; and Sarah Dyck, ed., *The Silence Echoes: Memoirs of Trauma and Tears* (Kitchener, ON: Pandora Press, 1997), preface.

5 For a noted exception, see Walter Sawatsky, *Soviet Evangelicals since World War II* (Newton, KS: Herald Press), 1981.

6 Frederic Jameson, "The Cultural Logic of Late Capitalism," in *Postmodernism, or The Cultural Logic of Late Capitalism* (Durham, NC: Duke University Press, 1992), 51.

7 Charles Taylor, *Sources of the Self: The Making of the Modern Identity* (Cambridge, MA: Harvard University Press, 1989); and Les Roberts, "Mapping Cultures: A Spatial Anthropology," in *Mapping Cultures: Place, Practice and Performance*, ed. Les Roberts (Houndmills: Palgrave MacMillan, 2012), 7.

8 Clifford Geertz, *The Interpretation of Culture: Selected Essays* (New York: Basic Books, 1973); and Catherine Brace, "Landscape and Identity," in *Studying Cultural Landscapes*, ed. Iain Robertson and Penny Richards (London: Arnold Publishers, 2003), 121.

9 Sergei Zhuk, "Making and Unmaking the 'Sacred Landscape' of Orthodox Russia – Identity Crisis and Religious Politics in the Ukrainian Provinces of the Late Russian Empire," in *Space, Place, and Power in Modern Russia: Essays in the New Spatial History*, ed. Mark Bassin, Christopher Ely, and Melissa Stockdale (DeKalb: Northern Illinois University Press, 2010), 209–11; and Natalya Venger, "Osobennosti formirovaniia mental'nykh kart 'naroda v puti,'" in *Eidos: Al'manakh teorii I Istorii Istoricheskoi nauki* (Kiev, 2013), 123–42.

10 Wayne Dowler, *Russia in 1913* (DeKalb: Northern Illinois University Press, 2010).

11 Joshua A. Sanborn, *Drafting the Russian Nation: Military Conscription, Total War, and Mass Politics, 1905–1925* (DeKalb: Northern Illinois University Press, 2011).

12 Page Herrlinger, *Working Souls: Russian Orthodoxy and Factory Labor in St. Petersburg 1881–1917* (Bloomington, IN: Slavica, 2007); and Heather J. Coleman, *Russian Baptists and Spiritual Revolution, 1905–1929* (Bloomington: Indiana University Press, 2005).

13 Tracy McDonald, *Face to the Village: The Riazan Countryside under Soviet Rule, 1921–1930* (Toronto: University of Toronto Press, 2011); Stephen Kotkin, *Magnetic Mountain: Stalinism as Civilization* (Berkeley: University

of California Press, 1997); Terry Martin, *The Affirmative Action Empire: Nations and Nationalism in the Soviet Union, 1923–1939* (Ithaca, NY: Cornell University Press, 2001); and Jochen Hellbeck, *Revolution on my Mind: Writing a Diary under Stalin* (Cambridge, MA: Harvard University Press, 2008).

14 Plokhy is a prodigious scholar. For the purposes of his chronological breadth alone, see Serhii Plokhy, *The Cossacks and Religion in Early Modern Ukraine* (Oxford: Oxford University Press, 2001); and Plokhy, *The Last Empire: The Final Days of the Soviet Union* (New York: Basic Books, 2014).

15 Serhii Plokhy, *The Origins of Slavic Nations: Premodern Identities in Russia, Ukraine and Belarus* (Cambridge: Cambridge University Press, 2006).

16 In one review, Subtelny calls this approach "a classic case of historiography adjusting to political change." See Subtelny's review in *The American Historical Review* 113, no. 1 (February 2008), 283–4.

17 Plokhy, *Origins of Slavic Nations*, see esp. 118–21, 360. More recently Plokhy has advanced the view that Ukraine's history has placed it at the "Gates of Europe," on the borderlands of diverse peoples and cultures. See Serhii Plokhy, *The Gates of Europe: A History of Ukraine* (New York: Basic Books, 2015), xix–xxii.

18 Paul Robert Magocsi, *A History of Ukraine: The Land and Its Peoples*, 2nd ed. (Toronto: University of Toronto Press, 2010).

19 Ibid., xxvi.

20 Serhii Plokhy, *Ukraine and Russia: Representations of the Past* (Toronto: University of Toronto Press, 2008).

21 Plokhy, *Ukraine and Russia*, 138.

22 Ibid.

23 Plokhy cites "Petropavlivka" as an example of a mixed-village; the one half was the Russian "Petrovka" and the other was the Ukrainian "Pavlivka" (ibid., 140).

24 Ibid., 141–2.

25 Ibid., esp. 147, 162.

26 T.P. Nazarova, "Agrotekhnicheskaia poomoshch Mennonite Central Committee v Rossii v period NEPa," in *Vestnik Volgogradskogo Gosudarstvennogo Universiteta* (2010, number 1), 35.

27 I.V. Cherkazianova, "Dissertatsionnye issledovania o Nemetskom naselenii SSSR (1920–1980gg.), in *Voprosy Germanskoi istorii* (Dnepropetrovsk, 2010), 127–42.

28 Detlef Brandes, *Von den Zaren adoptiert: Die deutschen Kolonisten und die Balkansiedler in Neurussland und Bessarabien 1751–1914* (Munich: R. Oldenbourg Verlag, 1993); and Dmytro Myeshkov, *Die*

Schwarzmeerdeutschen und ihre Welten 1781–1871 (Düsseldorf: Klartext, 2008).

29 On Mennonites in Orenburg, see E.F. Tiuliuliukin, *Rossiiskie Nemtsy v istorii Orenburzhia (konets XIX–nachalo XX v.)*, (Orenburg, 2001).

30 T.P. Nazarova, "Zarubezhnaia Mennonitskaia pomoshch golodaiushchemu naseleniiu Sovetskoi Rossii v 1920-e g.g." *Vestnik Tomskogo Gosudarstvennogo Universiteta* (No. 3, 2010) 72–9.

31 On Mennonites in Siberia, see the special issue of *Journal of Mennonite Studies*, Volume 30, 2012; and A.I. Savin, *Ėtnokonfessiia v sovetskom gosudarstve: mennonity Sibiri v 1920–1980-e gody* (Novosibirsk, 2006). On the background and context of the 2010 conference on Germans in Siberia, see Royden Loewen and Paul Toews, "Foreword," in *Journal of Mennonite Studies* (2012), 7–8.

32 Petr P. Wiebe, "The Mennonite Colonies of Siberia: From the Late Nineteenth to the Early Twentieth Century," in *Journal of Mennonite Studies* (2012), 33–4. Wiebe only refers to "Germans" in the final paragraph whereupon reference to Mennonites – the focus of the entire article – disappears entirely.

33 P.P. Vibe (Petr P. Wiebe), *Nemetskie kolonii v Sibiri: Sotsioal'no-economicheskii aspect* (Omsk: 2007), 7.

34 Faith Hillis, *Children of Rus': Right-Bank Ukraine and the Invention of a Russian Nation* (Ithaca, NY: Cornell University Press, 2013).

35 Sergei Zhuk, "In Search of the Millennium: The Convergence of Jews and Evangelical Christian Peasants in Late Imperial Russia," in Glenn Dynner, ed., *Holy Dissent: Jewish and Christian Mystics in Eastern Europe* (Detroit: Wayne State University Press, 2011), 337.

36 Sergei Zhuk, *Russia's Lost Reformation: Peasants, Millennialism, and Radical Sects in Southern Russia and Ukraine, 1830–1917* (Washington, DC: Woodrow Wilson Center Press, 2004).

37 Sergei Zhuk, "Making and Unmaking the 'Sacred Landscape' of Orthodox Russia. Identity Crisis and Religious Politics in the Ukrainian Provinces of the Late Russian Empire," in *Space, Place, and Power in Modern Russia: Essays in the New Spatial History*, ed. Mark Bassin, Christopher Ely and Melissa K. Stockdale (DeKalb: Northern Illinois University Press, 2010), 209.

38 Paul Werth, *The Tsar's Foreign Faiths: Toleration and the Fate of Religious Freedom in Imperial Russia* (Oxford: Oxford University Press, 2014); Paul Werth, *At the Margins of Orthodoxy: Mission, Governance, and Confessional Politics in Russia's Volga-Kama Region, 1827–1905* (Ithaca, NY: Cornell University Press, 2001); and Nicholas B. Breyfogle, *Heretics and Colonizers: Forging Russia's Empire in the South Caucasus* (Ithaca, NY: Cornell University Press, 2005).

39 Jacob A. Neufeld, *Path of Thorns: Soviet Mennonite Life under Communist and Nazi Rule*, ed. Harvey L. Dyck, trans. Harvey L. Dyck and Sarah Dyck (Toronto: University of Toronto Press, 2014).

40 John R. Staples, *Cross-Cultural Encounters on the Ukrainian Steppe: Settling the Molochna Basin, 1783–1861* (Toronto: University of Toronto Press, 2003), 172, 177. Cf. Leonard G. Friesen, *Rural Revolutions in Southern Ukraine: Peasants, Nobles, and Colonists, 1774–1905* (Cambridge, MA: HURI, 2008).

41 David Moon, *The Plough that Broke the Steppes: Agriculture and Environment on Russia's Grasslands, 1700–1914* (Oxford: Oxford University Press, 2013). See in particular how Moon begins his study (1).

42 Aileen Friesen, "The Case of a Siberian Sect: Mennonites and the Incomplete Transformation of Russia's Religious Structure," *Journal of Mennonite Studies* 30 (2012), 139–58.

43 Colin P. Neufeldt, "Separating the sheep from the goats: the role of Mennonites and non-Mennonites in the dekulakization of Khortitsa, Ukraine (1928–1930)," *Mennonite Quarterly Review* 83 (April 2009), 221–58.

44 Moon, *The Plough that Broke the Steppes.*

45 For an excellent example of the important insights gained by the Dnipropetrovsk Institute's interview project, see *Zhivi and Pomni: Istoriia Mennonitskikh Kolonii Ekaterinoslavshiny* (Live and Remember: the History of the Mennonite Colonies in the Ekaterinoslav Region) (Dnipropetrovsk National University: Institute of the Ukrainian-German Historical Researches, 2006).

46 James Urry, *None but Saints: The Transformation of Mennonite Life in Russia, 1789–1889* (Winnipeg: Windflower Communications, 1989).

47 Such an assessment is offered in Simon Dixon's review of Urry's *None but Saints* in *The Slavonic and East European Review* (October 1990), 762–3.

48 Albert W. Wardin Jr., *On the Edge: Baptists and Other Free Church Evangelicals in Tsarist Russia, 1855–1917* (Eugene, OR: Wipf & Stock, 2013).

49 "Some of the people who persecuted us were Mennonites. They turned against us and betrayed us. I saw my beautiful red coat being worn by another girl. The one that was confiscated. Her father was a village official, a Mennonite who became a Communist." A reflection from collectivization as recorded in Edith Elisabeth Friesen, *Journey into Freedom: One Family's Real-Life Drama* (Winnipeg: Raduga Publications, 2003), 20.

PART ONE

Overviews: New Approaches to Mennonite History

1 "Land of Opportunity, Sites of Devastation": Notes on the History of the Borozenko Daughter Colony

SVETLANA BOBYLEVA

In the past two decades, the history of the Russian Empire's Mennonite population has captured the attention of many Russian and Ukrainian historians, as is clear from the important contributions that colleagues such as Venger, Beznosova, and Cherkazianova have made to this volume.[1] This is due to the growth of a new Ukrainian national self-consciousness, which some have called "ethnic renaissance," and others "ethnic paradox." This has particular meaning for our Black Sea region, which has historically served as an occasionally difficult point of contact for Russia and Ukraine. How could it be otherwise for a region that is known historically both as "southern Ukraine" and "New Russia"? However, regardless of the name, this process of historical inquiry has highlighted the problem of inter-ethnic relations within the Russian Empire, and of how its multi-ethnicity contributed to the mental mapping of any one grouping, such as the Mennonites. We can also see how the landscape itself shaped Mennonite identities, how Mennonites dynamically engaged with the land they settled upon and the skies they settled under, and how they themselves were shaped and reshaped in the process.

Scholars in the Soviet Union often conflated the history of the Russian Empire's Mennonite population with the history of German colonists. Such an approach was understandable given the reality of much Imperial legislation in the late Imperial era, but it is hardly helpful to have those definitions cast back to the settlement period of the late eighteenth century. Shared linguistic and cultural-domestic factors as well as comparable stages of social-economic and political development also reinforced a sense of overlapping identities between Mennonites on the one hand and German Lutherans and Catholics on the other. More careful historical inquiry, however, indicates a complex picture. On the one hand, Mennonites differed significantly from the empire's Germans in their development and self-identification, first and foremost in religious matters. On the other, the line between Mennonites and Germans was increasingly blurred after 1900 as communal boundaries between them became more porous.

In addition, the history of Russia's Mennonite population is inherently connected with the political-economic developments that took place in the empire as a whole. For example, a recent study by Faith Hillis challenges the complex ways in which "Little Russian" intellectuals understood Ukrainian and Russian identities in right-bank Ukraine. Her insight, that "Little Russian" identities were multivalent, and welcomed by both Imperial servitors and Kievan intellectuals, allows us to imagine Mennonites who were loyal to the empire yet firmly rooted in the local identities of Ukraine. Lewis Siegelbaum and Leslie Moch demonstrate how dynamic population movements were across the empire from the late nineteenth century onward. I have been especially impressed by their determination to take a "living history" approach, one that uses recent interviews alongside the more classically defined historical sources of governmental directives and correspondences. Though they stress resettlement in the late nineteenth century as a time of relocation from European Russia to the Siberian steppe, my study of Borozenko suggests that resettlement within regions (or Ukraine itself) are equally worthy of investigation. David Moon's study of the great grasslands of Russia and Ukraine has inspired me to integrate the landscape of southern Ukraine into the history of its peoples. Whereas Moon has produced a finely honed environmental history of settlement, development, and climate change in the empire's vast steppe, my own study reads more like a preliminary sounding on one small corner of that vast steppe, a corner that was intimately connected with Ukraine's Mennonites. Finally, Mikhail Akulov's recent doctoral investigation invites us to rethink the role played by perhaps the most notorious of peasant anarchists in the revolutionary period: Nestor Makhno.[2]

Ukrainian scholars did not always have access to western specialists and their research, especially as it pertains to Mennonite studies. We first met with a group of Canadian, American, and German Mennonites who came for the international scholarly conference "Mennonites in Tsarist Russian and the Soviet Union" in 1999. At that time we did not think that the history of Ukrainian Mennonites would have an important place in our lives, or that it would cause us to reconsider how we understood the history of our region. At that time, Mennonite history was only one of the items on our scientific research plan, and a small one at that.

However, that conference brought us together with very interesting people, including Harvey Dyck, Paul Toews, John Staples, and Johannes Dyck. Such scholarly contact allowed our Ukrainian scholarly community to break out of its decades-long Soviet isolation. We soon learned that nearly every one of these scholars considered our homeland to have been their ancestral one at one time. We were struck by their friendliness and willingness to listen to others' opinions even as we quickly realized that not all viewpoints coincided with our own. Now, years later, we are grateful that Leonard Friesen has included the story of that remarkable first encounter in the appendix to this volume. Its significance for the scholarly community of southern Ukraine cannot be overstated, nor can our appreciation for the crucial initiatory role played by Harvey Dyck.

By 1989, researchers of the Oles Honchar Dnipropetrovsk National University Ukrainian-German Scientific Research Institute had already begun joint scholarly researches with the Göttingen Research Centre, headed at the time by Dr Alfred Eisfeld. We had initiated a series of historical-ethnographical expeditions in the former German colonies of our region. Since Mennonite settlements and German colonies were often located close to each other and the history of their existence was similar in many respects, they were also subjected to investigation. In that sense, our first forays into Mennonite history were almost accidental, though they soon gathered their own momentum.

The results of this labour became the book *Live and Remember...: A History of Mennonite Colonies of Katerynoslav Region*, published in 2006 with an edition of 500 copies.[3] This has become a rare book though requests for it continue. The material for this short history of twenty Mennonite colonies came from regional archives, an oral history project, and publications by foreign and domestic historians. That material, some of which is included in this chapter, adds an important perspective to the Mennonite experience in the Soviet period. As such, it supplements important work done by Neufeldt and Beznosov on Mennonites and collectivization, which has been included in the present work. Together, they significantly expand our understanding of Mennonite identity during the Stalinist revolution, though my own research makes it difficult to support a view of widespread Mennonite complicity.

It was during that massive interview project that we first noticed an extremely small amount of data on one of the groups of Mennonite daughter colonies, the so-called Borozenko villages. I have concluded from a search of historical materials and historiography that the history of these colonies had yet to be undertaken by either Ukrainian or western scholars. Several reasons account for this. For one, countless materials from the Nikolaipol (Novosofievka) district were destroyed during the hard war years. For another, Mennonite scholars have focused more on the larger and older "Mother" colonies of Khortitsa and Molochna. Nevertheless, we finally concluded that it was both possible and necessary to undertake the history of this daughter colony, if only to provide an alternative perspective on the Mennonite experience in southern Ukraine. In that sense, my contribution differs substantially from the approach taken by other contributors to this volume. Similar to Siegelbaum and Moch, I am interested in a case study of how Mennonite identities and societal interactions changed over the *longue durée*.

Tsarist officials had understood their state to be multi-ethnic for centuries, and so it can be concluded that multi-ethnicity was at the heart of their Imperial "mental map."[4] Such projections were not static however, as even the understanding of their "Russianness" changed over time, as Hillis has already demonstrated for right-bank Ukraine. To this one must add Nathaniel Knight's recent observation that St Petersburg never managed to reconcile its statist and imperial (i.e., Russian and non-Russian) projections of itself, a problem that was greatly exacerbated after 1900 by international developments.[5] The utility of a study that considered dynamic change over time defined the scope of my historical research, even as I narrowed my geographic focus to a handful of villages. Through the example of Borozenko, its establishment and eventual destruction, I will weave together a story of how Mennonites related to the land, both environmentally and economically, as well as to their neighbours. Through an exploration of life in Borozenko as Mennonites contended with post-emancipation land hunger, the rise of Russian nationalism, and the mobilization, occupation, and contested politicization of Borozenko, I intend to demonstrate the high degree to which Mennonite life was intertwined with the land and peoples of this region. Even so, they were never able to rid themselves of an identity torn between insider and outsider markings. Of course not all questions can be answered. In particular, I set aside questions of economic management in the villages and the daily experiences within the Borozenko colonies as we had already investigated them in *Live and*

Remember.[6] Instead, I will focus on matters of a socio-political nature which related directly to the fate of the Borozenko colonies.

Looking at the history of the Borozenko colonies, one first notices that they were founded in the 1860s. Why so, and how did it affect the destinies of the Empire's German-Mennonite population? For starters, serfdom was abolished in Russia in 1861 as the empire modernized economically, for which it first required social transformation. As Venger suggests in her chapter, Russia's adoption of a capitalist path of development was quite painful for the majority of the population. Social-economic innovations were poorly received as estates of the nobility were ruined from mismanagement, masses of peasants were dispossessed of their lands, and merchants experienced a financial crisis of their own. The economic processes of the 1860s–80s and Imperial Russia's headlong advance on its path of capitalization had a serious effect on the largest rural sector of the Empire's southern provinces – the Ukrainian peasantry.[7] Their land holdings shrank by almost a third, causing rural overpopulation and social tension. Peasant tensions further increased as nobles began to sell of their private estates to Mennonites and others, often to the initial detriment and displacement of local peasants.

Mennonite colonists also experienced considerable socio-economic turmoil in the post-emancipation era, even as many quickly and organically integrated into these new social-economic conditions. Commodity-monetary relations had already been developed in the Khortitsa and Molochna mother colonies over the previous half century. We see this in their market-oriented farms and in their earliest industrial enterprises (see Venger's chapter) which gave rise to a commercial-industrial bourgeoisie which generated a special economic dynamism for the entire region.[8] This remarkable transformation also had more negative results as Mennonite socio-economic stratification accelerated. As a result, most Mennonites in the mother colonies were landless by mid-century. The interpersonal relations among Mennonites that had previously been founded on a common ethno-religious basis had become more complex and divisive, and it was clear by then that there were multiple Mennonite experiences, starting with the vast distance that separated the haves and have-nots. Perhaps most surprisingly, by 1860 land was neither the sole nor the main determinant of Mennonite wealth.

Beznosova is correct to suggest that a landless Mennonite entrepreneurial elite had emerged in the mother colonies by mid-century. Even with their emergence, however, land remained the basis of economic activities for the vast majority of these colonist-agriculturalists. Many of the landless elite identified with the landscape around them as their enterprises, from milling to manufacturing, were linked to agricultural productivity. The right of primogeniture, with its indivisibility of land allotment, simultaneously strengthened overall Mennonite economic strength through the diversification of activity and the concentration of wealth, even as it set the stage for the Mennonites' geographic fragmentation. Both the very rich and the poor among the Mennonites sought opportunities beyond the mother colonies at the very time that estate lands began to flood the market due to peasant emancipation, alongside the nobility's disinclination to adapt by any other means.

For decades, the mother colonies persistently refused to divide the reserve lands or the full land allotments that had been initially granted to them, and they were successful until the 1860s, by which time the land shortages had acquired threatening proportions.[9] The significant demographic increases in the colonies further exacerbated a crisis in which both the landed and landless appealed to the state for support. In search of an internally managed solution, in 1866 the colonists began to divide up full land allotments. Now three groups represented the population of the mother colonies: the first, those with full allotments (65 desiatinas [equal to about 1 hectare]), half allotments (32 desiatinas), and quarter allotments (small, 12 desiatinas); the second, farmers in charge of lots with fewer than 12 desiatinas; and, the third, the Mennonite landless. The last two categories were obviously the most worrisome as their steady increase was tied directly to the growth of social tension in the colonies. In certain settlements the percentage of small farms and the landless had reached 56 per cent to 70.7 per cent of the families.[10] In response, the colonies sought out new land both within and beyond the original mother colonies to safeguard Mennonite self-identification as fundamentally egalitarian. With this goal, Mennonite colonists began to plough up sheep-grazing reserve land (pastures) in the mother colonies, they narrowed the ancient salt roads that passed through Molochna villages, and – in search of opportunities further afield – purchased new lands to create "daughter colonies."

Hunger for land and economic difficulties coincided with the splintering of relations and overall coherence in Mennonite religious life. Land that had been deemed to be in abundance at the point of settlement was now viewed as an increasingly scarce resource. At the same time, dynamics at work in the Ukrainian countryside after the emancipation of the serfs in 1861 challenged Mennonites to conceive of their home base in broader terms, well beyond the confines of the Khortitsa and Molochna settlements. All this prompted Mennonites to purchase lands near and far, including one massive parcel that the Khortitsa settlements acquired jointly from the landowner Borozenko, along with the *Kleine Gemeinde* of the Molochna settlements. The so-called Borozenko colonies, a tribute to the former owner, were founded on this land.

The Khortitsa mother colony founded six villages: Schöndorf, Nikolaital, Ebenfeld, Felsenbach, Eichengrund, and Hochstädt. The *Kleine Gemeinde* founded Heuboden, Blumenhof, Annafeld, Steinbach, Rosenfeld, and Neuanlage. In total, these settlements occupied 12,000 desiatinas of land.[11] In 1866, 2,000 desiatinas of this land belonged to the *Kleine Gemeinde*, which founded two more villages in 1866–7: Friedensfeld and Grünfeld. Hochfeld, a separate farm (*khutor*), was founded in 1872.[12] Three years earlier (in 1869), there had already been a split within the Molochna *Kleine Geminde*, as some of its members (sixteen people) headed by the elder A. Friesen resettled in the village Friedensfeld, where they later joined the Mennonite Brethren Church. Everything stated above allows us to make the following conclusion: the colonists bought the land from the noble Borso, which directly affected the interests of adjacent Ukrainian peasants who had previously worked these same lands. The abrupt entry of Mennonites into this micro-region would play a role in the fate of these settlements during the civil war period.

But why was the land sold to Mennonites and not to peasants who lived adjacent to it and who may have needed it more? The Mennonites' ability to pay for the proposed land, their well-known fiscal accountability, and the precision with which they undertook monetary matters prompted Borso to offer the land for sale to them. This initially irritated the neighbouring Ukrainians from the village of Sholokhovo even if the newly arrived Mennonites failed to notice it at the time. It did not help that the newly-founded Mennonite daughter colony of Borozenko was located in one of the region's most densely populated districts – Ekaterinoslav, in the province of the same name. The Ukrainian peasants of this district experienced an acute land shortage of their own because the Mennonites did not make lands available for lease as estate owners had previously done. In addition, the problem of competition in the land market in the province was so great that the Ekaterinoslav provincial zemstvo (elected assembly) in the 1880s moved to restrict German-Mennonite land tenure in the Russian Empire.[13] The timing and agency here is crucial because it suggests that local zemstvo representatives (peasant and noble) initiated nationalist concerns against Mennonite and German land acquisitions. If correct, the more draconian laws against "foreign" ownership that St Petersburg later initiated may have originated at the local level and moved up the administrative chain from there. These new regulations against further land acquisition by Germans and Mennonites did not immediately improve the peasants' lot, though some of this may have been because of weak enforcement. Private estates in the province owned by former colonists made up 10 per cent of all arable land by 1900, while the number of ethnic Germans was just 3.8 per cent of the population. Even more striking were the data for Ekaterinoslav district where German land ownership reached 19 per cent.[14]

Second, what can we say about the historical-social features that shaped the neighbouring Ukrainian village of Sholokhovo, which later played such a sinister role in the fate of several Mennonite settlements? The *Katerynoslavshchina* comprised the territory where the Zaporozhe *Sech* had been located previously. Sholokhovo itself had once been part of the ancient Zaporozhe floodplain where it had formed part of the ancient Zaporozhe Cossacks' land-base. In fact, the richest and most prosperous winter homes and farmsteads of Zaporozhe Cossack military officers had been located here since at least 1740. According to the 1782 census, 144 men and 71 women already lived in the village of Sholokhovo, which was by that time a possession of the Imperial Russian state. Even so, the village's population continued to grow. After the rout of the Zaporozhe *Sech*, Catherine II settled some of the Cossack warriors in Sholokhovo, though they stayed on the land unwillingly. Their turbulent past still simmered long after the fact, even as Zaporozhian violence waned over time. To the great detriment of former colonists, the revolutionary upheavals of the late nineteenth century stirred the memories and rekindled the resentments of these former Cossacks.

These were the best years for the Borozenko Mennonites but it was hardly the end of the story. The anti-German campaign on the eve of the First World War that officials directed against the "peaceful conquest" by Russian Germans, the subsequent introduction of draconian liquidation laws to counter German land acquisition, and the eviction of German-Mennonites from their properties all combined to place the German Mennonite community in a state of siege by 1916. Last, the Orthodox Church incited the area's peasants to adopt an "us versus them" approach to the area's colonists (including Mennonites among them). In short, actions taken by the Imperial Russian state before 1917 directly intruded on the well-being of the empire's ethno-religious minorities[15] and directly influenced the moral consciousness and behaviour of the peasantry during the civil war. Cross-cultural relations between Mennonites and their neighbours may have been relatively benign in Molochna, as John Staples and Leonard Friesen have both suggested, but they were much more volatile in Mennonite daughter colonies like Borozenko where conflicting cognitive maps of Ukraine were played out between peasant and colonist.[16]

In the eighteenth century, Montesquieu wrote, "Many things rule over people: climate, religion, laws, principles of the government, past examples, customs .... As a result of all these a nation's general spirit is established."[17] Taking this into account, we turn to the characteristic of the territory on which Mennonites and Germans founded their daughter colonies. All the enumerated settlements (with the exception of Grünfeld – Verkhnedneprovsk district and Steinbach – Kherson district, and Kherson province) were a part of Ekaterinoslav district and located in the southwestern part of Ekaterinoslav province. The Dnipro River skirted the district on the north, south, and east, providing a natural border on three sides. On the west side, the Bazavluk River separated Ekaterinoslav district from Kherson province. Since the colonists were generally occupied with agriculture, the natural-geographical and climatic conditions of this region were of great importance to their livelihood. The settlements were situated on the transition from the Dnipro highlands to the Black Sea lowlands, all of which contributed to its unique characteristics.

The Dnipro highlands were the source of many of the Dnipro's tributaries. The Black Sea lowlands were characterized by wide flat fields between rivers which themselves were crisscrossed by gently sloping gullies. The width of these hollows reached 300 to 500 metres. Mennonite settlements were on the banks of small, often dry creek beds of the Bazavluk and Solenaia Rivers, both of which were tributaries of the Dnipro River. The Bazavluk River now differs considerably qualitatively from what it was in the second half of the nineteenth century when it was deep and carried water swiftly to the Dnipro. Osier shrubs, Tatar maples, and oak trees grew along its banks. Both then and now it is characterized by high water and floods, which in the summer months gave lush grasses, well used by the population for pasturing livestock. Thanks to David Moon, we now have a much clearer picture of the diminution in southern Ukraine's once mighty rivers, what he calls "the drying out of the steppes," and its intimate connection to contemporary agricultural practices.[18]

The intensity of rising water levels averaged 20 to 120 centimetres per day during floods in the second half of the nineteenth century and in many respects depended on the amount of rainfall in the spring and snowfall in the winter. Spring floods occasionally started in February – though often in March – and even so water levels peaked two to three times during the spring run-offs. Mennonite diarists from the Borozenko settlements mentioned floods in the 1870s, and more generally make plain how thoroughly Mennonites identified with these lands.[19]

These villages were located in a moderate-continental climatic zone. Significant annual fluctuations in weather conditions had a direct effect on Mennonite economic activity within the Borozenko settlements.[20] Moderately wet years took turns with sharply arid ones. Destructive hot dry winds were frequent. Overall, the climate was characterized by relatively cold winters and hot summers. The combination of a limited moisture reserve at the beginning of spring alongside high temperatures in the summer months made the air dry and magnified the moisture deficiency, making agriculture a risky undertaking.

Climatic conditions played an essential role in the economic activity of the population. No wonder Mennonite diarists recorded so carefully the daily temperatures, the condition of snow cover in the fields, the water levels in nearby rivers, the ice drift on them, frost on the ground at the end of spring and start of fall, and wind directions.[21] No less important for the rural inhabitants was the constantly varying length of daylight hours. It is well known that settlers started work at dawn. The amount of daylight fell between 8.2 hours on winter solstice (22 December) to 16 hours on summer solstice (22 June) and reflected the wide variations in what a workday looked like. The average January temperature was –4.1C°, June +22.5C°. There were 172 days with temperatures higher than +10°.

Settlements on the Dnipro steppe felt the power and fury of the wind. Most often, the northwest winds of winter gave way to the arid summer winds of the Azores High, bringing drought-like conditions with them. Agriculturalists needed to shape their crop selections and cultivation styles accordingly if they were going to be successful. Mennonite settlers thus adapted early on to Borozenko's unique microclimate, and stopped cultivating tall crops which tended to be killed off before maturity. They also formed single-row villages that were slightly smaller than those found in Molochna as they adapted to limited sources of water and relatively wide variations in soil types and fertility.[22] Even then, farmers watched anxiously to see what rains would fall from May to September, as their economic well-being depended on adequate rainfall. At the same time, the region's aquifers were generally unsuitable for use by the population of the Borozenko colonies. Instead, they relied on water from their own dug wells to meet their household needs, though even then the arid conditions in the Borozenko settlements made it difficult to dig and maintain their wells. Ukrainian peasants in the area also knew the importance of ready access to water for their survival, which is why the older Sholokhovo settlement was located at the confluence of the Bazavluk and Solenaia Rivers. According to historian Royden Loewen, the Mennonites referred simply to that long-standing former Cossack village as "Schalag."[23] Mennonites in the region also learned a great deal from the peasants on how to combat periodic drought conditions, whether it was in constructing dams, to hold spring melt-offs or in cultivating vast watermelon fields, the famed *bashtans*, for the moisture they afforded them.[24] This ability to learn from peasants suggests also that Mennonites were by no means isolated and insulated from those around them. In fact, early Mennonite diarists from Borozenko indicate a relative ease of movement across the physical and human landscape that stretched from Odessa in the southwest to the "mother" colony of Molochna in the east.[25]

Today, travelling around the places of the former Borozenko colonies, one can see that Mennonites were more than mere rationalists. They were also able to appreciate beauty as practically all settlements were located in picturesque settings on this black-earthed southern steppe with its abundant meadows, well-tended gardens, and forested gully slopes. Mennonite memoirists later recalled the years of settlement and adjustment before 1900 as a "golden age" despite the reality of persistent crop failures (for every four fruitful years there were three lean ones thanks to a range of factors that included persistent drought, hordes of grain beetles, ground squirrels, and locusts).

How, then, was this a "golden age," especially if these decades saw increased pressures on Mennonites to integrate into Russian society? The memory of one's youth doubtless played a role, or perhaps it involved a more calculated appraisal by colonists who had survived rough beginnings in the Borozenko settlement. They had made the necessary adaptations and begun to realize at least some economic progress, even if it was at the price of increased integration into society. Borozenko Mennonites founded schools and established their religious life on a high plane, even after the entire *Kleine Gemeinde* settlement emigrated in 1874.[26] Those who stayed did not sit idle; they constructed and maintained their own flour mills and farms as grain cultivation reached unprecedented levels in this micro-region. Observers from outside of the Mennonite world were unequivocal in their own assessment, as they concluded that the vast majority of the settlement population, including those of the Mennonite daughter settlements, represented the strongest possible economic impetus to the region. Neighbouring Ukrainians, by comparison, were far less successful and many of these may have blamed their persistent poverty on these interlopers. Overall, the expansion of Mennonite daughter colonies across southern Ukraine expanded Mennonite self-identification with the region as a whole even as it challenged an erstwhile cultural isolationism.

The social-political life of the settlements at the dawn of the twentieth century was anything but placid as the tsarist regime's Russification policies undoubtedly affected the Borozenko colonies. As one aspect of it, imperial officials required that all systems of records management and language instruction in the settlement schools be undertaken in Russian. The villages themselves were renamed after 1890, a process of profound mental remapping that Mennonites had completed by the start of the First World War. Henceforth the Borozenko settlements were officially known as: Borozenkovo (previously Blumenhof), Mar'ino (Heuboden), Kuz'mitskoe (Steinbach), Shishkino (Annafeld), Ekaterinovka (Rosenfeld), Ivanovka (Neuanlage), Ol'gino (Schöndorf), Novosofievka (Nikolaital), Mariapol' (Felsenbach), Ul'ianovka (Ebenfeld), Petrovka (Eichengrund), Aleksandropol' (Hochstädt), and the homesteads Zelenyi (Grünfeld) and Gogolevka (Friedensfeld).

Together with the entire Russian Empire, the Borozenko colonists shared the hardships of the Russo-Japanese War, the 1905 revolution, the calamity of the First World War, and the two following revolutions (in February and October of 1917). However difficult these events were, the civil war that started in 1918 left the most tragic and bloody trail in the memory of those who survived.[27] An unprovoked massacre of the population took place in Borozenko. For example, on the night of 5 December 1919 all fifty-four individuals still living in the Mennonite village of Steinbach were murdered by peasant anarchists.[28] A number of Ukrainian researchers blame the annihilation of the Mennonites in the south on the latter's own willful creation of self-defence detachments (the *Selbstschutz*) which they subsequently deployed in active armed opposition to their attackers, and which contradicted the pacifist postulates of the Mennonite creed. But this does not fit with the events of 1919 in the Borozenko settlements when Mennonites did not undertake any armed resistance against the Makhnovists or any other armed gangs. Even so, the absence of any apparent rationale or social selectivity did not forestall the threatened annihilation of all colonists, and poses difficult questions and problems for researchers. Only a detailed micro-historical investigation can get at the answers needed.

What factors need to be raised if we are going to understand the Ukrainian population's relations with German-Mennonites during this era of world war, several empire-wide revolutions, and fierce civil war? How will this affect the changing nature of Mennonite self-perception, or of their previously strong identification with the region and empire? Even a partial list needs to include the following:

1. The place of multi-ethnic and regional dynamics within the general direction of late Imperial Russian history.
2. The psychology of the peasant masses, and the forces that influenced it.
3. The agrarian issue.
4. Religion, its institutions, and their role in the empire's history as a factor in Mennonite history in particular.
5. The impact that the First World War, the crisis of empire, and the revolutions that followed had on everything that happened.
6. The civil war in Russia and Ukraine in general, and specifically in Mennonite areas, which included Borozenko.
7. Imperial Russia's foreign policy and its influence on non-Russian peoples in the late Imperial period.
8. The Austro-Germanic presence in Ukraine during the First World War.

Domestic and foreign historians have amassed a prodigious number of studies on the above-mentioned problems. However, most researchers have analysed the issues through the prism of the empire's social-economic and political crises after 1900, especially after the onset of the Great War in 1914. Unfortunately this resulted in structurally fixed understandings, ones that did not allow historians to consider the behaviour of individual subjects.[29] Sadly, historians left individuals themselves, and individual responsibility, outside of their field of vision, simply excluding psychological aspects. Fortunately, we live at a time when psychological issues are seen as key to a full understanding. Contemporary research strategies also favour an interdisciplinary, multi-factor approach, one that takes into account wide variations within Ukraine as a whole and points to the uniqueness of southern Ukraine in particular. All of this becomes clear when we consider Borozenko and its environs as a microcosm of the whole.

To begin, we observe that a wide range of religious and ethnic groups lived in Ekaterinoslav province, as noted earlier. This reality inescapably defined its "mental map" (a concept introduced by E.C. Tolman in 1948). It is precisely this "mental map" that allows us to understand what took place in the Borozenko villages in 1918–19.

The agrarian issue. Access to land was one of Imperial Russia's most persistent challenges in the half-century before 1914. Agrarian overpopulation and acute internal social strife forced Mennonites to purchase and rent additional lands, as was already evident in the noticeable growth in increased Mennonite land ownership through daughter colonies and private estates from 1860 to 1880. In Ekaterinoslav district alone, and in the province of the same name where the fates of the Borozenko settlements were at issue, the German-Mennonite land ownership in these years steadily increased by 39,000 and 105,000 desiatinas respectively.[30] No wonder the Mennonites' self-perception of this pre-revolutionary era was akin to a golden age. The situation was aggravated by the constant increase in land prices and land rental rates; and all of this led to an acute shortage of land area available to Ukrainian peasants who lived along-side their German-Mennonite neighbours. It was in this context that the "German issue" emerged from those opposed to both Mennonite and German land expansion, as the distinction between these ethnic groupings was reduced to nil. If the economic component of this "German issue" had somehow disappeared, or if there had been evidence by 1914 of a reduction in German land tenure, it is reasonable to conclude that peasant hostility to Mennonites and Germans would have been minimized or disappeared altogether. But this did not happen.

Psychology of the masses. The Mennonite daughter colony's obvious economic success might have generated among the surrounding peasants a desire to understand the reason for it and to try to master the technologies of agricultural production and the principles of management for themselves. But, instead, it appeared to have provoked only feelings of envy which added an unwelcome dynamic to ethnic relations. The mentality of the Ukrainian peasantry which has often been portrayed in idyllic terms also has to be taken into account. Indeed, peasants were often hardworking, honest, charitable, and conscientious.[31] However, the dark side of the peasant mentalité was rooted in the negatively objective circumstances of rural life over the previous half-century, including the relatively late abolition of serfdom, the inadequacy of reforms in the 1870s, the widespread lack of peasant political rights, and the widespread illiteracy of the rural population (according to the 1897 census, literacy was only 17.4 per cent in rural areas).[32] Many other factors negatively affected the peasants' world-view, including the speed with which they were compelled to adjust to the Borozenko settlement after Mennonites purchased these lands in the mid-1860s, so soon after the peasants' purported emancipation.

More recently, scholars have undertaken a reassessment of Makhno's motivations in particular. Sean David Patterson has suggested that the "Makhnovist narrative" is rooted in peasant and Cossack concerns for social justice.[33] Patterson places considerable stock in Makhno's own memoir, whose "schematic narrative template" stressed his linkage to the collective memory of the Zaporozhian Cossacks and the search for social justice. Just as striking, he avoids any mention of ethnic animosity to Mennonites (whom he consistently refers to as "German colonists"), though the language of social class and privilege is constantly applied.[34] Though his work is refreshing, it does appear as if Patterson needed to be more critically engaged with Makhno's memoir as memoir. How can one deny its self-serving nature? A much more helpful perspective has recently been provided by Mikhail Akulev who likens the Makhno initiative to "warlordism." Akulev quotes Maknno's commitment already in the summer of 1918 to "merciless individual terror" that his peasant comrades intended to direct against Austro-German troops, Ukrainian troops, and previously privileged landlords who wished to reclaim their lands. Though he does not address Mennonites specifically, Akulev's work goes a long way to explain why the peasant response to Mennonites, and countless others, was so virulent.[35]

Taken together, one can easily see how such directly contrary mental maps of land and inhabitants would lead to the bloodshed of the civil war years, at which time the Mennonite colonists would be significantly outmatched and overpowered.

The government's nationalist policy. The empire's economic and social transformation in the second half of the nineteenth century coincided with a change in attitude by state bureaucrats, and even the dramatic change associated with the new tsar, Alexander III, whose suspicion of all things German was well known. No wonder imperial authorities encouraged a spirit of national enmity within society, and themselves became active participants when they formulated anti-German policies, especially after Germany's refusal to renew its "Reinsurance Treaty" with Russia in 1890. As the empire's anti-German sentiments mounted, few initially suspected how volatile and ultimately destructive this policy would turn out to be for the colonists – and for the Romanovs – who were dynastically connected to the German monarchy. As Beznosova has suggested in her contribution to this study, Imperial animosity towards Germany increased after Kaiser Wilhelm II refused to renew the Reinsurance Treaty with Russia in 1890. As Mennonites were no longer legally separated from German colonists after 1870, it meant that the Mennonite/German distinction diminished at the worst possible time for these formerly Dutch and Flemish Anabaptists.

Religion. The Russian Empire clearly experienced a religious crisis at the dawn of the twentieth century, as was also the case in western Europe. In Russia's case, the revolution, the Bolshevik victory, and the subsequent civil war appeared to overwhelm all restraints of Christian morality. The Christian principle of "thou shalt not kill" was relegated to the background and all the barbaric strength of the masses spontaneously shot to the surface, driven by war, revolution, and civil war. The new call in the countryside became "kill the alien." To be fair, available evidence suggests that not all of the Borozenko settlements fell victim to the carnage of these years, as Mennonite preachers occasionally persuaded roving gangs to spare their villages. Olga Rempel has written about this in her book *One of Many*. Rempel mentions the preacher Aron Toews, who, because of the steadfastness of his personality and religious convictions, saved the Friedensfeld residents from physical extermination during a mob attack. How to explain this? On the one hand, the power of persuasion by Mennonite preachers must have played a key role, and on the other hand, it is possible that religious sentiments by members of the peasant bandits made them reluctant to kill innocent villagers, German, Mennonite, or otherwise.

The social factor and the First World War. When the call to arms was issued in 1914, 12.8 million peasants entered active duty. Their households were suddenly deprived of male labour even as the state's demand for foodstuffs increased dramatically. Everywhere in Europe the new reality of "total war" took hold.[36] On 20 November 1916, the Minister of Agriculture, A.A. Ritter, gave the order on surplus appropriation. State initiated and punitive requisition of grains followed as ever more conscripts were ordered to serve the tsar in battle. This terrible war mobilized almost 40 per cent of male peasants – many of whom did not return – and changed the collective psychology of the peasants, as Joshua Sanborn has forcefully concluded.[37] A soldier-peasant could kill and be killed. To him, the old elites, political and otherwise, had lost their moral authority. Besides, rumours repeatedly circulated in government circles during the First World War that the peasant land issue would be resolved at the expense of the German colonists' landholdings.[38] And nothing excited Russian soldiers – themselves yesterday's peasants – more than the land issue. For the sake of a plot of land, they were ready to go with anyone and against anyone. The liquidation laws reinforced soldier/peasant expectations that they would acquire land that had previously belonged to the colonists,[39] and many concluded that the 1917 revolution had eliminated all prohibitions. As society disintegrated during the civil war, manifestations of amoral behaviour rose as the result of inadequate social, spiritual, and moral guidance. Moreover, the specifics of revolution, war, and civil war in Ukraine need to be taken into account as fronts changed repeatedly and as new loyalties were constantly being demanded.

The Austro-German forces in Ukraine and their policy on provisions and protecting property rights (including those of the colonists). The Austro-German presence in 1918 became a unique catalyst for inter-ethnic conflicts. The Germans, as V. Vinnichenko graphically stated, came to Ukraine not for the sake of the young (Ukrainian) farm girls' beautiful eyes but for its bread, sugar, and coal. The peasants did not want to surrender their bread on the terms offered by the Germans so the invaders took it by force. It became the first knot of a future conflict. The second knot was the decision to reinstate Mennonite property rights to land[40] and to compensate former owners for damages inflicted.[41] These decisions were implemented by special German and Austro-Hungarian detachments. German settlers, having lost their properties during the revolution, also resorted to the help offered by these occupying forces.[42] The third knot was the creation of the Mennonites' own military self-defence units which themselves were armed with the assistance of the Austro-German forces and which represented a revolutionary shift in how Mennonites were seen, and how they viewed themselves.[43] Taken together, these factors explain why Ukrainian peasants, including those under Makhno's command, pounced on the colonists after the departure of Austro-German forces from Ukrainian territory.

Southern Ukraine quickly became the theatre of a violent armed struggle between competing military-political powers as streams of blood flowed across its lands. This is when the fates of the

German-Mennonite population of the Borozenko colonies truly became tragic. Legal nihilism – the usual companion of the revolutionary destruction of statehood – worsened the unresolved status of the agrarian issue. Peasant paramilitary groups emerged across a countryside marked by ethnic fragmentation and religious heterogeneity, such that purported friends and enemies often lived side by side. One gang from Solonskoe committed atrocities in Grünfeld, and a peasant gang from the villages of Kozlik, Glushchenko, and Slashchev attacked Steinbach. The Ukrainian peasant anarchist Makhno personally visited Blumendorf. Indeed, Makhno's own personality capped an explosive mixture that stirred human emotions, encouraged national prejudices that aligned Mennonite colonists with the German empire, and stoked "primitive" prejudices of one against the other.

There is currently considerable interest in the question of Makhno's attitude toward the colonists, as well as in the person of Nestor Makhno himself. This is explained by the desire radically "to update the pantheon of national heroes" in modern-day Ukraine. Films about Makhno have been made, new publications have been released,[44] and halls have been set aside for museum expositions on the Makhno movement. What has caused this? Perhaps totalitarian thinking by its nature is one-dimensional, dogmatic, and aggressive, without nuance. Such views, it seems, may even survive the very regime that gave birth to them. Thus, a confrontational worldview exemplified by Makhno continues to exist in a post-totalitarian society and has given rise to a dichotomous view of the world.

The desire to re-examine the past in light of new historical sources previously inaccessible to researchers is positive in itself. However, it has created a "disease of historical insanity," a popular "spiritual striptease" of historians. A specific political charlatanism, which obviously became a substitute for scientific inquiry to some, erupted in full bloom. It was sad that new myths replaced old ones in the immediate aftermath of the Soviet Union's collapse, and instead of the previous falsifications we adopted ever more vulgar new ones. What was at issue might be called the shape of now-independent Ukraine's self-understanding and whether it would be defined by a defiant Ukrainianism associated with Makhno or a more cosmopolitan approach which Serhii Plokhy has thoughtfully explored. So it was with the interpretation of tragic events in the history of the Borozenko colonies during the civil war. In particular, the thesis of "Makhno the internationalist," and of his innocence of whatever horrors may have unfolded in these settlements, continues to this day.

However, archival documents and memoirs of first-hand witnesses give a frightfully different picture of what has been so heroically depicted in some post-independence historiography.[45] This is where Akulev's recent voice has been particularly valuable in setting Makhno's "revolutionary warlordism" in the context of a larger geopolitical fight for control in southern Ukraine. A classic example of the tragedy that befell the Borozenko colonies after 1917 is the fate of Steinbach, which was destroyed through the direct involvement of residents from the neighbouring village of Sholokhovo. In 1900, Sholokhovo was a crowded and industrially developed village. Some of its residents needed to find seasonal work because of the shortage of land available in the village itself. Thus, the Ukrainian population's discontent partly emerged because their own land crisis found its "half solution" when they were employed as seasonal labourers on German and Mennonite farms. What did the Ukrainian workers see there? They saw a good deal, including homes and utility structures of good quality, well-equipped settlements, agricultural machinery, highly productive cattle, well-groomed fields, and gardens. And finally, they observed that the residents of Steinbach differed substantially from their Ukrainian counterparts by the clothes they wore, their way of life, primness, and emotional restraint, but also their faith. The conciliating factor was the colonist's personal participation in labour. These farmers toiled tirelessly next to their hired Ukrainian labourers, and did so from morning till late evening. Mennonite employers also settled accounts honestly with their hired help. As a result, the anti-German sentiments that existed in Imperial Russian society at the end of the nineteenth century and into the twentieth had practically no concrete manifestation in the vicinity of the Borozenko settlements. Although the economic successes of the settlers undoubtedly caused a feeling of envy tinged with an ethnic component among the surrounding population, there is no indication that it gave rise to open antagonism at that time.

The situation abruptly changed during the civil war for the reasons mentioned above as Ukrainians became overtly aggressive to the inhabitants of Kuz'mitskoe (as Steinbach became known). And on 5 December 1919, the history of the Mennonite village came to an abrupt and tragic end when local Ukrainian peasants violently struck at this settlement and annihilated all its residents: every single person was murdered, from little ones to men and women. The Sholokhovo peasants – many of whom had previously laboured for German and Mennonite landowners – participated in these bloody events. They formed a part of

Makhno's detachments that were active in this area. "The horror of both the red and the white terror," V. Buldakov wrote, "faded against a background of peasant mass indifference." which degenerated into the "spontaneous sadism of the masses" during the civil war.[46] In the course of a recent historical-ethnographical expedition, the residents of Sholokhovo and neighbouring villages were interviewed (by M.L. Cherep, M.S. Kirpa, and M Kolesnik). They recounted their forebears' tragic treatment of the Germans and Mennonites and related what Sholokhovo residents had heard directly from their parents and other former witnesses of the December 1919 tragedy. Those interviewed in our time all condemned the savage bloodshed of that era, as their stories confirm the enduring nature of historical memory. Taran Anna Dmitrievna, born in 1916, asserted that some of the participants of the atrocious assault on Mennonite villagers partially lost their minds because of what they had seen and done. There was talk in particular about a certain Slashchev, who was remembered in the 1930s as a lunatic. At the same time, the analysis of his behaviour as conveyed by this respondent allows one to assume that his conduct was a kind of simulated madness that emerged from a desire to avoid the punishment of the tribunal. Later, KGB officers repeatedly interrogated the Sholokhovo residents as they attempted to identify those who had massacred the Mennonite villagers. Fifty-four people were killed in Steinbach and another sixty-seven in Ebenfeld. There were victims in virtually all of the Borozenko colonies, including those who had meddled in the political struggle. It must be said that the majority of Mennonites in the Borozenko colonies, when attacked, did not fight, for religious reasons.

The fratricidal war years claimed the lives of hundreds of thousands of people of different nationalities and faiths, many of whom had lived next to the Ukrainians for centuries. The population of the Borozenko colonies also fell due to the merciless grind of this war. These Mennonite colonists had lived and worked the lands of what they had previously deemed to be their little homeland. They understood themselves to be fully a part of the Russian empire, and fully alive to the landscape and diverse peoples of southern Ukraine. Even so, when the "shadow of Lucifer's wing" overshadowed Russia in the twentieth century, it also placed its diabolical seal on their fate and forced a revolutionary reworking of the cognitive maps of those who survived.

The revolutionary shocks of 1917 released the social energy of the masses and divided the world. The merciless destruction of all and everything began. The creative element was barely noticeable as brutalizing elements were everywhere, especially as the revolution followed on the heels of the ongoing Great War that had dragged on since 1914. Everything collapsed: law, traditions, and foundations. Violence, lawlessness, and killing became almost commonplace. The fratricidal civil war after the revolution threatened the Mennonite population with physical annihilation. They had become strangers and aliens in a land that had seemingly cast them out.

Ukraine became the theatre of a fierce armed struggle between the Whites and the Reds, and between supporters of Petliura, the Greens, and the Makhnovists, a struggle that, in the final analysis, turned into streams of blood. Children and women from the Borozenko daughter colony, the elderly infirm, and innocent young girls, young and old, were ruthlessly slaughtered in the autumn of 1919. Not all who perished were victims of the Makhnovists, however, since many armed gangs existed – even those only pseudo-politicized – and all of these mercilessly massacred the peaceful population. On the whole, the revolution and civil war years had a seriously adverse effect on all aspects of life in the Borozenko settlements. Though many lost their lives from direct attack, others died from the typhoid epidemic brought here by the armies of belligerents and "slayers" of the colonists in the winter of 1919–20.[47] One of the contemporaries who lived through these years later wrote: "It got to where one passed by many farmsteads and entire German colonies where not a single living soul was seen; everywhere one saw scattered ruins and traces of fire ... The steppe was completely abandoned, unplowed, overgrown with tall weeds and feather grass."[48] In sum, tsarist policies enacted both before and during the Great War, the devastation caused by the Austro-German armies, and the more episodic warlordism and gangsterism of the civil war years all contributed to the peasant population's loss of all moral-ethical principles – and made it possible for previously peaceful peasant neighbours to wreak havoc on their Mennonite neighbours.

Nor did this process stop with the end of the Civil War.[49] The terrible famine years of 1921–3 followed,[50] as did the initially repressive measures undertaken by Soviet authorities who viewed the prosperous rural elites as their adversaries. Practically all German-Mennonites were deemed kulaks by the new government, and they suffered economic sanctions accordingly. In time these gave way to violent measures and fierce repression as national-religious factors retreated before the post-1917 onslaught of a socio-economic juggernaut. The process of kulak dispossession affected the entire Ukrainian population without exception, including the Ukrainian peasantry. However, archival documents indicate that Germans and Mennonites were hit disproportionately in this process, as the Soviet government imposed extravagant requisition demands on them. In a sense, they were used as compensation for quotas not realized from Ukrainian villages, and it is interesting in this instance how Soviet authorities continued to view Mennonites in relation to their neighbours, even as that relationship had changed dramatically.[51]

German-Mennonites also suffered disproportionately during the process of land redistribution in 1920–1. For example, Soviet officials seized 59.5 per cent of Mennonite landholdings in the Novosofievka district.[52] In just twelve German and Mennonite districts of the southern region, 38.5 per cent of the land was confiscated. Each one of the Borozenko settlements experienced similar hardships. That aside, the land crisis was a genuine one in the region of the Borozenko settlements, and had both Imperial and Soviet causes, among them the natural population increase at the beginning of the century and the emergence of the land-poor in a number of settlements. Landlessness grew significantly during the civil war years as populations fled to larger settlements in search of refuge from gangs.

It is important to note that such significant demographic growth occurred at the very time lands were being appropriated from Mennonite villages. For example, in Miropol' at the end of the nineteenth century there were 41 people on 1,100 desiatinas of land, while in 1925 a total of 317 people had access to only 778 desiatinas; in Ol'gino at the end of the nineteenth century, 89 people lived on 800 desiatinas, while in 1925 with a population of 128 the land allotment was only desiatinas. Similar trends are evident in the history of virtually all settlements, as evidenced in the following diagrams.

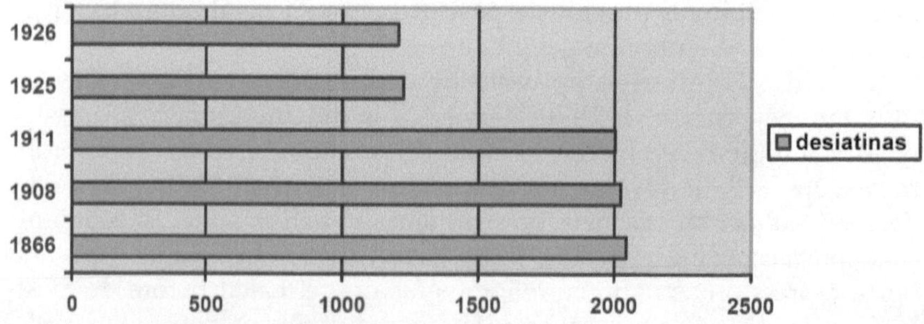

Eigengund (Sharapovka, Petrovka)

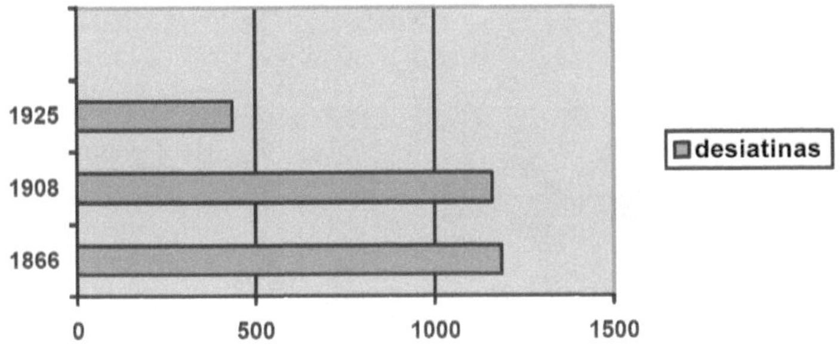

Heuboden (Mar'evka)

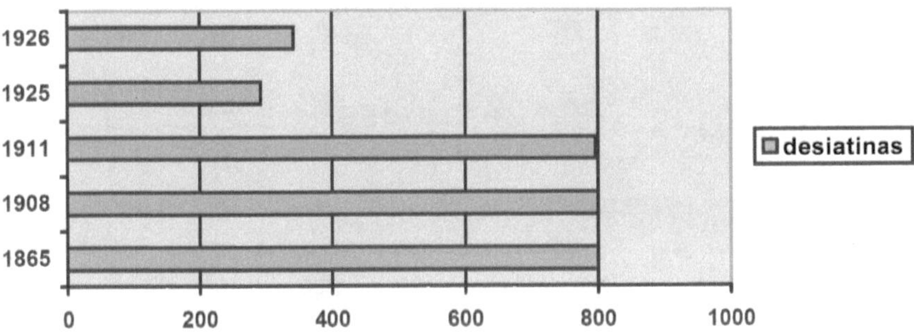

Schöndorf (Ol'gino, Novosofievka)

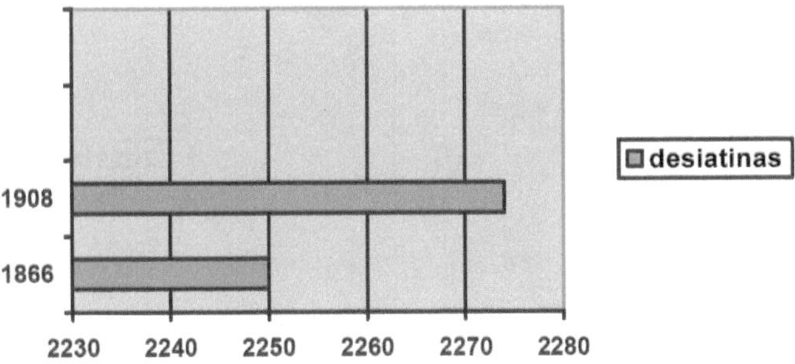

Neu-Hochstädt (Alexandropol')

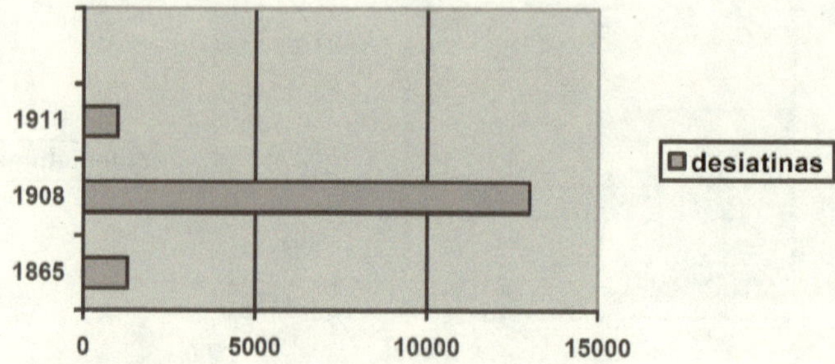

Ebenfeld (Ul'ianovka)

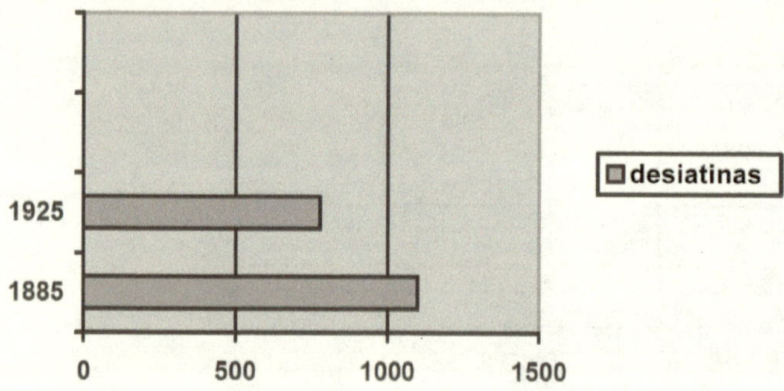

Friedensfeld (Miropol')

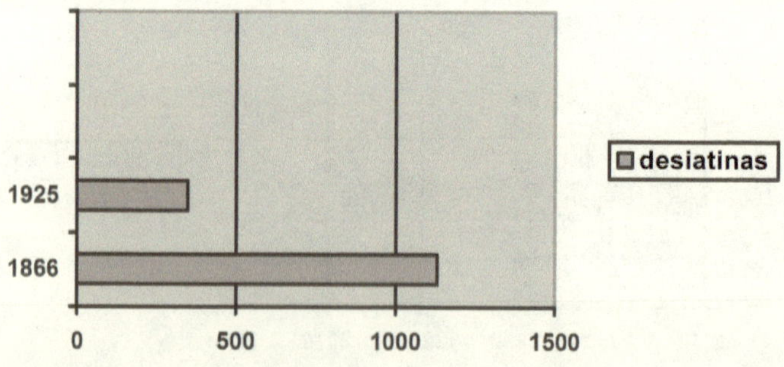

Rosenfeld (Glinianoe, Ekaterinovka)

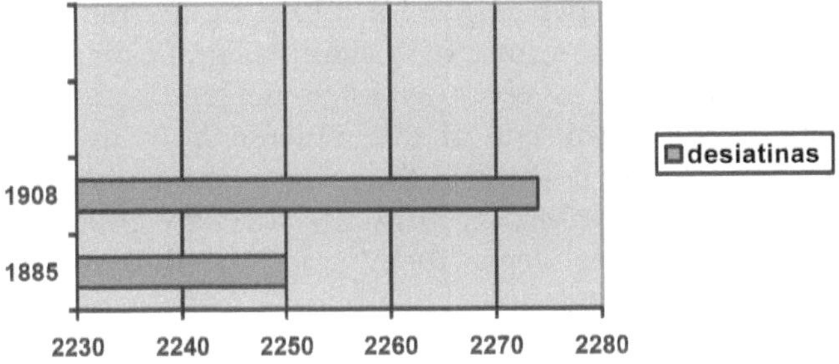

Hochstädt (Alexandropol')

Soviet officials did not establish clear-cut quotas for land use, which led to considerable variations in the land allotted for each mouth to feed across the settlements: it was 2.3 desiatinas in Alexandrovka and 6.7 desiatinas in Ol'gino. These indicators were even more striking compared to prerevolutionary ones when the number for Ol'gino was 70 desiatinas per person and 10.6 desiatinas per person in Alexandrovka. This situation could not but arouse the discontent of the Mennonites who had survived the revolution and civil war. Obviously, economic opportunities for Mennonites declined as their allotment sizes decreased. The Mennonites' ability to pay taxes fell as well and this, ironically, concerned Soviet officials. In all ways, then, Mennonites seemed estranged from their neighbours and from the state in the immediately post-revolutionary era, and it is not surprising that they now sought identifications and associations beyond Soviet Ukraine. Those Germans and Mennonites who had been hard hit but survived now appealed to foreign charitable organizations which increasingly became partners of the colonists. These included American Mennonite Relief; American Relief Administration; Algemene commissie voor Buitenlandssche Noorden, International; Russian Relief Executive; Relief Society for German Settlers of Azov-Black Sea Coasts; and the International Red Cross.[53] Soviet authorities could not allow this, and prompted the Ukraine Communist Party Provincial Committee to reassess the situation in Novosoviefka district. In 1922–3[54] a decision had already been made to terminate any further seizure of lands from the colonists and to return at least part of the lands previously taken – even at the expense of the government's own land fund.[55] However, similar resolutions most likely had only a propaganda value, as not a single settlement experienced a return to anything close to its pre-war level. In addition, one of the most significant changes that came from the increased involvement by Soviet land managers was the ethno-religious transformation of the settlements themselves. Ethnic Ukrainians now started to settle in the colonies more often, even if the process was slow in developing. But with each new Ukrainian household the dividing line between "them" and "us" that had previously been possible for all parties began to erode.

Soviet officials continued to ignore the Mennonites' interests in the administrative reforms that followed. A number of the territories with a German population base were included in regions that were ethnically mixed during the 1921–3 administrative-territorial reforms and further obscured imperial demographic distinctions. Thus, the Borozenko colonies were merged into the Sofievka region until February of 1931 when they were placed in the Stalindorf Jewish nationality region.[56] Stalindorf comprised twenty-three village Soviets: seven former Jewish colonies, thirty-three resettled Jewish communities, forty-seven Ukrainian villages, eleven Russian villages, and thirteen German ones. The German settlement occupied 9.7 per cent of the region's territory.

The difficulties of resettling could not but heighten the German-Mennonite population's desire to find refuge in places where there were no serious political, economic, and social disturbances. Many now identified with biblical images of the faithful as a pilgrim people, cut off from, and subject to, a fallen world. In 1923–6, several thousand Germans and Mennonites left Ukraine for America, Germany, Canada, and Australia.[33] In one instance the Ol'gino (Shendorf) residents planned to emigrate, but all returned. However, the kind of massive exodus of the population of Borozenko colonies that had taken place in the 1870s was not observed in the middle of the 1920s. Instead, the settlements survived even in the difficult years as the population tried to adapt to the relatively relaxed social-economic conditions of the NEP (New Economic Policy) years. The end of NEP marked a true turning point as the relatively stable system of cultural interaction collapsed. Now the destructive character of the Soviet government's politics held sway and Mennonites were overwhelmingly victimized by it, even if Neufeldt's conclusion in this volume – that select Mennonites themselves acted as agents of the Soviet state – is true. Regardless, collectivization brought with it the famine of 1931–3. These years of the so-called Great Turn left a deep unhealed wound in the nation's memory.

The former Borozenko colonies were hit by the Great Famine explored by Alexander Beznosov in these pages. Unfortunately, the exact numbers of Germans and Mennonites who died were not recorded. We do know that Ukrainians who lived in adjacent villages died of hunger. For example, in Ivanovka all five children of the local blacksmith – who were Russian – died of hunger. As for collectivization itself, the political-ideological basis of this policy for Ukraine was released on 20 March 1929 when the Central Committee of the Ukrainian Communist Party issued a decree entitled "About the economic, cultural and Soviet task in the German villages." Thereafter the Party carried out the eviction of dangerous "elements" in the Borozenko colonies that refused to join the new collective farms. The events in Mar'evka in particular gave evidence of the scale of what was underway as the properties of twenty-eight people were expropriated and twenty-two of the now former owners were exiled to Siberia as kulaks. All their remaining possessions were subsequently confiscated.

The campaign, which began in September of 1931 to liquidate the kulaks as a class, was accompanied by the arrest of the rural intelligentsia and clergy – those who could potentially consolidate and lead Germans, Mennonites, and others in opposition. The records of the village Soviets and of the proceedings from general meetings of collective farms – as well as other materials – identify a wide variety of "crimes," including participation in anti-Soviet actions, exploitation of the labours of others, anti-collectivization and anti-Soviet talks, religious advocacies, and failure to meet grain production quotas. Members of the management at the Karl Liebknecht Collective Farm (Alexandropol') were arrested and charged as former kulaks. They were accused of stoking an automobile with clean threshed wheat. The absurdity of the accusation is obvious, taking into account that this was 1932 and the desperate conditions of the time.[57] Wieler was arrested on the groundless charge that he had organized a criminal group of kulaks and their supporters, who had systematically plundered grain at the Thälmann Collective Farm (Novosofievka). The preacher Penner was also arrested in Novosofievka for having allegedly declared that "to steal in a collective farm is not a sin, and so not forbidden by God."[58] Analysis of the cases of repressed residents living in the former Borozenko colonies suggests that the principal means of repression at the start of the 1930s comprised arrests and imprisonment, with terms that ranged from three to five years. Besides imprisonment, authorities exiled those deemed anti-Soviet to Siberia. Perhaps surprisingly, there is no evidence to suggest that arrested and sentenced Mennonites from the Borozenko colony in the early 1930s were executed for their crimes. Even so, this was clearly a time when most Mennonites would have identified themselves as "Defenceless and Abandoned," as Friesen notes in his introduction to this volume. It should be noted that the scholarly investigation of the repressed continues.

The authorities persistently tried to overcome the political opposition that they deemed was present in the population. Since economic sanctions by themselves could not guarantee political loyalty, state officials also placed increased emphasis on propaganda-educational work. Much attention was given to the schools where teachers figured prominently.[59] Soviet authorities were concerned that these teachers might be reluctant to undertake the principal task before them: the training of a new generation in the manner required by a Stalinist state. Nor was this surprising, as the system of education practised by Germans and Mennonites in the colonies, and as explored here by Cherkazianova, had previously relied on the traditional foundation of interrelated social institutions whereby schools and churches were in complete harmony. The Church could hardly be expected to support a pedagogical approach that was committed to unbridled atheism. Thus, at the onset of the Stalinist revolution, the state decided to ban ecclesial authorities altogether.

School administrators in the Borozenko settlements also had to respond to the Soviet state's reversal of the NEP era policy of "indigenization," as Terry Martin has investigated previously.[60] Under "indigenization," all communication in Mennonite families had still been carried out in Plautdietsch, whereas the classical German language had been taught in school. However, the cultural revolution associated with the end of NEP and the Great Stalinist Transformation sharpened the political and ideological opposition of the Communist Party to local teachers over pedagogical content, methodology, and religious education. Mennonite and German teachers were retrained or purged, to be replaced by new personnel from among "socially steadfast elements."[61] Houses of worship previously located in school premises were now closed, as happened in Alexandropol' and Ivanovka. Authorities actively began to create a new socio-cultural infrastructure, one that was unequivocally loyal to the government. Clubhouses and hut-reading rooms (*избы-читальни*) suddenly cropped up in the villages of Ol'gino, Alexandrovka, Mar'evka, Marinopol' Miropol', Ivanovka, and Alexandropol'. School officials worked under strict ideological supervision to radically reshape their collections of books and newspapers, and it is here that Colin Neufeldt challenges us to rethink the role that selected Mennonites might have played in this expansion of Moscow's power into the settlements. Mennonites during NEP had worked hard to augment their school libraries, but almost exclusively with German language materials. Foreign charitable foundations had responded to appeals for assistance and since the mid-1920s had regularly sent book parcels to the colony. This had partially met local needs. Against this background, authorities ordered that Mennonite schools withdraw more than 100,000 books which had previously been acquired from Germany. Officials were primarily concerned with the religious orientation of those volumes. However, in their zeal to guard ideological purity, the authorities sometimes reached the point of absurdity. Therefore, they also decided to ban a wide range of books from entry to the Soviet Union that had also been published in Berlin, including "Snow Maiden," "Cinderella," and "Red Riding Hood."[62]

Young Pioneers and members of the Communist Union of Youth (*комсомольцы*) (in Ol'gino, Mar'evka, and Ivanovka), and even Ukrainian Community Party members (in Ol'gino and Miropol') began to appear in a number of the Borozenko villages by the mid-1930s. The emergence of these youth organizations was the result of work by regional *Komsomol* organizers to overcome religiosity in youth and encourage them instead to join the *Komsomol* and Pioneer organizations. As far back as 1925 it was noticed at the 9th Katerynoslav Provincial Conference of *Komsomol Ukraine* that not enough German youth had joined the *Komsomol*. "Such a state is explained," authorities concluded, "mainly by this inertness, which is caused by the so-called community life in German settlements when, for example, a Mennonite German community expels a young man from not only the community but also the family for joining the *Komsomol*." It was a situation that officials declared had to change, and it did, as in the end ideological influence started to filter in among Mennonite youth. As one indication of the speed with which this transpired, investigations undertaken in Novosofievka by the German military administration in 1941 concluded that 3 per cent of those polled were members of labour unions, *Komsomols*, and various public organizations.

Perhaps more surprising is the fact that teachers continued to instruct students in the German language in all our investigated villages up to 1938. Since language is one of the most important elements in the symbolism of ethnicity and often plays a key role in shaping identity, one can conclude that it still managed to fulfil this role in the Borozenko settlement well into the 1930s. This enabled the German and Mennonite population, under strong pressure to acculturate, to master new elements they had adopted as contact with the Ukrainian population increased. At the same time, Mennonites managed to preserve some aspects of their unique identity so as to avoid complete cultural assimilation.

The fate of these colonies became truly tragic with the arrival of National Socialism (fascism) after Hitler assumed full control of the German government in 1933. Alexander Beznosov has explored the significance of that inauguration in his contribution to this volume. For starters, the Stalinist repression of 1937–38 had a significant "German component" in its national spectrum. Now the arrested residents of German villages were politically stamped as "saboteurs," "spies," "counter-revolutionaries," and members of "fascist organizations." Henceforth, the decisions of the courts uniformly ruled that the accused and convicted should be executed.

Waves of lawlessness and death rolled along the lands of Ukraine, and the male population of the German villages was annihilated. An inquiry of these villages later undertaken by the German military administration under the command of Stumpp concluded that up to 50 to 70 per cent of the population was missing in many villages. Thirty thousand inhabitants of the Dnipropetrovsk oblast were arrested over a two-year period, and 7,857 of them were German (which would have included Mennonites). In fact, in the volume of victims who were repressed by the People's Commissariat for Internal Affairs (NKVD), Germans were only exceeded by Ukrainians. From indirect evidence of the tragedy that took place, there are data on the number of German families left without a father, as well as the number of families who had members arrested. For example, in Aleksandrovka, 98 per cent of the families were victims of repression, and 69.9 per cent of the families were without a father. In Ul'isnovka, to which 266 Germans were resettled at the beginning of the occupation, 29.7 per cent of the families did not have a father; in Petrovka – 60 per cent, Marinopol' – 53 per cent, Miropol' – 60 per cent, and Zelenyi – 54 per cent.[63]

If that was not enough, a new era of ordeals set in for the German and Mennonite populations, beginning with the German invasion of the Soviet Union in June of 1941. An insignificant part of the population of the former Borozenko colonies was evacuated when they were ordered to accompany machinery and cattle as it was relocated to the East. However, there was simply not enough time to fulfil the USSR State Defence Committee's order that the German-speaking population of Ukraine be deported along with implements and livestock to the eastern regions of the country. Thus, most of the Borozenko Germans and Mennonites remained in lands that were rapidly occupied by the German army in 1941.

We now have an opportunity to evaluate their moral-psychological state as their own stories and memoirs have been published in the West, but we also have the narrations provided by their former fellow villagers, with whom I have managed to communicate. None of the Ukrainian respondents mentioned any animosity by the Borozenko German population toward the Ukrainians from the beginning of the war. On the contrary, they described the occasions when German or Mennonite neighbours warned of impending bloodshed or when young people were in danger of being dispatched as slave labour to Germany. German women even saved the arrested former teachers and chairmen of collective farms (Petrovka) when their lives were in peril. It was as if the horrific inhumanity of the civil war era had itself perished in those years, to be replaced by neighbourly goodwill across ethnic lines. Facts remain facts, and years of war and occupation did not make irreconcilable enemies of residents of different nationalities. On the contrary, many Ukrainians were sympathetic to the German villagers who were exported to Germany in the autumn of 1943, and the feelings and goodwill seem to have been mutual.

In the post-war period, only a few Germans or Mennonites ever returned to Ukraine. And the former Mennonite and German settlements of southern Ukraine lost their national traits with the departure of the German population. A significant number of Germans and Mennonites, having left during the hard times, permanently forsook their little native land. Years passed, yet a recent renewed interest in their roots demonstrates that people's memories are much stronger than the residential buildings of their former colonies

The memory of those difficult and terrible years continues to live in the hearts of the relatives of the fallen, the deceased, and all honest people. Alexander Tvardovsky said: "He who insists on hiding the past will unlikely be in harmony with the future!" Now we have reached a stage where we can return to our past again and again. Acknowledging that past with its triumphs and hardships is the guarantor of our future. The history of the former daughter colonies of the Borozenko settlements should be made known to the living. In particular, we need to understand more how and why Mennonite colonists once identified so closely with the empire, the landscape, and the peoples of southern Ukraine. For the history to be told is not simply for the benefit of German Mennonites but also for all who care for the history of our common motherland. All of us need to know and love it, and to remember that nothing passes without a trace.

And may there be peace on earth.

NOTES

1 N.V. Venger, "Mennonitskoe predprinimatel'stvo v usloviiakh modernizatsii Iuga Rossii: mezhu kongregatsiei, klanom i rossiiskim obshchestvom (1789–2009)," (Dnepropetrovsk: Dnepropetrovskii national'nyi universitet, 2009); O.V. Beznosova, ":O chem umolchal P.M. Friesen? Mennonity i pravoslavnaia tserkov' v tsarskoi Rossi, 1860–1917" Voprosy germanskoi istorii (Dnepropetrovsk: RVV DNU, 2006), 23–45; A.I. Beznosov, "Kolonistskoe naselenie i vooruzhennaia bor'ba na iuge Ukrainy (konets 1918–osen' 1919)," Voprosy germanskoi istorii (Dnepropetrovsk: RVV DNU, 2005), 71–96; S.I. Bobyleva, "Obshchestvennoe mnenie Rossii kontsa 18th – nachala 20th veka o rossiiskikh nemtsakh," in *Istoriia nemetskoi kolonizatsii v Krymu i na Iuge Ukrainy v xix–xx veka: Materialy Mezhdunarodnoi nauchnoi konferentsii, posviashchennoi 200-letiiu pereseleniia nemtsev v Krym. 6–10 June 2004*, edited by Iu. N. Laptev (Simferopol,' 2007), 204–35; M.V. Belikov, "Mennonitskie kolonii Iuga Ukrainy (1789–1917)" (Disertatsiia na zdobuttia naukovogo stupenia kandidata istorichnikh nauk za spetsial'nistiu 07.00.01). Istoriia Ukraini (Zaporizh'skii natsional'nii universitet. Zaporizhzhia, 2005).

2 Faith Hillis, *Children of Rus': Right-Bank Ukraine and the Invention of a Russian Nation* (Ithaca, NY: Cornell University Press, 2013); Lewis Siegelbaum and Leslie Moch, *Broad Is My Native Land: Repertoires and Regimes of Migration in Russia's Twentieth Century* (Ithaca, NY: Cornell University Press, 2014), esp. ch. 1; David Moon, *The Plough that Broke the Steppes: Agriculture and Environment on Russia's Grasslands, 1700–1914* (Oxford: Oxford University Press, 2013); and Mikhail Akulov, "War without Fronts: Atamans and Commissars in Ukraine, 1917–1919" (PhD diss., Harvard University, 2013).

3 Bobyleva, ed., *Zhivi i pomni ...: Istoriia Mennonitskikh kolonii Ekaterinoslavshchiny* (Dnepropetrovsk, 2006).

4 R.M. Downs and David Stea, *Maps in Minds: Reflection on Cognitive Mapping* (New York: Harper & Row, 1977).

5 Nathaniel Knight, "Ethnicity, Nationality and the Masses; Narodnost' and Modernity in Imperial Russia," in *Russian Modernity: Politics, Knowledge, Practices*, ed. David L. Hoffmann and Yanni Kotsonis (New York: St Martin's Press, 2000), 59.

6 Bobyleva, *Zhivi i pomni.*

7 On these events for all of southern Ukraine, see Leonard Friesen, *Rural Revolutions in Southern Ukraine: Peasants, Nobles, and Colonists, 1774–1905* (Cambridge, MA: Harvard University Press for Harvard Ukrainian Research Institute, 2008), ch. 4.

8 Nataliya V. Venger, "Agrarna kolonizatsiia? Do pitannia pro formuvannia 'osoblivoi' ekonomichnoi zoni na teritorii sil's'kogospodars'kikh mennonits'kikh kolonii Pivdnia Ukraini (persha polovina 19th stolittia)," *Ukrains'kii selianin: zb. nauk. Stat* (Cherkasi: Cherkas'kii natsional'nii universitet, 2004), 63–8.

9 L. Padalka, "Zemlevladeniia nemtsev – byvshikh kolonistov v Khersonskoi gybernii" *Sbornik Khersonskogo zemstva* (Kherson, 1891), 17.

10 A.A. Velitsyn (Paltov A.A.), *Nemtsy v Rossii: Ocherki istoricheskogo razvitiia i nastoiashchego polozheniia nemetskikh kolonii na Iuge i Vostoke Rossii* (St Petersburg, 1893), 125; Vestnik Evropy, (vol. 3, part 4, 1866), 710.

11 D. Reger and A. Plett, *Diese Steine* (Steinbach, MB: Crossway Publications, 2001), 375.

12 Researchers disagree on the founding data of the settlements. For example, Dr Stumpp gave 1862 as the beginning of Friedensfeld (see Richard H. Walth, *Oblomki vcemirnoi istorii* [Essen, 1994], 356); *The Mennonite Encyclopedia* (Kansas: The Mennonite Encyclopedia, 1955), vol. 1, 391, says 1866. The encyclopaedic dictionary of V. Diesendorf's "Nemtsy Rossii: Naselennye punkty i mesta poseleniia" (Moscow: ENR, 2006), 410, points to 1867.

13 P.N. Sokolova, ed., *Sistematicheskii svod postanovlenii Katerynoslavskogo Gubernskogo Zemskogo Sobraniia. 1866–1913. Part 2, 1890–1913 – Vyp II* (Katerynoslav, 1916), 1024.

14 Beznosov, "Sotsial'no-ekonomicheskoe i obshchestvenno-politicheskoe razvitie nemetkikh poselenii Iuga Ukrainy v nachale 20th veka," in *Voprosy germanskoi istorii* (Dnepropetrovsk: DNU, 2000), 117.

15 Bobyleva, "K voprosy o prichinakh tragicheskikh sobytii v mennonitskikh koloniiakh Iuga Ukrainy v gody grazhdanskoi voiny," in *Rossiiskie nemtsy v inonatsional'nom okruzhenii: problemy adaptatsii, vsaimovliianiia, tolerantnosti* (Moscow, 2005), 289–303.

16 John R. Staples, *Cross-Cultural Encounters on the Ukrainian Steppes: Settling the Molochna Basin, 1783–1861* (Toronto: University of Toronto Press, 2003), esp. chs. 2–3; and Friesen, *Rural Revolutions*, 39–43, 139–43.

17 C. Montesquieu, *Izbrannye proizvedeniia* (Moscow, 1955), 412.
18 Moon, *The Plough that Broke the Steppes*, 152–7.
19 H. Goerz, *The Molotschna Settlement* (Winnipeg, MB: CMBC Publications and Manitoba Mennonite Historical Society, 1993).
20 Ibid.
21 Ibid.
22 Royden K. Loewen, *Family, Church, and Market: A Mennonite Community in the Old and the New Worlds, 1850–1930* (Toronto: University of Toronto Press, 1993), 22.
23 Loewen, *Family, Church, and Market*, 20.
24 Moon, *The Plough that Broke the Steppes*, 211, and Friesen, *Rural Revolutions*, 182.
25 Delbert F. Plett, "Jakob M. Barkman 1824–75: Father of Steinbach," in *Preservings* 9, no. 2 (1996), 2–4.
26 There is a strong treatment of the Kleine Gemeinde emigration in Loewen (1996), chs. 3–4; and Delbert F. Plett, *Pioneers and Pilgrims: The Mennonite Kleine Gemeinde in Manitoba, Nebraska and Kansas, 1874 to 1882* (Steinbach, MB: D.F. Plett Publications, 1990).
27 Ibid.
28 S.I. Bobyleva, "A History of the Borozenko Settlement," n.d. in possession of author, 149.
29 S.I. Bobyleva and T.L. Petrova, "Kto vinovat? Rossiiskoe obshchestvo i 'nemetskii' v gody pervoi mirovoi voiny," in *Visnik Dnipropetrovs'kogo universitetu, series: Istoriia ta arkheologiia*, no 8–9, (Dnipropetrovsk, 2009), 83–4.
30 Dvadtsat' tret'e ocherednoe Katerynoslavskoe uesdnoe zemskoe sobranie, 5–10 October 1889, (Ekaterinoskav: 1891), 42.
31 S.V. Obolenskaia, *Narodnoe chtenie i narodnyi chitatel' v Rossii kontsa 19th veka* (Odissei, 1997 – Moscow, 1998), 208.
32 Ibid., 9.
33 Sean David Patterson, "The Makhnos of Memory: Mennonite and Makhnovist Narratives of the Civil War in Ukraine, 1917–1921" (MA thesis, University of Manitoba, 2013).
34 Patterson, "The Makhnos of Memory," 28, 39, 47.
35 Akulev, iii, 162.
36 Roger Chickering and Stig Förster, eds., *Great War, Total War: Combat and Mobilization on the Western Front, 1914–1918* (Cambridge: Cambridge University Press, 2000); and Joshua Sanborn, *Imperial Apocalypse: The Great War and the Destruction of the Russian Empire* (Oxford: Oxford University Press, 2014).

37 Joshua Sanborn, *Drafting the Russian Nation: Military Conscription, Total War, and Mass Politics, 1905–1925* (Dekalb: Northern Illinois University Press, 2011).

38 Rossiia v mirovoi voine (v tsifrakh), (Moscow, 1925), 16–22.

39 GARF, f. 102: Department politsii (1846–1917): Osobyi otdel, op. 316 (1915), d. 343, "O nemetskom zacil'e v Rossii 02.1915-12.1915," 7, 26.

40 "Konstitutsiini akti Ukraini. 1917–1920. Nevidomi konstitutsii Ukraini," in *Filosofs'ka i sotsiologichna dymka* (Kiev, 1992), 82–3.

41 B.V. Malinovskii, "Nekotorye aspekty vsaimootnoshenii nemtsev-kolonistov Iuga Ukrainy i voisk Tsentral'nykh derzhav v otsenke predstavitelei gosudarstvennoi administratsii Ukrainskoi Derzhavy getmana P.P. Skoropadskogo" in *Voprosy germanskoi istorii: Germaniia i mir: problemy mezhetnicheskikh kontaktov i gosudarstvennykh vsaimootnoshenii: Vol. 1. Istoriia* (Dnepropetrovsk: DGU, 1998), 81.

42 N. Makhno, *Vospominaniia*: 3 books, Book 2–3 (Kiev: Ukraina, 1991), 20–4; and *Grazhdanskaia voina na Katerynoslavshchine (February 1918–1920): Dokumenty i materialy* (Dnepropetrovsk: Promin'), 35–6.

43 Malinovskii, "Nekotorye aspekty," 82–3.

44 P.A. Arshinov, *Istoriia makhnovskogo dvizheniia (1918–1921)*, (Moscow: TERRA; Knizhnaia lavka–RTR, 1996), Series "Tainy istorii v romanakh, povestiakh i dokumentakh"; A.V. Belash and V.F. Belash, *Dorogi Nestora Makhno* (Kiev: Reklamno-izdatel'skii tsentr "Prosa,"), 1993; and V.V. Komin, *Nestor Makhno: mify i real'nost'* (Kalinin, 1990).

45 *Grazhdanskaia voina na Katerynoslavshchine (February 1918–1920): Dokumenty i materialy* (Dnepropetrovsk: Promin', 1968).

46 V. Byldakov, *Krasnaia smuta* (Moscow, 1997), 237.

47 Goerz, *The Molotschna Settlement*.

48 I. Danilov, "Vospominaniia o moei podnevol'noi sluzhbe u bol'shevikov," in *Arkhiv Rossiiskoi revoliutsii*, vol. 15–16 (Moscow, 1993), 1814.

49 Goerz, *The Molotschna Settlement*.

50 Bobyleva and Petrova, "Kto vinovat?," 83ff.

51 GARF, f. 1318, op. 1, d. 1033, l. 17.

52 *Tsentral'nyi gosudarstvennyi arkhiv vysshikh organov vlasti i upravleniia Ukrainy*, f. 413, op. 1, d. 130, l. 171.

53 DADO, f. II - 1, op. 1, d. 1928, l. 52.

54 Ibid., f. II - 1, op. 1, d. 1528, l. 38; d. 635, l. 73.

55 Ibid., f. II - 1, op. 1, d. 1525, l. 113.

56 B. Kagan, *Stalindorf* (Kiev: Radians'ke budivnitstvo i pravo, 1935).

57 Ibid., 47.

58 Ibid.

59 GADO, f. II - 1, op. 1, d. 2235, l. 104.
60 Terry Martin, *The Affirmative Action Empire: Nations and Nationalism in the Soviet Union, 1923–1939* (Ithaca, NY: Cornell University Press, 2001).
61 Ibid., f. II - 1, op. 1, d. 1525, l. 103.
62 Ibid., f. II - 11, op. 1, d. 316, l. 27.
63 R.H. Walth, *Oblomki vcemirnoi istorii: Rossiiskie nemtsy mezhdu Stalinym i Gitlerom*, 2nd ed. (Essen, 1996), 119.

2 Afforestation as Performance Art: Johann Cornies' Aesthetics of Civilization

JOHN R. STAPLES

In June 1837, Johann Cornies left his home in New Russia and travelled to Pyatigorsk in the Caucasus Mountains. There he joined his friend and mentor Andrei Fadeev to begin a survey of peasant conditions in the Kuban region.

Pyatigorsk held a special place in the Russian imagination. Its hot springs attracted the wealthy and famous who came as much for the society as they did to take the baths. The celebrated Russian poet Mikhail Lermontov, exiled from St Petersburg, arrived in Pyatigorsk just days after Cornies, and his description of the hazy blue "amphitheatre of mountains," the "silver chain of snowy peaks," and the air "pure and fresh, as the kiss of a child" captures the region's breathtaking beauty.[1]

Cornies was not immune to the wonders of Pyatigorsk. He wrote vividly to an old friend in Prussia: "I am here at the foot of beautiful Mount Bisten in the Caucasus, located in a romantic region with glorious views of the Caucasus Mountains that are covered with eternal snow. Elbrus, the highest of these mountains, rises majestically far above the clouds."[2] But in this wild beauty Cornies saw danger: "The inhabitants of this region live in constant fear of Circassians on fleet-footed horses bent on kidnapping many of their members and dragging them off to the mountains .... The deep valleys and forests that grow here more luxuriantly than in any place I have ever visited serve as secret hiding places."[3]

The association of wildness with danger that Cornies identified in Pyatigorsk reflected a central element of his world view: he dedicated his life to taming the wild world of New Russia. This sometimes meant "civilizing" nomadic people and sometimes mapping uncharted land, but at its root was a desire to make the world orderly.

When anthropologist James Urry labelled Johann Cornies the "prophet of progress" he captured in a single powerful phrase an entire historiographical tradition that depicts Cornies as an agent of the Tsarist state's modernizing agenda.[4] In this tradition, Cornies emerges as a secular and secularizing figure, undermining traditional Mennonite religious and community values even as he laid the foundations of future Mennonite economic prosperity. This depiction of Cornies, and of Tsarist Mennonite history in general, echoes a larger historiographical tradition that identifies the state as the principal agent of change in the Empire and leaves little room for local agency.[5]

Urry's depiction of Cornies captures an important truth about Cornies' role in the Mennonite community. He was the state's most important agent in the Molochna Mennonite settlement, and his reform program placed him at odds with conservative Mennonite religious leaders. In the 1840s, backed by the state, he wholly undermined the political power of the religious conservatives and helped depose the conservative majority's most important leader, Jacob Warkentin.

Nowhere in the historiography are Cornies' personal motivations deeply plumbed. Even early twentieth-century accounts that hold Cornies up as a Mennonite hero depict little more than a man who, fed up with Mennonite "backwardness," forged a path forward to prosperity.[6] Urry moves beyond this Mennonite hagiography to situate Cornies' reforms in the scholarship of modernization, revealing the ways that economic changes undermined the Mennonites' traditional culture. My initial account of Cornies' reforms leaned heavily on Urry's depiction of the internal dynamics of the Mennonite community and tried to situate this Mennonite story in the larger Tsarist picture.[7]

Close attention to Cornies' own accounts of frontier "backwardness" and his reform mission force a reframing of the Tsarist Mennonite story. Urry ironically labels the secularizing Cornies a "prophet" to his religious community, but I will argue here that Cornies was profoundly influenced by pietism, which provided him with a religious framework into which he incorporated the Tsarist reform agenda. Blending the Tsarist designation of Mennonites as a didactic model for other frontier communities with a pietist vision of the Christian community as a "city upon a hill," Cornies constructed his own unique aesthetics of civilization.

Cornies was sixteen when he immigrated to Russia. He had lived long enough in the Vistula River Delta under Prussian rule to have a clear sense of what historian Marc Raeff has called the "well-ordered police state."[8] Land in the delta was carefully allocated, and water in the swampy lowlands was closely managed by dike societies; this was an old, highly developed, closely managed agricultural region.

The Molochna river basin in New Russia could not have been more different. The region had only passed into Russian hands in 1783, with the first permanent villages appearing in the following year. The first Mennonites immigrated in 1804, and when Cornies arrived they had barely had time to build their homes and plant a few fields. Around them other villages were also springing up: to the southwest, Russian Doukhobor sectarians; to the west, Lutheran and Catholic peasants from across the German states; to the southeast, semi-nomadic members of the Nogai Tatar Horde who transmigrated along the coast of Sea of Azov.

Soon after his arrival in the Molochna, the young Cornies became a merchant, hauling butter across the steppe to cities in the Crimea. The most vivid account of this period of his life comes from his biographer David Epp, who describes Cornies racing across the steppe pursued by armed Nogai Tatars.[9] This depiction may well be apocryphal, but it accurately reflects an important element of Cornies' understanding of his new home. The steppe, just like the Caucasus Mountains, was wild and dangerous; he would later call it a place of "great darkness."[10] Cornies meant this as a metaphor for what he perceived as Tatar ignorance, but his choice of words is striking: the open steppe with its seemingly endless vistas more often evokes metaphors of light, a "sky-blue steppe," as Lermontov described it.[11]

Cornies' first public role in his Molochna community was as the settlement's land surveyor, a position to which he was appointed in 1817. It was a job that allowed him, functionally and symbolically, to impose order on the wild land. Land surveying became a life-long passion for Cornies. He never attempted to master its technical complexities, instead forcing his son to take up the profession of surveying and map-making under the training of private tutors in Ekaterinoslav and Moscow. Johann Jr showed little aptitude or desire for this career – he sent drawings of flowers home to his mother from Ekaterinoslav, and left more drawings to adorn the walls of his Moscow host, the Moravian Brethren merchant Traugott Blueher, but his maps left no mark, and back home he disappeared into obscurity.[12] Perhaps forcing him to become a map-maker was his father's way to try to tame, and make useful, his artistic talent. After all, pietists were always suspicious of art for beauty's sake, and of the vanity of artists who presumed to interpret

God's creation.[13] Cornies' aesthetics found beauty in the more prosaic form of ordering the world.

Land surveying began with simple goals – the assignment of 65 desiatina land allotments to Mennonite immigrants – but it forced Cornies to think seriously about the complexities of ordering life in New Russia. Land derived its value from its productive capacity, and Cornies devoted himself to understanding the environmental constraints that governed agriculture in his region. He investigated ground-water levels, overseeing well-digging across the region to determine what sites would support new villages. He paid close attention to precipitation and promoted dam projects to provide water for hay meadows. He conducted detailed studies of native steppe plants, and experimented with wide varieties of crops to find the most productive commercial varieties. By the late 1830s he had become expert on crop rotation systems, attuned to both the limitations of the soil and the potential of fodder crops and fallow fields to preserve and increase productivity.[14]

These efforts to order the environment had the clear economic motive of increasing productivity and wealth, and while Cornies took the lead in implementing changes, the impetus often came from the Guardianship Committee for Foreign Colonists that oversaw the Mennonites and other settlers in New Russia. However, Cornies' purpose was not only economic, and the underlying values that shaped his reform efforts were distinctly his own. Nowhere is this clearer than in his projects to "civilize" the Nogai Tatar Horde. It is here that Cornies first explicitly associated order with civilization; in identifying the ordering of the natural world with the "civilizing" of the "wild" Nogai Tatars, Cornies' vision of order migrated to the human realm.

Cornies had a long-standing interest in the Nogai Tatars. It was they who allegedly pursued him across the steppe in his youth, but he had also encountered them in friendlier surroundings, for his father was a natural healer to whom the Nogai Tatars came for herbal remedies. Cornies' wealth was founded on the land he leased at Iushanle, where, beginning in 1812, he grazed large herds of sheep, often under the care of hired Nogai Tatar shepherds. Most important, in 1822 the Swiss pietist Daniel Schlatter came to the Molochna and took up residence among the Nogais, hoping to evangelize them. While he lived with a Nogai landowner, Schlatter became a close personal friend of Cornies and one of his most important intellectual influences.

Schlatter was raised in St Gallen, Switzerland, where he was deeply immersed in the pan-European pietist community of the early nineteenth century.[15] His aunt, Anna Bernet-Schlatter, was a leading figure in European pietism. Daniel Schlatter was strongly influenced by his famous aunt, and he listed among his principal intellectual influences her friend and mentor Johann Caspar Lavater.[16] Lavater was a prominent pietist preacher and religious writer, but he owed his greatest fame to his *Essays on Physiognomy*.[17] This influential volume argued that it was possible to understand people's moral character from the scientific analysis of their physical appearance. While this seems to situate *Essays on Physiognomy* in the secular scientific milieu of the Enlightenment, in fact Lavater's work is more often "a sermon on the goodness of God and that goodness as reflected in the constitution and action of created things."[18] Lavater wrote that "God has ever branded vice with deformity, and adorned virtue with inimitable beauty."[19]

When Lavater equated beauty with virtue, he was constructing an aesthetics of civilization. The most famous expression of that aesthetics came in his drawing of the metamorphosis of a frog into Apollo. This drawing placed the natural world on one end of a scale of civilization, and Apollo, the epitome of high western culture, at the other end. The choice of Apollo, Greek god of music, poetry, and art, stressed the degree to which Lavater understood civilization in aesthetic terms.[20]

I use "aesthetics" here in a very basic sense, as a set of principles "concerned with beauty or the appreciation of beauty."[21] Lavater offers an aesthetics of civilization in which beauty is an abstract value associated with civilization and modernity. For Cornies, this aesthetic concept relating beauty, civilization, and modernity became closely entwined with ordering a disorderly world in New Russia. There is no explicit evidence that Cornies ever read Lavater's work, or even knew the Swiss Pietist's name, but beginning in the mid-1820s Cornies began to pay close attention to the physical attributes of the people in surrounding communities, and he directly relate these attributes to their civilizational status and potential.[22] Such observations occurred shortly after the arrival of Schlatter, who both informed Cornies' understanding of the Nogais, and himself described their physiognomy in explicitly Lavaterian terms.[23]

Lavater's work was never accepted by contemporaries in the scientific community, who recognised his lack of scientific rigour. Nevertheless, he gained broad popularity in Europe. In Russia, luminaries such as Prince Aleksander Golitsyn and other prominent pietists avidly read his work, in part because of his melding of pietist sensibilities with the rationalist values of the Enlightenment. In Daniel Schlatter's hands,

Lavater's theories penetrated to the Molochna where they provided Johann Cornies with an important idea, encouraging him to think that people and their world could be changed at the most fundamental level.

Lavater's influence is apparent in Cornies' 1825 essay "The Nogai Tatars in Russia."[24] This essay's general argument was that the Nogais' uncivilized condition was both caused by, and reflected in, their economic backwardness, revealed most clearly in nomadism. Cornies saw nomadism as irrationally disordered, for he had no understanding of nomadism as a rational response to environmental conditions.[25] It was simply a product of "the inclination to a lazy, changeable, unrestrained life still clinging to" the Nogais.[26] Ending the practice was the first step to reducing their "prejudice, superstition and fanaticism, ... making the Nogais more receptive to moral improvement, culture of the spirit, and all institutions that contribute to the happiness of human society and therefore also to the state."[27] In this judgment Cornies was closely attuned to broader Christian missionary attitudes toward nomadic peoples. As Brian Stanley has noted, missionaries adopted a view of nomadism as "one of the distinguishing marks of the degeneration of humankind from the settled and cultivating mode of existence that characterized the Garden of Eden."[28]

Lavater's work was pseudo-science, and at any rate Cornies probably only knew it second-hand, so unsurprisingly Cornies' essay about the Nogais does not offer a sophisticated argument about their physiognomy. What it does reveal is a new-found concern with physical appearance – revealingly identified explicitly as "physiognomy" – expressed in the specific context of an essay about the Nogais' potential for economic development. In a section entitled "Character and Physical Stature of the Nogais," Cornies writes that the Crimean Tatars (most of whom practiced sedentary agriculture) "can be distinguished from [the Nogais] for their culture, cleanliness, and more attractive physiognomy."[29] As for the Nogais themselves, he praises their strength, their posture, and their "snow white" teeth, and he notes that Nogai "girls and very young women" have "well-proportioned physiognomies, lively eyes, pretty noses, small mouths, long necks, especially beautiful teeth, and black hair."[30]

Cornies' account of Nogai women is revealing, because he considered their mistreatment to be particularly damning evidence of Nogai incivility. He writes that Nogai woman are "left with little more than animal instincts, which must have the most detrimental physical and moral effects on [their] children."[31] The consequence for women was that "as they get older, they usually only reveal traces of earlier beauty in wasted, pale faces. The female gender wilts very early and carries the stamp of apathy [and] ignorance."[32] While Lavater's civilizational aesthetic is implied in this passage, Cornies' primitive understanding of Lavater's ideas is also apparent. Taken literally, Cornies' description might suggest that Nogai women were civilized when they were young and became uncivilized as they aged, a progression that goes well beyond Lavater's general claim that physical beauty reflects virtue. Yet Lavater's larger point, that appearance, moral character, and civilization are linked, is still apparent in Cornies' linkage of "animal instincts" to physical deterioration.

Cornies saw in the Nogais' physiognomy and their nomadism a symptom of their uncivilized condition, but he also saw in them the potential to become civilized. This was already in evidence in his 1825 essay, where Cornies proposed a series of reforms, including forcing the Nogais to sow grain crops, and providing schools that might slowly wean them away from what he termed their "superstitions." Here again Cornies echoed the prescriptions of evangelical missionaries, undoubtedly influenced by Schlatter. But in the 1830s, when he moved from proposing reforms to implementing them, it was Cornies' own civilizational aesthetics that took centre stage. This is most clearly revealed in his personal initiative in establishing a model Nogai village called Akkerman.[33]

Akkerman was Cornies' vision of an orderly peasant village. He helped select the village site; planned the layout of the home plots, streets, and fields; and offered systematic instruction on the proper balance between grain crops and livestock. The basic assumption was that people forced to order their lives within "civilized" boundaries would in fact become civilized, and that as the obvious merits of civilization became evident, other Nogais would imitate Akkerman.

Cornies' plan for Akkerman is a depiction of what he understood to be the aesthetics of civilization. It was not enough that the Nogais grow grain and raise fine-wooled sheep – it was also necessary that the places where they lived take on the appearance of the homes and villages of "civilized" people. Cornies described precisely what a civilized, orderly village and its individual homes should look like, from the dimensions of their front porches to a requirement that their doors, shutters, and window-frames be properly painted.[34]

While the Akkerman project provides the clearest depiction of Cornies' aesthetics of civilization, by the 1830s Cornies was also busily engaged in trying to reorder Mennonite life. The explicit tie between civilization and order that Cornies made in relation to the Nogais implicitly suggests a sharp criticism of Mennonites: apparently he believed that Mennonites too were uncivilized, disorderly, and in need of reform.

The wedge issue through which Cornies began re-ordering Mennonite life was afforestation. One of the starkest contrasts between the Vistula and the Molochna was the lack of trees in New Russia, and it was only natural that Cornies' attempt to civilize the Molochna's inhabitants should begin with efforts to bring forests to the steppe. This coincided tidily with the Russian state's economic agenda, for it recognized the many ways that trees benefited peasants.[35] Mennonites already recognized the economic benefits of growing trees, and from their first years of settlement they had planted fruit trees. In 1825, when Tsar Alexander I visited the settlement, he urged the Mennonites to increase their efforts to plant trees, and in 1828 the Ministry of Internal Affairs launched a project to establish forestry societies across New Russia.

Trees were both a state mandate and an economic boon, and naturally Cornies – as the state's best agent in the Molochna – took up the cause with zeal. He established a tree nursery on his land at Iushanle in 1830, and in 1831 he accepted the post of chairman of a newly established Forestry Society with the authority to carefully supervise and expand afforestation in the Molochna.[36]

For Cornies, afforestation was not simply utilitarian: it also had an explicitly aesthetic character. Civilization possessed a proper appearance, and trees, like painted window frames, were one of its elements. In 1841 he wrote: "Where fields are cultivated by industrious men of the land they provide a picture of abundance and well-being. Villages and yards with good soils but lacking fruit trees, on the other hand, betray lazy and ignorant inhabitants and are not worthy of respect .... As soon as people from time immemorial left their savage state and became cultivators of the soil, they have developed orchards."[37]

Cornies was not satisfied with forcing Mennonites to plant useful trees on their fullholdings: by the end of the 1830s the Forestry Society began insisting that Mennonites also plant attractive trees on public land. He ordered that villages line their streets, and eventually the roads that linked the villages in the settlement, with trees. In annual reports on Mennonite progress he proudly reported to the Ministry of State Domains that "our villages are growing more beautiful, with trees planted along streets and elsewhere."[38]

The Forestry Society's demands for systematic tree-planting for economic purposes provoked some opposition from Mennonites, though hardly wholesale revolt, as is sometimes claimed. Most Mennonites accepted the value of planting trees, and indeed their success had attracted Tsar Alexander's praise long before the Forestry Society came into existence. However, the expansion of the program to tree-planting for aesthetic reasons pushed Cornies onto more uncertain ground.

Hostility to Cornies' civic beautification program grew in proportion to his increasing power to force Mennonites to accept his orders. In 1836 the Forestry Society was subsumed into a new, much more powerful organization called the Agricultural Society. This gave Cornies broad powers to reform agriculture. Its most characteristic and intrusive element was the re-ordering of field rotations: Cornies forced all Mennonite fullholders to adopt a four-field crop rotation. This sharply increased Mennonite agricultural productivity, but it also sharply increased the physical demands on Mennonite peasants, for as Cornies observed, "as the many easy days of sheep breeding are significantly reduced we embrace a way of life in which man must literally eat his bread by the sweat of his brow."[39] It may have been the single most important and labour-intensive reform that Cornies implemented. Yet here again there is no evidence that the field rotations themselves provoked any opposition. Mennonites, after all, were farmers, who never shied away from hard work and who recognized good agricultural practices when they saw them.

Far more provocative were the inspection tours that Cornies and other members of the Agricultural Society carried out in the settlement. These tours were intended to ensure that the Society's orders regarding forestry and agriculture were obeyed. At first they focused on identifying fullholders who were not following Society orders. For example, reports from an 1836 inspection identify concerns about twenty-two householders. In most of these cases the Society reported that the fullholders were beyond recovery. Dirk Boldt of Neukirch was "a slacker … addicted to drink"; Jacob Baerg of Marienthal was "unmotivated and [had] no prospects"; in Wernersdorf there was "no hope for improvement in the farming of three householders, Kaethler, Engbrecht and Giesbrecht."[40] But over time, the Society extended its focus to village aesthetics, insisting, for example, that Gnadenheim "beautify the area around community buildings" by "planting … various useful trees," or that Gnadenfeld plant trees along footpaths "to beautify the village."[41]

Society reports identified the economic consequences of disorder, but they also focused on the *appearance* of disorder. One of Cornies' key concerns was that Mennonites visibly fulfil their role as model colonists. This "model" status was what justified Mennonite privileges, and in a state that, under Tsar Nicholas, was moving sharply toward a homogenizing vision of national identity under the policy of "Official Nationality," *demonstrable* success was important.

The state's insistence that Mennonites play the role of model colonists was at the core of political and religious tensions in Russian Mennonite life. Religious conservatives insisted that Mennonites were a static model, invited to Russia because of their already-established characteristics, and were required only to continue to live moral, industrious agricultural lives as a model to others. Progressives, pushed by the state and led by Cornies, insisted that the model was a moving target, subject to new state policies in a changing world. Cornies, who knew the mind of official Russia better than any other Mennonite, saw a progressive model as essential to preserving Mennonite privileges.[42]

The Mennonite model was intended to produce change by consequence of its appearance. The conservative version of the model insisted that the model was a fixed, natural order of things, rooted in a fixed vision of primitive Christian life. It was not "aesthetic," for it could not be subject to interpretation: it was founded on a single absolute Christian value. Cornies' version of the model was, by comparison, explicitly aesthetic, subject to change rooted in the changing values of its intended audience. The model was officially intended for an audience of other colonists, but Cornies knew that it had a second important audience: the state officials who controlled Mennonite privileges. He wrote that "individuals and statesmen who travel through our villages and honour us with their visits, judge entire regions by their appearance."[43]

Cornies was highly attuned to this state audience for the Mennonite model, and he carefully staged a Mennonite performance of civilization for official visitors. The Molochna was a relatively isolated place, and visits from high officials were consequently rare. Because officials usually came with retinues, their visits required advanced local planning, a job that invariably fell to Cornies. He anxiously sought news of planned visits and prepared careful itineraries for the visitors. Village mayors were given orders that villagers should "behave politely and decently to distinguished visitors," and Mennonites were admonished about proper clothing and behaviour.[44]

The Molochna performance of civilization had two key acts: the Nogai model village of Akkerman, and Cornies' estate at Iushanle. Akkerman was set in the midst of Nogai territory, so as visitors were led to the model village they could observe Nogais in their natural, "primitive" state. Arriving at Akkerman, they found the Nogais transformed into civilized people, with proper homes and painted window frames. At the climax of the performance the audiences were invited to enter a Nogai home and observe real live Nogais *in situ*.[45]

The larger Mennonite settlement provided the setting for the second act, Iushanle. The settlement, with its bustling agricultural economy, was already an impressive sight to visitors. Its trees, so rare on the steppe, drew particular praise, and visitors often called the settlement an "oasis." But on the tours that Cornies staged for visitors, Iushanle was the performed settlement's centrepiece, a 3,800-desiatina estate with a home, office, barns, corrals, orchards, and tree nurseries. It was a quintessential "laboratory of modernity," where Cornies grew experimental crops, experimented with livestock breeding, tried out new barn feeding methods, and trained peasant apprentices.[46]

Petr Keppen, the Ministry of State Domains official who became one of Cornies' most important patrons, described the Molochna Mennonite tour in his journal after his first visit in 1837. He had never met Cornies, though Fadeev, his Ministry colleague, had provided him with an introduction by mail. Keppen arrived in Halbstadt, the settlement's administrative centre, and was immediately taken in hand by Cornies, who swept the visitor away to Iushanle.[47] What followed was a whirlwind tour of the settlement, which left Keppen overwhelmed by the fineness of the Iushanle estate (he described in detail its interior walls painted in "various colours"), and by Akkerman, the shining example of Cornies' success in "civilizing" the Nogais. Accounts of official visits in the 1840s describe similar carefully staged tours.

The Iushanle performance helped to establish an image of the Mennonites as model subjects in official minds, making an argument for preserving Mennonite privileges. In the 1840s the Mennonites became a national marvel, held up in journals, newspapers, and Ministry circulars as a model of peasant progress to which all Russian officials should aspire for the peasants they administered. Cornies gained a national reputation as an architect of civilizational reform, a status recognized with his prestigious appointment to the Learned Committee of the Ministry of State Domains.[48]

The danger of this performed identity was that it established expectations that would have to be met. When Cornies introduced Russian officials to his Iushanle laboratory, he established an expectation that the entire Mennonite settlement would equally act as a laboratory. By performing Mennonite identity as progressive, Cornies created expectations that Mennonites would continue to model progress. He staked his own status in official circles on the continuing successful performance. Yet the image was a consciously idealized one, part of a carefully constructed aesthetics of civilization that did not accurately reflect the Mennonite settlement as a whole. Cornies well knew this – the Agricultural Society's village inspections revealed the weak performances of bit players, while mounting political challenges from leading actors threatened to close down the theatre.

The tension between the real and performed Mennonite settlements reached the breaking point in the Warkentin Affair. In 1841 a long-running dispute between Cornies and Jacob Warkentin, the settlement's leading conservative and Elder of the Large Flemish Congregation, reached its climax. Warkentin led a rebellion against Agricultural Society authority, first through defiance of Society directives, and then in the elections for District Mayor. The Guardianship Committee stepped in and forced the election of a reform-friendly mayor; it then deposed Warkentin and dissolved the Large Flemish Congregation, forcing the creation of three smaller congregations in its place.[49]

These events were scandalous in their own time and provoked a wave of outrage and recriminations in the broader Russian and Prussian Mennonite communities. In the big picture, however, their significance has never been very clear. Cornies enjoyed virtually unchallenged authority from 1841 until his death in 1848, but after that the power of the Agricultural Society waned, so the Affair had only brief political consequences. As for the religious significance, although in the moment direct state interference in Mennonite religious affairs prompted apocalyptic language from Warkentin's supporters, the religious upheavals brought on by the creation of the Mennonite Brethren in the late 1850s and 1860s soon relegated the Warkentin Affair to minor status in the larger Mennonite story.

The Warkentin Affair is conventionally recounted as a dispute between religious and secular authority, and in practice this is what it became; Cornies, allied with the state's Guardianship Committee, oversaw the dismantling of the Large Flemish Congregation and imposed the Agricultural Society's reform agenda on the Mennonite Settlement.

Curiously, closer examination of the dispute reveals that the issue that sparked the revolt was not Cornies' most important agricultural reforms, but his aesthetic vision of a properly ordered world. Perhaps the reason that this issue has never attracted close attention is that it seems too prosaic to be taken seriously. What Warkentin's Large Flemish Congregation first rebelled against in 1841 was brick buildings.

In Cornies' account of the Warkentin Affair, he wrote that the issue that "particularly offended" the Warkentin Party and sparked the political crisis was the "new, attractive and more appropriate building style using fired brick for houses and barns. This style was strongly supported by the Society because it gave our villages a more cheerful and beautiful appearance."[50] Abraham Friesen, Elder of the Kleine Gemeinde, confirmed this in a letter to his brother-in-law Heinrich Neufeld, one of Warkentin's strongest supporters. Friesen identified the event that sparked the Warkentin revolt as the refusal of a congregational member to build his home of bricks in the newly prescribed manner.[51]

Cornies had begun constructing buildings from brick with tile roofs at his Iushanle and Tashchenak estates in 1837, and he was soon pushing for all new construction in the Molochna to follow suit. In 1837 he insisted that the new Ohrloff church be constructed from brick in a "new, tasteful design," and in 1839 he required that the entire new village of Landskrone be constructed from brick.[52] In 1842, the Agricultural Society mandated brick-and-tile for all new construction in the settlement.[53] There were economic justifications for these regulations. For one thing they helped prevent fires such as the one that destroyed nine houses in Sparrau in 1839.[54] The regulations also provided jobs for the landless, both through the manufacture of brick and tile and the labour intensive work of bricklaying. But as Cornies made clear in 1842, bricks were first-and-foremost about aesthetics, an important expression of his concern with the aesthetics of civilization.

If Cornies understood brick and tile in terms of aesthetics, the Warkentin Affair reveals that Molochna conservatives shared his understanding. Opposition to ostentation in clothing and buildings was a deeply rooted element of Mennonite religious beliefs, and Cornies' aim to beautify the Molochna by brick construction was controversial on these grounds alone. Building the Ohrloff Church – Cornies' home church – of bricks was a particularly pointed challenge to this tradition. Just as, for Cornies, brick buildings were part of a larger aesthetic of orderly civilization, for Warkentin and his supporters, bricks were an unacceptable extension of Cornies' re-ordering of the world. Warkentin insisted that the Mennonite model remain static because he and other conservatives understood the Mennonite way-of-life as a survival of the primitive Christian community. It was not an economic model in a laboratory of modernity – it was a model of God's kingdom on earth. This is why, among the economic reforms and political challenges that Cornies championed in the late 1830s, his aesthetic reforms emerged as a key conservative concern.

Cornies wrote that Warkentin and his supporters, by promoting disobedience to "our legal authorities" and blocking economic reforms that were intended to promote "the country's welfare and the community's success," were turning "God's blessings away from us, [keeping] the land from producing its fruits and [causing] our livestock to die of hunger."[55] This echoes a recurring theme in all of Cornies' justifications of his reforming role in the settlement: as he had written during agricultural crises in 1825 and 1833, God used hardships to promote change.[56] By corollary, God would send hardships to punish the failure to change.

Warkentin and Cornies alike understood conflict over aesthetics as a religious conflict. Emblematic of this, when Cornies wrote about the relationship of wildness and danger from Pyatigorsk, he addressed his letters, not to friends and family in the Molochna, but to his key western pietist confidants, Daniel Schlatter and David Epp. These letters show that for Cornies there was a conscious connection between ordering the frontier and his pietist religious views. This is hardly surprising: the missionary impulse that brought Schlatter and other pietists to the Molochna employed exactly the language of darkness and light that Cornies used in these letters.[57]

Pietism claimed for itself a civilizing role that frequently echoed the modernizing agenda of the Enlightenment even as it tried to reject the secularizing implications of that agenda.[58] Cornies' plans to civilize the Nogais fit neatly into a broader missionary discourse that characterized indigenous peoples as part of a "vast moral waste" and viewed the incorporation of such people into the peasantry as the Christian antidote.[59]

Less explicit, but more important to the state-prescribed Mennonite role of the Mennonites as model colonists, was the idea of a Christian "city upon a hill." In the Sermon on the Mount, Jesus told his audience that "You are the light of the world. A city that is set on a hill cannot be hidden."[60] The city upon a hill, as a depiction of a model Christian community, shared the ambiguity of the Russian state's injunction to the Mennonites to be model colonists. It was most famously invoked by John Winthrop's sermon "A Model of Christian Charity," given to Puritans fleeing the religious constraints of England. In that context it clearly envisioned a static model, for early Puritan colonization of America was not a missionary enterprise. The relevance of this example for religiously conservative Mennonites fleeing Prussia for the Russian frontier is obvious. In the hands of pietist leader Hermann Franke the city upon a hill took on new, evangelical significance. Franke envisioned Halle as the city upon a hill from which a second Reformation would emanate. His plan was to educate and send forth an army of clergy to win over the world to a renewed faith. This explicitly missionary vision saw the city upon a hill, not as a static model, but as a beachhead for transformative Christian missionary work.[61]

Schlatter, who was so central to Cornies' intellectual development, came from a European missionary culture that sought out missionary hilltops on the colonial frontier. Schlatter came to the Molochna on the recommendation of Ebeneezer Henderson, a British and Foreign Bible Society representative who visited the Molochna in 1818, and who described the Molochna Mennonite settlement is terms that vividly evoke the promise that evangelical missionary movements saw in the Molochna Mennonites: "Placed in the centre of an extensive territory, where they are surrounded by Russians of various sects, Germans, Greeks, Bulgarians, Tatars, and Jews, we could not but regard them as destined by Divine Providence to shine as lights in a dark place.'[62]

There is a clear parallel between this pietist missionary perception of Molochna Mennonites and the Russian state's perception of them. The Mennonites' signal success in establishing an orderly, prosperous frontier community made them an irresistible recruitment target for both secular and religious civilizational projects. It is no wonder that Jacob Warkentin and his conservative congregation saw little difference between the two.

Most accounts of Johann Cornies identify him as an agent of secular state authority who undermined congregational authority in his community. Such accounts focus on the utilitarian nature of his economic reforms and his alliance with the Guardianship Committee in disputes with Jacob Warkentin. Attention to Cornies' aesthetics of civilization demands a reconsideration of this consensus.

When Cornies imposed order on the wildness that surrounded him, he did not frame his purpose solely in utilitarian economic terms. Civilization, as he understood it, possessed an aesthetics. This was true both in the sense that he saw beauty in order (and danger in disorder), but equally in his explicit efforts to stage the performance of order.

The conscious performance of civilization is perhaps the most astonishing element of this story. It shows that Cornies was not simply acting as an agent of state interests. Instead he actively deceived the state by imposing an interpretive lens on what state representatives saw when they visited the Molochna. This represented a sophisticated understanding of the state's modernization policies, which depended on model colonists to play a didactic role in regional development. Cornies fought to preserve Mennonite privileges by staging performances of modernity, an interpretive act that was explicitly aesthetic. For all that this embroiled him in deep controversies in the Mennonite community, his efforts are clear evidence that he was no mere agent of the state.

Of course Cornies' aesthetics of civilization was not just a performance – it also provides important evidence of the role that pietism played in shaping his world view. Part of the prevailing image of Cornies is as a secular and secularizing figure, but his aesthetics were clearly and profoundly affected by pietism. The foundations emerged from the pietist ideas of Lavater, introduced to Cornies by the pietist Schlatter. As Cornies applied these ideas to his community, they evolved to reflect a pietist version of the didactic model – not of the Mennonite settlement as an agency of economic modernization, but rather as a "city upon a hill," an oasis of salvation in the New Russian spiritual desert.

NOTES

1 M. Yu. Lermontov, *A Hero of Our Time*, trans. Paul Foote (Baltimore: Penguin, 1966), 91. On Pyatigorsk, see Benjamin D. Morgan, "Topographic Transmissions and How to Talk about Them: The Case of the Southern Spa in Nineteenth Century Russian Fiction," *Modern Languages Open*, 2.

2 Johann Cornies to David Epp, 15 July 1837, State Archive of the Odessa Region (hereafter SAOR), f. 89, o. 1, d. 47.

3 Ibid.

4 James Urry, *None but Saints: The Transformation of Mennonite Life in Russia, 1789–1899* (Winnipeg: Windflower Communications, 1989).

5 On the historiography of Imperial Russia and its Mennonites, see *Transformation on the Southern Ukrainian Steppe: Letters and Papers of Johann Cornies, Volume I: 1812–1835*, trans. Ingrid I. Epp, ed. Harvey L. Dyck, Ingrid I. Epp, and John R. Staples (Toronto: University of Toronto Press, 2015), xxii [hereafter Dyck, Epp, and Staples, *Transformation*].

6 See, e.g., David Epp, *Johann Cornies*, trans. Peter Pauls (Winnipeg: CMBC, 1995); Franz Isaac, *Die Molotschnaer Mennoniten* (Halbstadt, 1908); P.M. Friesen, *The Mennonite Brotherhood in Russia (1789–1910)* (Fresno, CA: Board of Christian Literature, General Conference of Mennonite Brethren Churches, 1978).

7 John R. Staples, *Cross-Cultural Encounters on the Ukrainian Steppe: Settling the Molochna Basin, 1783–1861* (Toronto: University of Toronto Press, 2003), particularly 107–43.

8 Marc Raeff, *The Well-Ordered Police State: Social and Institutional Change through Law in the Germanies and Russia, 1600–1800* (New Haven, CT: Yale University Press, 1983).

9 Epp, *Johann Cornies*, 9.

10 Johann Cornies to Daniel Schlatter, 22 July 1837, SAOR f. 89, op. 1, d. 432.

11 Quoted in V.F. Petrenko and E.A. Korotchenko, "Metaphor as a Basic Mechanism of Art (Painting)," *Psychology in Russia: State of the Art* 5 (2012): 531–67. http://psychologyinrussia.com/volumes/?article=1208, accessed 27 Sept. 2015.

12 His mother, Anganetha, had the drawing of flowers framed and hung – see Johann Cornies to Johann Cornies Jr, 27 November 1833, in Dyck, Epp, and Staples, *Transformation*, 345. His drawings still hung on the walls of his Moscow host, Traugott Blueher, six years after he returned home – see Traugott Blueher to Johann Cornies, SAOR f. 89, op. 1, d. 911. 7 May 1843.

13 Barry Stephenson, *Veneration and Revolt: Hermann Hesse and Swabian Pietism* (Waterloo, ON: Wilfred Laurier University Press, 2009), 46–8.

14 Staples, *Cross-Cultural Encounters*, 118–23.

15 Schlatter describes his background in the preface to his *Bruchstücke aus einigen Reisen nach dem südlichen Russland in den Jahren 1822 bis 1828* (St Gallen: Huber & Comp., 1836). Among Cornies' papers is a brief "Biography of Daniel Schlatter" (undated, probably 1826), in Dyck, Epp, and Staples, *Transformation*, 49–50.

16 Schlatter, *Bruchstücke*, xi.

17 Johann Casper Lavater, *Essays on Physiognomy Designed to Promote the Knowledge and the Love of Mankind*, trans. Thomas Holcroft (London: B. Blake, 1840). Originally published as *Physiognomische Fragmente zur Beförderung der Menschenkenntniß und Menschenliebe* (Leipzig: Weidmanns Erben und Reich, 1776).

18 John Graham, "Lavater's Physiognomy in England," *Journal of the History of Ideas* 22, no. 4 (1961), 563.

19 Lavater, *Essays on Physiognomy*, 49.

20 On Lavater's aesthetics, see, e.g., Miriam Claude Meije, *The Anthropology of Petrus Camper (1722–1789)* (Amsterdam: Rodopi, 2014), 115–23.

21 *Oxford English Dictionary, cv* "Aesthetics."

22 For example, Cornies also wrote about the physical appearance of the Doukhobors and its relationship to their moral character. See "The Doukhobors in the Molochnaia Area," in Dyck, Epp, and Staples, *Transformation*, 501.

23 See Schlatter's description of Nogai "Anatomy, Physiognomy, and Intelligence," *Bruchstücke*, 88–92.

24 Cornies, "The Nogai Tatars in Russia," in Dyck, Epp, and Staples, *Transformation*, 457–93.

25 There is a long, still influential scholarly tradition characterizing nomadism as irrational. More recent scholarship argues for the economic rationality of nomadism under arid conditions. For a summary of the literature, see Marius Warg Næss, "Are Nomadic Pastoralists Non-Rational?" (7 July 2015), http://pastoralism-climate-change-policy.com/.

26 Cornies, "The Nogai Tatars in Russia," in Dyck, Epp, and Staples, *Transformation*, 463.

27 Ibid.

28 Brian Stanley, "Christianity and Civilization in English Evangelical Mission Thought, 1792–1857," in *Christian Missions and the Enlightenment*, ed. Stanley (Grand Rapids, MI: William B. Eerdmanns, 2001), 188.

29 Cornies, "The Nogai Tatars in Russia," in Dyck, Epp, and Staples, *Transformation*, 469.

30 Ibid., 470–1.

31 Ibid., 485.

32 Ibid., 471.

33 Cornies, "Pravila neobkhodimye k sobliudeniiu, pri ustroistve iz Nogaiskoi derevni akerman v obraztsovuiu ili primernuiu koloniiu" (1842), SAOR f. 89, op. 1, d. 818. This Russian copy is dated 1842, but internal evidence shows it originated in 1832. For a fuller account of Cornies' involvement with the Nogais, see Staples, "'On Civilizing the Nogais': Mennonite-Nogai Economic Relations, 1825–1860," *Mennonite Quarterly Review* 74, no. 2 (2000): 229–56.

34 Ibid.

35 On the state's efforts to transform the steppe, see David Moon, *The Plough that Broke the Steppes: Agriculture and Environment on Russia's Grasslands, 1700–1914* (Oxford: Oxford University Press, 2013). Moon provides an excellent overview of state afforestation program (173–205). He also notes Cornies' role in improving crop agriculture (277–280).

36 The establishment of the Forestry Society is conventionally dated to 1830, but while the Guardianship Committee ordered the creation of a Society in February 1829, the Society Charter was not issued until 1831. See Guardianship Committee to District Office, 23 July 1829, in Dyck, Epp, and Staples, *Transformation*, 179–80; and Andrei Fadeev to Johann Cornies, 13 July 1831, in Dyck, Epp, and Staples, *Transformation*, 227–35. Regarding Cornies' Iushanle nursery, see Cornies to Fadeev, 3 December 1830, in Dyck, Epp, and Staples, *Transformation*, 196.

37 Forestry Society to village offices, 16 January 1841, SAOR f. 89, op. 1, d. 750.

38 Report of progress made in agriculture and the trades during the year 1842 in the Molochna Mennonite District, 4 January 1843, SAOR f. 89, op. 1, d. 915.

39 Johann Cornies to Andrei M. Fadeev, 26 June 1839, SAOR f. 89, op. 1, d. 521.

40 Forestry Society Records from February, 1836, March 1836, SAOR f. 89, op. 1, d. 368.

41 Forestry Society to H. Wiens, March 1843, SAOR f. 89, op. 1, d. 954. Forestry Society to Gnadenfeld Village Office, September 1843, SAOR f. 89, op. 1, d. 960: Forestry Society to H. Wiens, [March 1843]; SAOR 89–1-954/31: Forestry Society to Gnadenfeld Village Office, September 1843.

42 The significance of the *Privilegium* and the Mennonite role of model is summarized in Dyck, Epp, and Staples, *Transformation*, xxix–xxx. For a more detailed account, see Staples, "Religion, Politics, and the Mennonite Privilegium: Reconsidering the Warkentin Affair," *Journal of Mennonite Studies* 21 (2003): 71–88. On the larger history of *Privilegiums*, see James Urry, *Mennonites, Politics, and Peoplehood: Europe-Russia-Canada 1525–1980* (Winnipeg: University of Manitoba Press, 2006). On the state's use of colonists as didactic models, see Roger Bartlett, *Human Capital: The Settlement of Foreigners in Russia, 1762–1804* (Cambridge: Cambridge University Press, 1980).

43 Forestry Society to village offices, 16 January 1841, SAOR f. 89, op. 1, d. 750.

44 Johann Cornies to District Offices, undated draft, probably June 1843, SAOR f. 89, op. 1, d. 750.

45 See, e.g., Cornies' description of Crown Prince Alexander's (the future Tsar Alexander II) inspection of Akkerman, Johann Cornies to Andrei M. Fadeev, 20 October 1837, SAOR f. 89, op. 1, d. 432.

46 Regarding the role of colonies as "laboratories of modernity," see Anne Laura Stoler and Frederick Cooper, "Between Metropole and Colony:

Rethinking a Research Agenda," in *Tensions of Empire: Colonial Cultures in Bourgeois Worlds*, ed. Stoler and Cooper (Berkeley: University of California Press, 1997), 5.

47 Keppen, "Mennonit Ivan Iv. Kornis i ego zavedenie," Archive of the Russian Academy of Sciences, f. 30, d. 1, op. 226.

48 Cornies was appointed to this committee in 1836 – see Andrei M. Fadeev to Johann Cornies, 3 January 1836, SAOR f. 89, op. 1, d. 367.

49 The Warkentin Affair is described in detail in Staples, "Religion, Politics, and the Mennonite Privilegium."

50 Cornies, "Description of the Warkentin Matter," n.d. (by context, probably July 1842), SAOR f. 89, op. 1, d. 813.

51 Abraham Friesen to Heinrich Neufeld, reproduced in Delbert Plett, *The Golden Years: The Mennonite Kleine Gemeinde in Russia (1812–1849)* (Steinbach, MB: DFP Publications, 1985), 286. Friesen repeated this characterization in a number of letters over the following years. See, for example, his "A simple declaration with respect to the farewell address of the former Aeltester Heinrich Wiens," in Plett, *Golden Years*, 308.

52 Regarding Landskrone, see Johann Cornies to Andrei M. Fadeev, 26 June 1839, SAOR f. 89, op. 1, d. 521. Regarding the Ohrloff Church, see Johann Cornies to Andrei M. Fadeev, 28 January 1837, SAOR f. 89, op. 1, d. 432.

53 Johann Cornies to Mariupul Mennonite District Office, 28 October 1842, SAOR f. 89, op. 1, d. 813. This directive was addressed to the Mariupol Mennonites, but it referenced orders also pertaining to the Molochna settlement.

54 Johann Cornies to Peter Koeppen, 12 August 1839, see SAOR f. 89, op. 1, d. 521.

55 From congregation members Johann Cornies, Gerhard Enns, and Jacob Martens to Bernhard Fast, n.d. (probably 28 January 1842), SAOR f. 89, op. 1, d. 845.

56 Johann Cornies to Traugott Blueher, December 1824, in Dyck, Epp, and Staples, *Transformation*, 19–20; Cornies to Fadeev, 13 September 1833, Dyck, Epp, and Staples, *Transformation*, 338–9.

57 Jane Samson, "Ethnology and Theology: Nineteenth-Century Mission Dilemmas in the South Pacific," in Stanley, *Christian Missions*, 103–4.

58 On the relationship between Evangelical Christian missions and the Enlightenment, see Stanley, "Christian Missions and the Enlightenment," 1–21.

59 John L. Comaroff, "Images of Empire, Contests of Conscience: Models of Colonial Domination in South Africa," in *Tensions of Empire: Colonial Cultures in a Bourgeois World*, ed. Cooper and Stoler (Berkeley: University of California Press, 1997), 175.

60 Matthew 5:14.

61 Anthony J. La Vopa, *Grace, Talent, and Merit: Poor Students, Clerical Careers, and Professional Ideology in Eighteenth-Century Germany* (Cambridge: Cambridge University Press, 1988), 139–41.

62 E. Henderson, *Biblical Researches and Travels in Russia* (London: James Nisbet, 1826), 386. Missionaries from the Basle Mission Society echoed this assessment, writing enthusiastically of Odessa as a "strong and fertile" base for missionary work, and of "the possibility of grounding an expansion of Evangelical work from the scattered German colonies" (quoted in Wilhelm Schlatter, *Geschichte der Basler Mission 1815–1915. Mit besonderer Berücksichtigung der ungedruckten Quellen*. Vol. 1 of 3. *Die heimatgeschichte der Basler Mission* [Basel: Vertrag der Basler Missionsbuchhandlung, 1916], 96, 100).

PART TWO

Imperial Mennonite Isolationism Revisited

3 Mennonite Schools and the Russian Empire: The Transformation of Church-State Relations in Education, 1789–1917

IRINA (JANZEN) CHERKAZIANOVA

The study of education among Mennonite colonists in Imperial Russia – a subject that is as important as it is complex – provides tremendous insight into the spiritual life of these foreign colonists, thus supplementing conclusions reached by Oksana Beznosova in chapter 4 of this volume. Education was at the core of Mennonite life in the colonies because it brought together so many social, economic, and spiritual factors. Not surprisingly then, schools were an important site for the dynamic interactions of state, church, and societal actors, most especially in the era of school reforms. Not only did Mennonites include education at the centre of their self-understanding or "cognitive map,"[1] it also played a vital and dynamic role in how the state viewed these colonists from the point of settlement to 1917 and beyond. As this volume has repeatedly argued, scholars have often overlooked this vital aspect of Mennonite engagement with the larger society by unduly relying on in-group sources. This chapter contributes to the historiographic sea change and presents a new paradigm for how Mennonites interacted with the Russian state over time that is grounded in previously under-used archival sources as well as recent scholarly findings on the history and culture of Germans and Mennonites across the former Soviet Union.[2]

The church had long played a leading role in Mennonite schools, as it did throughout the traditional Mennonite villages of the Russian Empire. However, the state's role in the regulation of education among young people increased as Mennonite colonies industrialized and diversified over the nineteenth century. Coincidentally, state authorities worked to create uniformity of training and identical educational programs across the empire as they sought standardized approaches to the organization of schooling, including a common language of instruction

(Russian). On the one hand, this was supposed to simplify the educational process. On the other hand, the state needed literate, educated citizens who could, in accordance with their social status, take part intelligently in national socio-economic, political, and public processes. Such a linguistic uniformity seemed unattainable in the mid-nineteenth century given the sheer vastness of the Russian Empire coupled with its multinational composition. Yet no other strategy seemed plausible as soon as Russia embarked on the path of capitalist development. It is, therefore, not surprising that conflicts involving state, church, and society on educational matters also increased at this time as state intervention increased and empire-wide reforms were implemented. In the process, Mennonites were challenged to reconsider who they were in relation to the empire, to their faith, and to the complex Germano-Dutch nature of their origins. Mennonites had only imperfectly and incompletely sorted through these issues when the revolutionary undoing of the empire in 1917 forced an entirely new turn of the wheel.

We can ascertain three periods at the intersection of these three components of church, state, and society in the pre-revolutionary educational history of Russia's Mennonites and Germans: 1) from the moment the first colonists appeared in Russia up to the early 1830s; 2) from the 1830s to the 1880s; and 3) from the end of the nineteenth century to 1917.

In the first period – up to the early 1830s – the state did not interfere in the educational sphere of the colonists, which parallels the findings that Venger has reached between the state and Mennonite entrepreneurs during this initial phase.[3] Instead, tsarist authorities chose what they deemed the optimal means of organizing their new subjects as they permitted the church and community to oversee the religious and educational instruction of the colonists. Theoretically, such a path was also preferable for the state because it ruled out any possibility for conflict between St Petersburg and religious organizations, Mennonite or otherwise. It also reduced the chance of enmity between Mennonite teachers and clergy given the overwhelming influence enjoyed by the latter in this initial stage. In practice, however, the Imperial Russian government could hardly do otherwise because it lacked a viable alternative in the shape of state-centred educational initiatives. This confirms Paul Werth's recent findings that the empire governed its subjects by co-opting its "foreign" faiths at a time when no realistic alternative existed.[4] For example, the first state-sponsored township (*volost*) schools were only introduced into the empire during the 1830s. In fact, as late as 1825, more than 130 district towns had no schools at all, and the situation was much worse in rural areas.[5] Thus, the church, clergy, and community of the colonists themselves all played key and complementary roles in colonist educational matters in this initial period, in ways that served everybody's interests.

Mennonites and German colonists later viewed this initial lack of imperial tutelage as a golden era. It allowed them to formulate their own educational institutions from the moment of settlement, as reflected in the presence of schools in almost every village. Beznosova has already shown how difficult the initial years were as the unprecedented opportunity to establish their own schools proved both boon and bane. In time, a Mennonite cognitive map of relatively independent colonies superseded an earlier self-image of Mennonites as well integrated into Polish/Prussian society. But once underway, the pace of growth in the number of schools differed between the Volga and the New Russian settlements. From 1838 to 1857, the number of schools in New Russia (as southern Ukraine was known) increased from 153 to 251, but only increased from 107 to 125 in the Volga region.[6] According to the calculations of James Urry, enrolment of Mennonite children from Molochna (where 80 per cent of school-age children attended school) had even surpassed Prussian schooling in the 1830s, as it had in the ratio of teachers to students. Thus, the ratio of teachers to students in Mennonite schools in 1831 and 1837 was 1:42 and 1:46 respectively, while in Prussia it was 1:75 in the early 1840s.[7] The table below shows that Mennonites invested large funds into their elementary schools compared with the empire's German and Bulgarian colonists.

The expenditure of funds by south Russian colonists on education in 1845[8]

Assignment of expenditure	Mennonites (67 colonies)	Germans (131 colonies)	Bulgarians (92 colonies)
Salary of teachers	6,538 r. 46 k.	9,813 r. 20 k.	5,384 r. 34 k.
Upkeep of students studying on public funds	558 r. 25 k.	2 r.	311 r. 11 k.
Upkeep of students preparing for the post of clerk	497 r. 43 k.	248 r. 39 k.	No information
Upkeep of students studying gardening and forestry	No information	114 r. 28 k.	61 r. 30 k.
TOTAL	7,594 r. 14 k.	10,177 r. 87 k.	5,756 r. 75 k.
Average flow of funds to one settlement	113 r. 35 k.	77 r. 69 k.	62 r. 57 k.

The variances in material prosperity between Mennonites and other colonists could explain these differences, but spiritual and organizational factors were no less important. The peculiarities of Mennonite church organization, based on the principle of "congregationalism," were also almost certainly a factor. The absence of vertical authorities in their "church-communities" and their corresponding autonomy allowed them to make their own locally generated decisions, even as this threatened an overall coherence. All of this reinforced Mennonites' identification of themselves as a relatively autonomous people grounded in the principle of self-organization and independence of oversight. General problems within the colonies were resolved by democratic means, most often during a general meeting of the inhabitants or at a church conference. Nevertheless, church leaders played a vital role throughout, which reinforced a strong sense of inner cohesiveness and coherence. In that vein, almost all teachers were preachers in this earliest phase, which contrasted sharply with the position of sexton-schoolmaster in the Lutheran and Catholic colonies, a position that remained distinct from but heavily dependent upon the clergy.

Lutheran and Catholic clergy consolidated their leading role in educational matters in 1840 with the passage of "Regulations for Schools and Catechismal Instructions among Foreign Colonists in Saratov Province." Lutheran clergy developed this draft law in the 1830s and state authorities subsequently approved it as they also instructed Orthodox parish schools to found parish schools in their jurisdictions.[9] The emergence of these regulations formalized the legal position of the Evangelical Lutheran Church and – together with the approval of church regulations in 1832 – allowed the Lutheran Church to receive official status as one of the empire's recognized state churches. Gradually state officials extended these regulations to the empire's Catholics. Not surprisingly, they also had an effect on how officials formulated state policy on Mennonite educational practices. In fact, these 1840 regulations comprised the only law that governed educational life across the colonies from their introduction to the end of the nineteenth century. In addition, they also came to provide the blueprint by which church and community interacted on educational matters within the colonies.

An analysis of this first period makes it plain that the authorities did not interfere in cultural or linguistic matters within the colonies as both parties adopted de facto cognitive maps that stressed independence of oversight and action. State officials, for example, did not decree the language of instruction or the process by which Mennonites appointed its teachers, nor did it challenge distinct school traditions. In most instances, officials were content to reinforce established practices among various school organizations and allow Mennonites to regulate schools from within their own systems. N.P. Malinovskii, a figure in national education from the early twentieth century, provided the following apt description of the empire's educational policies in the early nineteenth century: "[A]t that time it did not occur to state officials that they utilize the school with a view to Russification."[10]

State officials took the first steps to regulate colonists' educational practices in the 1830s as they inaugurated a new phase in their relationship with the empire's colonists and began to bring so-called enlightenment principles of governance to the countryside.[11] Officials henceforth began to intervene in the organization of traditional schools and the pedagogical content delivered, especially when it concerned the language of instruction. If the opening of a village school remained – as before – a matter between the community and the church, the responsibility for the operation and control of those same schools now shifted to the state, which was intent on disseminating the Russian language among the colonists.

As noted above, state officials first attempted to influence the organization of the internal life of German primary schools when they approved the regulations of 1840. Thereafter, the state influenced colonists' education most markedly when it created central secondary schools. In so doing, authorities wanted to regulate the economic life and administration of the colonies in the southern provinces, and it reasoned that colonists' businesses would suffer if colonists did not know Russian or were unable to translate documents from one language to another.

Although officials had intended to found the first school for training Russian-speaking specialists in southern Ukraine, officials in the Volga region were actually the first to take the initiative. On 30 August 1834, they simultaneously inaugurated two educational institutions in Lesnoi Karamysh and Ekaterinenstadt. Before long, colonists transferred the experience of the Volga region back to the southern provinces, a transfer made possible by officials in the Ministry of Internal Affairs and its counterpart in State Domains, under whose authority the colonists were placed in 1838. As a general policy, local authorities were henceforth required to institute concurrent measures in colonist villages across the Volga region and southern Ukraine. This suggests that St Petersburg was working with a broader empire-wide cultural mapping than one focused on distinctly Ukrainian or Russian regional aspects. It also suggests that colonists may have played a role in minimizing national distinctions within their regions.[12]

On 20 June1835, Superintendent Kh. G. Pelekh of the Ekaterinoslav Office of the Guardianship Committee on Foreign Settlements of Southern Russia (the so-called Guardians Committee) – itself subordinate to the Ministry of Internal Affairs – ordered the Molochna Mennonite district to open at least one school with Russian as the language of instruction. Indeed, the committee hoped for more such schools, though at the initiative of the colonists themselves. These schools were to be located in areas of high population density within the colonies, and Mennonites opened the first such school in Halbstadt (Berdiansk district) – the largest of the Mennonite villages – in 1835. Though such instructions cannot be linked directly to the Russification initiatives of the late nineteenth century, they did suggest the influence of "Official Nationality" policy under Tsar Nicholas I on the colonies. Nathaniel Knight has demonstrated how, far from being a reactionary policy, this initiative was "indicative of modernity" with its emergent notion of *narodnost'*.[13]

Mennonites responded positively to this linguistic injunction, which suggests either that they had acquired a more integrative understanding of their "Russian" identity within little more than one generation of settlement, or that culturally integrated Mennonites from Poland/Prussia sought the same when they settled in New Russia. Nor should this have surprised anyone. Mennonites were, after all, relatively prosperous by the 1830s. They were also deeply loyal to the imperial order, and many were convinced that mastering the Russian language would give them an important economic advantage in the region. In addition, on the initiative of the Ministry of State Domains in 1838, Mennonites also began to debate whether to construct new central schools. Based on a study of village-community decisions, the Guardians Committee investigated colonists' intentions. For example, the Molochna German colonists were interested in the construction of one new school for which they were prepared to retain a teacher, but recent crop failures had hampered their ability to raise the necessary funds for the building. German colonists closest to Odessa even refused to hire a teacher. By contrast, the Molochna Mennonites expressed their readiness to open a school in Tiegerweide along the new guidelines, and after that in other villages. They also agreed to support Russian-language teachers with a salary from 500 to 600 rubles per annum.[14] The opening of a central school in Khortitsa in 1842 revealed the harmonious interaction of church and secular structures among the region's Mennonites. On the instructions of the Guardians Committee, the church conference, together with civil leaders and district officials, collaborated on the project to found a Russian-language school. To that end they put together a construction plan and cost estimates. The Guardians Committee approved the documents on 6 November 1841 and soon after Mennonites opened the first such school.[15] Officials next approved the "Statute of the School in the Sarata Settlement" in Bessarabia (the Werner School) on 23 October 1842, a community that had been settled by German Lutherans and Catholics,[16] and then established a central school in Prishib (Melitopol district) on 18 July 1846. These central schools soon became important centres for preparing teachers for German schools across southern Russia and Ukraine.

The Guardians Committee formulated measures for disseminating the Russian language in all schools following the establishment of these first central schools, and on 5 March 1842 submitted a related note to the Ministry of State Domains. It went one giant step further than previous initiatives when it proposed that Russian be placed on an equal footing with German in all rural schools, a position that was immediately challenged by colonists across the Volga region and into southern Ukraine. Contested personnel issues and curriculum content now rose to the surface, motivating state officials to create unified requirements and common programs for all primary schools. Officials believed that increased state tutelage would preserve the continuity between the lower level of education (rural primary schools) and the new, higher type of centralized training school. Even so, roadblocks remained. Ben Eklof argues that even within the state there were multiple visions and administrations engaged in school formation under Nicholas I.[17] The opening of central schools clearly emphasized another problem that state officials faced: their recognition that isolated teachers were often at the mercy of local clergy, let alone the population itself. Here lay the rub. If the Church deemed a teacher to be little more than an assistant to the clergy, the state saw in the new cohort of German and Mennonite teachers – graduates of the new central schools – important agents of cultural Russification. By mid-century, authorities therefore increasingly strove to make teachers independent from both the clergy and local populace.

An additional problem arose when state officials realized they needed many more new teachers for the further dissemination of the Russian language among the colonists, which itself would require more central pedagogical schools. They soon built such schools across Kherson province in southern Ukraine, specifically for the residents of Liebental, Berezan, and Glückstal : in Grossliebental for Lutherans, and in Landau for Catholics.[18] Yet the shortage of qualified teachers necessitated delays even here. Hence, the school in Grossliebental did not open until 1869, though when it did it was modelled after the experience of the Ekaterinenstadt school in Saratov province. Again we can see how southern Ukraine and the Lower Volga were deemed part of one piece. Fourteen central schools were already operating in this broad prairie swathe by 1885, including three in Kherson province, two in Bessarabia, five in Tavrida, two in Ekaterinoslav, one in Saratov, and one in Samara.[19] Despite the state's intentions, officials had yet to introduce an empire-wide law that might have regulated the functioning of these central schools, nor had they comprehensively articulated what Russification would entail for the colonists. Even so, the very existence of these centralized educational institutions created a foundation for strengthening the role that the Russian language played in the life of the colonists well beyond pedagogical matters.

The increasingly supervisory role that state officials played in colonist schools from the 1830s on inevitably limited the influence of Mennonite church leaders who sought to preserve the traditional schools and their role within them, and who were reluctant to make radical changes to the existing order. Yet despite the best efforts of the clergy, the control structures for Mennonite schooling began to take on a new shape in the 1840s. Officials introduced a new law in 1843 that transferred the management of schools in the Molochna Mennonite district from the exclusive control of the religious leaders to the Agricultural Society, which had been organized by the state in 1831[20] (and was known until 1848 as "The Society for Promotion of Agriculture and Industry"). The association was presided over by Johann Cornies (1789–1848). Historian John Staples explains that Cornies participated actively on the heels of his "great awakening," and his later enthusiasm for the concepts of pietism. Staples believes that precisely this renewed religious orientation allowed Cornies to look at the world differently, to abandon the conservative mentality of the first Mennonite colonists who had rejected the welfare of the world, and to promote religious service through economic engagement "in the world."[21] For our purposes, it is important to note that the collision of identity markers within the Mennonite colonies had become as significant as the ones that identified the relationship between Mennonites and the state.

Cornies oversaw public education in the Molochna Mennonite colonies for five years until his death in 1848. He visited and inspected schools, reworked curricula, and oversaw teachers' conferences. With these innovations he tried to weaken the authority still exercised by church leaders and thus bring the schools closer to the realities of contemporary Russian life.[22] In 1837, Cornies met with the academician Petr Keppen, who at the time was conducting an inspection of the German colonies. They discussed Cornies' proposal to create a special settlement of artisans in the Molochna district, a settlement that was, in fact, founded in 1841 as Neu-Halbstadt. In sum, Mennonite schooling progressed considerably thanks to the activities of such weighty individuals as Cornies, as well as by his successors P. Wiebe, D. Cornies, and P. Schmidt, in a manner that coincided with St Petersburg's changing expectations of colonist education.

A third and final period in the development of relations between the imperial state, the church, and the community of Mennonite colonists on the school question began after the middle of the nineteenth century, coinciding with the bourgeois modernization of the empire as a whole. As such, it confirms the periodization that Beznosova and Venger have also used in this volume. The "Great Reforms" of the 1860s inevitably prompted state servitors to alter the administrative system of the empire's foreign colonists and their respective educational institutions. Therefore, it is necessary to examine the German school reform from two points of view: in the context of the modernization of education across the empire in the 1860s and 1870s and of the overarching administrative reform of the colonists which began in the 1870s. Up to this time, the ethno-linguistic identity of everyone within the empire had been of secondary importance to their social estate (i.e., the fact that they were legally neither peasant nor noble, but "colonist") and religious affiliation.[23] However, now "non-Russianness" was more and more associated with language, and nationality based on one's own language became the main criterion for differentiation between Russians and non-Russians, as well as between the different non-Russian peoples. One of the most important consequences of the reforms was that officials now denied the Church any oversight of Mennonite schools, which they henceforth consolidated with schools of all types under the Ministry of National Education.

The transfer of schools from the Ministry of State Domains to the Ministry of National Education began in 1867 with former state peasant schools. The transition of "non-Russian" schools (Bashkir, Tatar,

Kyrgyz) took place in 1874, and Bulgarian schools in 1877. At the end of this process, the decree of 2 June 1897 switched Armenian-Georgian schools over to the authority of St Petersburg.[24]

The administrative reform of 1871 preceded the transition of Mennonite and German schools to state tutelage. Under the new law, officials subordinated colonists to the rules and institutions as applied to all rural inhabitants across the empire. These now-former colonists henceforth received their new legal status as villager-owners (*poselian-sobstvennikii*). Mennonites, along with everyone else, now had to conduct all of their business correspondence related to community management in Russian. From 1881 to 1892, officials transferred German schools to the Ministry of National Education in stages, starting with the central and rural Mennonite schools, according to the law of 2 May 1881. The law itself was entitled: "On the transfer to the authority of the Ministry of National Education of the central and rural schools in the former Bulgarian and German settlements, as well as schools in the settlements of Jewish farmers in the Bessarabia, Ekaterinoslav, Tavrida, Kherson, Samara, and Saratov provinces." For the clergy, only the right to oversee religious education remained intact. From that time on, the adoption of Russian in Mennonite schools gathered significant momentum.

Mennonite loyalty to the empire, to their own central schools, and to the Russian language did not mean that these erstwhile colonists were ready to have all school subjects taught in Russian. This transition took place only after officials had transferred the schools to the jurisdiction of the Ministry of National Education in the late 1880s. The first central school in southern Ukraine to switch its teaching to Russian was located in Prishib.[25] Khortitsa School introduced a Russian-language teacher in 1871, though the overall language of instruction only shifted to Russian toward the end of the 1880s. By 1886, Halbstadt was teaching every subject in Russian except religion, German, and mathematics, though officials had switched mathematics to Russian within two years of the new regulations. The shift to largely Russian instruction took place in Gnadenfeld in 1887 and a year later in Orloff.[26] J.J. Hildebrandt calls 1886 the year of the introduction of Russian as the language of instruction in Mennonite schools of the southern colonies,[27] which in fact was not quite so. By that year, only pupils in the central schools were receiving their instruction in Russian, and even then, administrators had not introduced Russian classes simultaneously to everyone. By 1 January 1900, Russian officials had concluded that all German primary schools in south Russia were giving Russian-language instruction except the two schools for the deaf.[28] The relative speed by which Mennonites made this transition can be seen by the fact that the Russian language was not generally taught by the Tatars (505 schools), the Jews (116), or the Karaites (10) at this same time.[29] It says a great deal about how Mennonite self-identity was not linguistically defined, at least not entirely, by the dawn of the twentieth century.

Government textbooks in Russian began to displace previous books after schools were transferred to the authority of the Ministry of National Education. However, Mennonites continued to produce textbooks in German language and religious instruction, as before, with active participation by the clergy. By the end of the nineteenth century, the largest publishing houses issuing textbooks for German colonists were in Odessa and Riga, as well as in the settlements of Halbstadt and Prishib. Printers in Berdiansk only released the first catechism for Mennonite schools published in Russia in 1874. This suggests that Mennonites had come to identify at least somewhat with Germany at the very time that Germany's relations with the Russian Empire had begun to sour. The Berdiansk catechism was an identical reprint from the Prussian edition.[30] For a long time, the first books of mathematical problems (*Rechentafeln*) and a songbook (*Choralus*) for Mennonite schools also came from Germany.[31] Later, the teacher W. Neufeld revised the *Choralus* and reissued it in Halbstadt. In fact, Mennonites had begun to show great initiative in developing their own textbooks by the dawn of the twentieth century. For example, Mennonite teachers after 1900 prepared a textbook on the history of the homeland (*Hilfsbüchlein beim ersten Unterricht in Heimatkunde*), which they had printed in Leipzig. They intended the text for schools of the Halbstadt and Gnadenfeld districts of Tavrida province; the authors of this timely history depicted the Mennonite settlements at Molochna as akin to a "Little Motherland."[32] At the General Mennonite Conference in 1913, contest judges awarded three prizes for the best Mennonite history curriculum for a school course,[33] all of which showed the high interest of communities in the preparation of appropriate German-language textbooks.

The democratization of life in the 1860s contributed to the development of community activities in school affairs, as German self-organizational skills were most evident when they established school boards. The Molochna Mennonite Council (Soviet) with its centre in Halbstadt stood out. A group of teachers had organized it on 5 November 1869 as a special administrative organ to control and manage the Mennonite educational institutions of southern Ukraine.[34] The council had offices in Ekaterinoslav and Kherson provinces. In 1881, seventy Mennonite schools in Tavrida province and thirty schools of other provinces were under its authority.[35] Of the fifty years of the council's existence, the most successful were the years 1884 to 1897 under the direction of Johann Klatt (1884–7, 1896–7) and Peter Heese (1887–96). The success of the Molochna Council was most evident in the condition of the central schools themselves, their material wealth, and their level of instruction. Mennonites spent up to 24,000 rubles annually on school maintenance for 166 students (in 1881), i.e., up to 144 rubles per year per student, exceeding even the total funds that the state gymnasiums and junior gymnasiums had spent on their students.

Delegates at the General Conference of Mennonites in the Empire constantly discussed school-related issues. Church leaders of Ekaterinoslav, Samara, and Tavrida provinces convened the first such conference in June 1879 in Neu-Halbstadt. Participants decided to send Andreas Voth, the chair of the Molochna School Board, to Odessa to discuss Mennonite school issues with Governor-General E.I. Totleben.[36] On 17 November 1882, at the first General Mennonite Conference, delegates decided to hold an annual joint conference of church leaders and teachers.[37] That conference convened in Halbstadt on 21–2 May 1885 in connection with the government's intention to prepare new regulations for colonists' schools. The Halbstadt delegates composed a written appeal to the government wherein they requested the preservation of the church school status among Mennonite schools.[38] Delegates at a subsequent conference in Neukirch on 13–14 October 1893 pondered the introduction of a new biblical history text for primary schools as well as new readers for their central schools. They further proposed that two manuscripts be forwarded to the Khortitsa School Board for approval, and that administrators submit their content to higher authorities for their consideration. Thereafter, school leaders printed and introduced the new texts into their schools.[39] Even so, Mennonites continued to feel misgivings as the end of the century neared. Delegates who gathered in Petershagen on 26–7 September 1895 voiced alarm at the deterioration in religious and German instruction in their schools, both of which had remained central to Mennonites even as Russian language proficiency had been added. This reduction in quality was particularly evident in those schools with only one Russian teacher, to which delegates proposed that all schools should have at least one German as well as one Russian teacher in each school.[40]

Mennonites thus responded as flexibly as possible to government school reforms, repeatedly demonstrating a loyalty and willingness to compromise. Observers noted that Mennonites had a stronger grasp of Russian compared to other German colonists, an indication that they had long regarded the state language as a tool to achieve their goals while safeguarding their rights. Mennonites acquired Russian language as a necessary and desirable step, but no less as a compromise that could forestall the state's intrusion into their unique spiritual identity. At the same time, the Mennonites' voluntary mastery of Russian did not indicate that they had been Russified, or, even more, assimilated, as Mennonites continued to implement measures designed to conserve their native tongue and unique identity.

State officials increased their pressure on German and Mennonite schools towards the end of the nineteenth century as the former colonists lost their right to appoint teachers, as they had done since the initial point of settlement. It is no wonder that more schools now adopted Russian as the language of instruction, as by 1900 school inspectors represented the state itself in their oversight of Mennonite education. The Ministry of National Education rated Mennonite and German schools after 1900 as being "among the unsatisfactory," on par with Jewish schools in the Warsaw school district or Muslim *maktabs* and *madrasahs*.[41] We are, however, convinced that this evaluation by the ministry needs to be approached with caution; otherwise, it cannot account for why the Saratov-Werner School, the Tarutyne School, the Sarepta School for Girls, as well as primary schools from Tavrida province, all participated in the Paris World Fair in 1900.[42] The primary schools of the Berdiansk district (Tavrida province) – among which a significant share were Mennonite – were awarded the grand prize by the fair's Department of Primary Education.[43] Under the circumstances, the ministry may have primarily directed its "unsatisfactory" assessment at church schools in the Volga region, which officials may have wrongly concluded were representative of German and Mennonite schools across the empire. Such an assessment may also reflect an emergent anti-German position within the Russian bureaucracy, one that would reach full flower in the coming decade.

State authorities may not have been alone in their negative assessment of German schools, as colonists themselves had concluded by 1900 that better teacher training was urgently needed. For their part, clergy argued for the establishment of special educational institutions (seminaries) under their control to train sextons (for Lutherans and Roman

Catholics) and preachers (for Mennonites). The idea itself was not new as some clergy had previously raised it, though it came forward again when H. Unruh and I. Dyck – representatives of the Molochna and Khortitsa Mennonites respectively – raised it at a church conference on 20 November 1901. Submitted to the administrator of the Odessa school district, it called for the establishment of a two-year Mennonite seminary in Gnadenfeld district. They appended draft regulations and curriculum for the seminary to the request,[44] though they realized that approval would likely not be forthcoming given the increasingly negative perception of Mennonites.

Democratic concessions in the area of religion and public life in the years of the 1905 Russian revolution led to the unprecedented growth of national and cultural associations across the empire as faith-based educational initiatives also regained strength. However, the government deemed the non-Orthodox variations to be little more than separatist aspirations on the part of those colonists who joined in. Officials now warned of "the cultural dominance of foreign-born and foreign-faith elements" which they considered a direct threat to state interests. Hence, authorities increased their distrust of Mennonite faith and practice at the very time when Mennonites were increasingly prominent in a variety of spheres. St Petersburg's increased suspicion also means that the Mennonite determination to link its culture with the German language had moved from a matter of imperial indifference in 1800 to a block to empire-wide administrative integration in 1870 to a threat to the empire and its people by 1900. In response to this perceived threat, the draft bill of 23 February 1907, introduced by the Ministry of Internal Affairs, ranked Mennonites among the empire's sects, not religions, a crucial distinction for all involved, as both Sergei Zhuk and Paul Werth have demonstrated.[45] This new status threatened the Mennonites' religious legitimacy within the empire and influenced the multifaceted way in which officials engaged with Mennonites and their institutions, schools included. Consequently, Mennonites protested this new sectarian designation, insisting that they were legitimate representatives of the Protestant denomination and not a mere sect. On 7 February 1908, representatives of the Mennonite Molochna community protested the bill in a signed petition that they submitted to Herman Abramovich Bergmann, a State Duma deputy.[46] Bergmann – a Mennonite estate owner from Ekaterinoslav province – served as a deputy to the third and fourth State Dumas from 1907 to 1917, and as a member of the Duma Committee on Religious Affairs. As such, he was a vital conduit through which Mennonites repeatedly tried to lobby their interests.

Mennonites continued to fight in the last years of the empire for the return of their right to appoint teachers in primary schools and to teach in German. The Duma faction of the Union of 17 October, which included deputies of German colonists (H.A. Bergmann, L.H. Lütz, V.E. Falz-Fein), insisted on the colonists' right to teach in their mother tongue during the whole period of primary school. Delegates at the Schönsee Conference of Mennonite church communities of the Russian Empire on 26–8 October 1910 dealt specifically with the management of parish registers and school affairs. In a memorandum to the Minister of Internal Affairs, the conference participants insisted on the return of their right to appoint teachers in schools that the communities themselves had founded and maintained. They also requested that they once again be permitted to use school premises for prayer meetings.[47]

The director of the Department of Spiritual Affairs of Foreign Faiths of the Ministry of Internal Affairs, A.N. Kharuzin, responded for the Ministry of Internal Affairs on issues concerning religion, church practice, and Mennonite schools. Regarding the schools, he wrote warningly, "Being endowed very generously in the material sense and often located in areas with indigenous Russian and Orthodox population, [Mennonite schools] – in the absence or scarcity of district public schools in that same region that largely paralyze their influence – are a hotbed of education in the spirit of narrow German tribal and religious separatism."[48]

Mennonite central schools concerned state authorities because the advancement in Mennonite pedagogy had long since gone from an emphasis on primary education to one that now focused on education at the secondary level. Most teaching candidates for those upper-level schools had been educated abroad – often at German universities – and had only passed the standard examination upon their return to teach in the empire. The Ministry of Internal Affairs was particularly concerned that a number of foreign "sectarian spiritual-educational institutions" had shaped an entire generation of preachers for Russia, including those who taught in the empire's Mennonite schools.

Based on these considerations, the authorities were prepared to respond favourably to the Mennonites' request to set up Bible classes in Friedenthal village in Kherson district, the Baptist desire for new classes in the Zhitomir district, and Evangelicals who wanted to establish similar schools in St Petersburg. However, the ministry also advised that the state should control all these steps and thereafter oversee matters systematically and consistently.

The Ministry of National Education was not the only state body that influenced national schools. The Ministry of Internal Affairs also played a significant role. Central here was P.A. Stolypin, who organized an empire-wide counteroffensive after the imperial humiliations of the 1905–7 revolution. Stolypin directly targeted ethnic societies and associations after 1907, including the ones that popular and localized educational leaders had initiated. Even so, authorities in St Petersburg soon reached their limit. In a 20 January 1910 circular to the governors, the Minister of Internal Affairs proposed that no more "foreign-born societies" be registered in the empire, and that any pretext be used to close already existing societies.[49] This, ipso facto, opened the door for police brutality should they meet any resistance.

The state's release of this circular initiated a verification process in the provinces that challenged the legitimacy of schools for sectarians, a category that now included Mennonites. Throughout 1910–11, for example, the governor of Akmola province in Central Asia closed every school in his jurisdiction that had operated without the permission of the school district administrator.[50] Nothing more clearly illustrates the way in which officials in the Ministry of Internal Affairs used this new directive than the story of the registration of the Charter of the Omsk Mennonite School Board. In the course of a single year (from March 1911 to March 1912), the Mennonite Charter – intended for the Akmola Provincial Office for the Affairs of Societies and Associations – was returned several times for revision. Officials were primarily concerned that the Omsk Mennonite School Board in Siberia was religiously motivated, which was particularly troubling as it proposed that non-Mennonites be admitted to its membership.[51] In fact, state servitors had long suspected that Mennonites were engaged in illegal missionary activity among the Orthodox. On 12 May 1912, the founders of the board lodged a complaint with the senate. The Akmola governor who presented the complaint reported that the board's purely religious character would do "indubitable damage to the Orthodox population of the province" because of the growth of religious sectarianism in the region.[52] On 5 April 1913, the senate decided not to take action on the Mennonites' complaint.

The anti-German campaign, which developed during the First World War, was a serious trial for the all Germans and Mennonites in the empire and parallels Venger's findings for Mennonite entrepreneurs, as well as Beznosova's on churches, even as my conclusion parts way with Venger especially. A ban on the use of German in public places introduced in autumn of 1914 was one of the most important steps in the empire's anti-German internal policies. Colonists suffered for this in all aspects of their lives including the ability to preach church sermons in German. This ban on the use of the German language came even before the "liquidation laws" of 2 February and 13 December 1915 threatened to eliminate all German land tenure and land use in the empire.

The more prosperous Mennonites now undertook a number of steps to prove their Dutch origin to protect their property. In particular, they used G.G. Pisarevskii's book *From the History of Foreign Colonization of Russia in the Eighteenth Century*, published in 1909 by the Moscow Archaeological Institute, in which scientists of the institute certified that Mennonites and Lutherans had emigrated from the free city of Danzig in 1789, though the ancestors of the Mennonites were actually from the Netherlands. Mennonites set down another plank in their own "Dutch" defence when the published the historical essay "Who are the Mennonites?"[53] More research is needed before we can determine how significantly this renewed formal emphasis on their Dutch heritage affected the Mennonites' own cognitive maps, especially at a time when many had long fostered ties with Germany.

The anti-German campaign in the empire intensified as the war progressed. It acquired organized forms in March of 1916 when B.V Stürmer, the chair of the Council of Ministers, created the Special Committee on the Struggle with "German Domination." This Special Committee also made a representation to the State Duma where it discussed all issues concerning Russian Germans, including school life. Even before that, German schools were most threatened by the passage of legislation in December of 1914 that forbade German language instruction in schools across the empire. The situation worsened in 1915 when officials approved the "liquidation laws," which threatened the very existence of those schools located on private Mennonite lands because depriving landowners of their property would also strip their schools of essential fiscal sources. State bureaucrats enumerated all colonists' schools in 1915, though by that time Germans and Mennonites had closed a number of their schools in the front-line regions of the empire. Meanwhile, Russian teachers began to replace Mennonite and German teachers in schools located further inland from the war front.

A particularly grave situation for German schools emerged in school districts that were in the zone of military operations or in front-line areas of Warsaw, Vilna, Riga, Odessa, Kiev, Kharkov, the Caucasus, and Petrograd – the very places where the majority of the empire's German schools were concentrated. Officials had applied the liquidation laws to these areas in the first instance; henceforth, the deportation of the German population also began here. The commanders of the military zones made the most of their unlimited power in these regions as their orders alone decided the fate of schools and trustees in these districts.

On 5 November 1914, the governor general and commander of the Odessa military district, M.I. Ebelob, sent the trustee of the Odessa school district a missive in which he questioned the patriotism of the German students. The general urged the state to remove all politically and morally unreliable teachers to provide the empire's children with the best education possible. He further recommended that authorities place schools under martial law in the region if they deemed their teachers untrustworthy. At least one trustee in the district interpreted this message as a guide to action – and schools began to close. Officials had closed 75 schools by 1 March 1915 in the Ekaterinoslav district directorate alone as well as another 112 schools in three other directorates.[54] The head of the Bessarabia School Board was particularly zealous: he had closed all 85 German schools by 1 July 1915 and dismissed 99 teachers.[55] Of these, he dismissed 52 teachers because they lacked sufficient knowledge of Russian and 29 as "undesirable elements."[56] Only the Tavrida Board was slow to close schools. In my view, this was tied to the fact that Mennonites here, distinguished by their loyalty to the authorities and a high level of Russian, formed a considerable part of the province's school districts. Nevertheless, in 1915, three central schools were closed in Crimea (also part of Tavrida province) due to insufficient funds: in Neusatz, Karassan (the Mennonite centre of the Crimea), and Spat.

By way of comparison within the empire, dramatic events also unfolded in the Mennonite school at the Omsk-Post Station (the Novo-Omsk School). Attempts by the Mennonites to set up a central school on its foundation ended in failure and the colonists were instead compelled to transform it in 1914 into a higher primary school. Mennonites took all the costs for its upkeep upon themselves but the educational authorities determined the internal order. Soon, however, supervisors had dismissed the German teachers and replaced them with Russian ones. As a first step they appointed G.J. Heide, a Russian teacher, as principal. At the same time Heide was also a preacher in the Mennonite community in the Chunaevka settlement of the Omsk district. By 1916, state officials had exiled him to Tobolsk province after he argued with the public school inspector.[57] That incident had followed on the heels of the closure of the Novo-Omsk school itself in the spring of 1915, which had played into Heide's protest.[58] Soon the local board opened a new school in the same building, though state officials now deemed it a Russian school.

At the same time, a number of publicists began to defend the cause of German colonists from unfair attacks. Among them, Moscow Professor K.E. Lindemann (1844–1929) criticized the liquidation laws. In particular, he examined the damage to German schools in connection with the application of the laws on 2 February and 13 December 1915.[59] According to the professor, there were 2,068 German colonies in the empire in 1915, of which about 1,000 suffered from the liquidation laws. Lindemann believed that in the 100-*verst* frontier in the Odessa school district and in the province of the Don Host, authorities would be able to close a staggering 363 schools with 11,585 students if officials ever applied these laws.[60] For example, Mennonite funds alone supported no fewer than 32 schools with 41 teachers and 1,422 children in Halbstadt (Mennonite) district. Annual maintenance of the schools cost 96,502 rubles, but they received only a paltry 25 rubles from the zemstvo for the purchase of visual aids.[61] In another appeal, pastor J.H. Stach vividly demonstrated the high level of development among the German colonies and their vital contribution to the development of the Russian economy and culture. He especially stressed the Germans' strong mastery of Russian and the high pedagogical standards of Mennonite schools in Tavrida province.[62]

With imperial tensions at such a fever pitch, it is not entirely surprising that many of the empire's Germans, Mennonites included, welcomed the overthrow of the Russian autocracy when it came. They hoped for better days, and initially had reason to believe that would happen when the liquidation laws were suspended on 11 March 1917 by the Provisional Government.[63] Soon the new regime also repealed selected restrictions concerning school and university education. On 20 March 1917, the newly formed Provisional Government decreed "On the abolition of religious and ethnic restrictions," which permitted the use of languages and dialects other than Russian in the business correspondence of private companies, for instruction in private schools of any kind, and in trade registers.[64] A resolution on 14 July 1917 entitled "On freedom of worship" legislatively consolidated the freedom of choice of faith and the right of religious organizations to religious-social, preaching, charitable, and educational activities. In all of these ways, 1917 marked a dramatic turning point in the history of education among the former German and Mennonite colonists of the Russian Empire.

To sum up, state policy regarding Mennonite and German schools changed drastically in the course of several generations. In the process, state perceptions of Mennonites and other minorities underwent revolutionary shifts, as did Mennonites' perceptions of themselves. Each turn of the wheel compelled Mennonites to reconsider how they would project their collective identity to the realm. Were they German or had they been Germanicized? Were they primarily a religious entity, in which case the voice of their religious leaders should be paramount, or were they a socio-cultural minority that was founded on faith? Much depended on the answer to these questions. In the end, of the partnerships established at the beginning of the nineteenth century, nothing remained in the war years after 1914. Policy changes introduced in the 1870s and 1880s with respect to schooling for Mennonites and Germans were connected not only to social reasons (implementing administrative reforms, changing the social status of these former colonists) but also to policy changes by state officials directed at national minorities in general and the German population in particular. Thereafter, the policy of Russification of education became more apparent with each passing year. Nor did any of this unfold in splendid isolation, as officials always linked the "German issue" within the empire to the formation of the German state in 1871 and its revolutionary impact on Russian foreign policy. Even emigration did not seem to solve the problem facing Mennonites and the pivotal role played by Mennonite schools in shaping their collective identity. This was evident from the experience of those who immigrated to Canada in 1874, who immediately sought to safeguard their oversight over their "parochial schools," what Royden Loewen has called a central aspect of their "institutional completeness."[65] Even so, Canada was far removed from the potential threat resulting from a united Germany. The Russian state was not as fortunate and it responded accordingly.

Ironically, state suspicion of Mennonites coincided with state suspicion of Germany at a time when increasing numbers of Mennonites were able to study in German universities. No wonder Germans and Mennonites only secured modest rights to use German as their language of instruction after the failed 1905 revolution, though Prime Minister Stolypin quickly swept even these away when he came to power in 1907. It was one thing to be German, but quite another when combined with the sectarian label, and Mennonite attempts to self-identify as Dutch were deemed by many as little more than a futile ruse that could not alter perceptions sufficiently within and beyond the Mennonite villages to make a difference.

Tsarist officials deemed the empire's Germans to be "internal enemies" during the First World War and they responded accordingly. In addition to religious restrictions already identified by Beznosova in chapter 4, the state also introduced repressive educational measures and closed schools as a result. At the same time, they either delayed the opening of new schools or forbade them outright. Russian teachers replaced German ones, and concessions attained by colonists on the language of instruction in the midst of the 1905 revolution were repealed. Against such an extensive onslaught, it is only surprising that laws forbidding German in school were never applied to religious doctrine, which Mennonites were able to teach in German even in the most difficult times.

In all of these ways, the Russian government's national policy in the second half of the nineteenth century dramatically reconfigured the relationship of all three parties – the imperial state, the Mennonite church, and the Mennonite community – on issues of education. The main conflict centred around teachers and the language of instruction. The church occupied a paramount place in the spiritual life of the Mennonite population and the clergy played a significant role in the development of the traditional religious school as well as in the preservation of the language and culture of the colonists. For its part, the church consistently defended Mennonite interests in the face of increasing government pressure. At the same time, the relationship between church and state concerning who had ultimate control on matters of education within the colonies themselves was always a dialectical one. The Mennonite community actively shaped and reshaped children's education, and ultimately ensured the welfare of both the schools and their teachers despite ever-mounting pressures. There were also some successes here on the local level, as the Russification of Mennonite and German schools overall was a gradual one, for instance when it came to the use of Russian as a language of instruction. Thus, active "cultural Russification" of German schools began later in comparison with the empire's other ethnic schools.

The experience of Mennonite schools in the Russian Empire allows one to reach important methodological conclusions about the importance of education to the Mennonite cognitive map, even when under siege. No wonder the Mennonite church and the community were able to create and maintain a system of primary and secondary education even without the participation or full support of the state. However, the ongoing flourishing of that same system depended on the degree to which Mennonite church and civil leaders were able to interact with imperial authorities and it is clear that Mennonites repeatedly adjusted their image-representations as part of this century-long conversation with state officials, even as they consistently sought to safeguard core identity markers. As it happened, increased state pressure before and after 1900 transformed Mennonite schools once again into a dramatically contested space in their struggle to survive as an ethnos. By then, however, the school was not the sort of space that these Mennonites were prepared to give up without a fight.

NOTES

1 Les Roberts, "Cinematic Cartography: Projecting Place through Film," in *Mapping Cultures: Place, Practice, Performance*, ed. Les Roberts (Houndmills: Palgrave Macmillan, 2012), 76–8; and Roger M. Downs and David Stea, *Maps in Minds: Reflections on Cognitive Mapping* (New York: Harper & Row, 1977), 6–8.

2 See Irina Vasil'evna Cherkaz'ianova, *Letopis' dissertatsii po istorii i culture rossiiskikh nemtsev (1960-e–2009 gg.)* (St Petersburg, 2009).

3 For a more detailed discussion of this period see my *Shkol'noe obrazovanie rossiiskikh nemtsev (problem razvitiia i sokhraneniia nemetskoi shkoly v Sibiri v XVIII-XX vv.)* (St Petersburg, 2004).

4 Paul W. Werth, *The Tsar's Foreign Faiths: Toleration and the Fate of Religious Freedom in Russia* (Oxford: Oxford University Press, 2014).

5 Ben Eklof, *Russian Peasant Schools: Officialdom, Village Culture, and Popular Pedagogy, 1861–1914* (Berkeley: University of California Press, 1986), 24–32.

6 Calculation made by the author according to the Table of educational institutions of all departments of the Russian Empire. – St Petersburg, 1838; Rossiiskii gosudarstvennyi istoricheskii arkhiv (RGIA), f.383, op.7, d.6364; f. 383, op. 9, d.8056; f.383, op.20, d.27730.

7 James Urry, *Nur die Heilege: Mennoniten in Russland, 1789–1889* (Steinbach, 2005), 180.

8 The table was drawn by the author according to RGIA, f.383, op.9, d.8056, Appendix 1, l.64.

9 Eklof, *Russian Peasant Schools*, 29.
10 N.P. Malinovskii, *Zakonodatel'stvo ob inorodcheskoi shkole. Inorodcheskaia shkola: Sb. statei i materialov po voprosam inorodcheskoi shkoly*, ed. G.G. Tumim and V.A. Zelenko, (Petrograd, 1916), 123.
11 Marc Raeff, *The Well-Ordered Police State: Social and Institutional Change Through Law in the Germanies and Russia, 1600–1800* (New Haven, CT: Yale University Press, 1983).
12 For a rather different approach, see the section entitled "Landscape and National Identity" in Catherine Brace, "Landscape and Identity," in *Studying Cultural Landscapes*, ed. Iain Robertson and Penny Richards (London: Hodder Arnold, 2003), 127–33.
13 Nathaniel Knight, "Ethnicity Nationality and the Masses: *Narodnost'* and Modernity in Imperial Russia," in *Russian Modernity: Politics, Knowledge, Practices*, ed. David L. Hoffmann and Yanni Kotsonis (New York: St Martin's Press, 2000), 54.
14 RGIA, f.383, op.1, d.404, l.11–13.
15 A. Neufeld, *Die Chortitzer Zentralschule. 1842–1892* (Berdjansk, 1893), 7.
16 *Polnyi svod zakonov Rossiiskoi imperii* (PSZ). 2nd Code. Vol. 17, no 16117; and http://www.grhs.org/vr/vhistory/sarata.htm.
17 Eklof, *Russian Peasant Schools*, 27.
18 RGIA, f.383, op.16, d.20049, l.1–1об.
19 Ibid., f.733, op.230, d.85, l.2.
20 P. Braun, *Der Molochnaer Mennoniten-Schulrat. 1869–1919. Zum Gedenktag seines 50jährigen Bestehens* (Göttingen, 2001), 19.
21 See John R. Staples, "Pietism and Progress in the Molochna: The 'Great Awakening' of Johann Cornies," paper given at *Molochna 2004: Mennonites and Their Neighbours (1804–2004). An International Conference.* Zaporizhzhia, Ukraine. 2–5 June 2004 (Zaporizhzhia, 2004), 93.
22 For details see *Ocherki istorii nemtsev i mennonitov Iuga Ukrainy (konets XVIII – pervaia polovina XIX vv.)* (Dnepropetrovsk, 1999), 152–4.
23 Elise Wirtschafter, *Social Identity in Imperial Russia* (DeKalb: Northern Illinois University Press, 1997).
24 On educational reforms after 1861 see Eklof, *Russian Peasant Schools*, ch. 2.
25 *Otchet o sostoianii Prishibskogo tsentral'nogo uchilishcha za 1885–1887 uchebnye gody* (Halbstadt, 1887), 4.
26 See P.M. Friesen, *Die Alt-Evangelische Mennonitische Brüderschaft in Rußland* (Halbstadt, 1911), 608.
27 See J.J. Hildebrandt, *J.J. Hildebrandt's Zeittafel: Chronologische Zeittafel* (Steinbach, 2004), 262.

28 Obshchii ocherk sostoianiia narodnykh uchilishch Tavricheskoi gubernii, Sevastopol'skogo i Kerchenskogo gradonachal'stv za 1898 i 1899 gody (Simferopol', 1900), 6.
29 Ibid.
30 Friesen, *Die Alt-Evangelische Mennonitische Brüderschaft*, 669.
31 Ibid., 670.
32 RGIA, f.821, op.5, d.1043, l.S.41 ob.
33 *Beschlüsse der von den geistlichen und anderen Vertreter der Mennonitengemeinden Russlands abgehalten Konferenzen für die Jahre 1879 bis 1913* (Berdjansk, 1914), 155.
34 RGIA, f.821, op.133, d.1010. l.110–111 (Polozhenie o Molochanskom uchilishchnom sovete. Copy).
35 *Obshchii ocherk sostoianiia narodnykh uchilishch Tavricheskoi gubernii za 1881 god* (Berdiansk, 1882), 27.
36 Ibid., 5.
37 Ibid., 6.
38 *Beschlüsse der von den geistlichen*, 19.
39 Ibid., 52.
40 Ibid., 62.
41 See *Obzor deiatel'nosti vedomstva Ministerstva narodnogo prosveshcheniia za vremia tsarstvovaniia imperatora Aleksandra III (Mart 2 1881–Oktiabr 20, 1894)* (St Petersburg, 1901), 408.
42 V.I. Varmakovskii, "Otdel nachal'nogo obucheniia i vospitaniia na Parizhskoi vystavke 1900 goda," in *Zhurnal Ministerstva narodnogo prosveshcheniia* (*ZhMNP*), no. 10 (1900), 118–19.
43 "Pis'mo iz Parizha," in *ZhMNP* no. 11 (1900), 38.
44 RGIA, f.821, op.5, d.940, l.134–9 obj.
45 Werth, *The Tsar's Foreign Faiths*, ch. 9; and Sergei Zhuk, "In Search of the Millennium: The Convergence of Jews and Ukrainian Evangelical Peasants in Late Imperial Russia," in *Holy Dissent: Jewish and Christian Mystics in Eastern Europe*, ed. Glenn Dynner (Detroit: Wayne State University Press, 2011), 336–49.
46 See *Dokumenty, otnosiashchiesia k veroispovednym voprosam mennonitov* (Halbstadt, 1910).
47 RGIA, f.821, op.133, d.1010, l.67–67 ob.
48 *Natsional'noe obrazovanie v Rossii: kontseptsii, vzgliady, mneniia. 1905–1938 гг., Part 1, 1905–1917*, ed. A.F. Kiselev (Moscow, 1998), 210.
49 See P.A. Pozhigailo, ed., *P.A. Stolypin: Perepiska* (Moscow, 2007), 668–9.

50 Tsentral'nyi gosudarstvennyi arkhiv Respubliki Kazakhstan (TsGARK), f.369, op.1, d.9137, l.6–7, 9, 15, 23.
51 TsGARK, d.2966, l.11–12, 23, 25, 33.
52 Ibid., l. 41.
53 *Kto takie Mennonity? Kratkii istoricheskii ocherk* (Halbstadt, 1915).
54 RIGA, f.733, op.186, d.2324, l.59 ob.
55 Ibid., l.83.
56 "Vedomost' so svedeniiami ob uchashchikhsia v kolonistskikh shkolakh Odesskogo uchebnogo okruga," *Tsirkuliar po Odesskomu uchebnomu okrugu* no. 1 (1916), Neofitsial'noe otdelenie, 19.
57 Arkhiv Upravleniia Federal'noi cluzhby bezopasnosti po Omskoi oblasti, d.P-9538, l. 19 ob.
58 RGIA, f.733, op.182, d.89, l.33 ob.
59 See K.E. Lindemann, *Zakony 2 fevralia i 13 dekabria 1915 (ob ogranichenii nemetskogo zemlevladeniia v Rossii) i ikh vliianie na ekonomicheskoe sostoianie Iuzhnoi Rossii* (Moscow, 1916), 123–6.
60 Ibid., 124.
61 Ibid., 104.
62 See J.H. Stach, *Ocherki po istorii i sovremennoi zhizni iuzhnorusskikh kolonii* (Moscow, 1916).
63 Decree of the Provisional government of 11 March 1917, "O priostanovlenii ispolneniia uzakonenii o zemlevladenii i zemlepol'zovanii avstriiskikh, vengerskikh i germanskikh vykhodtsev," in *Vestnik Vremennogo pravitel'stva* (14 March 1917).
64 *Vestnik Vremennogo pravitel'stva* no. 15 (1917); *Tsirkuliar po Odesskomu uchebnomu okrugu* no. 4/5 (Odessa, 1917), 154–7.
65 Royden Loewen, "New Themes in an Old Story: Transplanted Mennonites as Group Settlers in North America, 1874–1879," *Journal of American Ethnic History* 11, no. 2 (1992): 10.

4 A Foreign Faith, but of What Sort? The Mennonite Church and the Russian Empire, 1789–1917

OKSANA BEZNOSOVA

"The Mennonites freely administer the affairs of their faith according to their customs and rites."[1]

– From the official statues on foreign faiths in Russia, 1896

Mennonites occupy an intriguing page in the history of the relations between the Russian autocratic state and its numerous ethnic and religious groups. During the 130 years of their history in the empire, Russian Mennonites experienced a drastic change in their status, from having initially been granted full religious freedom to being deemed a barely tolerated sect by 1914. Such a dramatic shift could not help but attract scholarly attention, even though those same scholars have thus far failed to adequately account for it. To some extent this failure to understand is not surprising given that most scholars have tended to examine Mennonite history in isolation from the overall political situation in the Russian Empire, a point clearly articulated elsewhere in this volume. At the same time, Mennonite historians have not incorporated important insights that a growing body of historians, including Mikhail Dolbilov, Paul Werth, and Robert Crews, have brought to our understanding of the Russian state's evolving approach to "the Tsar's foreign faiths."[2] This scholarly neglect is especially noticeable in the study of Mennonite church life during the colonist period (1789–1871) when Mennonite church communities were investigated solely as a "thing in themselves." James Urry reinforced such views recently with his suggestion that Mennonites separated themselves from the larger world, that Mennonites in the first half of the nineteenth century "were not well integrated into Russian society and culture."[3] Such an approach, in my opinion, ignores conclusions reached separately by Werth and

Crew which challenge us to reconsider the paradigmatic value of Mennonite isolationism. It also significantly narrows the epistemological possibilities of researchers and hinders our ability to account for the dramatic shifts in government policies in the late nineteenth and early twentieth centuries.

Another common historiographical feature of Mennonite studies in the Russian Empire (and in the various countries that succeeded the subsequent Soviet demise) is the interest in them as creators of the famous "Mennonite economic miracle." This resulted in the paradoxical conclusion that Mennonites could be deemed economically integrated, yet culturally and politically removed from the constantly changing realities of the empire. Both of these historiographical traditions originated in the nineteenth century and have subsequently been interrogated, as is evident by Nataliya Venger's contribution in chapter 5. Venger, Bobyleva, and Cherkazianova have all demonstrated that new insights await those willing to dig into the rich archival collections housed across Russia and Ukraine. These previously neglected or inaccessible documents reveal the contradictory and ambiguous process by which the empire's religious policies shaped many aspects of Mennonite religious culture. This chapter will analyse tsarist officials' perceptions of the inner life of Mennonite church communities during the so-called colonist period on the basis of insufficiently explored and previous unknown archival documents of the Russian Empire's state authorities. It provides an important window into the changing cognitive maps[4] that Mennonites created to define themselves on their own terms and in relation to the society around them. Our work also uses the recent scholarly work undertaken by Albert W. Wardin Jr on Russian sectarians and by Heather Coleman on Russian Baptists to interrogate the relationship between empire and faith.[5]

The Russian State in the Colonist Period (1789–1871)

Religious Tolerance and Political Expectations

Mennonites who settled in "New Russia" (as southern Ukraine was known then) in 1789 and after were legally categorized as foreign colonists – a special, privileged part of the empire's population. Their settlements were subject to the administrative care if not outright control of the Ministry of State Domains[6] through its regional office, the Office of Guardianship (later converted into the Guardianship Committee).

The archives of the above-mentioned institutions[7] contain a variety of documents on Mennonite matters. At the same time, Mennonites were also deemed a religious group, and their members held a special religious-legal status in the Russian Empire according to the 6 September 1800 charter of Paul I.[8] The Hutterites also received the same status on 23 May 1801, according to the decree of Alexander I.[9]

It is easy to see why most historians have stressed Mennonite isolation and autonomy within the empire. Mennonites were promised exemption from military service in perpetuity as a condition of settlement, though their communities were also granted full autonomy in church and internal community affairs, including "the right to their own internal police and jurisdiction on offences and claims between members of the community."[10] This formulation implied the right to administer punishment for those who had transgressed the moral code within the community as determined by Mennonite ecclesial law. Mennonite authorities maintained public order in their communities and oversaw civil conflicts when they arose. The investigation of criminal offences took place under civil law. Settlement authorities (the Office of Guardianship, the Guardianship Committee) probed administrative transgressions against the rules of settlement regulations and intervened when conflicts involved the surrounding population. It can be concluded that from the outset the Mennonite cognitive map was like a dance between two poles, being both a legal (European colonist) and a religious (Mennonite faith) entity.[11] Though this did not immediately result in a state of perpetual conflict, such discord did arise at key points in history, as it did during the years Johann Cornies held power.

In connection with such broad rights of internal autonomy, the church life of the Mennonites was not subjected to guardianship and control by the Ministry of State Domains, as it was in the first years of their resettlement from Prussia (until 1810). Instead, they enjoyed seemingly unfettered religious freedom as they did initially over education, as Cherkazianova makes plain. That said, authorities did not assist Mennonites in the long-term material support of church life, though in the initial ten-year (1789–99) settlement period, the church elder of the Khortitsa colony, as well as other "foreign religious" clergies, received a 133 to 300 ruble cash benefit from the New Russian Treasury.[12] Ministry officials did demand an annual "progress record of schools and clergy" from Mennonites, though they regarded educational institutions in particular as exemplary because of the colonists' ability to thrive without imperial assistance.[13]

Mennonites adapted well to the state of affairs of church life that existed during the colonist period on the whole. If the agreement of 1786–1825 contained an obligatory clause granting Mennonites religious freedom and church autonomy, then the similar 1851 agreement with the government about future resettlement to Samara province simply granted them the same rights elsewhere in the empire.[14] However, Mennonite religious identities in the Russian Empire – despite almost complete religious freedom and church autonomy – had their own complications and contradictions, for here they faced administrative procedures and challenges different from the west European ones they had been accustomed to. First of all, Mennonites and other foreign colonists had to develop self-government in their new settlements within the Russian Empire. Thus village (secular) self-government was introduced along with the traditional Mennonite church rule, as the dance between the two poles was institutionalized.[15] As a result, Mennonite village elders vied with Mennonite church leaders for authority in matters of church discipline. Overall administrative supervision (except for actual church matters),[16] was performed by agencies of the Guardianship Committee, as was the case for all foreign colonists before the reforms of 1871. But the initial political battlegrounds were in the villages themselves, as Mennonite secular leaders felt that church elders constantly meddled in village matters. These, by way of perspective, had traditionally been placed under ecclesiastical control in their previous communities in Poland and Prussia.

What was going on here? Historians Robert Crews and Paul Werth have both demonstrated how St Petersburg's stance of religious toleration was offset by several expectations: first, that there would be a certain cohesion exercised within all of the foreign faiths akin to what existed within Orthodoxy; and second, that church leaders would demonstrate broad support for the empire's polity. As far as St Petersburg was concerned, religious tolerance had nothing to do with later notions of individual liberal openness and more to do with contemporary understandings of the late-eighteenth-century *Rechtsstaat*.[17] Dolbilov sees the roots of this policy in Peter the Great's drive to create a secular Russian state and its implications for all Christians, first and foremost the Russian Orthodox.[18]

On 16 May 1803 (less than two years after Paul I's famous decree on Mennonite privileges), the remarkable clause that "*there is to be no interference by the spiritual teachers of the Mennonites, performing the duty of their rank according to the rules of their creed, in secular and other affairs unseemly to the Priestly office*"[19] was introduced into the empire's legislation. The confrontation between Mennonite secular and church elders therefore grew in subsequent decades, especially as the secular elders moved to expand their powers. The sharp antagonism between church and secular authorities in the colonies led to a split of the Mennonite community into a majority of more tolerant Mennonites and a small number of supporters of strict isolationism from secular innovations. In 1812–19, the isolationists organized a special *Kleine Gemeinde* ("Small Congregation") whose members did not recognize the secular Mennonite self-government.[20] However, at the end of the 1850s, the *Kleine Gemeinde* elder Johann Friesen also took part in the work of the Molochna Church Convention[21] by which his "Small Community" demonstrated that they had moved on from their previously intransigent positions.

The Mennonite identity between the two poles was challenged by the *Kleine Gemeinde,* just as it was from the outset by the Flemish and Frisian congregations because it pointed to a lack of coherence within the one "pole." Yet another challenge arose when Mennonite secular and religious leaders contested which of them had the ultimate authority. This struggle between church and village elders worsened dramatically during the time of Johann Cornies when the Agricultural Society – created on his initiative – extended its activities to the schools, which had previously been controlled exclusively by church elders.[22] In extreme cases (e.g., in the conflicts between Johann Cornies and Jacob Warkentin, church elder of the Molochna Flemish congregations), the Guardianship Committee was forced to intervene. Each time authorities were compelled to rethink previous assumptions about Mennonite cohesiveness. Much to the chagrin of Mennonite spiritual leaders, when asked to adjudicate the committee tended to support Mennonite representatives of the secular government.[23] The committee's (and through it the government's) intervention was proof that Mennonite spiritual authorities by the mid nineteenth century were sometimes unable to resolve internal disciplinary problems within the colonies. In the opinion of Russian officials, the elders imposed "much too soft" punishments (normally as a moral censure only) on guilty brothers in faith,[24] as a result of which the latter "felt absolutely unpunished."[25] A classic example of this state of affairs was the case in the village Tiegenhagen of Molochna district in 1841 when church elder Warkentin tried unsuccessfully to reason with the chronic alcoholic Johann Bolt. Warkentin resisted the demands of both village elders and Molochna district authorities that Bolt be banished from Russia for his behaviour.[26] Nevertheless, Warkentin continued to defend his way of resolving disciplinary problems. In the end, the elders – such as Warkentin and spiritual teacher Wiens – who were most contentious and least inclined to compromise with secular authorities were themselves temporarily exiled from the empire by authorities.[27] As a sign of a societal shift, many Mennonites themselves opposed Warkentin's despotic tendencies and pretension to absolute control. Even those who had previously supported Warkentin in his conflict with Johann Cornies soon rejected him.[28] Ultimately this led to internal friction in Molochna's big Flemish community, which Warkentin oversaw, and resulted in its subsequent split into several independent communities.[29] Thus, much to the surprise of imperial authorities, Mennonite religious identities were complex and conflicted from the beginning. It remained to be seen how Mennonites would respond when challenges came their way from beyond their colonies. Would such crises serve as agents of unification or further discord?

The Religious "Explosion" in the Middle of the Nineteenth Century as a Mennonite "Social Revolution"

The religious conflicts and schisms that emerged in the Mennonite colonies in the mid nineteenth century were strongly shaped by a peculiar undercurrent within the colonies themselves: Mennonite inheritance practices. Established in the second half of the eighteenth century, the Mennonites' land-use system resulted in an inequitable power relationship between the "full owners" and the "landless" settlers. Although this situation was handled relatively painlessly among the region's Lutherans and Catholics, it caused a sharp disagreement among the Mennonites which was manifested in confessional discord.

The end result of Mennonite inheritance practices violated the traditional equality of rights that had been enjoyed by members of the Anabaptist community. The division of villagers into "full allotment owners" and the landless placed the latter in a marginal position politically, whether they were teachers, large-scale factory owners, or large landed estate owners (who lived outside the colonies). This left a negative imprint on the life of the church community because right up to the religious schisms of the 1860s, church elders were elected, as a rule, from full allotment owners, which also violated the equal rights supposedly enjoyed by all members of the congregation. The conflicts on these grounds acquired special acuteness in the Molochna mother colony of Tavrida province. Molochna also stood out among the other colonies by the prosperity of its overall population as well as by the number of landless, which, in 1851, accounted for two-thirds of all its villagers. Numbers for Khortitsa were also deemed alarmingly high by mid-century.[30]

The social division along full allotment owners and the landless also shaped the main parties that opposed each other in the religious struggle of the second half of the nineteenth century: the conservative spiritual elders selected from full allotment owners on the one hand and the radically inclined landless young people on the other. Even the well-known Russian scholar and civil servant, Alexander Klaus, in the mid-nineteenth century, paid attention to this feature of the social life of the Russian Empire's Mennonite community during the colonist period. And as recently as the 1980s, British researcher James Urry very successfully applied the theory of social contradictions to the study of religious life. Based on the study of data pertaining to the social origin of the 1850–60 religious movement's participants among the Molochna Mennonites, Urry advanced the idea that social factors were the driving force behind these new religious movements, though it must be said that the view he was repudiating was a simplistic view that saw the Mennonite Brethren as a socio-economic movement of the poor Mennonite landless. Quite the contrary. In Urry's words, "the Brethren therefore belonged largely to that minority group of educated, landless, upwardly mobile group."[31]

To make sense of this apparent contradiction, bear in mind that being landless in a colonist environment did not mean being poor. Thus, a significant number of participants of the religious movements were entrepreneurs, millers, and owners of private farmsteads, all of which suggested that some supporters of the new religious movements were prosperous. In addition, many also enjoyed a relatively high level of education, as landless village school teachers were also active in these new religious movements. Although these teachers were not the most prosperous members of the Mennonite community, their education was sufficiently high to ensure them respect in society and a reasonable standard of living. Therefore, Soviet researcher V.N. Arestov's conclusion that "not the Mennonite landlords and industrialists, but members of the poor Mennonite environment started to lead" missionary activity among the Orthodox[32] seems unreasonable. The whole paradox of the situation lies in "the Mennonite landlords and industrialists" being melded into the category of "landless" settlers who were forced to purchase land at their own expense and to found their new enterprises on it. For example, one of the most active members of the new Mennonite Brethren movement, the former blacksmith Abraham Unger, was an educated and wealthy man who had founded a factory in the Einlage village of Ekaterinoslav province in 1861, which had a strong reputation throughout the entire southern region for its production of covered wagons.[33]

This theory finds its full corroboration across the Khortitsa mother colony of Ekaterinoslav province. Of the five leaders involved in the 1854–5 and 1861–3 Khortitsa "awakenings," one was initially a blacksmith and later an entrepreneur (Abraham Unger); the rest were school teachers. If anything distinguished Molochna from Khortitsa it was that the latter tended to produce younger leaders. All of Khortitsa's leaders had been born in the empire. None were recent immigrants. This was in part because the Khortitsa colony had been settled much earlier than the Molochna colony, and was more conservative in spirit.

Therefore, and despite the dramatic differences in social status between the full allotment owners and the landless in the new Mennonite communities (including the Mennonite Brethren and Templers), it remains the case that Mennonites of landless status (including prominent private landowners and entrepreneurs) participated almost exclusively in the initial stages of the new religious movements. Thus, we confidently assert that social factors were crucial for the development of non-reform processes within the Mennonite community in the Russian Empire. Their presence resulted in a peculiarly "Russian" version of the development of evangelicalism in the Mennonite community. However, this distinctively social stimulus to a religious irruption was less evident after the era of the Great Reforms in the 1860s culminated in the abolition of the Mennonites' special settler/colonist status in 1871. Thereafter, Mennonite religious developments were more closely aligned with larger developments underway in the empire's other German-Protestant populations. It is perhaps surprising that the speed with which new religious movements emerged did not slow down after 1871, which suggests that social factors were by no means the most important driving forces at work. In short, Mennonites actively participated in a distinctly social (bourgeois-democratic) revolution during the reform era, one that placed a new Mennonite "third estate" – their intellectual and business elite – among their spiritual leaders. They, in turn, were subsequently able to play a vital role within the Mennonite settlements. By this means, the whole community adapted to widespread changes underway within the empire as the epoch of state-initiated reform at mid-century gave way to an era of capitalist modernization.

State Authorities and Intra-Mennonite Conflict

In their church affairs, and in contrast to other Protestants, Mennonites were not subject to the overt control of either the Ministry of State Domains or the Ministry of Internal Affairs during the initial (colonist) period. In cases of acute church conflicts that could not be resolved on the spot, Mennonites appealed directly to the Minister of Internal Affairs because they "d[id] not have and have never had any of their own higher authority."[34] Since there were no experts on Mennonite religious affairs in the empire at this time, the ministry took no action on these petitions and recommended instead that the contending parties resolve such conflicts within the community. In short, those government agencies with oversight of the Mennonite colonies were noticeably reluctant to intervene in conflicts they deemed internal to Mennonite life within the empire. As a rule, the Orthodox and Lutherans who worked in the Offices of Guardianship did not consider themselves competent enough to resolve Mennonites' religious crises. For example, in 1813 when the conflicts in the big Flemish community at Molochna became acute, Mennonites finally requested the Office of Guardianship to mediate. However, this Office, as represented by inspector Carl von Lau, dissociated itself from the case and instead directed the Khortitsa church elders to serve as justices of the peace. They were then instructed "to try as much as possible to reconcile the contending parties and decide on measures, which would serve as a solid agreement for many and to unite the brothers in faith," adding at the same time the formidable resolution: "otherwise, the Office will accept no further complaints on this subject from the Mennonites, but will already be forced on the first adverse action of the Mennonites or their elder Enns to take coercive means, which will serve to upset the good opinion the authorities have of these people and lead to infamy."[35] The independent efforts of the Mennonites to resolve this conflict in the big Flemish community led to its split in 1812–24 into three independent congregations: Kleine Gemeinde, Lichtenau-Petershagen, and Ohrloff.[36] Since the Mennonites did not object in principle to such a separation, the guardianship agencies ultimately sanctioned their legitimacy. It is also telling that Flemish Mennonite colonists in southern Ukraine as early as 1813 understood themselves to have been sufficiently integrated within the empire to appeal to state authorities to resolve a domestic tension.

In 1810, a special Department of Spiritual Affairs of Foreign Faiths (*Departament Dukhovnykh del inostannykh ispovedanii*) was established[37] to which St Petersburg transferred the general observation (as opposed to active monitoring) of Mennonite religious affairs. Therefore, a significant mass of documents pertaining to the relationship of Mennonites (as members of a distinct religious group) with the authorities remains within the archival collection of this institution.[38] Its main task was to coordinate the religious life of non-Orthodox communities within the empire's religious system in which the Orthodox Church enjoyed a preeminent position. As only the Orthodox could engage in missionary activity (to strengthen and spread its influence), all other faiths were not only obligated to desist but also to submit to Orthodox interests on this matter. Therefore, with the organization of a new religious community or the construction of a house of prayer, the representatives of the other faiths were required to provide a written statement of their creed to the local civil administration (which for foreign colonists meant that it be directed to the Guardianship Committee or Office). The respective civil authorities then passed these statements on to the local spiritual consistory of the Orthodox Church to ensure that "no harm to the interests of the Orthodox Church" resulted from the new religious community, institution of prayer, or public organization.

Mennonites also had to do this. They also submitted petitions for the construction of new houses of worship to the Guardianship Committee. Copies of the resolution of petitions were sent to the Department of Spiritual Affairs and the Ministry of Domains, and included references to the economic aspects of the construction activities. So the lion's share of the sources for this period comprised, on the one hand, authorization documentation of this kind, and on the other hand, overview notes on the legal status of Mennonites and general observations on developments within Mennonite districts. It is interesting to note that, in the opinion of the officials, Molochna was distinguished by its material well-being, Samara was considered the most advanced because of its ability to apply new technologies, and Khortitsa stood out for its residents' purported high morals.[39] On the whole, officials appraised Mennonite moral and ethical quality highly and the government continued to maintain that the inner life of the Mennonite settlements did not need external intervention.[40]

The means by which ecclesial matters were resolved changed after 1830 when the Evangelical Lutheran Church in Russia received official status and, as an institution, occupied a prominent place in the empire's religious system. The Minister of Internal Affairs henceforth began to consult the opinion of the General Consistory of the Evangelical-Lutheran Church without preliminary permission so it could resolve contentious issues in Protestant ecclesial affairs. As a result, state officials after 1830 who dealt with problems within Mennonite communities first extrapolated on their religious life from concepts that were unique to the Lutheran Church. Negligent translators began to introduce such conceptual nonsense as the "Mennonite *parish*," and "Mennonite *pastors*"[41] (both of which later also passed into Russian historiography). No wonder there was such misunderstanding and misinterpretation by both contemporary authorities and subsequent researchers concerning religious phenomena that existed exclusively in Mennonite church life.[42] This deference to Lutheran authorities after 1830 may have satisfied Russian bureaucrats but Mennonites were dissatisfied. They continued to maintain that their religious disputes should not be settled by representatives of other faiths, itself a fascinating distinction in Mennonite self-understanding. If anything annoyed Russian officials it was their own assessment that – according to imperial law – Mennonites "were granted complete freedom to resolve church affairs," yet their representatives had often proven incapable of doing just that.[43]

On the other hand, the administrative-supervisory functions of the Department of Spiritual Affairs were legislatively limited. Therefore, agencies of guardianship, as representatives of the Russian government, only rarely interfered in Mennonite church affairs. They confirmed the appointment of church elders, for example, but only after they had been selected by the communities themselves. They investigated disputes between those same elders and the Mennonites' own civil administration, between individual Mennonites and church or village elders, and so on. There are surprisingly few cases (not more than three dozen) in the archives of instances that dealt directly with the internal religious life of the Mennonite communities during the colonist period.[44] Though it is possible, for example, to encounter a richly diverse official documentation on religious unrest in the German Protestant colonies in the 1850s, the vicissitudes of the "religious revival" in Mennonite Khortitsa in 1853–5 became known to researchers only through latter recollections by eyewitnesses.[45] The Khortitsa district government report submitted by the authorities only mentioned it almost a decade later, when the

Mennonite Brethren movement of the 1860s had already taken hold.[46] Similarly, Albert W. Wardin Jr. has clearly linked the Mennonite religious revival of the 1850s to evangelical winds that had blown through the region's Lutheran Germans in the 1840s.[47]

During the worst of the Mennonites' church crisis of the 1860s and 1870s, the government essentially refused to interfere in internal church matters despite a fierce "war of discrediting evidence" which pitted "old" and "new" Mennonites against each other. According to the figurative expression of the famous Orthodox missionary Bishop Alexis (A. Ia. Dorodnitssyn),

> for the Russian government this religious dispute among the Mennonites had no special significance, as it had on this subject its own point of view, on the strength of which one thing in dogmatic respect was demanded from religious societies of foreign faiths, so that in the creed of the present religious society there was nothing contrary to the basic principles of Christianity, morality, and civil order.[48]

Therefore, despite the desperate calls of the "old" Mennonites, the government decided to follow the path of least resistance, even as Cherkazianova shows how the state began to intervene in educational matters at the same time. On religious affairs, the state adopted the proposal of the Novorossiysk and Bessarabia governor general P.E. Kotzebue to support the resettlement in Kuban of 100 member families of the Mennonite Brethren Church.[49] The record of correspondence makes plain that officials continued to hope throughout the 1860s that the flames of religious conflicts and schisms enveloping the Mennonite community would be extinguished by relocating religious dissidents onto vacant land so that the problem would be resolved on its own terms. As Werth has observed, these same officials were especially confused in the Mennonite case as all parties identified themselves as the true and "orthodox" Mennonite faith, making it impossible to determine which was the sectarian movement among them.[50]

Coincidentally, the era of religious conflict and schism coincided with the Great (socio-political) Reforms in the Russian Empire, and contributed to the overcoming of the Mennonites' religious reticence to proselytise. The onset of active Mennonite missionary activity had a visible effect on the religious life of the various ethnic and confessional subgroupings that surrounded them. In 1862–4, there was already a state of excitement for the first court cases on the missionary activity of the Mennonite Brethren. Their activity had undermined the missionary activity of the Orthodox Church and was regarded by the authorities as a threat to the very foundations of Russian statehood. This circumstance forced the government and the Guardianship Committee in the last decade of the existence of the colonist system to intervene more actively in Mennonite religious affairs, as the official correspondence beginning in 1860 testifies to.[51] It became clear to Russian officials by the 1870s that it was impossible to resolve religious conflict within the Mennonite community with measures that presumed ethno-confessional isolation. That era had clearly passed after the Mennonite pietistic renewal movement of the 1850s had quickened their missionizing impulse, from which countless peasants had abandoned Orthodoxy in favour of Shtundism and other sectarian beliefs.[52] In response, those with oversight in the religious sphere on behalf of the empire now moved from a policy of non-interventionism in Mennonite affairs to large-scale reform that suggested active state engagement as the state's cognitive map of these former colonists had changed considerably.

Mennonites and the Reforms of 1871 and 1874

Legal and Social Consequences

The Russian Empire's religious policy underwent significant changes throughout the nineteenth century though the pace accelerated during the Great Reforms of the 1860s and 1870s as the state's ultimate goal became the administrative unification of the empire's rural population. To that end, St Petersburg equalized the rights of all foreign colonists (including all followers of "foreign" faiths) together with those of former serfs and state peasants. It was in this decade that government officials moved from a policy of non-intervention in Mennonite religious affairs to one in which they gradually attacked colonists' traditional rights and privileges. It was also at this time that the designation of "foreign" faiths began to take on a different meaning for St Petersburg. Scholars such as Darius Staliūnas and Mikhail Dolbilov have focused on this as the era of Russification with all its contradictory impulses. What did it mean to become Russianized? For some, the shift was a linguistic one; for others, who believed that the only true Russians were Orthodox, it was religious.[53] Either way, it marked a dramatic sea change for an empire seeking to recover from the humiliation of defeat in the Crimean War. According to Werth, the designation of "foreign" as late as 1868 was intended to confirm the primacy of the Orthodox Church more than to alienate non-Orthodox (and non-Christian among them) believers. For that reason, it was possible to be both "foreign" and "indigenous" within the empire.[54] However, "foreign" did begin to take on an increasingly threatening meaning for the empire after that as Russia's own nationalist movement gathered momentum.

In our attempt to assess how much rural society was actually transformed by these reforms we would do well to recall the peculiarities of Russian society – which Alfred Rieber quite correctly called "The Sedimentary Society." Rieber argued that the presence of significant feudal vestiges (the fragmentation of society into classes and groups with special rights and privileges) meant that reforms in Imperial Russia affected only the most superficial "layers" of public relations, leaving unchanged the basic "type" (*poroda*) or traditional structure of the Russian society of that era.[55] Therefore, before proceeding to analyse the consequences of the reforms of the 1870s, it is necessary to clearly define what had changed as a result of these reforms, and what remained as before.

The implementation of a new course of domestic policy not only put an end to the Mennonites' colonist status (as well as for other foreign settlers) across the Russian Empire; it also significantly reduced their erstwhile religious rights and freedoms. The most significant changes happened in the differentiation of secular and church rights which resulted in a considerable contraction of the Mennonite church authority in its organizational and supervisory functions. Investigation of all misdemeanours under the category of criminal offences and civil delinquency were henceforth withdrawn from community control. Earlier, the investigation and punishment of minor offences and crimes among Mennonites had taken place within the communities – and only traditional moral punishments (such as excommunication) were imposed.[56] Henceforth all these powers were transferred to the authority of local civil or judicial administrations where matters were dealt with on general civil grounds. Candidates for church elders who had previously been merely confirmed in their posts by Guardianship agencies were now subjected to mandatory approval by the local civil administration. According to the new regulations, Mennonite ecclesial leaders were required not only to swear an oath (Mennonites were permitted simply to pledge themselves) but also, like the clergy of all other faiths, to report politically untrustworthy persons within their communities to the government. Church elders were still required to maintain the

Mennonite communities' registries, but henceforth in the Russian language and following uniformly prescribed civil patterns. From this point forward, Mennonite communities were also subject to unprecedented regular inspection through provincial boards of administration.

At the same time, and in the framework of the ongoing development of internal educational reform, the village school was removed from the exclusive control of Mennonite church elders (as also happened at this time for all the other colonists). All training (except lessons on the laws of God and the mother tongue itself) was converted to Russian by law. This of course mirrors the findings reached by Venger and Cherkazianova.

Given these changes, it is perhaps surprising that Mennonites on the whole approved of the Colonist Reform of 1871. They now expected to receive the same rights as the empire's other subjects, as well as certain civil liberties and opportunities (in particular, the freedom of movement within the empire which had previously been strictly limited under the terms of settlement regulations). Although the implementation of the reforms in the area of communal land ownership caused some agitation (especially in the Molochna), even there it considerably expanded opportunities for social and spatial mobility, which was an obvious advantage for the now former colonists (Mennonites). The new legislation was less about integrating a previously separate people who had lived in isolated communities. Mennonites, after all, had been integrated from the very point of settlement. What had changed were the means by which that integration would be accomplished in an age where corporate identities were being radically revised, if not eliminated.

Encouraged by the Mennonites' positive reaction, imperial authorities began actively to explore the ground concerning military reform, especially as they already had the Prussian example in resolving preexisting problems. The government's consultations at the end of the 1860s, "particularly," as the Novorossiysk and Bessarabia governor-general P.E. Kotzebue emphasized in his report, "with the most influential and prosperous Mennonites from Molochna," showed that a considerable portion of the Mennonites, "with the exception of just religious fanatics,"[57] were prepared to accept the proposed changes. Importantly, these even included extending military service to them through exclusively alternative forms (first forestry, and then also sanitary service in field forces). However, during recurrent negotiations on this issue in the Molochna colony, the improper behaviour of one of the

Ministry of State Domain officials (Colonel Barthelemy) – who made an inappropriate joke – led to false rumours and serious unrest. Kotzebue claimed that Mennonites had suddenly exaggerated the government's actual plans and concerns for them.[58] Almost a third of the Mennonite territory in the empire was abandoned forever through emigration as a result of the downturn in these negotiations before the Mennonite population finally managed to move on.

The empire's implementation of its military reform after 1871 undoubtedly signified one of the most vivid transformations of the former religious-legal system and dramatically challenged Mennonites' self-perception as colonists. Though this shift suggested integration, it came at a great cost to previously cherished privileges. For one, obligatory military service was expanded in 1874 to Mennonites and other colonists-pacifists across the empire.[59] As a whole, these changes signalled a new era characterized by a steady but consistent attack on Mennonites' religious rights. Mennonite historiography has tended to treat the legislative shifts in the late imperial era as a willful manifestation of the Russian government's blatant arbitrariness, one that violated all the obligations and promises that the government had made to Mennonites to persuade them to resettle to southern Ukraine in the first place. Nevertheless, the study of, on the one hand, the archival correspondence from different state echelons concerning the revision of Mennonite religious status, and on the other hand, the reality that the Mennonite community of that time was a social organism that had entered a new stage in its church-community development, leads to the conclusion that the government's process of revising the Mennonites' religious status was neither straightforward nor antagonistic. Instead, Mennonites were as much actors as victims in this dramatic transformation of the state's religious policy.

In the second half of the nineteenth century, the Mennonites' previous tendency to fracture into disparate religious subgroupings decreased significantly as a greater internal tolerance came into display. This was most evident in a broad-based unification movement that gathered speed before 1900, which, interestingly, coincides with Venger's findings on the economic front. The first signs of bureaucratization within Mennonite church life were also evident in precisely these years, all of which had previously been deemed under the authority of protocols and the various regulatory records of the "Babylon establishment." Thus, the Mennonite community showed more and more signs of a shift from "a settlement of believers" to a settlement of churches "within a Mennonite society whose identity was primarily ethno-cultural, a society that itself existed within the vast and modernizing Russian Empire.

Though all changes introduced by the reforms of the 1870s were hardly met with approval by all Mennonites, it is clear that they were not met with any serious resistance. In short, the experience of carrying out these reforms had demonstrated to the government that almost the entire Mennonite community had come to accept them, even though they had been implemented with little enthusiasm, while some had emigrated altogether. Even so, the future path of Mennonite administrative integration seemed set.

Mennonite Church Polity after the Convention of 1851

Internal discipline within communities-churches was supervised from the outset not only by church leaders but also by village elders, who occasionally competed fiercely with each other and challenged a narrow understanding of Mennonites as primarily a faith-based people. It is not surprising that a new generation of Mennonite leaders responded to these new internal social conditions at the end of Cornies' era in the 1840s. They sought to modernize their methods of self-government by introducing a revised Church Convention in 1851 (the convention was a body of Mennonite elders that had previously served as advisors to help solve religious problems). For, as both state officials and Mennonites themselves acknowledged, the absence of any supreme superior arbiter had a detrimental effect on their ability to solve the most important issues of their community.[60] Robert Crews argues that it was this lack of centrally recognized authority within Protestant churches that had prompted the Russian state to intervene by the 1830s. Though Crews does not speak directly to the Mennonite case, my own research suggests that it applied there as well.[61]

This lack of a centrally recognized authority on even church matters meant that individual Mennonite ecclesial leaders could reinterpret the understanding of church discipline (and self-discipline), thereby threatening the cohesion of the whole. Russian officials had unanimously observed for years that the peculiar structure of Mennonite colonies made quarrels and disputes on religious grounds between either Mennonite communities or individuals "a quite ordinary phenomenon in their life."[62] According to Crews, the state's attempt to institutionalize administrative uniformity for the empire's Protestants in 1832 had actually increased conflicts as harmonious relations became more elusive than ever.[63]

Not all such initiatives were so broadly cast. Mennonite deliberations in 1851 were deemed a success as they conferred certain disciplinary powers to their own Church Convention. The majority of Mennonites approved of this new initiative and on 7 April 1851 the Guardianship Committee headed by Keller (a Lutheran) also approved the Church Convention's new authority. All hoped that henceforth Mennonite church affairs would be resolved at the local level by Mennonites themselves.[64]

The main objective of the renewed Church Convention – whose subdivisions acted absolutely independently in the Frisian and the Flemish congregations of the Khortitsa and Molochna colonies – was to resolve religious disputes and strengthen church discipline. However, not having a clearly defined scope of authority, the Church Convention (in which the different communities constantly fought for influence) often also assumed those functions, which, according to Mennonite custom, only a general assembly of the communities possessed. So when the renegade religious movement was founded at the beginning of 1860, the founders of the Molochna Mennonite Brethren split were expelled as members and were stripped of their rights as Mennonites. That decision was made by the Molochna Church Convention, not by the general (civic) assembly of their home communities. Ironically, it was precisely this event that provided the leaders of this fledgling Mennonite community with the opportunity to found their own (Brethren) community.[65] On the other hand, such actions of the Convention led to its fiercest criticism and the démarche of the Lange brothers' group which grew in 1863 into an independent community of the Mennonite Templers.[66] As a result, the Church Convention was already torn by internal opposition by the end of the 1860s and demoralized by accusations that it had assumed "papal authority"; that it suffered from greed for money, moral decay; and that it was paralysed and practically unable to function.[67]

In those years a question had arisen for state authorities at the very time that they had begun to design and implement wide-scale reform across the empire, about the forms of interaction between the state and the Mennonite communities and the lack of congruence for the latter in their relations with the state. These disputes, and the struggle to establish a clear framework for their relations with state authorities, reflected the trend whereby Mennonite society before 1900 became a diverse church-based society as opposed to a monolithic, insular world unto itself. Put another way, it revealed the degree to which Mennonites had become socially institutionalized to Imperial Russian realities, and marked their transformation from an overarching religious community to a social community of churches and other institutions. The most striking manifestation of this shift was the attempted establishment of the 1851 Church Convention with extraordinary powers to secure a distinctively supreme church-administrative authority within the increasingly diverse conglomerate of Mennonite communities in the Russian Empire. Thus, the 1851 Convention marked a first transitional stage to a modern form of socially-based organization for Mennonite church life. Though the 1851 convention was later deemed a failure, it nevertheless marked an important stage in the development of more secular-based and unifying authorities within Mennonite settlements as old cognitive maps were overturned and new ones introduced.

This transition from an indivisible Mennonite community to "one or more churches within a community" led to the emergence of a whole host of new religious groups (new Mennonites) as a distinctive answer to the socio-cultural conditions of life in the Russian Empire. This "answer" was largely negative because the new religious groups refused to obey the old organs of power. This led to a very real administrative anarchy in Mennonite settlements as not only did members of the old and the new faiths not recognize each other as "Mennonites," they also tried in every possible way to discredit each other in the eyes of state officials. The religious movement of the 1860s and 70s also became a distinctively social revolution when these new Mennonites refused to recognize the division of Mennonite landowners into full- and half-allotment holders. The Colonist Reform of 1871 had the same vector as it equalized all Mennonites in social as well as in church rights.

Thus, the change of the government's religious policy was caused, first of all, by the inability of Mennonite leaders to set acceptable assurances and limitations on the religious freedom enjoyed by all Mennonites. On the contrary, government officials had been aware since at least the middle of the nineteenth century that Mennonites were unable to cope independently with their internal church (as in, first of all, church-administrative) problems, as John Staples has previously pointed out. It is no wonder, then, that a number of developments had so fractured the Mennonite community into a conglomerate of complementary detached autonomous communities by the late nineteenth century that it had practically exhausted its ability to manage itself. Aileen Friesen has demonstrated how the state's own response to the Mennonite religious schisms of the mid-nineteenth century reflected the government's own inability to speak with one voice. Fragmentation, it seemed, was not limited to Mennonites; authorities also expressed a wide range of divergent views, from the local to the imperial level, and across the various ministries engaged.[68]

If anything prompted Mennonites to want to resolve these challenges, it was the mounting awareness across the Mennonite communities before 1900 that they needed to speak with one Mennonite voice before the state authorities. This was initially felt most acutely by the "new" sects which had fought a desperate struggle for their Mennonite rights between 1871 and 1879. Therefore, the need to coordinate their efforts across divided communities prompted the call for a joint conference of the Mennonite brotherhood. The Mennonite Brethren Church was the first to come to this realization. It began to conduct such conferences annually, though a sign of the challenges before them was evident in 1873 when the first conference (held in Andreasfeld village, Alexandrovsk district, and Ekaterinoslav province) received the designation "Mennonite Brethren Federal Congregation." The old Mennonites also started to convene such conferences after 1883.

Towards Confrontation: Imperial Religious Policy and Mennonite Coherence after 1880

Major changes to the empire's religious structures and relations were inevitably caught up with the government's decision to press on with the modernization of Russian society as a whole. Contemporary notions of the universal citizen as an individual agent demanded no less. On 6 August 1880, officials established the Department of Spiritual Affairs of Foreign Faiths as an independent institution, though on 16 March 1881 it was again included in the Ministry of Internal Affairs as part of a general Department of Spiritual Affairs. In the end the oversight (still not active religious monitoring!) of Mennonite religious affairs was transferred to this agency.

A number of changes in religious policy coincided with these institutional shifts, for many reasons. Right up to the 1880s, Russian officials treated Mennonites in a manner that could have been characterized as one of favourable indifference. Mennonites had always been legally deemed as "acceptable (permissible), though of foreign Christian faith."

Thus, despite plans of radical reforms in different areas, it is doubtful that state officials harboured plans to limit Mennonite religious rights (evidenced by the official recognition in 1880 of all new Mennonite sects as also legally "Mennonites"). The relationship that emerged in the post-reform era between Mennonites (as a religious community) and the Russian state initially suited both sides and provided Mennonites with a much more favourable position than they had enjoyed in the German empire during the last Mennonite emigration.

However, the relationship between Mennonites and the Russian government fundamentally changed at the beginning of the 1890s, to a great extent at the initiative of Mennonites themselves. By this time, and to a greater degree than was evident in all other faiths in the Russian Empire, the Mennonite communities had passed through practically all stages of maturing from an all-embracing community to a church within a larger ethno-cultural community and multi-ethnic empire. This social transformation was accompanied by successfully rooting the Mennonite church within the empire's evolving religious system. Mennonite relations with the larger world of the empire changed accordingly, most especially as the growing influence of pietism drew Mennonites in a new direction: external missionary work. From the government's perspective, these new developments were not totally unexpected. The dismantling of the colonist system had transformed the inhabitants of these formerly isolated foreign settlements into proselytizers of the surrounding "larger world." Therefore, the new Mennonite sects that emerged in the late nineteenth century were all driven to proselytise. The era of religious schisms within the Mennonite settlements coincided with a time of wider socio-political reforms in the Russian Empire, and contributed to overcoming the religious reticence of the Mennonites themselves. It transformed their missionary activity into a noticeable phenomenon in the religious life of their neighbours who themselves represented an increasingly wide range of faiths and nationalities; nor does the archival record support the generally accepted assumption that the Mennonite Brethren were the sole missionaries. The extant documents that contain numerous complaints against Mennonites of diverse sects attests to this, even if the absolute domination of the Mennonite Brethren in this undertaking is also evident.[69]

Government officials especially worried about the spread of pacifist ideas among the troops as events moved towards a great war in 1914. Even though it had made a number of religiously-based concessions in the revolutionary upheaval of 1905, the government sprang into action after that same revolutionary tide had abated. It now sought to establish direct state control (monitoring) over the internal affairs of all religious communities, as had long been the case for the Orthodox Church. Officials took the first step in this process in 1910 when they issued new regulations for the registration and functioning of non-ecclesial religious communities. Recently Paul Werth concluded that it was in 1910 that the state abandoned a conciliatory approach to foreign faiths that had begun after the revolution of 1905. Nor was such a shift surprising with German-language faiths given the empire's steadily deteriorating relations with Germany.[70] In response to this new imperial onslaught, Mennonites convened the First All-Mennonite Conference and finally began to work vigorously to unite all of the Mennonite congregations so as to present a unified front before the imperial government. Despite the Mennonites' stubborn resistance, the situation rapidly deteriorated. In its next steps, in 1913–14 the government asserted its complete control over all religious communities when it established a general policy of universalisation. Officials claimed that this policy was the logical expression of Russia's status as a vast "Eurasian empire." The beginning of the First World War and the expansion of Russia's anti-German campaign destroyed any hope that the Mennonites would be able to maintain even the significantly reduced religious rights that they had received as a result of the 1871–4 reforms. In this context, fuelled by the patriotic fervour at the outbreak of war, Mennonites had every reason to conclude that they would soon have their legal status reduced to that of a barely-tolerated sect. In that sense, my findings do not concur with Cherkazianova's conclusion that Mennonites were somewhat immune from anti-German legislation at this time because of the support offered to them by provincial officials. As I see it, the circle was completed by 1914: if at first the Mennonites had escaped from Poland and Prussia to find what they so desired in the Russian Empire – religious freedom and independent self-government – within barely more than a hundred years Mennonites were again threatened by the very real prospect of being deemed religious and social misfits. Nor were they alone in this transition. Heather Coleman has demonstrated that the empire's Baptists also viewed the years after 1905 especially as "an open storm."[71]

Towards the beginning of the twentieth century, then, the internal political situation in the Russian Empire changed for the worse for Mennonites of all denominations, and forced all of them to pursue inter-Mennonite cooperation. By 1900, a new generation of Mennonite believers had come of age, and the recriminations that had characterized the era of religious schisms had largely faded. For the first time in forty years, it seemed that peaceful coexistence of representatives of the different persuasions (clearly shown by the growing popularity of the Alliance Churches) was within reach. One might call this Mennonite self-perception as more cosmopolitan, and less narrowly universalist, as the issue of who had the truly orthodox Mennonite faith was set aside. The need for a joint challenge to the government's plans for further retrenchment of Mennonite rights and freedom brought the Mennonites closer to calling an All-Mennonite General Conference, the first of which was held on 26–7 October 1910 in the village Schönsee at Molochna. In the process of its implementation, questions on school matters, health service, and others were discussed. However, the most important matters dealt with upholding the community's shared interests before state representatives. Delegates called for coordinating efforts and implementing representation functions, and to that end, the "Committee on Faith" (Glaubenskomission) – a consultative-representative body of Mennonite communities of all denominations in the Russian Empire – was appointed. This committee was called upon to present and protect Mennonites' shared interests before Russian officials. Its first chairman was the elected church elder of the Ekaterinoslav Mennonite congregation (a subsidiary of the Khortitsa Flemish community), David (Heinrich) Epp. Heinrich Braun, the director of the Raduga Publishing Company, also joined the committee on behalf of the Mennonite Brethren. This committee had offices in all of the mother church-colonies and fulfilled the role of a "presidium" or "council of brothers," whose decisions were accountable to and whose actions were evaluated at the annual conferences of Mennonite congregations (Allgemeine Mennonitische Bundeskonferenz). These, in turn, gathered representatives of the older church (Kirchliche) as well as the new Mennonite congregations to consolidate all Mennonite congregations in Russia. Although the traditional principles of Mennonite congregational polity were strictly observed in the organization of these organs of Mennonite self-government, their activities successfully and efficiently enabled Russian Mennonites to coordinate their efforts in confronting the increasingly aggressive challenges of the "external" world.

Conclusions

On the whole, we need to rethink our understanding of how Mennonites related to the larger empire in the initial period of settlement, and we need to do so in light of recent historiographical insights. Mennonites were anything but a people unto themselves, somehow at a great remove from the empire itself. They were, from the moment of settlement, integrated into a *Rechtsstaat* that organized its disparate society by a host of means, including religious affiliation. Such an organizational strategy allowed for the so-called foreign faiths to be integrated into the empire at a time when liberal notions of the sentient individual had not taken root. Under the circumstances, most Mennonites could live and die in southern Ukraine thinking that they were a distinct and isolated people, and they could maintain that perspective as long as the state did not change its organizational strategy, or as long as Mennonites (or all other religious communities for that matter) did not cross the line from narrowly religious to more broadly political activity. Russian officials during this Colonist Period regarded Mennonites with favourable indifference as long as they played their role as loyal servitors of the empire. This provides important parallels with work by Venger and Cherkazianova in this volume, though it must be said that seeming indifference was born of an overall favourable regard that officials had for Mennonite colonists.

Changes in both Mennonite and Imperial Russian society transformed that relationship between Mennonites and the state, even as it did for literally everyone else in the empire. In the larger picture, St Petersburg responded to its humiliating defeat in the Crimean War by seeking the total transformation of the empire, starting with the emancipation of the peasantry in 1861. It followed that erstwhile legal distinctions enjoyed by the empire's colonists would also have to go as the state modernized, and as it melded all non-noble rural society into a single peasant social estate (soslovie). On a more immediate level, the state was more inclined to rethink its relationship with "foreign" faiths given the inability of, especially, Protestants to maintain order within their own faith communities. Such was surely the case for Mennonites, much to their own and the state's chagrin, given the plethora of religious and social divisions that had arisen in the first half of the nineteenth century. Thus, by mid-century both Mennonites and the state were seeking to redefine their relationship, albeit in very different ways. Therefore the authorities welcomed the Mennonites' attempt to modernize their traditional methods of self-government (as in the revision to the original Church Convention).

That said, the government was already clearly aware by the middle of the nineteenth century that the Mennonites themselves were unable to deal independently with the problems that arose from the peculiar symbiosis of virtually unlimited freedom of faith on the one hand, and their simultaneous need to maintain strict civil administrative order on the other. Even so, the state did not intervene until Mennonites violated their own initial terms of settlement, which happened when they began to proselytise the empire's Orthodox peasants. Albert W. Wardin Jr has demonstrated how state concern about Mennonite exploitation of "the Russian peasants" and their support of "Germanism" reached a fever pitch after 1900 as these erstwhile Mennonite colonists were now openly identified as part of a foreign culture and religion.[72] "Foreign" gradually took on a new meaning in the decades immediately before 1900 as Russian nationalists gained ground, and it was this development that so perplexed contemporary Mennonites (and many observers). An examination of religious life among Mennonites in southern Ukraine also reinforces the scholarly work of Serhii Plokhy, who has concluded that modern Ukrainian identity has developed out of "historically, culturally, and religiously diverse regions."[73] Surely it was that very diversity that the imperial Russian state found so threatening before and after 1900. For, as with the "Children of Rus" and Faith Hillis's study of Slavs in Kiev and right-bank Ukraine for this period, Mennonites also had little difficulty in seeing themselves as a distinct but fiercely loyal people.[74] But once the question of loyalty had entered into the bureaucratic mindset it was a difficult one to expunge, all the more so for those deemed Germanic after the rise of Germany. Changes in the government's religious policy in the second half of the nineteenth century thus corresponded to the ongoing transformation and development of the Mennonite communities as a social organism. By the beginning of the twentieth century, Mennonites had already reached the stage of social (i.e., ecclesial) maturity that fit well with the system of inter-religious relations that had emerged in the empire as a whole. They had moved from a state of completely insularity to one whereby they sought actively to engage and transform the outside world in accordance with their own rules of life. This might have worked well had Russia gone the way of a modern liberal society that respected equal rights. Some hope for just that development was evident when the tsar approved legislation in the spring of 1905 placing all religions on an equal footing, and fully legalized conversion from one faith to another.[75] The times demanded no less a radical concession as Russia found itself mired in a terrible war with Japan coupled with a revolutionary upsurge across the empire. Under the circumstances, why would Mennonites not have continued to expand their base within the empire, and continue to undertake missionary activity among the Orthodox?

Paul Werth has shown better than most that such an outcome was not to be, in large part because a second ideology battled with liberal reform in these years, and eventually overcame it. This was the empire, which was rooted in a particular version of what it meant to be Russian, that is, linked to Orthodoxy and the Russian nationality. By 1910 the latter movement had won out, in part because of the strong support given it by Tsar Nicholas II.[76] No wonder all foreign faiths felt increasingly under siege after 1910 and most especially after the Great War broke out in 1914. Mennonites were among those under suspicion as "foreign" and "Russian" were now deemed to be mutually exclusive. Under the circumstances, dark days were sure to lie ahead for them.

NOTES

1 *Svod uchrezhdenii i ustavov upravlenuia dukhovnykh del inostrannykh ispovedanii khristianskikh i inovernykh. Svod zakonov Rossiiskoi imperi* (St Petersburg, 1896), vol. 11, chapter 5, Article 903.

2 Mikhail Dolbilov, *Russkii krai, chuzhaia vera: Etnokonfessional'naia politika imperii v Litve I Belorussii pri Aleksandre II* (Moscow: Novoe literaturnoe obozrenie, 2010); Paul W. Werth, *The Tsar's Foreign Faiths: Toleration and the Fate of Religious Freedom in Russia* (Oxford: Oxford University Press, 2014); and Robert Crews, "Empire and the Confessional State: Islam and Religious Politics in Nineteenth-Century Russia," *American Historical Review* 108, no. 1 (2003): 50–83.

3 James Urry, *Mennonites, Politics, and Peoplehood: Europe, Russia, Canada, 1525 to 1980* (Winnipeg: University of Manitoba Press, 2006), 6, 95, among numerous other references.

4 Nataliya Venger has also used this important concept in her own work with respect to Mennonites in Ukraine. As an introduction to cognitive maps, see Roger M. Downs and David Stea, *Maps in Minds: Reflections on Cognitive Mapping* (New York: Harper & Row, 1977).

5 See especially Albert W. Wardin Jr, *On the Edge: Baptists and Other Free Church Evangelicals in Tsarist Russia, 1855–1917* (Eugene, OR: Wipf & Stock, 2013); and Heather Coleman, *Russian Baptists and Spiritual Revolution, 1905–1929* (Bloomington: Indiana University Press, 2005).

6 The only exceptions were the Mennonite settlements in Volyn and Kiev provinces because they were located on privately owned lands, as well as the Samara Mennonite settlements by the Volga River. Although the last one also settled on government land, since their settlements in the Samara province were too far from the city of Saratov (where the Office of Guardianship Volga Colonists was), it was decided not to set up another office and the functions of administrative-economic guardianship of the Mennonites were passed along to the specially created department of the Office of the Samara Governor.

7 Fond N°381 (Ministerstvo gosudarstvennykh imushchestv) and 383 (1 Departament Ministerstva gosudarstvennykh imushchestv) Rossiiskogo gosudarstvennogo istoricheskogo arkhiva (RGIA, St Petersburg, Russia), N°6 (Popechitel'nyi Komitet) Gosarkhiva Odesskoi olasti (Odessa, Ukraine), N°134 (Ekaterinoslavskaia kontora opekunstva inostrannykh poselentsev) Gosarkhiva Dnepropetrovskoi oblasti (Dnepropetrovsk, Ukraine).

8 *Polnyi svod zakonov Rossiiskoi imperii.* – Sobranie 1 (PSZ), N°19545 from 6 September 1800; *Svod uchrezhdenii i ustavov upravleniia dukhovnykh del inostrannykh ispovedanii khristianskikh i inosvernykh.* – ch. 5, 903. PSZ (1896, vol. 11), 171; *K voprosu o proiskhozhdenii mennonitov. Materialy sobrannye D.G. Epp i Chlenom Gosudarstvennom Dumy G.A. Bergmanom* (Petrograd, 1916).

9 After this, official documents often started to call the Hutterites the "Radichev Mennonite Brethrens."

10 PSZ, N°19545 from 6 September 1800.

11 I thank the press's anonymous reviewer for helping to clarify, and temper, this distinction.

12 *Rozklad vidatkiv na 1798 rik po Novorosiis'koi gubernii; Rozklad vidatkiv na 1799 rik po Novorosiis'koi gubernii; and D.I. Iavornits'kii, Do istorii Stepovoi Ukraini* (N°173) 256, (N°215), 346, (N°219), 362, and (N°258), 421. In 1790–1, this position was held in the Khortitsa Flemish community by Jakob [Bernhard?] Penner, and in 1791–9 by Johann Wiebe. In the Khortitsa Frisian community the church leader in 1792–4 was Kornelius Froese. However, the above-mentioned documents refer to the salary of only one "Mennonite pastor." These were the so-called preferential years (the first ten years after resettlement), when the state took upon itself all the expenses for settling foreign immigrants. When the period expired, their payments from the state stopped. According to Mennonite tradition, church elders did not receive salaries for church services or "payment for religious rites" from the community (officials of the Guardianship

Committee made special notes about this in the lists of colonist pastors and parishes: RGIA, f.821, op.6, d.20, l.1ob-8).

13 Community tax on maintenance of school buildings and teachers was the same as the charge on supplies for community registers, repairs of houses of worship, and public buildings. At the beginning of the twentieth century, this sum in the Khortitsa church-communities (both Flemish and Frisian) was made up of 4 kopecks from each 1,000 rubles of a declared property householder. See Predpisanie Khortitskogo volostnogo pravleniia sel'skim starostam. 13 March 1913 (N°2155); and Gosarkhiv Zaporozhskoi oblasti, f.P-121, op.1, d.145, l.3ob).

14 RGIA, f.383, op.13, d.14397, l.18ob.

15 The Hutterites were the exception as they were able to convince the Guardianship Offices that though the church elder was the head of the community, his special assistants fulfilled the function of village elders.

16 Gosudarstvennyi arkhiv Odesskoi olasti, f.6, op.4, d.23650, l.3; RGIA, f.383, op.29, d.159, l.84ob; and RGIA, f.821, op.5, d.975, l.26–27ob, 31ob.

17 Crews, "Empire and the Confessional State," 56; and Werth, *The Tsar's Foreign Faiths*, 71.

18 Dolbilov, *Russkii krai, chuzhaia vera*, 44–55.

19 *Svod uchrezhdenii i ustavov upravleniia dukhovnykh del inostrannykh ispovedanii khristianskikh i inosvernykh*, 904.

20 John Friesen, "Mennonite Churches and Religious Developments in Russia, 1789–1850," in *Mennonites in Russia, 1788–1988: Essays in Honour of Gerhard Lohrenz*, ed. John Friesen (Winnipeg: CMBC Publications, 1989), 59–64.

21 J. Friesen was one of the two elders who, at a meeting of the Molochna Church Convention on 11 March 1861, voted against the exclusion of the Brethren community from Mennonite rank.

22 Gosudarstvennyi arkhiv Odesskoi olasti, f.6, op.3, d.15623. For the definitive work to date on historiography regarding Johann Cornies, see Harvey L. Dyck, "Russian Servitor and Mennonite Hero: Light and Shade in Images of Johann Cornies," *Journal of Mennonite Studies* (1984), 9–28.

23 John R. Staples, "Religiia, politika i mennonitskaia Zhalovannaia gramota v nachale XIX veka v Rossii: Peresmotr dela Varkentina," in *Voprosy germanskoi istorii* (Dnepropetrovsk, 2003), 4–22; RGIA, f.383, op.10, d.9431; op.12, d.12327; op.19, d.25437.

24 RGIA, f.383, op.10, d.9431, l.1–4.

25 Gosudarstvennyi arkhiv Odesskoi olasti, f.6, op.1, d.5976, l.16–18.

26 Ibid., f.6, op.1, d.5976.

27 RGIA, f.383, op.10, d.9431, l.7, 13; d.9341; op.19, d.25437; and Urry, *Mennonites, Politics and Peoplehood*, 92–3.

28 RGIA, f.383, op.10, d.9431, l.3–4; and Staples, "Religiia," 18–19.

29 J. Warkentin was elected church elder in 1824 in the Big Flemish community of Molochna (Lichtenau congregation), formed in the same year as a result of the split of the Molochna mother church (Orloff-Petershagen-Halbstadt). In 1841, the Lichtenau congregation led by J. Warkentin split up, from which on 2 September 1841 the Lichtenau-Peteshagen congregation was founded. The remaining former congregation organized the new Margenau-Schönsee Church on 18 June 1842. See P.M. Friesen, *The Mennonite Brotherhood in Russia, 1789–1910*, 2nd ed. (Fresno: Board of Christian Literature, 1980), 166–9, 892–4; and Friesen, "Mennonite Churches and Religious Developments in Russia," 69.

30 Harvey L. Dyck, ed. and trans., *A Mennonite in Russia: The Diaries of Jacob D. Epp, 1851–1880* (Toronto: University of Toronto Press, 1991), 34.

31 James Urry, "The Social Background to the Emergence of the Mennonite Brethren in Nineteenth Century Russia," *Journal of Mennonite Studies* 6 (1988), 26–8.

32 V.N. Arestov, *Baptism bez maski* (Kharkov: KGU, 1982), 25.

33 Heinrich Epp, *Notizen aus dem Leben und Wirken des verstorbenen Ältesten Abraham Unger, dem Gründer der Einlager Mennoniten Brüdergemeinde,* (Halbstadt, 1907).

34 Curiously, Russian officials considered precisely this factor as the main cause of the emergence of religious movements among the Mennonites in the 1860s. See RGIA, f.821, op.5, d.940, l.12ob–13; d.976, l.9ob, 75ob.

35 Gosudarstvennyi arkhiv Odesskoi olasti, f.6, op.1, d.746, l.3.

36 In 1812, the Kleine Gemeinde was formed by church leader Klaas Reimer, and in 1824 there was a split in the Molochna ("parent") church-community (Orloff-Petershagen-Halbstadt), and from there the new Lichtenau congregation headed by elder J. Warkentin took approximately two-thirds of the members of the former congregation, which opposed active contacts with the pietists. In the former community (Orloff), made up approximately of one-third of the previous structure headed by the elder B. Fast, remained those who were positively disposed to him.

37 On 25 July 1810, the Main Department of Spiritual Affairs of Foreign Faiths was founded. In 1817, it was a part of the Ministry of Spiritual Affairs and Public Education, which in 1824 was transformed into the Ministry of Public Education with spiritual affairs of only foreign religions subordinated to it. On 2 February 1832, it was attached to the Ministry of Internal Affairs as the Department of Spiritual Affairs of Foreign Faiths. On 6 August 1880, this Department was detached as an independent institution. On 16 March 1881 it again was part of the Ministry of Internal

Affairs (S.N. Balk and V.V. Bedin, eds., *Tsentral'nyi gosudarstvennyi istoricheskii arkhiv SSSR v Leningrade. Putevodetel'* (Leningrad, 1956), 125.

38 RGIA, f.821, op.5.

39 The primary source apparently had in mind the number of transgressions committed.

40 RGIA, f.821, op.5, d.1043, l.22–22ob.

41 Ibid., f.821, op.5, d.940, l.15, d.981, l.17, d.1043, l.8ob; Iavornits'kii (N°CLXXIII), 256; (N°CCXV), 346; (N°CCXIX), 362; (N°CCLVIII), 421; and other files. "Opisanie Menonistskikh kolonii v Rossii" in *Zhurnal Ministerstva gosudarstvennykh imushchestv* (1842, Book 1), 35 and others.

42 A. Klaus, *Nashi kolonii. Opyty i materialy po istorii i statistiki inostrannoi kolonizatsii v Rossii* (St Petersburg, 1869), 157; and V.I. Iasevich-Borodaevskaia, "Sektanstvo v Ekaterinoslavskoi gubernii" in *Bor'ba za veru* (St Petersburg, 1912), 282.

43 Gosudarstvennyi arkhiv Odesskoi olasti, f.6, op.3, d.746, l.1–18; RGIA, f.821, op.5, d.940, l.12–13; d.976, l.9ob, 75ob; RGIA, f.821, op.5, d.1043, l.3ob; and RGIA f.383, op.12, d.12327, l.41–41ob.

44 These files are mainly stored in the collections of the Popechitel'nogo Komiteta (Gosudarstvennyi arkhiv Odesskoi olasti, f.6); Departamenta Ministerstva gosudarstvennykh imushchestv (RGIA, f.383); and the Departamenta dukhovnykh del inostrannykh ispovedanii (RGIA, f.821).

45 C. Hildebrandt, "Aus der Kronsweider Eweckungzeit," in "The Early Mennonite Bretheren. Some outside views," ed. John A. Toews, *Mennonite Quarterly Review* 58 (April 1984), 83–123; Gosudarstvennyi arkhiv Odesskoi olasti, f.1, op.249, d.465, l.8–11ob; RGIA, f.821, op.5, d.976, l.4–4ob, 41–2; and P. M. Friesen (1980), 281–2.

46 "Donesenie Inspektory kolonii iuzhnoi Rossii g. Villeru Khortitskogo volostnogo pravleniia sovmestno s dukhovnymi starshinami Gergardom Dik i Iakovom Gil'debrandtom ot September 11 1862 za N°2345" in Aleksii (Dorodnitsyn), ed., *Materialy dlia istorii i issledovaniia religiozno-ratsionalisticheskogo dvizheniia na Iuge Rossii vo vtoroi polovine XIX stoletiia* (Kazan, 1908), N°4, 6–17.

47 Wardin Jr, *On the Edge*, 56–61.

48 Aleksii (Dorodnitsyn), *Religiozno-ratsionalisticheskoe dvizhenie na Iuge Rossii vo vtoroi polovine XIX stoletiia* (Kazan, 1909), 136.

49 RGIA, f.821, op.5, d.976, l.84–86ob.

50 Werth, *The Tsar's Foreign Faiths*, 95–6.

51 Cf. Gosudarstvennyi arkhiv Odesskoi olasti, f.1, op.249, d.465; f.6, op.5, d.279, 746; and RGIA, f.821, op.5, d.976, 976, 981.

52 Wardin Jr, *On the Edge*, ch. 9–10.

53 Darius Staliūnas, *Making Russians: Meaning and Practice of Russification in Lithuania and Belarus after 1863* (Amsterdam: Rodopi, 2007), 179; and Dolbilov, *Russkii krai, chuzhaia vera*, ch. 8.
54 Werth, *The Tsar's Foreign Faiths*, 56.
55 A.J. Rieber, "The Sedimentary Society," in *Between Tsar and People: Educated Society and the Quest for Public Identity in Late Imperial Russia*, ed. E.W. Clowes, S.D. Kassow, and J.L. West (Princeton: Princeton University Press, 1991), 343–66.
56 Thanks to the law on internal policing, reports of minor crimes and offences of Mennonite were resolved within their communities and did not fall into the general summary. On the whole, before 1801, two grave crimes were reported by the authorities at Khortitsa district authorities and fifty-eight at Molochna from 1800 to 1818. There were many fewer and different kinds of administrative violations and criminal offences than in the German colonies but much more than among the Bulgarians, Swedes, Swiss, Serbs, and Jews. See O.V. Konovalova, "Kolonisty Iuga Rossii v konflikte s zakonom (1800–1818)," in *Voprosy germanskoi istorii: sbornik nauchnykh trudov* (Dnepropetrovsk: Porogi, 2007), 98–105. Among the delinquencies committed by Mennonites and known to authorities, misdemeanours of an administrative (such as insubordination to village elders) or economic nature (such as keeping illegal drinking establishments, failure to repay debts) prevailed.
57 Among them were the Hutterites, the Mennonites of the Kleine Gemeinde, and parts of those of Khortitsa.
58 RGIA, f.821, op.5, d.996, l.20–21ob.
59 For a fascinating firsthand account of the impact this legislation on Ukraine's Mennonites see Dyck, *A Mennonite in Russia*, book 4. Cf. Royden Loewen, *Family, Church, and Market: A Mennonite Community in the Old and New Worlds, 1850–1930* (Toronto: University of Toronto Press, 1993), 61–6.
60 RGIA, f.821, op.5, d.940, l.12ob –13; d.976, l.9ob, 75ob.
61 Crews, "Empire and the Confessional State," 74.
62 RGIA, f.821, op.5, d.940, l.12–13; d.976, l.9ob, 75ob; and RGIA d.1043, l.3ob; f.383, op.12, d.12327, l.41–41ob.
63 Crews, "Empire and the Confessional State," 62.
64 RGIA, f.821, op.5, d.981, l.7–7ob; Klaus, 175; and S.D. Bondar', *Sekta mennonitov v Rossii: (v sviazi s istoriei Nemetskoi kolonizatsii na iug Rossii* (Petrograd, 1916), 106.
65 Friesen, *The Mennonite Brotherhood in Russia*, 231–2; and RGIA, f.821, op.5, d.976, l.30–1, 79–80ob.

66 Bondar', *Sekta mennonitov v Rossii*, 106–7; and RGIA, f.821, op.5, d.981, l.34–34ob.
67 RGIA, f.821, op.5, d.981, l.7–34ob; and James Urry, *None but Saints: The Transformation of Mennonite Life in Russia 1789–1889* (Winnipeg, Hyperion, 1989), 188.
68 Aileen Friesen, "Religious Policy in the Russian Borderlands: The 1860s Mennonite Schism" (Edmonton: University of Alberta, 2007), unpublished MA, 104.
69 Hans Kasdorf, *Flammen Unausloeschlich: Mission Der Mennoniten under Zaren und Sowjets 1789–1989* (Bielefeld: Logos Verlag, 1991). I thank an anonymous reviewer for drawing this source to my attention.
70 Werth, *The Tsar's Foreign Faiths*, 248–54.
71 Coleman, *Russian Baptists and Spiritual Revolution*, 27, n.1.
72 Wardin Jr, *On the Edge*, 481–2.
73 Serhii Plokhy, *The Origins of the Slavic Nations: Premodern Identities in Russia, Ukraine, and Belarus* (Cambridge: Cambridge University Press, 2006), 360.
74 Faith Hillis, *Children of Rus': Right-Bank Ukraine and the Invention of a Russian Nation* (Ithaca: Cornell University Press, 2014).
75 Werth, *The Tsar's Foreign Faiths*, 208.
76 Ibid., 254.

5 Mennonite Entrepreneurs and Russian Nationalists in the Russian Empire, 1830–1917

NATALIYA VENGER

Entrepreneurship was one of the activities in which Mennonites proved themselves within the Russian Empire. From the outset, entrepreneurs from this ethno-religious sect benefited from the terms granted by St Petersburg during the Mennonite colonization process that stretched from 1789 to the first half of the nineteenth century. Mennonites understood that these terms favoured them and contributed to the successful economic well-being of their colonies. Before long, entrepreneurial activity became a key part of their identity, even as Russian officials reached a similar conclusion.[1] In the first half of the nineteenth century, the Russian state assisted in the development of the industrial activity of various colonist groupings, including Mennonites, Germans, Bulgarians, and Greeks. In the process it used the practical skills of these recent immigrants as a major resource for the development of southern Ukraine as well as for the modernization of the empire as a whole. In fact, the Russian state continued to support multi-ethnic entrepreneurship with various economic, administrative, and social policies[2] until Russian nationalists gained the upper hand in the late nineteenth century. Henceforth, colonist entrepreneurs were constantly threatened by increased sanctions against them.

Most scholars agree that this nationalist phenomenon manifested itself in the empire during the period of "Official Nationality" in the 1830s.[3] It gradually evolved from a primarily broad-based ideological orientation to one that exerted a powerful influence on practical policies under Alexander III.[4] Not surprisingly, the empire's various social and ethnic groups had to bring themselves into the Russian nationalists' orbit after mid-century, though the process was occasionally a difficult one. The state's decision to modernize the empire in a manner that reinforced Russian nationalism gave it more of a confrontational character from the outset, especially in southern Ukraine where numerous ethnicities abounded. State officials molded the empire's national policy and closely monitored ethnic groups deemed to be non-Russian and possibly disloyal. Such a designation mattered, especially when those ethnic groupings had ties with potentially hostile foreign powers such as Germany. By 1900, that was, of course, the case with Russia's Germans, and it was also seen to be the case with Mennonites. Thus, imperial servitors gambled as they introduced their nationalist initiatives because they threatened the cohesiveness of the very empire they ruled, and the nation they wished to create.

Russian nationalists in the late nineteenth century were also concerned with those ethnic communities that had relatively high cultural and economic potential, and that were deemed to have a large impact on the vital political and economic interests of Russians themselves. For this reason, Russian nationalistic sentiment focused increasingly on both Mennonite entrepreneurs and their associates – the socially active group of Mennonites who performed the functions of elite representatives – spoke on behalf of Mennonites across the empire and lobbied for their interests. Unfortunately, the ongoing economic success of Mennonite industry stirred up more and more fervent opposition from Russian entrepreneurs, political figures, and nationalist ideologues, and provoked increasingly negative sentiments across Russian society. These trends culminated in the period of the First World War (1914–17) when Mennonite entrepreneurship, along with other displays of ethnicity within industrial activity as a whole, became the object of open economic and political discrimination.

The aim of the present study is to examine the dynamic interrelationship of Russian nationalism as a political ideology on the one hand and how Mennonite entrepreneurs from southern Ukraine responded to the emergence of Russian nationalism up to the end of the First World War on the other. To investigate the problem, I proceed from the fact that dynamic relations between Mennonite entrepreneurs and Russian nationalists cannot be understood outside the context of the development of this ethnic group's colonies in the Russian Empire. Russian nationalists always focused on the Mennonite colonies as a whole – and not on separate social groupings within the colonies. All of this underscores the fact that Mennonite entrepreneurs – who played such a vital role in their communities as well as beyond – also affected the formation of those proto- and early nationalistic sentiments which individual Russian nationalists would later exploit to justify their position vis-à-vis Mennonites as a whole.

Proto-nationalist Identities, Early Nationalism, and Entrepreneurial Activity: The Prehistory of the Conflict

As noted above, the process of establishing ethnic and, in particular, Mennonite economic activity was connected with colonization in southern Ukraine and the privileges[5] that Mennonites received as one of the economically promising groups in this relatively unsettled region. The incentive policy attached to colonization[6] meant that individual ethnic groups acquired significant tangible assets that were not provided to the indigenous or incoming peasant populations. Subsequent social opposition within the region was directly tied to the state's means of solving the problem of colonization and the corresponding redistribution of resources. Apparently, this issue was secretly discussed and protested by educated members of Russian society involved in colonization, and sparked the first anti-colonization views – well before the nationalist voice had been raised. Under the conditions of absolutism, however, and given the absence of a voice for civil society, the bearers of these sentiments – mostly officials and possibly some landed nobles – remained silent in the face of the positive initial reviews of the colonization process. At the same time, Mennonites were one of several groups of colonists who made the case for the privileges they received.[7]

Some indirect information is available about the existence of such alternative positions from the earliest days. For example, Court Councillor S.C. Contenius wrote disapprovingly about a certain Charles Hablitz in his report to A.E. Richelieu, then governor general of New Russia. Hablitz occupied the post of steward of the Dispatch Office of State Economy, Guardianship of Foreign and Rural Departments of the Ministry of Internal Affairs. Contenius, who directed the Office of Guardianship for Foreign Settlers in New Russia, declared: "It seems that your friend does not much like colonies and colonists ... I do not really understand such patriotism ... such patriotism will never be yours nor mine."[8] Thus, a colonization policy originally built on a system of unequal rights and privileges provoked the rudiments of negative sentiments about colonization and settlers.

Mennonites involuntarily became a focal point for Russian protonationalistic sentiments when they generated two very distinct identity markers (*obraz-prezentatsiia*) of their community from outside.[9] The first had an official origin and was initiated by authorities during the colonization process itself; it was positive. The surrounding populace generated the second identity marker themselves when they first encountered

Mennonite colonists. Since those encounters took on many different forms, and included conflict,[10] the content of these identity markers varied tremendously. Most of the neighbouring residents typically placed Mennonites between the two poles of sympathy and antipathy, depending on how successfully they had interacted with them.

Since entrepreneurial activity was the most active way by which Mennonites engaged others, it bore direct responsibility for the outcomes of communication and the overall image of the community. It is important for us to accept that conflicts or other results of interactions were not necessarily inevitable in ethnic interactions, though they did erupt over time. The initial peasant relations with the first Mennonite entrepreneurs and artisans in southern Ukraine formed certain fixed impressions – including negative ones – and they did so regarding Mennonites as a whole rather than only the entrepreneurs in question. These identity markers were mainly ethnic ones and remained intact in peasant memory for years after. They manifested themselves occasionally in social conflicts, and Russian officials were later able to exploit these very stereotypes to their own ends. Speaking retrospectively about the causes of ethnic conflict in the late imperial era, we must recognize that many peasants deemed colonists "aliens." This served as the spontaneous preferential memory of the negative, even as it may have been rooted in the peasants' strong sense of ethnic self-preservation: that they needed to know who the outsiders were to avoid related threats in the future. In short, many peasants regarded Mennonites as "a thing unto themselves" – unknown – and thus a potential threat.

Society's negative reaction to Mennonite entrepreneurs at this earliest stage of proto-nationalism is unintelligible unless one recalls that Russians have traditionally had a negative attitude towards entrepreneurs in general. Researchers observe that, in imperial Russia's status-driven society, the merchant social-estate could not get respect either from hereditary nobles or simple peasants – both sectors viewed them as commoners who had lost touch with the land. As noted by some Russian researchers, the attitude towards entrepreneurs in Russia took the form of a "spirit of hostility," which emerged from the "supra-economic" ethics of orthodoxy and communal psychology.[11] Despite the presence of two contrary depictions of Mennonites from the outset, it was the official, positive, image of the ethno-religious sect that dominated for decades. Legal conditions for the development of Mennonite economic activity also remained highly favourable for these colonists.[12]

The national policy of the Russian state until the mid-nineteenth century was characterized by tolerant and pragmatic relations with non-Russian peoples and other fringe nationals. The authorities regarded the most affluent groups of Mennonite society as valuable regional elites who were loyal to the Russian monarchy.[13] Gradually, however, the orderly relations within the empire began to change. The first manifestations of Russian nationalism, associated with the Polish uprising of 1830–1, did not involve any measures concerning the colonists, as state officials did not deem them to threaten the internal stability of the state. For example, in June 1837, a decree was issued that reminded the empire's governors of their obligation to adhere strictly to the legislation regarding privileges granted to the colonists, though the very mention of it suggests some mention of emerging threat.[14]

However, only a year later, in 1838, state officials promulgated a law that mandated Russian language instruction in all non-Russian schools, the first evidence of a change in the internal strategy of the state towards foreign colonists. In the Mennonite case, there is evidence from Cherkazianova in chapter 3 that they may have supported this law given their desire to be active within the empire as a whole. As one of the manifestations of this new policy – an echo of the Polish uprising – officials stressed that this new degree should not challenge the religious and ethnic identity of the colonists. Instead, the authorities insisted that the new law was intended to stimulate contacts between the colonists and those living in the surrounding areas. The goal was to integrate colonists into Imperial Russian society. It was ultimately intended to allow Mennonites to fulfil the stated imperial wish that these colonists fulfil an "exemplary" and "didactic" mission in the region, just as Tsar Paul I had intended in his 1801 "Charter." Nor were Mennonites unresponsive to this mission for they understood that their "privileges" were most likely to be protected if this mission was fulfilled.[15] Imperial Russia was on the threshold of a new political course which became apparent after the second Polish uprising of 1863, as Paul Werth has also concluded.[16]

Imperial Reforms for Societal Unification and the Phenomenon of Colonist-phobia (*kolonistofobia*) – A New Identity Marker for Mennonite Communities

The Imperial state initiated a bold new course in relation to non-Russian peoples when in mid-century it began to expand and intensify the regulation of non-Russian ethnic groupings, including Mennonites. Officials at this time introduced measures designed to unify the realm linguistically and to initiate the administrative integration of non-Russian parts of the empire along with their populations. At the same time, the Polish question put before Imperial Russian society the problem of social justice in the distribution of rights between the Russian and non-Russian populations. This, in my opinion, was the single greatest influence in the development of Russian nationalistic discourse.

Early nationalists – Iu.F. Samarin (1819–76), I.S. Aksakov (1823–86), and M.N. Katkov (1818–87) – were publicists and public figures who served as the first ideologists of the "German question" in Russia. All had previously advanced the thesis of "unequalized legitimacy," but the times called for a radical revision.[17] This triumvirate analysed the past and present of the Baltic German settlements and concluded that the empire's German population attained "the triumph of the German nationality with coercion and forced Germanization."[18] By this means, Germans had managed to create a "political nationality" through their undue political influence which now threatened the international well-being of the Russian Empire.[19] M.N. Katkov combined the threat posed by the Ostsee Germans, the colonists generally, and the state's lax border policy to assert that the time was ripe for a state-initiated reform that would strengthen and unify the empire. Katkov was convinced that all ethnic groups within the state should have equal rights, which was hardly the case at the moment.[20] How could it be, Katkov opined, when the present state policy on foreign colonists was so imperfect and prejudicial in their favour? In his words: "[T]he Germans, the Mennonites, and the Bulgarians have been poignantly separated out according to the regulations set up for them." As Katkov warned, the colonists had proceeded from their initial terms and legal regulations to establish a de facto "state within a state." Now, having grown accustomed to their isolated state, Russians should expect these colonists to react negatively to the prospect of integrative reforms.[21] The discussion, which subsequently unfolded in increasingly strident Russian nationalist discourse, influenced the content and justification for the reforms for administrative unification (the laws that eliminated the distinct colonist status in 1871)[22] and the requirement that Mennonites henceforth serve in the military (1874).[23] In the early 1860s, the authorities had already created the "Commission on the System of Public Administration of Foreign Colonists," whose purpose was to prepare the colonies for these very reforms.[24]

Meanwhile, Mennonite entrepreneurs became a more and more noticeable phenomenon in the empire as they successfully built up their capital, founded new factories, and purchased more land. Thus, these entrepreneurs seemed to confirm the slogans of the nationalists, who, as with Aksakov, saw in everything "the unremitting force of Germanization and denationalization of the Russian borderlands."[25] The appearance of Mennonite entrepreneurs in cities and the countryside in the empire's south appeared to foreshadow future conflicts. Mennonite flour-milling production reached its greatest influence in the territory of Tavrida and Ekaterinoslav provinces, where they comprised an impressive 30 per cent of total production. By 1900, Mennonite factories were manufacturing a staggering 58 per cent of Ekaterinoslav's provincial output in machine-building products.[26] By 1914, there were 157 large Mennonite enterprises (57 factories, 100 mills) in the territory of Ekaterinoslav province.[27] In 1908, 291 businesses, valued at 1,766,165 rubles, were located in the villages of Halbstadt and Gnadenfeld districts of Tavrida province.[28]

These successes by Mennonite entrepreneurs simultaneously stirred the imagination of Russian nationalists and roused the concern of their potential competitors. On the other hand, at the initial stage of reforms for modernization, the state was inclined to accommodate Mennonites because of their entrepreneurial skills and demonstrated success. Like it or not, Mennonites were initially given a unique immunity from nationalism. The state welcomed the economic success of the colonies, and Russian nationalists – before it rose to the level of state policy (which, in my opinion, happened during the reign of Alexander III and was consolidated during the premiership of P.A. Stolypin) – hesitated to go on the offensive. Nationalists were simply too aware of the empire's economic vulnerability and the important contributions being made by their colonist "enemies." Instead, officials initially confined themselves to the tactics of observation and critique.

At the same time, Mennonite entrepreneurs occupied an increasingly significant position in the social hierarchy of the Mennonite community where they became a genuine secular elite and demonstrated their readiness to perform leadership functions. As Bobyleva suggests in chapter 1, this structural transformation coincided with a newfound confidence across the Mennonite community after mid-century. This increased role by Mennonite entrepreneurs was demonstrated when Mennonites opposed the imperial reforms of the 1870s. Together with religious leaders and representatives of the teaching intelligentsia, entrepreneurs led delegations that lobbied for the interests of the colonies. Mennonites were alarmed at the preliminary stage of reforms, which included a new law on universal military service, and they responded adroitly.

Leonhard Sudermann, an entrepreneur and leader of the Berdiansk community, headed one such deputation to St Petersburg.[29] He took a radical position and denied the possibility of any Mennonite concessions to the threatened end of their state-protected pacifist exemption. Authorities were equally tough.[30] In response, as a side effect of these reforms, many Mennonites emigrated to North America,[31] and thus undertook a distinctive act of Mennonite civil disobedience. Yet that very response influenced a further nationalist awakening among Mennonite colonists.

Overall, this initial reform period ended favourably for the Mennonites,[32] an indication that state officials under Alexander II were reluctant to jeopardize the ongoing development of the colonies. However, the enduring conflict did introduce substantial changes in Mennonite relations with Russian and Ukrainian society, even more so than with imperial authorities. Justifying their actions on reforming the colonies, the authorities used elements of "anti-colonist propaganda" for the first time, provoking (voluntarily or involuntarily) elements of "anti-colonist consciousness" (colonist-phobia) in the region. This colonist-phobia resulted in a new and highly negative identity marker that outsiders had for Mennonites, some elements of which were supported by a nationalism from below. It reinforced the view that Mennonites owed their prosperity to the extravagant privileges they received when they settled in the Black Sea steppe and had thereafter continued to enrich themselves, amassing property and former estates, all the while treating the indigenous peasant population with contempt. Critics charged that Mennonites were largely unpatriotic and capable of betraying the interests of the imperial state. Colonist-phobia threatened adverse consequences for Ukraine's Mennonite Germans as authorities who had often used their colonist status as a positive identity marker up to the 1860s now changed course and launched their "anti-colonist" propaganda.

"Anti-colonist consciousness" retained its significance even after 1874 when it became a breeding ground for another complex phenomenon of Imperial Russian reality – the "German question." The merging of "anti-colonist consciousness" elements with that of the "German question" (originally associated with the Baltic Germans)[33] and the transformation of the latter into a rallying point for Russian socio-political nationalists was caused by real political and economic prerequisites. The rise of Pan-Germanist movements in the mid-nineteenth century was certainly an important factor,[34] but it was in the 1880s – after the unification of Germany and the formation of the anti-Russian bloc[35] – that imperial authorities became especially wary of their German colonists. The anti-German tune sounded even more expressively in the nationalist policies initiated under Tsar Alexander III (1881–94).[36] In the development of the "German question," internal and external geopolitical factors fuelled and mutually influenced each other and contributed to the conflict's escalation. This rapidly emerging "German question" was accompanied by a growing confrontation between the empire's Germans on one side and Russian landholders and entrepreneurs on the other. And it came at a time when German (and Mennonite) agriculturalists and industrialists were experiencing extraordinary rates of growth across the empire, though it was most pronounced in southern Ukraine.

My research shows that authorities must have realized that Mennonites were an ethno-religious community that strove for homogeneity while generating immense wealth. Mennonites had successfully preserved their essential autonomy through a sophisticated tactic of assimilation and had refused to integrate culturally into society as a whole. That said, St Petersburg's attempt to incorporate erstwhile colonists into the state's socio-economic system built on the social estates of peasant and noble was neither radical nor consistent. Instead, it took on a spontaneous, reactive, and fragmented character. Put another way, the actions carried out by the government in the so-called Reform Era were mainly of a disjointed administrative-legal character and had little in common with the policies of Russification and assimilation that were coincidental with it. In many instances authorities would not have opposed the right of Mennonites to preserve their identity. Many would have endorsed the Mennonite version of ethnic self-consciousness as long as it could have been combined with loyalty to the empire and dynasty. It should also be noted that Mennonites were one of the last of the ethnic groups to fall in line with the new policy (after the Poles, Greeks, and so on).[37] Imperial patience in their instance was undoubtedly a reflection of the longstanding trust that Mennonites had garnered from Russian authorities.

Colonist-phobia and the "German question" were subjects of constant public discussion from 1880 to 1917, as became clearly apparent in political essays published at that time. Politicians, public figures, and academics wrote in both journalistic and scientific publications with different degrees of objectivity. Supporters of the critically inclined group (M.N. Katkov, I.S. Aksakov, A.A. Paltov (Velitsyn), G.A. Evreinov, S.P. Shelukhin, and I.I. Sergeev) disputed the conclusion that the colonization process had realized positive results. Instead, they advanced and supported the theory of "peaceful conquest" of the Russian empire by the Germans, a category that almost always included Mennonites. Gradually, such negative identity markers helped to consolidate the "anti-colonist consciousness" in Russian public opinion.[38]

In stark contrast, voices were also heard in defence of the German-speaking population of the empire. *Mir Bozhii* (The World of God), a Russian-language magazine, boldly supported the empire's German population in 1902. One unidentified author wrote an article entitled "The German Colonies in New Russia" (Southern Ukraine) in which he observed that "the success of the German colonists incited hostility against their population and administration." The magazine's publishers saw the root of the problem as follows: "Instead of raising our own spiritual and economic standard, we try in every way possible to lower this standard among the colonists."[39] Pamphlets with apologetic content were prepared by politicians and public figures that, for various reasons, defended the interests of this ethno-religious group, among them F. Brun, P.A. Kamenskii, and later J. Stach and K. Lindemann.[40] Mennonites themselves used these publications as part of a larger strategy as they responded to accusations which they deemed groundless.

The "German question" was inseparable from the emergence of Germany as a European power, especially after relations soured following Berlin's decision not to renew the Reinsurance Treaty in 1890. The abrupt cooling of relations on the international stage initially focused itself within the empire on the land problem, though it soon morphed elsewhere.[41] Russia's rate of industrial development had grown considerably by 1913 when it produced 5.3 per cent of the world's industrial output. In absolute volume, this came close to the industrial production of France (6.4 per cent), which the Russian Empire exceeded in the smelting of steel, the production of machinery, and the manufacture of cotton fabrics.[42] Yet up to the last third of the nineteenth century, entrepreneurs still had unlimited opportunities to apply their talents and capital. By contrast, the expansion of German land ownership, in the south especially, suggested that a definite limit had been reached in its availability. In southern Ukraine alone, Mennonites founded twenty-three daughter colonies from 1832 to 1904, including the Borozenko settlement that Bobyleva has investigated for this volume. According to the data of P.M. Friesen, Mennonites owned a staggering 713,213 desiatinas of land by 1907.[43]

Anti-German sentiments at this stage of the conflict did not affect the business interests of either Mennonites or German colonists; however, indisputably, they had an effect on the religious and ethnic isolation that Mennonites had begun to feel. It seemed that the future would not be as kind as the past. German-speaking citizens of the Russian Empire tended to respond by relying even more on internal ties within the colonies than they had done in the past. Mennonite industrial corporations were more inclined to organize on confessional lines, even if this occasionally strained their career ambitions. This parallels conclusions reached in this volume by Beznosova and Cherkazianova. Far more dangerous was the hidden work and destructive effect that anti-German sentiments had on social cohesion across the region. Increased ill-will was evident between Mennonites and others after 1900 despite the fact that the accusations of disloyalty of the empire's Mennonites and Germans were groundless.

Enterprises that belonged to entrepreneurs with German last names by the turn of the century were under constant surveillance. Thus, in 1900, factory inspectors conducted a study of internal relations in enterprises where foreigners or other non-Russian specialists filled executive positions. The senior factory inspector of Ekaterinoslav province observed in his report that "the directors-foreigners and their assistants-partners hate and despise the Russian workers ... The workers pay them back in kind."[44] He further claimed that his conclusions were "very typical of all the major factories in Ekaterinoslav province."[45] As an example, he gave an account of the supervisor of the mechanical department of Ekaterinoslav's machine-building plant, Hesse, who was often "unfair to workers. Dozens of assorted inspections and complaints against him confirm that he utterly scorns both Russian laws and Russian workers."[46] In his turn, the senior factory inspector of Kherson province was more charitable to former colonists when he concluded that "cases where Russian workers are mistreated by masters and managers-foreigners in the Kherson province are isolated acts."[47]

Mennonites themselves provided material for accusations of disloyalty. Rather revealing was a conflict that took place in July of 1910 in Khortitza village. On the eve of the birthday celebration of His Imperial Highness, the heir to the Tsar and Grand Duke Alexei Nikolaevich, the district police officer Shevchenko warned the business owners of Khortitsa village that they needed to put up state flags on factory buildings. As the officer reported, A.A. Wallmann, as well as other Mennonite entrepreneurs, refused to comply with this order. The entrepreneurs defended their position when they testified that they, as Protestants, regarded flags as an unnecessary attribute, and not as evidence of their devotion to the tsar and the Fatherland.[48] In an explanatory note, the officer accounted for Wallmann's position and explained how the businessman had become so influential: "A.A. Wallmann, who possesses a large fortune and is very popular among the German population, is highly influential. In all important cases, Wallmann's opinion is always sought in the end, and only what he has endorsed is done."[49] The internal memorandum concludes with the police officer's verdict: "The above-stated actions of the German population headed by Wallmann demoralize the local population living in Khortitsa, which consists mainly of the working class."[50] Of significance is the fact that by 1910 local officials no longer distinguished between Mennonites and Germans.

Therefore, the report concluded that Wallmann was dangerous as a major business owner and "a German," as he subjected all factory workers to his influence and created an unstable situation in the village. Other Khortitsa entrepreneurs – Hildebrandt, Heese, and Ens – were also drawn into the conflict. The investigation did not anticipate any immediate consequences, but recommended that authorities should be mindful of this troubling situation. Particularly revealing is one of the expressions used by the police officer: "On the obscene relations of Wallmann and his subordinates of German origin." This sentence speaks volumes about the contemporary lexical code which once again testifies to the volatility of the "German question" in the public consciousness. Undoubtedly, the position taken by Wallmann may have been short-sighted. At the very least, it indicates that Mennonite entrepreneurs, in the four years before the beginning of the anti-German campaign, felt quite calm and confident, even as they paid close attention to extreme manifestations of Russian nationalism. It is significant that the Niebuhr dynasty – very well known in the south[51] – which owned eleven flour mills in Ekaterinoslav province alone, passed the statutes of its "Sanatorium Alexanderbad" on 25 February 1913. For a year and a half before the military conflict, the list of shareholders included subjects from Germany – members of the Böttcher house – a fact that would soon become the very basis for the enterprise's appropriation.[52] It suggested at the very least that Mennonite entrepreneurs were moving comfortably in (imperial) German circles by the eve of the First World War.

The reality of colonist-phobia was once again confirmed in 1910 and 1912 when authorities first attempted to restrict German land ownership by means of existing legislation. As is known, the Mennonites, having learned from their previous mistakes pertaining to political inactivity, participated energetically in the elections for the second to the fourth State Dumas (1907–17). They lobbied alongside the empire's Germans for their interests in the Third Duma, especially at meetings where proposed bills were discussed.[53] The German group within the "Union of October 17" Party led the way. K. Lindemann, a Baltic German who had been born in Nizhny Novgorod, was identified as a leading actor in this initiative.[54] The state's inability to impose its will before 1914 did not settle anything when it came to existing anti-German sentiments.[55] No wonder Mennonites after the revolution remained politically engaged and strategically savvy. This astuteness, as Toews argues in this volume, was a transferable skill, and would be put to good use by Abraham Friesen in the effort to re-establish the Russian Mennonite world in Canada.

The First World War, Nationalism, and Mennonite Entrepreneurs

The Russian Empire's entry into the First World War against Germany changed everything as the campaign to combat "German dominance" took on an urgent and empire-wide character. Legislative bodies in St Petersburg – the Duma foremost among them – initiated, enacted, and partially implemented a series of legislative acts from 1914 to 1917 known as "The Liquidation (Extraordinary) Legislation." By this omnibus initiative, officials sought to restrict the activity of all nationalities within the empire who were linked to states at war with the Russian Empire. For instance, restrictions on non-Russian land use, land ownership, and capital transactions were substantially increased. Taken as a whole, the liquidation legislation exemplified an internal economic war waged by Russian nationalists against, in particular, large concentrations of Germans and Mennonites located in southern Ukraine. In hindsight, this omnibus legislation was clearly unfair and counterproductive as it benefited only the interests of selected social groups which had long demanded the "redistribution" of economic positions. Since entrepreneurs were owners first of all, the emergency legislation directly infringed upon their interests.

On 22 September 1914, the Registered Supreme Decree of the State Senate was published, introducing a temporary ban on the acquisition of real estate by enemy subjects of the empire.[56] At the same time, the Ministry of Internal Affairs and the Ministry of Justice began to draw up legislation to limit the civil rights of German citizens of Russia. The leading role in their development and adoption belonged to the heads of the ministries: N.A. Maklakov and I.G. Shcheglovitov. On 2 February 1915, the Council of Ministers adopted laws including: "On land tenure and land use of Austrian, Hungarian, German, or Turkish subjects in the Russian state";[57] "On termination of land tenure and land use of Austrian, Hungarian, or German immigrants in border areas";[58] and "On land tenure and land use of certain classes consisting of Austrian, Hungarian, or German immigrants with Russian citizenship."[59] These laws did not apply to those who had acquired citizenship before 1 January 1880, that is, former German colonists and Mennonites. However, society demonstrated its willingness to go further, following the appeals of such public figures as A.S. Rezanov, author of *Nemetskoe shpionstvo* (German espionage)" (1915). Rezanov maintained that "German espionage was organically joined with German industry," and called upon the public to take action, including illegally.[60]

On 13 December 1915, the Council of Ministers passed the decree "On some changes and amendments to the law of 2 February 1915 on land tenure and land use of subjects of states at war with Russia, as well as Austrian, Hungarian, or German immigrants."[61] The law expanded the area of legislative influence to Ekaterinoslav and Tavrida provinces and directly affected colonist ownership. It called for the compulsory sale of property and the application of appropriation (itself a restriction on the disposal of property). Such a restriction concerned only Germans and Mennonites registered to a rural society; it excluded Germans (and Mennonites) who lived in cities, a category that subsumed a significant number of entrepreneurs. Neither did the laws extend to the families of colonist military personnel or retired officers, or individuals who participated in hostilities and had been decorated. In practice, however, this rule was often violated. At the beginning of 1916, German colonists and Molochna Mennonites followed directions to register their properties, a bad omen under the circumstances, indicating that the authorities intended to bring the plan to its logical conclusion.[62]

According to the information of the "Committee for the fight against German domination," 15,598 farms in the territory of Ekaterinoslav, Tavrida, and Kherson provinces with a total area of 1,899,217 desiatinas (on 30 May 1916) were subject to liquidation on the basis of the laws of 2 February and 13 December 1915.[63] Since most of the Mennonite entrepreneurs were also landowners, the laws affected their properties as well. Let us recall that a significant number of small and medium-sized Mennonite enterprises were located directly on the lands under their ownership. Curiously, the fate of these businesses had been specified in the legislation.

However, these were only the first steps. At the initial stage of the war, nationalistic members of the bourgeoisie had already turned to the government with a call for more decisive actions, demanding that the Russian economy become less cosmopolitan and "more Russian."[64] Similar sentiments provided the government with a "mandate" to introduce additional legislation.

Special measures were proposed simultaneously with the liquidation policy in the area of land tenure. As announced, these measures were developed specifically for German enterprises, though all were subsequently applied against the empire's former colonists. Among them, the following laws should be mentioned:

1) 16 March 1915: "On the appointment of government inspectors for the supervision of activities of some commercial-industrial establishments" (where the rights and limitations of the subjects of the states at war with Russia were extended to their commercial enterprises, as well as for any personal businesses with hired labourers);
2) 10 May 1915: "On the elimination of commercial enterprises belonging to subjects of hostile states";
3) 2 January 1916: "On measures against evasion by subjects of the enemy from actions of restrictive legitimization on the maintenance of commercial-industrial enterprises";
4) 12 January 1916: "On the management and operation of appropriated (transferred to the temporary administration) enterprises and property";
5) 16 January 1916: "On the government's supervision of activities of commercial-industrial enterprises, the owners of which are nationals of hostile states";
6) 22 October 1916: "On changes in the existing regulations on the procedure of management and operation of appropriated enterprises and property"; and
7) 25 October 1916: the position of the Council of Ministers "On the procedure of liquidation of industrial enterprises situated on land subject to takeover that belong to nationals and expatriates of hostile states."[65]

Despite its empire-wide mandate, the practical implementation of the liquidation laws in certain regions depended on the willingness and ability of local authorities to implement them. Officials acted most aggressively if they deemed that the "German question" had become problematic in their province or region. Even if that were not the case, they also responded if public opinion there demanded it, or if they were personally and negatively disposed to the Germans in their midst.

Thus the situation took different shapes as authorities somewhat arbitrarily implemented the legislation in individual provinces across southern Ukraine. Part of the problem is that public opinion on the situation and the corresponding legislative initiative was decidedly mixed and inconstant. In February of 1914, a meeting of the zemstvo members in Tavrida province sent a delegation to St Petersburg to warn the government not to approve decisions that were short-sighted from the point of view of the state. A discussion of the laws of 13 December 1915 at a January 1916 session of the Tavrida provincial assembly ended when the state's intentions were censured.[66] However, in February 1915, on the initiative of the centre, the Provincial Office for the Implementation of the Emergency Legislation was founded. Soon the liquidation lists began to be published, and auctions were conducted in the Simferopol and Halbstadt rural districts (in particular, the villages of Altona, Tiege, Ohrloff, Alexanderwohl, Blumenfeld, Neu-Halbstadt, and Münsterberg). By the winter of 1917, 4 million rubles had been realized from the forced sale of these properties.[67]

In January of 1916, a determined Ekaterinoslav provincial zemstvo assembly decided to petition for the dissemination of the law of 13 December across the empire.[68] As a sign of protest, Deputy G.A. Bergmann declared a "dissenting opinion," when he stated that "Russian subjects who are Germans have been and remain citizens loyal to Russia ... These citizens are so honest and hardworking that they cannot possibly be a harmful element in the country."

As P. Heese, owner of the flour-milling industry, described the situation in the city of Ekaterinoslav, "[W]hen the Russian government announced that Mennonites are no longer worthy citizens of Russia but enemies ..., the hardships began."[69] However, due to their influence in the city, Mennonites managed to maintain a favourable social climate.[70] When the tsar visited the city of Ekaterinoslav on 31 January 1915, an escort that included prominent Mennonites accompanied Nicholas II on a trip around the city. One of them, G. Bergmann, presented 10,000 rubles to Nicholas on behalf of his congregation.[71] Summing up his own descriptions, P. Heese concluded: "Not everything has emerged so badly for us, and from time to time we even felt that respect was shown to members of the German culture."[72]

The liquidation laws had opened the way for many abuses and tyrannical acts by the authorities against Mennonite owners as a whole and entrepreneurs in particular. Zemstvos targeted not only landowners but also Mennonites who owned properties, including factories, mills, and shops. In 1916, the Alexandrovsk district zemstvo board in the provincial zemstvo report justified the need to purchase the villages of Kichkas, Kantserovka, and Nieder Khortitsa. An assessment of the buildings in these villages was carried out, according to which their value amounted to 2,210,705 rubles.[73] Even though villagers of Khortitsa and Kichkas at a gathering decided "not to sell the village voluntarily," a joint meeting of the Alexandrovsk town council and the "Special commission on the issue of acquisition by the municipal government of land with all buildings of villagers-owners of Kichkas located on them" took place on 29 December 1916. On 2 February 1917, the period for voluntary sale of property by villagers had expired. The commission concluded that it was still necessary to establish a percentage reduction of Mennonite properties. It aimed at 30 per cent for industrial enterprises and 20 per cent for land and small farmstead buildings. Thus, the total amount assigned to the sale value of properties in Kichkas village was set at 1,846,460 rubles (instead of the real value of 2,701,550 rubles).[74]

The government paid special attention to machine-building enterprises under Mennonite ownership. A report of the Committee of the Southwestern Front, "On the production of local agricultural machinery and implements," prepared in 1917, stated that the majority of factories of this specialisation were owned by so-called foreigners. An attached note, dated 10 January 1917, from the president of the Alexandrovsk district zemstvo, referring to Mennonite machine-building enterprises in Kichkas, concluded that officials still believed that the owners "acquire[d] a huge profit." The author assured readers that "the acquisition of these industries by the Zemstvo would appear to be a valuable contribution to Russian life."[75]

The situation in Bakhmut district turned out to be especially unfavourable for Mennonites who wished to preserve their properties as local authorities conducted an evaluation of all land allotments in

Santurianovskii and Zhelezniianskii townships, paying no attention to the real value of the enterprises concentrated in these areas. For example, a 2,400 sazhen [1 sazhen = 2.34 metres] plot located near a steam-mill owned by J.D. Kasdorf (Kondratevka Colony) was estimated at 283 rubles whereas a similar one (2,400 sazhens) owned by A.J. Herzen was set at 186 rubles.[76] Officials then made cash offers as compensation to the owners of these lands based on these assessments, neither of which approximated their real value.

Anti-German propaganda and the corresponding liquidation legislation produced additional political problems for the country as the protracted nature of the war resulted in ever-worsening conditions across the empire. Industry in particular experienced considerable difficulties. It is understandable that the constant appeals to fight against "enemy domination" bore fruit in workers who often turned against the Russian-German owners of enterprises in their midst. In central Russia, for example, at the end of 1914–15, factory inspectors and police repeatedly recorded information on worker strikes where the sole demand had been that German and Austrian members of the administration in selected enterprises be removed.[77] Anti-German sentiments were expressed not only in the form of strikes, but also in the attacks on shops and businesses owned by non-Russian nationals. In Moscow, for example, 700 shops and offices suffered accordingly.[78] Anti-German sentiments in the work environment became particularly acute in May to June 1915,[79] much to the alarm of the authorities of Ekaterinoslav province. In June 1915, the governor sent a telegram to the local chief of police in which he declared: "In recent times following the devastation of German shops in Moscow, persistent rumours have circulated among the population of the province entrusted to me that there is to be a pogrom of German villagers. The population's resentment against this sector has grown not only because of the war, but also because German villagers live apart under the best of conditions and do not bear any burden in the current war, which the indigenous Russian population must then bear in its entirety."[80]

Local authorities were especially concerned by a communication from the Alexandrovsk police with information on peasants of the Voznesenka village in Alexandrovsk uezd who intended to organize a pogrom in the Khortitsa region on 20 June 1915. In view of this, the Ekaterinoslav governor warned, "If the local administration treats them leniently and does not stop them, it can strengthen the population's faith in the impunity of the pogroms against the Germans and in all kinds of illegal actions. The disorder can adopt a spontaneous character."[81] As can be seen from the governor's answer, the state was much less concerned about national enmity than by social disorder as such, which – it was felt – could result from these pogroms and thereafter be difficult to stop.

Mennonites responded with a campaign as they actively sought to defend their rights. Congregations and individuals prepared petitions which were sent to the relevant authorities. They also prepared and distributed pamphlets to explain and lobby their concerns. As noted by Beznosova in this volume, Mennonites began to stress their Dutch origin, releasing *Who are the Mennonites?* by P. Braun and *The Question of the Origin of the Mennonites* by D. Epp and H. Bergmann.[82] Provincial and district courts were overwhelmed by appeals that Mennonite properties be removed from the liquidation lists. Complaints of the same nature also made their way to the "Committee on the fight against German domination." Within a year of its founding the committee had considered no fewer than 630 such petitions, of which only 17 were accepted.[83]

Mennonite entrepreneurs were particularly active in the campaign to defend their rights. On 17 January 1917, J. Thiessen and A. Braun, authorized representatives of the Ekaterinoslav and Tavrida provinces respectively, appealed on behalf of their congregation to Tsar Nicholas II. A note, "On the liquidation of Mennonite land," was attached to the appeal. It contained information about numerous violations, for example, that had happened as authorities implemented the new legislation. By unjust means the state had seized not only agricultural lands, but also businesses and manufacturing enterprises. They argued that these measures did more harm than good to the empire. J. Thiessen warned that the inevitable consequence of this policy would be the "complete devastation of an impressive cultural sector ... and it should be immediately eliminated as it threatened even enterprises that worked for defence, such as: flour mills, and factories that produced ammunition for military needs, carriages for the army, engines, and others." And further: "There is very little hope that the liquidation authority has not but ruined much-needed plants and factories."[84]

The tactic that the Mennonites followed under the circumstances was fully justified and logical. Not certain of their ability to exert real influence to block legislation and placate public sentiment, they at least tried to buy time, and they did occasionally experience positive results. Officials responded to the influx of these petitions when they launched an inquiry into the status of Mennonites in Ekaterinoslav province. The "special committee" instructed the Ekaterinoslav provincial gendarmerie authority to provide information on Mennonites in light of the concerns raised. On 24 September 1915, the Ekaterinoslav governor V.A. Kolobov wrote that, in his opinion, Herman Bergmann's petition was absolutely unjustified because Germans who had lived in the province for more than one hundred years "completely ignore the local Russian population and keep themselves apart." He further observed that "on the factories belonging to Germans and Mennonites ... the whole administration and the highest-paid employees are Germans. The Russians are only given work as unskilled labourers."[85] In this way, V.A. Kolobov tried to persuade Petrograd (as St Petersburg had been renamed in 1914) that Mennonites represented an internal danger to the state. Disclaiming the significance of the public and philanthropic activities of the entrepreneurs, Kolobov stated that "their donations are insignificant, and always 'decoratively' arranged, serving as advertisements in order to solicit privileges." The note concluded that the religious differences among Lutherans, Catholics, and Mennonites did not appear to be the basis for their national isolation. Consequently, the Kolobov concluded that there was every reason to employ extraordinary legislation against the ethnic-religious sects.

It seemed that the whole empire was up in arms against the empire's Germans and Mennonites: the authorities, the nobility, the Russian bourgeoisie, and the peasantry all demanded that German and Mennonite lands be appropriated. But two unanticipated circumstances interfered in the anti-colonist campaign: first, the military economy, and second, the timing involved. First, the army's need of artillery was constantly growing as a total war effort was desperately required. Meanwhile, many Russian enterprises were on the syndicalist path which resulted in significant price increases for their products.[86] For this reason, the Military-Industrial Committee searched for more compliant manufacturers. It would be correct to assert that Russia's misfortune in the war preserved entrepreneurial ownership among the colonists as the need to procure armaments and provisions provided an opportunity for many Mennonite enterprises to continue their production activities.

At the same time, a few political parties of the State Duma supported the former colonists. For example, one of the deputies of the Kadet Party [Constitutional Democrats] observed correctly that the present meaning of the German issue had never been completely clarified: "To anyone, the word is thrown around without a precise definition of its meaning and is repeated by all strata of the Russian society in accordance with their personal beliefs, personal views, personal likes and dislikes, and this slogan in the mouth of the individual acquires a different meaning, sometimes even the opposite of what was intended."[87] This quote actually confirms that the "German question" had become a field for wild speculation and localized tensions, one that many believed had weakened the state itself. In this regard, the Kadet representative from Petrograd, F.I. Rodichev, remarked ironically that "Russia has to fight not so much against German dominance as against Russian dominance."[88]

Towards the beginning of 1916, there were also new and no less convincing calls in support of the business representatives of this ethnic group. The Moscow Merchant Society, which conducted studies on the role of German capital in the economy of the different Russian provinces, came to a very balanced conclusion. They maintained, through largely unbiased analysis, that German-speaking entrepreneurs did evince special features that allowed them to be successful in business. The report declared that Russian industrialists needed to learn how the Germans within the empire produced goods without defects, as well as how best to reduce production costs without a corresponding loss of quality. Additional lessons could be learned on how to maintain a courteous attitude to all customers, and how to most efficiently adapt the products produced for the market by tailoring them to the prospective purchaser.

The Society's investigation thus confirmed that the success of the German entrepreneurs in Russia had less to do with special conditions and privileges than with their hard work, knowledge, and dedication to service.[89] In their statements to the Eighth Congress, members of the Council of Congresses of Representatives of Industry and Commerce wrote: "A national policy which hampers the development of domestic productive forces and plunges us all in a great dependence on labour tied to the land can be called anything you like, but not national."[90]

The First World War's disastrous impact on Russia's economy, the military losses endured, and the souring of public opinion had all contributed irrationally to the implementation of the liquidation bills. Even so, they were severely criticised at the State Duma sessions on 29 February and 4 and 8 March 1916. In view of this, the Council of Ministers was forced to adopt a more conciliatory tone. At the beginning of March 1916, the local authorities moved the dates of implementation of the liquidation laws from 1915 to the end of 1916. A new decree, N° 87 dated 15 July 1916, preserved the property of the colonists when they themselves – or one of their family members – had participated in the battles of the southern army or navy. On 25 August 1916, a statute by the Council of Ministers was passed with the name "On some changes and amendments to the existing law on the restriction of hostile land ownership and land use." The Council of Ministers further postponed the implementation of the law until the summer of 1917 for households that had said in the summer of 1916 that they wanted to sow and harvest winter crops. Ministry of Internal Affairs officials who had previously been sent to the provinces to monitor the implementation of legislation were recalled.[91]

The conciliatory nature of the August 1916 legislation directly affected German and Mennonite industrialists as the Ministry of Commerce and Industry subsequently suspended for two years the public sale of land on which all industrial establishments were situated. It was further anticipated that even this deadline would be extended for factories involved in defence manufacturing.[92] This was meant to address in part the work of the "Committee on the Struggle against German Domination" which in June of 1916 had issued several decrees of "a coercive nature" against Germans and Mennonites, even though Mennonites continued to argue against inclusion with Russia's Germans. Their efforts appear to have been rewarded in January of 1917 when the Minister of Justice, N.A. Dobrovolskii, received the consent of Nicholas II to revise the terms of the emergency legislation.[93] The Mennonite petition was now transferred to the chairman of the Council of Ministers to form an interdepartmental commission on the subject of revisions to the Mennonite case and to undertake a comprehensive verification of their statements that they were, in fact, of Dutch origin.[94] Although the Commission of A.S. Stashinskii concluded that Mennonites were, in fact, Germans, it was unable to influence the course of subsequent events. In February 1917, the application of the liquidation laws was extended to the whole territory of the Russian empire. At the same time, a printed notice declared that state authorities had exempted Mennonites from a forced takeover in the southern provinces. According to materials of the "Special Committee" in the Ekaterinoslav province, thirty-five commercial and industrial establishments were liquidated, but none of them was actually appropriated from their owners.[95] Finally, on 11 March 1917, the Provisional Government adopted the decree "On suspending the use of the laws on land tenure and land use of Austrian, Hungarian, and German immigrants."[96]

Many factors. then, accounted for the conservation of Mennonite entrepreneurship during the period of the liquidation legislation: the degree of fame of each specific enterprise, its specialization, the personal qualities of the owner and his connections, the willingness of Mennonites to undertake military production, and the self-organization and lobbying efforts of Mennonite business clans. Often individual entrepreneurs escaped financial ruin solely because of their personal contacts and their ability to conduct a dialogue with the Russian community and to be persuasive in this dialogue.

After the war had begun, colonists' enterprises became the object of scrutiny by the Commissions in Special Records Management under Government Supervision.[97] This agency examined the presence of "enemy capital" in the activities of these enterprises. Capital and management were studied from the point of view of their possible danger or usefulness for the development of the imperial war economy. From 611 corporations suspected of collaboration of German and Austrian capital, 96 were liquidated and 19 enterprises were transferred to other owners. In this context, the circumstances for enterprises were most favourable for survival when those under scrutiny manufactured defence products in support of Russia's military actions. For example, the investigation into the Lepp and Wallmann firm, which had been pursued by the Special Records Management under Government Supervision of commercial-industrial enterprises, was discontinued when it began to produce military products at its plants.[98] In November 1916, an organizational merger of the Lepp and Wallmann plants and the factories of A.J. Koop was carried out for this purpose. The new initiative that was formed, Lepp, Wallmann, and Koop, signed a number of agreements with the St Petersburg Main Artillery administration and the Ekaterinoslav military-industrial committee on the production of shells of different modifications. In 1916, Koop's plant produced goods in the amount of 1,366,651 rubles, including defence goods valued at 1,326,651 rubles. The volume of production from this enterprise, which had previously manufactured only agricultural machinery, soon quintupled its pre-war level. During the war (according to information obtained from an April 1918 questionnaire), Koop produced military goods in the amount of 143,574 rubles.[99] By 1917, the annual production of the Lepps had reached 1,557,530 rubles.[100] The corporation's worth by that time had doubled since the start of the war, reaching 2,400,000 rubles.[101]

New and unprecedented contracts for military orders allowed Mennonites not only to preserve their holdings but also created tolerable conditions for their factories to function normally under wartime conditions, at a time when the demand for peacetime products had fallen sharply. The various war departments, as well as the military-industrial committees, replaced the contracts. The Alexandrovsk military-industrial committee in particular presented itself as the most active organization in the territory of the southern provinces.

For the production of defence products, the company Hildebrand and Pries (Khortitsa), the Krieger oil engines plant, and the Unger vehicular factory (Osterwick) were also involved. According to the reports of factory inspectors, the enterprise Koop and Helker increased its production by 15 per cent.[102] In Tavrida province, fifteen industrial enterprises merged for the joint production of shells. H.H. Schröder, the director of Schröder and Co. headed the association. The largest mills of the partnership, Niebuhr and Co., (a conglomeration of six plants) worked virtually non-stop for defence needs.[103] In July 1916, the Ekaterinoslav Mennonite mills received military orders;[104] so did the Dyck flour mills of Feodosiia district and the Tavrida-American Association steam flour mill of J. J. Dyck and P. Mantler (Nelgovka settlement).[105] It should be noted that factories that received military orders were under a special patronage arrangement with the government, and therefore protected.

Only the most powerful Mennonite enterprises, those that had established a reputation in the pre-war period and had owners with enough personal connections to the relevant departments in St Petersburg, were able to get such enormous military orders. For example, the chief of Simferopol Police reported that local enterprises could not secure contracts with the defence ministry based on merit alone.[106] What makes this shift to military-based production all the more remarkable is that it challenges Beznosova's conclusions in this volume that by 1914 Mennonites were most commonly associated with their pacifist position.

A special feature of the overall situation for the development of ethnic entrepreneurship in 1914–17 was that every entrepreneur had to fight independently for himself and his enterprise. The relative success of the Mennonites of Ekaterinoslav and Alexandrovsk was in many respects determined by the mutual support they offered each other, and the determined consistency of their actions. According to the information of Ekaterinoslav's City Duma, entrepreneur and public figure Johann Esau was a crucial link between Mennonites and the state. As a member of the commission for fuel supply in charge of the organization of warehouse premises, the delivery of horses, carts, hospital equipment, and much more,[107] Esau's agency ensured the transfer of orders to Mennonite industries.

The clash with state nationalism demanded more flexibility from the Mennonites. In this context, we should also mention the ethical side of this problem. As is well-known, pacifism was one of the paradigmatic directives of religious Mennonitism and this is certainly at the core of Beznosova's conclusion. In fact, entrepreneurs did more than simply accept the offer to manufacture military products. They also actively sought out such opportunities even though they varied from the classical Mennonite position, itself an indication that Mennonite entrepreneurs were governed by a meta-cultural world view. On the other hand, the process of transitivity inevitably drew into its orbit the whole population of the colonies. Evidence of this can be shown by the reaction of the rest of the congregations, from whom no condemnation of the entrepreneurs' actions was observed. The compromising behaviour of the Mennonites in this situation reflected a distinctly conformist way out of the conflict, at least with respect to Imperial Russian society. It raises the question of whether the core Mennonite identity marker had shifted away from narrowly religious foundations to an identity more rooted within secular relations. It seems as if they contested less their religious freedoms and a "sacred landscape" than their right to develop a different form of civil society, most especially in as ethnically diverse a setting as southern Ukraine.[108] In this sense, my findings suggest a vision of Ukrainian societal development that parallels the work and findings of historian Serhii Plokhy, most especially in his "peoples' history" of southern Ukraine.[109] In this particular instance at least, Mennonite entrepreneurs had demonstrated their ability and willingness to reconcile ethnic entrepreneurship and imperial politics, at a time when the latter was shaped by great-power nationalist forces. Had events unfolded otherwise, this socio-economic integration might have provided Mennonites with a reliable foundation for their survival and future development as vital entrepreneurs within the empire.

Conclusion

The problem of "Mennonite entrepreneurship and nationalism" unfolded as part of the "German question," a contemporary social phenomenon with deep historical roots. It had become a key element in Russia's nationalist discourse by the late nineteenth century with no signs of abating. The "German question" erupted in bitter debates about how best to secure the empire's development given its heterogeneous population, and how to most effectively ensure the economic integration of the German-speaking population. The "German question" was deemed a crucial factor in the uneven development of the outlying districts, and in the vexing question of what it might mean to be a loyal "Russian" subject when one had roots in countless distinct ethnic groupings within the empire.

The origins of this question originated in the earliest state practices adopted by the Russian Empire before Mennonites first set foot in southern Ukraine. At that time, the imperial centre had extended comparatively favourable terms to attract many ethnic groups to immigrate to the borderlands of Southern Ukraine. Both central and peripheral elites within the empire cooperated to make this possible. Yet it was this very principle of broad inter-ethnic consensus building that was so vilified as imperial Russian nationalism emerged. The formation of the late-nineteenth-century "German question" was connected with the specifics of Russian nationalism, which focused more on the themes of social justice in the distribution of rights than on the goal of uniting diverse peoples into a single Russian state. Nationalists maintained that many of Russia's challenges resulted from state officials who had asked the eternal Russian question "Who is to blame?" more often than "What should we do now?" Nationalists believed that all of this was beside the point at best, and at worst allowed ethnic minorities to claim obedience to St Petersburg even as their actions threatened the future of the empire itself. Among those deemed "guilty" by Russian nationalists, as a rule, were the most successful ethnic groups and communities, and they included the Mennonites.

In their theoretical constructions, the nationalists did not rely on substantiated facts. They pointed instead to possible threats to the integrity of the state, which – as the ideology of nationalism postulated – was likely to come from a strong, successful, and possibly "hidden" enemy. Entrepreneurial practice was a key indicator of the Mennonites' success in the empire, and resulted in Mennonite industry becoming one of the catalysts for the development of the "German question" in Russia in general. In the opinion of the nationalists, the loyalty of a potential enemy (in our case, the Mennonite entrepreneurs who had accumulated significant financial and material wealth) was anything but assured in 1900 despite having demonstrated their loyalty to the empire in the past. Instead, they feared that the loyal former colonist today would become the enemy tomorrow. Therefore, the nationalists believed that the threat should be averted by preventive measures. Nationalists maintained that Mennonite entrepreneurs presented a potentially dangerous enemy which made them a convenient object for criticism and active supervision. The fact that Mennonites were successful in various areas of entrepreneurial activity (including the agricultural and industrial sectors) alarmed Russian nationalists and created a comprehensive social base for potential conflict.

Mennonite entrepreneurs, supported by the state, successfully resisted Russian nationalism in its earliest stages of development (up to 1880). As Mennonite industry consolidated, its entrepreneurs turned into an ethnic elite community, by which they effectively represented the interests of their fellow colonists. It was the nationalists' annoyance with the activities of this entrepreneurial elite that determined how the conflict would be played out after 1880. After the campaign of the 1860s and 1870s, the attitude towards members of the Mennonite community started to change as their loyalty was questioned by an increasingly strident nationalist discourse under Alexander III. Later, these attitudes spread to the whole of Russian society, which, at the law-making stage, resulted in a new negative image of this ethno-religious sect.

The difficulties of the transition to modernization led to the gradual convergence of nationalism and pragmatic politics. This process, traceable in the last third of the nineteenth century in the direction of legal unification, had little effect on ethnic entrepreneurs who contributed directly to the empire's economic gains of the early twentieth century. However, all of these concerns were exacerbated with the onset of World War I, as the problem was framed as an issue of "foreign" ownership with potentially seditious ends. No wonder Mennonite entrepreneurs actively responded to this charge. Russian nationalists crossed a line with the development and adoption of the liquidation legislation as they proposed restrictive measures not only against foreign nationals, but also against German-speaking citizens of the Russian Empire. Nationalist proponents managed to convince many within Imperial Russian society of the correctness of their actions by engaging supporters from all social levels.

At the same time, despite the unequal distribution of strength in the conflict from 1914 to 1917, the "Russian nationalist–Mennonite entrepreneur" confrontation did not end with the defeat of the latter. Mennonites continued to make their case in the highest political circles of the empire as Mennonite industrialists played a decisive role during the war. In the end, their connections with influential elites across

Russian society slowed the pace by which the legislation was implemented. But it also provided large Mennonite businesses with lucrative military orders, which allowed them to preserve their ownership and expand their wealth. This last development not only corresponded with the interests of Mennonite entrepreneurs, but also exerted an indirect influence on the future well-being of the whole community. Still, a clash with a state-centred nationalism that demanded loyalty from the Mennonites and other ethnic groups did come at a significant cost to the community. Besides the loss of small-scale production, Mennonites experienced a blow to the basis of their identity as their pacifist identity marker was challenged from within.

The liquidation of property under the nationalists' scenario significantly damaged not only the Russian economy during a time of war, but also delayed the development of a broad-based civil society within southern Ukraine. Even a partial limitation on Mennonites' entrepreneurial activities negatively affected the region's modernization as it slowed down the processes of imperial economic, retooling, recovery, and reacceleration. Nationalists tainted as illegitimate the strongest, most socially active and industrious ethnic and social leaders, the very ones who might have made the sort of breakthrough that the empire so desperately needed after 1914. As a result, the state – which now conceived of itself as a single, complete, indivisible modernizing community – paid dearly for the ambitious slogans and alienating actions of its nationalistic-minded politicians. In the attempt to engage Russia in an undoubtedly important discussion of the empire's future development, nationalists put the right questions in front of society, but they often gave the wrong answers. The fallacy of these answers was confirmed in practice, because, as history and, in particular, the events analysed here have shown, it led to a split within society, not to its cohesive mobilization.

The larger public's role bode ill for the future of the imperial Russian state as it, by and large, either kept silent or supported the advancement of the laws that trampled on the rights of some of its citizens. Thus the project to create a unified Russian nation – the last version of which was presented by P.A. Stolypin[110] – seemed unlikely to succeed after 1900. As conditions worsened dramatically society-wide fissures revealed how incapable Russia was of responding cohesively to a state of "total war" after 1914. Thereafter it seemed equally incapable of adjusting to civil war conditions; it supported the unlawful actions of political forces which seized temporary power, and willfully disregarded the interests of some for the benefit and ambitions of others. Subsequent events confirmed the truth of how inauspicious this would be for the empire.

NOTES

1 Nataliya V. Venger, "Vozniknovenie i razvitie chastnoi predprinimatel'skoi deiatel'nosti na territorii mennonitskikh kolonii," in *Voprosy germanskoi istorii* (Dnepropetrovsk, 2002), 30–51; Venger, "Agrarna kolonizatsiia? Do pitaniia pro formuvaniia "osoblivoi" ekonomichnoi zoni na teritorii sil's'kogospodars'kikh menonitskikh kolonii Pivdnia Ukraini (persha polovina XIX stolittia)," in *Ukrains'kii selianin* (Cherkasi, 2004), 63–8; David G. Rempel, "The Mennonite Commonwealth in Russia: A Sketch of its Founding and Endurance, 1789–1919," in *Mennonite Quarterly Review*, 47, no. 4 (1973): 259–308. I have previously written about mental maps in Venger, "Osobennosti formirovaniia mental'nykh kart 'naroda v puti,'" in *Eidos: Al'manakh teorii I Istorii Istoricheskoi nauki* (Kiev, 2013), 123–42.
2 Ethnic entrepreneurship is a phenomenon of social adaptation of members of certain ethnic groups, who, being in a state of emigration, mobilize the means available to them in the business sector. The phenomenon of ethnic entrepreneurship was formed in the Russian Empire under conditions of colonization and subsequent comfortable habitation of certain religious and ethnic groups.
3 Boris N. Mironov, *Sotsial'naia istoriia Rossii perioda imperii (XVIII – nachalo XX veka)*, Vol. 1 (St Petersburg: Dmitrii Bulanin, 1999), 28–34.
4 A.I. Miller, *"Ukrainskii vopros" v politike vlastei i russkom obshchestvennom mnenii*, (St Petersburg: Aleteiia, 2000), 10. For an excellent overview of this transition see Paul W. Werth, *The Tsar's Foreign Faiths: Toleration and the Fate of Religious Freedom in Russia* (Oxford: Oxford University Press, 2014).
5 Rempel, "The Mennonite Commonwealth in Russia," 259–308.
6 Not only Russian autocrats (Catherine II, Paul I, Alexander I, Nicholas I) were apologists of the program, but also Russian officials with direct relationship with colonization including Duke A.E. de Richelieu (Kherson Military Governor and Governor of Civil Administration of Ekaterinoslav, Kherson, and Tavrida provinces), S.M. Contenius (Chief Judge of the Novorossiia Office of Guardianship of Foreign Settlers from 1800–18), A.M. Fadeev (senior member of the Ekaterinoslav Office of Foreign Colonists), I.N. Inzov (Chief Administrator of Colonists of the Southern Region of Russia in 1818–42), and A. Klaus (official of the Ministry of State Domains and a historian of colonization).

7 The earliest works on the history of colonization, which provided a positive assessment of the economic status of Mennonite settlements in the first half of the nineteenth century, were scientific publications by A. Skal'kovskii (director of the Main Statistical Committee of New Russia and a member of the Odessa Society of History and Antiquities), and the work of August Haxthausen. The first official historian of German colonization, as recognized by contemporary researchers, is Alexander Klaus (1843–91). See A. Skal'kovskii, *Opyt statisticheskogo opisaniia Novorossiiskogo kraia*, 2 vol. (Odessa, 1850–3); August Haxthausen, *Issledovanie vnutrennikh otnoshenii narodnoi zhizni i osobennosti sel'skikh uchrezhdenii Rossii*, trans. L.I. Ragozin in 3 vol. (Moscow, 1870), though the volumes were originally published in German from 1847–53; and A. Klaus, *Nashi kolonii: Opyty i materialy po ictorii i statistike inostrannoi kolonizatsii v Rossii* (St Petersburg, 1869).

8 *Pisma gertsoga Armana Emmanuilovicha de Rishel'e Samuilu Khristianovichu Konteniusu, 1803–1814*, compiled and edited by O.V. Konovalova (Odessa: OKFA, 1999), 34.

9 *Obraz-prezentatsiia* (image-presentation) refers in this context to the image of an ethnic group, appearing unexpectedly in the society as a result of neighbouring residence, observation, cooperation, or external cultivation.

10 Rossiiskii gosudarstvennyi istoricheskii arkhiv (RGIA), f.383, op.29, d.370, ll.1–82; and Gosudarstvennyi arkhiv Odesskoi Oblasti (GAOO), f.89, op.1, d.1465, l.6.

11 L. Goricheva, "Ekonomicheskie problemy i natsional'noe samosoznanie," *Voprosy ekonomiki* (1993, N° 8), 44–53; and A. Sobolevskaia, "Dukhovnye istoki rossiiskogo predprinimatel'stva," *Voprosy ekonomiki* (1993, N° 8), 88–105.

12 A policy on the promotion of ethnic entrepreneurship initiated by the Manifestos of Catherine II. Cf. "O pozvolenii vsem inostrantsam, krome zhidov, vykhodit' i selit'sia v Rossii, i o svobodnom vozvrashchenii v svoe otechestvo russkikh liudei, bezhavshikh za granitsu (4 December 1762)," *Polnoe sobranie zakonov Rossiiskoi Imperii* (*PSZ*), 1st ed., (St Petersburg, 1930), vol. 16, 126–7; and "O dozvolenii vsem inostrantsam, v Rossiiu v'ezzhaiushchim, poseliatsia, v kotorykh Guberniiakh oni pozhelaiut, i o darovannykh im pravakh" (22 July 1763), *PSZ*, vol. 16, 313–16. Others followed including "Prositel'nymi stat'iami Mennonitov"and especially "Zhalovannaia gramota mennonistam, vodvorennym v Novorossiiskoi rubernii. Vysochaishaia gramota mennonitam o podtverzhdenii obeshannoi im svobody v otpravlenii veroispovedaniia po tserkovnym ikh ustanovleniiam i obychaiam" (6 September 1800),

PSZ, vol. 26, 286–7. Legislation from 1812 concerned the possibility of withdrawing from colonist status and moving to other classes, including the merchant class. The law of 1846 concerned the withdrawal of territorial limits on the development of entrepreneurial activity. See "Otmena sushchestvuiushchego zapreshcheniia na otpusk Novorossiiskikh kolonistov dlia zarabotkov dalee predelov Novorossiiskogo kraia" (9 December 1846), *PSZ*, vol. 21, 628.

13 See, for example, A.M. Fadeev, *Vospominaniia*, vol. 1 (Odessa, 1897), 51–3, 63, 82–8, 104–6, 211. See also John R. Staples, *Cross-Cultural Encounters on the Ukrainian Steppe: Settling the Molochna Basin, 1783–1861* (Toronto: University of Toronto Press, 2003), 107–42; and Harvey L. Dyck, "Russian Servitor and Mennonite Hero: Light and Shadow in Images of Johann Cornies," *Journal of Mennonite Studies* 2 (1984): 9–43.

14 "Nakaz grazhdanskim gubernatoram ob obiazannosti grazhdanskikh gubernatorov po okhranenii prav i l'got, darovannykh inostrannym kolonistam" (3 June 1837), *PSZ*, vol. 12, 361–438.

15 Staples, "Religiia, politika i mennonitskaia Zhalovannaia gramota v nachale XIX veka v Rossii: Peresmotr dela Varkentina," in *Voprosy germanskoi istorii*, (Dnepropetrovsk, 2003), 4–22.

16 Werth, *The Tsar's Foreign Faiths*, 150–3.

17 Iu. F. Samarin was the first to raise the problem of Russia's outskirts in the context of the German population's special status in the publications *Rizhskie pis'ma* (1848), and *Okrainy Rossii: Russkoe Baltiiskoe pomor'e* (1868–76). Ivan S. Aksakov asserted that Samarin's work on Russia's borderlands was of the utmost importance. In particular, he declared that Samarin "expresses deeply what to [Aksakav] is a strong need to bring a deliberately Russian state policy to the other … borderlands." The works of Ivan S. Aksakov pertaining to problems caused by the Ostsee Germans were published in the journals *Moskva* and *Den'* from 1862 to 1885.

18 Ivan S. Aksakov, "V prave li pribaltiiskie nemtsy protestovat' protiv reform russkogo pravitel'stva vo imia printsipa natsional'nosti" (23.09.1867) in Ivan S. Aksakov, *Polnoe sobranie sochinenii*, vol. 6, *Pribaltiiskii vopros. Vnutrennie dela Rossii* (Moscow, 1887), 30.

19 Aksakov, "V kakom smysle ostzeiskie nemtsy dorozhat svoimi otzhivshimi privilegiiami" (September 1868) in Aksakov, *Polnoe sobranie sochinenii*, 102.

20 *Moskovskie vedomosti* (*MV*) (No. 51, 1864), 136.

21 Ibid.

22 "Vysochaishe utverzhdennye pravila ob ustroistve poselian-sosbstvennikov (byvshikh kolonistov), vodvorennykh na kazennykh

zemliakh v guberniiakh: Sankt-Peterburgskoi, Novgorodskoi, Samarskoi, Saratovskoi, Voronezhskoi, Chernigovskoi, Poltavskoi, Ekaterinoslavskoi, Khersonskoi, Tavricheskoi i v oblasti Bessarabskoi" (14 June 1871), *PSZ*, vol. 46, 813–19.

23 "Pravila ob otbyvanii obiazatel'noi sluzhby mennonitami," *PSZ*, vol. 50, 146–7.

24 *MV* (No. 51, 1864), 118.

25 Aksakov, *Polnoe sobranie sochinenii*, 413–16.

26 Nataliya V. Venger, *Mennonitskoe predprinimaterl'stvo v usloviiakh modernizatsii Iuga Rossii: mezhdu kongregatsiei, klanom i rossiiskim obshchestvom (1789–1920)* (Dnepropetrovsk, 2008), 296–333.

27 RGIA, f.821, op.133, d.319.

28 Tsentral'nyi gosudarstvennyi istoricheskii arkiv vysshikh organov vlasti i upravleniia Ukrainy (Kiev) (TGAVOU), f.5, op.1, d.967, l.88.

29 Venger, *Mennonitskoe*, 224–5.

30 Harry Loewen, "A House Divided: Russian Mennonite Non-resistance and Emigration in the 1870s," in *Mennonites in Russia, 1788–1988: Essays in Honour of Gerhard Lohrenz*, ed. John Friesen (Winnipeg: CMBC Publications, 1989); and Peter M. Friesen, *The Mennonite Brotherhood in Russia (1789–1911)*, 2nd ed. (Fresno: Protestant Spiritual Tradition, 1978), 587–8.

31 P. Albert Koop, "Some Economic Aspects of Mennonite migration: With Special Emphasis on the 1870s Migration from Russia to North America," *Mennonite Quarterly Review* 55 (1981): 143–56.

32 Putting the colonists under the joint jurisdiction of the provincial and district agencies for peasant affairs as well as the local one, the authorities did not completely reject the "incentive" policy of the colonists. "Rules about the system of villagers-owners" contained three main points important for understanding the essence of the reform: 1) colonists-villagers obeyed the joint authorities of the provincial and district agencies for peasant affairs as well as the local agency; 2) kept all of their personal benefits, "which they hitherto enjoyed"; and 3) kept the ownership of everything standing on their allotment of land. Recognizing the colonists' right to conduct business activity and the related necessity of temporary absence from the colonies, the authorities introduced the practice of "small rural meetings." Its convocation was allowed if a separate settlement "had a large number of populations" or the quota of members of a meeting could not be provided because of the lack of people on reason of their involvement in commercial-industrial activities. (RGIA, f.1181, d.71, ll.102–3, 136–9). See also Venger, "Mennonity i vlast' v konflikte 1860–1870: pros i cons reform unifikatsii," in *Grazhdanskaia identichnost' i vnutrennii mir*

rossiiskikh nemtsev v gody Velikoi otechestvennoi voiny i v istoricheskoi pamiati potomkov (Moscow 2011), 449–67.

33 Nataliya V. Venger, "'Nimets'ke pitaniia' v otsintis I.S. Aksakova ta Iu. F. Samarina: Dialog z rosiis'kim suspil'stvom u desiatilittia 'velikikh refrom' (1860–1870)," in *Voprosy nemetskoi istorii* (Dnepropetrovsk, 2011), 53–72.

34 Eric Lohr, *Nationalizing the Russian Empire: The Campaign against Enemy Aliens during World War I* (Cambridge, MA: Harvard University Press, 2003), 220.

35 V.I. Bovykin, *Ocherki istorii vneshnei politiki Rossii. Konets XIX–1917* (Moscow, 1960), 7.

36 K. Golovin, *Moi vospominaniia*, vol. 2 (St Petersburg, 1908), 46–7; I.A. Murav'ev ed., *Alexandr tretii: Vospominaniia. Dnevniki. Pis'ma* (St Petersburg, 2001), 268; O. Barkovets and A. Krylov-Tolstikovich, *Neizvestnyi imperator Alexandr III: Ocherki zhizni, liubvi i smerti* (Moscow, 2003).

37 A. Ged'o, *Sotsial'no-ekonomichnii rosvitok grets'kikh gromad Ukraini seredini XVII–XIX stolittia: dzhereloznavchii aspect* (Donetsk, 2006), 39.

38 A.A. Velitsin, *Nemtsy v Rossii* (St Petersburg, 1893); G.A. Evreinov, Rossiiskie nemtsy (Petrograd, 1915); I.I. Sergeev, *Mirnoe zavoevanie Rossii nemtsami: Doklad, prochitannyi v chrezvychainom obshchem sobranii "Obshchestva 1914"* (Petrograd, 1915); and S.P. Shelukhin, *Nemetskaia kolonizatsiia na IUge Rossii* (Odessa, 1915). See also Nataliya V. Venger, "Kolonizatsiia i problemy reformirovaniia kolonistov v rossiiskom natsionalisticheskom duskurse," in *Nemtsy Sibiri: istoriia i kul'tura* (Omsk, 2010), 264–71; Harvey L. Dyck, "Russian Mennonitism and the Challenge of Russian Nationalism, 1889" *Mennonite Quarterly Review* 56 (1982): 307–17; and David G. Rempel, "The Expropriation of the German Colonists in South Russia during the Great War," *Journal of Modern History* 4 (1932): 49–67.

39 "Nemetskie kolonii v Novorossii," *Mir Bozhii* 1 (1902): 22.

40 F. Brun, *Chernomor'e: Sbornik issledovanii po istorii geografii Iuzhnoi Rossii, 1852–1877*, Part 2 (Odessa, 1880); P.A. Kamenskii, *Vopros ili nedorasumenie: k voprosu ob inostrannykh poseleniiakh na iuge Rossii* (Moscow, 1895); K.E. Lindemann, *Prekrashchenie zemlevladeniia i zemlepol'zovaniia poselian-sobstvennikov: Ukazy 2 fevralia i 13 dekabria 1915 i 10, 15 iiunia i 19 avgusta 1916 i ikh vliianie na ekonomicheskoe sostoianie Iuznoi Rossii* (Moscow, 1917); and Ia. Shtakh, *Ocherki iz istorii i sovremennoi zhizni iuzhnorusskikh kolonistov* (Moscow, 1916).

41 To some extent, the "German question" was fuelled by the aggravated and complex religious situation in the empire, the spreading influence of baptism, the proselytism of the Mennonites, and also the German law on dual citizenship allowing persons of German nationality residing outside the borders of the Reich to preserve the right to German citizenship.

42 *Predprinimatel'stvo i predprinimateli Rossii: ot istokov do nachala XX veka*, ed. V. I. Bovykin, V.V. Zhuravlev, and Iu. A. Petrov (Moscow, 1997), 56.
43 Friesen, *The Mennonite Brotherhood in Russia*, 865.
44 Tsentral'nyi Gosudarstvennyi istoricheskii arkhiv Ukrainy (Kiev) (TGIAK), f.575, op.1, ch.1, d.243, l.2.
45 Ibid.
46 Ibid., l.3.
47 Ibid., l.7.
48 Ibid.
49 Ibid.
50 Ibid.
51 Nataliya V. Venger, "Dinastiia Niburov i ee vklad v ekonomicheskoe rasvitie regiona," in *Nemtsy Priazov'ia i Pricherno-mor'ia:Istoriia i sovremennost': k 200-letiiu pereseleniia* (Donetsk, 2004), 55–65; and Nataliya V. Verger, "Mukomol'noe proizvodstvo" in *Nemtsy Rossii: Entsiklopediia*, vol. 2 (Moscow, 1999), 572–5.
52 RGIA, f.23, op.28, d.22, ll.1–29.
53 Terry Martin, *The Mennonites and the Russian State Duma, 1905–1914* (Seattle: The Donald W. Treadgold Papers in Russian, East European and Central Asian Studies, 1996), 34–42.
54 Alfred Eisfeld, "Karl Lindeman: politicheskaia i obshchestvennaia deiatel'nost' moskovskogo uchenogo" in *Nemtsy Moskvy: istoricheskii vklad v kul'turu stolitsy* (Moscow, 1997), 268–91.
55 S.V. Baakh, "Transformatsiia soderzhaniia nemetskogo voprosa v kontekste deiatel'nosti Gosudarstvennoi Dumy (1906–1917)" in *Rossiiskoe gosudarstvo, obshchestvo i etnicheskie nemtsy: osnovnye etapy i kharakter vzaimootnosheniia: Materialy XI mezhdunarodnoi konferentsii. Moskva, 1–3 November 2006* (Moscow, 2007), 189–200.
56 RGIA, f.1483, op.1, d.1, l.5.
57 The first of the presented laws deprived subjects of the rights of land ownership and land use if they hailed from countries at war with Russia (according to K. Lindemann, it amounted to about 300,000 desiatinas). Landowners of this category were asked to submit voluntarily to the will of the law, namely to sell their property within six months. After this time, the property could be auctioned off. Until 2 February 1916, authorities also planned to liquidate all lease obligations of foreign nationals of the states of Germany, Austro-Hungary, Turkey. See *Sobranie uzakonenii i rasporiazhenii pravitel'stva, izdavaemoe v Pravitel'stvuiushchem Senate v 1915*, Otdel 1 (Petrograd, 1915), 559–64.
58 According to the provisions of the second law, a zone of 100–150 versts [1 verst = 3,500 feet] was established along the borders with Germany,

Austria-Hungary, Finland, and also along the coast of the Baltic, Black, Azov seas (including the Crimea and the Caucasus), where land ownership and land use of immigrants, with Russian citizenship, from Germany and Austria-Hungary were liquidated. For voluntary fulfilment of the law, there was a period of ten to sixteen months from the date of the promulgation of lists of possessions subject to disposal. In case of owner refusal, the legislation permitted the forced seizure of lands and their sale by auction. The legislation also specified the category of land, which fell under the influence of the legal act: the action of the law applied to the property of rural societies as well that owned by individuals. In the 100-kilometre border zone, 859 colonies of Bessarabia, Kherson, and Ekaterinoslav provinces (a total 982,789 desiatinas of land) fell under the influence of the law of 2 February 1915. Included were 283 colonies of Tavrida province (about 520,000 desiatinas). See ibid., 564–6.

59 The law, adopted on 2 February 1915, "On land tenure and land use of certain classes, consisting of Austrian, Hungarian, or German immigrants with Russian citizenship," prevented further expansion of land use and land ownership by Germans in Russia. According to the law, Germans were forbidden to acquire any real estate outside the cities. The influence of the laws of February 2 was extended to 130,000 people. See ibid., 566–8.

60 A.S. Rezanov, *Nemetskoe shpionstvo* (Moscow, 1915), 209.

61 *Sobranie uzakonenii i rasporiazhenii pravitel'stva, izdavaemoe v Pravitel'stvuiushchem Senate v 1915. Otdel 1* (Petrograd, 1915), 2749.

62 In the whole empire, according to the calculations of the Ministry of Internal Affairs, 2,068 settlements were taken over. Among them – properties of expatriates of countries at war – 2,950,852 desiatinas; properties of nationals of hostile countries – 71405, for a total of 3,256,733 desiatinas. The law of 13 December 1915 affected the interests of about 330,000 people who lived in the southern provinces, 70,000 Volynian Germans expelled on order of the military authorities in the summer and fall of 1915, as well as the German-speaking population of Kiev province, Podolia province, and the Polish provinces (a total of about 500,000 people).

63 RGIA, f.1483, op.1, d.16, d.34.

64 Lohr, *Nationalizing the Russian Empire*, 27.

65 RGIA, f.23, op.28, d.3090, ll.1–5, 7, 17 ob., 25–6; *Sobranie uzakonenii i rasporiazhenii pravitel'stva, izdavaemoe v Pravitel'stvuiushchem Senate za 1915*, 2 vols. (Petrograd, 1916–17).

66 Iu. Laptev, "Polozhenie nemtsev v Krymu v gody Pervoi mirovoi voiny" in *Nemtsy v Krymu* (Simferpol', 2000), 63–72.

67 Lindemann, *Prekrashchenie zemlevladeniia i zemlepol'zovaniia poselian-sobstvennikov*, 384.
68 O. Hamm, *Memoirs of Ignatyevo in the Light of Historical Change* (Saskatoon, 1984), 109.
69 Peter Heese, "Jekaterinoslav," Mennonite Heritage Center Archive, vol. 5015, Small Archives, 9.
70 Ibid., 10.
71 *Ves' Ekaterinoslav. 1915* (Ekaterinoslav, 1915), v.
72 Hesse, "Jekaterinoslav," 11.
73 TGIAK, f.715, op.1, d.2259, l.14.
74 Ibid., ll.2, 6.
75 Ibid., l.6.
76 Gosudarstvennyi oblastnoi arkhiv Donetskoi oblasti (GADoO), f.101, op.1, d.3, ll.49, 64.
77 Iu. I. Kir'ianov, "Rabochie Rossii i voinạ: novye podkhody k analizu problemi" in *Pervaia mirovaia voina: Prolog XX veka* (Moscow: Nauka, 1999), 434.
78 David G. Rempel and Cornelia Rempel Carlson, *A Mennonite Family in Tsarist Russia and the Soviet Union, 1789–1923* (Toronto: University of Toronto Press, 2002), 168.
79 Kir'ianov, "Rabochie Rossii i voina," 434.
80 Gosudarstvennyi oblastnoi arkhiv Dnepropetrovskoi oblasti (GADO), f.11, op.1, d.1294, l.10.
81 GADO, f.11, op.1, d.1294, ll.10, 20. Imperial authorities had good reason to fear that spontaneous acts of violence could eventually be directed to them. For the prehistory to this, see Charters Wynn, *Workers, Strikes and Pogroms: The Donbass-Dnepr Bend in Late Imperial Russia, 1870–1905* (Princeton: Princeton University Press, 1992).
82 Calvin W. Redekop, "Business," in *The Mennonite Encyclopedia*, vol. 5 (Scottsdale: Herald Press, 1991), 38.
83 RGIA, f.1276, op.12, d.1447; and RGIA, f.1483, op.1, d.20, ll.10–2.
84 Ibid., f.1483, op.1, d.20, ll.19–27.
85 Ibid., f.821, op.133, d.319, ll.25–7.
86 O.R. Airapetov, *Generaly, liberaly i predprinimateli: rabota na front i na revoliutsiiu (1907–1917)* (Moscow, Tri kvadrata, 2003).
87 Baakh, "Transformatsiia soderzhaniia," 7.
88 Ibid., 8.
89 *Doklad komissii po vyiasneniiu mer bor'by s germanskim i avstro-vengerskim vliianiem v oblasti torgovli i promyshlennosti* (Moscow, 1915), 62.
90 *Promyshlennost' i torgovlia v zakonodatel'nykh uchrezhdeniiakh v 1913–1914*, vol. 2 (St Petersburg, 1914), xx.

91 Lindemann, *Prekrashchenie zemlevladeniia i zemlepol'zovaniia poselian-sobstvennikov*, 31, 250.
92 Ibid., 96, 104–5, 245.
93 RGIA, f.1276, op.1, d.1455, l.8.
94 Ibid., f.1483, op.1, d.20, l.16.
95 Ibid., f.1483, op.1, d.16, l.107.
96 Sobranie uzakonenii i rasporiazhenii pravitel'stva 1917 (Petrograd, 1917), 558–60.
97 RGIA, f.23, op.28, d.1216, ll.33–4.
98 Gosudarstvennyi arkhiv Zaporozhskoi oblasti (GAZO), f.30, op.1, d.190, l.56.
99 GADO, f.158, op.1, d.107, l.37.
100 GAZO, f.158, op.1, d.98, l.202.
101 Ibid., f.158, op.1, d.98, l.202.
102 TGIAK, f.2090, op.1, ch.1, d.423, l.72.
103 GAZO, f.32, op.1, d.481, l.21.
104 TGIAK, f.2090, op.1, ch.1, d.423, l.76.
105 Ibid., f.2090, op.1, ch.1, d.423, l.76.
106 Gosudarstvennyi arkhiv Avtonomnoi Respubliki Krym (Simferopol') (GAARK), f.143, op.1, d.5, l.1.
107 Hesse, *Jekaterinoslav*.
108 The "sacred landscape" borrows terminology from Sergei Zhuk. Cf. Sergei Zhuk, "Making and Unmaking the 'Sacred Landscape' of Orthodox Russia–Identity Crisis and Religious Politics in the Ukrainian Provinces of the Late Russian Empire," in *Space, Place, and Power in Modern Russia: Essays in the New Spatial History*, ed. Mark Bassin, Christopher Ely, and Melissa K. Stockdale (DeKalb: Northern Illinois University Press, 2010), ch. 8.
109 Serhii Plokhy, *Ukraine and Russia: Representations of the Past* (Toronto: University of Toronto Press, 2008), ch. 8.
110 Venger, "Nimets'ke pitannia v svitogliadi ta polititsi P.A. Stolipina: aprobatsiia vladoiu," in *Aktual'ni problemi vitchiznianoi ta vsesvit'noi istorii: Naukovi zapiski RDGU*, 22 (Rivne, 2011), 173–80.

PART THREE

Mennonite Identities in Diaspora

6 Mennonite Identities in a New Land: Abraham A. Friesen and the Russian Mennonite Migration of the 1920s

JOHN B. TOEWS

An isolated cemetery in Rabbit Lake, Saskatchewan marks the grave of A.A. Friesen, a member of the so-called Study Commission sent abroad by Ukrainian Mennonites in 1919. When he died on 20 September 1948, residents remembered him only as the former manager of the local lumberyard and possibly knew little of his role in the emigration of the 1920s. Fortunately, surviving family records as well as the archival records of the Canadian Mennonite Board of Colonization (CMBC) and the A.A. Friesen Collection significantly expand our knowledge and understanding of this remarkable person, often misunderstood by the very constituency he tried to serve.[1]

But why include a study of this individual in a volume primarily concerned with Mennonite identity in Ukraine? The question is a fair one. I argue that A.A. Friesen provides a valuable vantage point on the nature of the so-called Russian Mennonite identity at the onset of the Soviet era. Though I cannot suggest that Friesen was at all typical of his generation, I do maintain that he represents a particular vision of what Russian Mennonite society had become by 1917. For instance, I will present here an individual who was comparatively cosmopolitan and critical of those co-religionists who had maintained an isolationist stance to the Russian empire and the society all around them. He especially criticised those Mennonites who by 1914 understood themselves to be Germanic and who wore their alienation from Russian culture as a badge of honour. Last, Friesen's journey from southern Ukraine to North America reveals both the varieties of acculturation that Mennonites faced, but also the great diversity of peoples who by 1920 identified themselves as Mennonite. Friesen was amazed at the highly fractious nature of the North American Mennonite world, even as he struggled with deep divisions within the Mennonite world of his birth. In the end, he would be unable to overcome the conflicts that occasionally surrounded him, but by that time he had, ironically, accomplished all that he had set out to do. That is the story to which we now turn.

A.A. Friesen was born on 15 February 1885, in the Molochna village of Schönau in the Black Sea steppe lands of the Russian Empire. At the age of seven, he entered the village elementary school and completed the customary six-year program in 1898. That fall he enrolled in the Ohrloff Central School, graduating in the spring of 1901. During the 1902–3 school years, he completed the pedagogical program at the Halbstadt Teachers' College, which qualified him as an elementary school teacher. From 1904 to 1906, he attended the Classical Gymnasium in Ekaterinoslav. This was followed by four years of study at the Imperial Novorossiisk University in Odessa. By this time Friesen had been broadly exposed to Russian and German literature as well as such languages as Latin, Greek, and Old Slavonic. The university also provided him with a broad knowledge of science. In 1910 he was appointed physics and chemistry teacher at the Mennonite College of Commerce in Halbstadt, where he taught until the end of 1919.[2]

There appear to be no surviving materials documenting Friesen's tenure at the Halbstadt College. Later memories portrayed him as a strict demanding teacher not particularly tolerant of lazy students. During the course of his education, Friesen specialized in agronomy. His talents in this field possibly motivated the Congress of German Colonists meeting in Prishib near Halbstadt on 14 May 1918 to elect Friesen as a delegate to examine lands in Germany and the Baltic countries for possible settlement. Information gathered during that trip was presented to the Second All-Mennonite Congress held in Ohrloff (18–21 September 1918). It was perhaps this "excellent report" that caused him to be elected as a member of the interim executive of the Congress. Subsequently, political chaos put an end to the aspirations of the Mennonite Congress movement. Apparently, for delegates attending a hastily called meeting in Rueckenau, Molochna late in 1919, the selection of Friesen as the chairperson of a study commission to explore potential settlement sites abroad seemed self-evident. By then Ukraine had already endured a lengthy period of war, civil war, and anarchy. A brief occupation of Ukraine by Bolshevik forces ended in April 1918 when German and Austrian occupation forces moved in under the terms of the Treaty of Brest-Litovsk (3 March 1918). Their withdrawal late in 1918 exposed the Ukrainian Mennonite settlements to ongoing instability thanks to the civil war as well as the depredations of Nestor Makhno's ruthless partisan army. Amid the ongoing chaos, Friesen and the other members left Ukraine on 1 January 1920, travelling by way of Crimea and Constantinople.[3]

When they finally arrived in Europe in April 1920, they contacted their co-religionists in Germany, Holland, and Switzerland. The delegation arrived in New York on 13 June 1920 and began visiting Mennonite communities in Canada and United States. After B.H. Unruh returned to Germany, Friesen became the pivotal figure in North America, exploring settlement possibilities for his Russian Mennonite constituency.

Friesen's diary lists the ports of call – Basel, Karlsruhe, Heilbrönn, Lautenbach, Stuttgart, Wernigerode, Berlin, and Emden. Then came the contacts with Dutch Mennonite leaders in The Hague, Utrecht, Amsterdam, and Rotterdam. Twelve days of turbulent seas characterized their journey from Plymouth to New York. Now came the visits to Eastern Mennonite centres such as Lancaster, Bluffton, and Berne. In Bluffton, Friesen met Dr Mosiman, president of Bluffton College, a significant contact for Friesen personally. By mid-July, he had spent some days with H.P. Krehbiel in Newton, Kansas and P.C. Hiebert in Hillsboro. While in Kansas he and Study Commission member C.H. Warkentin toured possible settlement sites. On 7 August, Friesen's diary simply notes, "Off to the north," meaning visits to Mennonite communities in Minnesota and South Dakota.[4]

In a personal letter to his fiancée Maria Goossen, still in Ukraine, he summarized his first exposure to the American Mennonite scene. As he journeyed west, he "stopped wherever there were Mennonite churches, until we finally came to Hillsboro, the center of the Russian Mennonites."[5] Reflecting on his visit to Elkhart, Indiana, some ten days earlier, Friesen observed: "There are 16 different [Mennonite] groups in America that, until now, have had no contact with each other. I think we have managed to unite all these independent groups together in a common relief agency serving us in Russia."[6]

Abraham had been in America for just over a year. He felt like a man caught between two worlds. In Ukraine, he had been molded in an environment that was both Slavic and German, and he had achieved significant intellectual credentials in that world. Here, as an immigrant, he would have to begin at the lowest rung. The Russian/Ukrainian Mennonite world had offered an all-encompassing familial, social, and economic security. Being Mennonite in that sense was significantly different from being Mennonite in America, where cultural inroads into the varied Mennonite communities threatened, in his estimation, a distinctive Mennonite identity. How was he to understand this complexity? More than a year later, in another letter to Maria, he hinted at his inner turmoil. "My faith that Someone Higher is in control sustains me."[7]

At least twice in his letters to Maria, he observed that if he remained in the United States he would not want to live among Mennonites but among Americans. Perhaps the American Mennonites in their varied responses to the surrounding culture contrasted too sharply with the stable, progressive Russian-Mennonite world he remembered from his student days. In the not too distant future, the normally resolute, clear-thinking Friesen would have to address the concerns of his constituency abroad and do so apart from his personal reservations and private struggles. Fortunately, one of his deepest personal concerns found resolution when Maria arrived safely in Rosthern, Saskatchewan in midsummer of 1922.

The members of the Study Commission, who left for Europe and North America late in 1919, could not have anticipated the complexity of their assignment. This was especially true of A.A. Friesen, its chairperson. The commission arrived in New York on 13 June 1920. By 1 November, B.H. Unruh had returned to Germany. Headquartered in Karlsruhe, he would generate a voluminous correspondence that detailed the varied crises confronting Russian Mennonites over almost four decades. Yet it was left to Friesen to unravel the enormous complexity of the American Mennonite scene, as well as the difficulties confronting any resettlement of the Russian Mennonites. It proved a difficult assignment.

It was after Unruh left that Friesen began to explore immigration possibilities in the United States. The problem of assessing potentially helpful organizations and persons must have proved daunting. What of the Mennonite Immigration Bureau in Newton, Kansas? Its secretary, H.P. Krehbiel, was an energetic promoter of Mennonite settlement in the United States. Was he an answer to the Russian Mennonite dilemma?[8] What was Friesen to make of the representatives of the various Mennonite groups that met with him in Newton, Kansas on 14 July 1920 in the interests of colonization? Who carried on the dialogue on that occasion – Unruh or Friesen – a dialogue that produced a meeting of all Mennonite relief committees in Elkhart, Indiana on 27 July 1920? On that day, the birth of the Mennonite Central Committee addressed one of the Study Commission's concerns – material aid for the devastated and starving Mennonite settlements in Ukraine.

The other agenda, colonization, was much more difficult to address. How was Friesen to assess and relate to the Mennonite Executive Committee for Colonization organized in Newton on 24 November 1920? Possibly, unknown to him at this point was the fact that American sentiment against European immigrants soon resulted in strict quotas based on nationality; nor could he anticipate both individual and constituency opposition to a large-scale Russian Mennonite immigration. Meanwhile, he was to explore potential settlement sites for an anxious population back home. Accompanied by American representatives G.G. Hiebert and J.W. Wiens, as well as Study Commission colleague C.H. Warkentin, Friesen embarked on a lengthy journey to Mexico during the winter months of 1920–1. In his initial and later reports, while mentioning issues like geography and climate, he focused on what he considered more basic issues – constitutional stability and Mennonite cultural continuity.[9] Friesen reiterated the same themes in a document he completed on 25 June 1921. The manuscript revealed significant insights into the ongoing Russian Mennonite experience and the daunting prospects of charting an unknown future. "The feeling of accountability often makes me tremble when new steps are to be undertaken whose outcome cannot be properly evaluated."[10]

Abraham briefly sketched what he considered the essential components of the story of Mennonite settlement in southern Ukraine: the displacement of indigenous people and the attempt to preserve the German colonists as a separate entity, religiously, culturally, and economically. His conclusion: "Out of a purely confessional people a national entity emerged with its own tradition." Later, when pan-Slavism generated suspicion of all things German, the colonists struggled for self-preservation, focusing on language and schools. It was a determined, persistent battle, ultimately not for confessional reasons, but rather an attempt to become a national minority. "We were not fighting for our faith but for the preservation of our existing state (nation)." A politically stable Russia would have forced two alternatives upon the Russian Mennonites: an ongoing, ultimately futile struggle for self-preservation or the acceptance of Russian national culture that entailed the loss of the German language. Friesen, perhaps reflecting his personal exposure to Russian language and literature, had no doubts as to what would have been the better choice. "When I view the situation from afar, it seems to me we should have extracted the highest ideals of Russian culture, acknowledged them and made them our own." For him, the Old Mennonites in America had, in their two-century history, accepted "the national language and understood the highest ideals of the nation." They absorbed the very best of American culture yet remained confessionally sound. If Russian Mennonites were able to emigrate, they must not isolate themselves from the dominant society. If they remained in Russia, Mennonites needed to solve "our greatest problem, namely our relationship to the Russian nation and culture." In his view, any attempts at self-preservation based on being German must be rejected, regardless of where a new homeland might be found: "Today there is no country in the world in which we can live in isolation. We must actively participate in the life of the nation if we want to survive. The question is: with which state can we bond most easily, with which nation do our values best harmonize?"

If potential emigrants accepted this pathway, Friesen felt, "the nationality question amid American and Canadian culture is forever solved and all our energies can focus on the development and maturation of congregational life." Whether they left or stayed in Russia, the Mennonites had no choice. "We can no longer be quiet in the land." There was no room for any anti-national or anti-cultural stance. "In the future if we stay, we must play the role in Russia that the Quakers play in England and America." Perhaps this line of thinking explained why, in his private letters, Friesen preferred to live among Americans, not Mennonites, if he remained on this continent. There is no evidence to suggest that his personal views negatively affected his emigration work.

Most of his co-religionists did not share Friesen's view on assimilation. Surviving documents in which prospective emigrants rationalized their reasons for wanting to leave were mostly penned in the wake of the 1921–2 famine.[11] Naturally, physical survival became a dominant concern. Pressured by a militant atheism, parents and community leaders were likewise concerned with the loss of control over their schools, as well as the prohibitions against religious instruction of any kind. Community leaders worried about a precipitous decline in public morality as evidenced by a weakened sense of right and wrong and a lack of community benevolence. Whatever the motivation for leaving, most Mennonite emigration leaders expressed a preference for the existing model of closed settlements as had been adopted in southern Ukraine. Friesen, by contrast, advocated abandoning that pattern in favour of a new broadly applicable paradigm. His views, if widely known, might have alienated members of his constituency in Ukraine.

Once in Canada, Friesen became something of a man behind the scenes. He was there at an informal meeting in Herbert, Saskatchewan in June 1921, exploring how to rescind the order-in-council (1919) barring Mennonites, Hutterites, and Doukhobors from entering Canada. He was a member of the first unsuccessful delegation to Ottawa in the fall of 1921 and joined others in a second Ottawa trip in March 1922 that tried to present a new cognitive map of Mennonites to Canadian authorities. Friesen was present when a permanent immigration committee was organized in Gretna, Manitoba in May 1922. When the project was finalized as the Canadian Mennonite Board of Colonization, he was appointed as correspondence secretary.[12] Few in the outside world would ever know what massive correspondence the assignment involved. It was also a role too easily overlooked and forgotten. Friesen found himself in a somewhat ambiguous situation. He was still a member of the now geographically scattered Study Commission. Most of the correspondence from abroad for this agency landed on his desk. Meanwhile, in Rosthern he was employed by the Board of Colonization. Eventually pressures from all sides would trigger his resignation from both agencies.

It was Friesen who carried on the bulk of the correspondence with B.H. Unruh in Germany and B.B. Janz in Ukraine. When, in addition to the Ukrainian Mennonite Union, the All-Russian Mennonite Agricultural Union was organized in Soviet Ukraine and also became active in emigration, they too were added to his mailing list. This international correspondence was especially wearisome because of mailing delays. Janz's correspondence was sent via German diplomatic mail from the German consulate in Kharkiv. Arriving in Berlin, it went to B.H. Unruh, who forwarded it to Friesen's desk in Rosthern. The return mailing route was equally time-consuming. Critical inquiries might take months to resolve. Short telegrams sometimes allayed fears and anxieties, yet, due to the need for secrecy amid an increasingly paranoid Bolshevik regime, they could not supply all the needed information.

Sandwiched between Friesen's official correspondence housed in the Winnipeg and North Newton files are scores of individual letters in which people privately express their concerns about emigration and settlement sites. For example, in the late spring of 1921 the newly organized "Mennonite Council of North Caucasus" informed Friesen that its original purpose was to free young Mennonite men from military service, but it was now concerned with civil, economic, and emigration matters.[13] In reply, Friesen detailed the difficulties currently associated with immigration to Canada and the United States and gently warned the group that the emigration question must be decided by the

Russian Mennonite constituency collectively.[14] A similar reply was sent in response to repeated inquiries from anxious emigrants in the Omsk and Slavgorod regions.[15] When H.H. Schroeder wrote from Constantinople requesting information about the arrival of American Mennonite relief, Friesen sent four consecutive letters, all of which remained unanswered.[16]

Once the rather shy and retiring Friesen was securely surrounded by the walls of the board offices in the somewhat remote town of Rosthern, Saskatchewan, he should have been freed from the former stress of moving about in – what was for him – a largely foreign Canadian Mennonite world. Surely as correspondence secretary he was now free from public scrutiny and criticism. The great public cause of Russian Mennonite emigration and the many criticisms it generated in North America would be, and were, ably defended by great public figures like David Toews. Friesen expressed his gratitude for this protection on several occasions. Some Canadian Mennonites, perhaps fearing personal liability, were horrified by the Canadian Pacific Railway (CPR) contract signed by David Toews whereby CPR agreed to transport Mennonite immigrants across Canada in exchange for payment to be made after settlement. While organized protests emerged in Canada, more subtle and more damaging happenings emerged south of the border. Some of these targeted A.A. Friesen directly.

Several American Mennonite publications did much to publicize the plight of the Russian Mennonites. These included *Die Mennonitische Rundschau*, published in Scottsdale, Pennsylvania; *Der Herold* in Newton, Kansas; and *Vorwärts* in Hillsboro, Kansas. All carried regular reports on the desperate conditions and food shortage in Russia, as well as news of relief efforts initiated by Mennonites in North America. *Vorwärts*, edited by Abraham Schellenberg, was especially generous in its coverage. The same was true of the Mennonite Brethren denominational publication, *Zionsbote*, which he also edited. In mid-September 1922, he reiterated his *Vorwärts* editorial policy stating that it was "a paper for everyone" and as such eschewed any personal or partisan viewpoints.[17] Yet it was not long after making such a pronouncement that Schellenberg decided to join a partisan dispute[18] involving the Board of Colonization and dissidents in the Saskatchewan constituency. A report of the meetings (26 July and 4 August) protesting the signing of the CPR contract by David Toews and Gerhard Ens on behalf of the Canadian Mennonite Board of Colonization on 24 July in Montreal was published in *Der Zionsbote*.[19] Far from being good news from Zion it ascribed selfish motives to the signatories. Then, under the rather dubious title, "A Word of Clarification," Schellenberg allowed the protest leader, J.P. Friesen, to publish a rebuttal to David Toews. Toews had tried earlier to refute various accusations against the contract in *Der Zionsbote*.[20]

Schellenberg published both Toews's *Zionsbote* defence and J.P. Friesen's response in *Vorwärts* with its broader Mennonite circulation. The names of Gerhard Ens and A.A. Friesen were mentioned, almost implying that they were part of the contract process headed by David Toews. Schellenberg penned a brief editorial on 5 January 1923. Commenting on the high cost of the contract with the CPR, he wondered whether "with Friesen and Ens" in leadership there would be sufficient trust and [financial] means for such an endeavour if sentiments elsewhere are as they are here."[21] It was deplorable, the editor felt, that these men did not enjoy public trust. He claimed he had received letters from Canada expressing concern about the enormous cost of the proposed contract, though he admitted there were some letters of support. With a touch of editorial caprice, *Vorwärts* then declared that it would desist from further comment on the issue. In a concluding sentence, Schellenberg wished immigration leaders success, but warned that any pressure on their part would hinder the project. Whatever his motives, the editor seriously damaged the reputation of A.A. Friesen in the eyes of his inter-Mennonite readership and placed an embattled project further in jeopardy. There was little either Friesen or Ens could do to defend themselves. No specifics were given as to why there was a lack of public trust. It was ironic that the groundswell of opposition to emigration came from the Mennonite constituency that had left southern Ukraine almost five decades earlier. Perhaps it was a case of the opinions of a few prejudicing the many. As if all of this were not enough, another blow came from an unexpected source – Friesen's Ukrainian Mennonite constituency. It was probably more painful and personally humiliating than anything he had experienced up to this point.

Ironically, a crisis among potential emigrants in faraway Khortytsia threatened to undermine Friesen's role as a member of the Study Commission. Anarchy and civil war had devastated the Khortytsia district. Rampaging bands acting individually or under the banner of Nestor Makhno systematically ravaged the villages. The few surviving eyewitness reports from the period portray unimaginable carnage.[22] Little wonder that the Khortytsia inhabitants were assigned the highest priority in any potential emigration. The failure of the proposed 1922 exodus proved a crushing blow to the increasingly discouraged and destitute villagers. Few could comprehend the bureaucratic nightmare encountered by emigration leaders at every level of government. In addition, Ukrainian autonomy was being steadily eroded as Moscow consolidated its power. Janz, in a letter to North American colonization authorities, reflected the quandary of Mennonites in Ukraine when he wrote: "Must we send out new delegates? Seek new ways?"[23] It was more a cry of desperation than a vote of non-confidence in Friesen.

During the second half of 1922, B.B. Janz's letters abroad constantly warned of the growing impatience of potential emigrants. Little did he suspect that this restlessness would soon emerge as an organized revolt. Collective anxiety, private ambition, and a lack of information were possible catalysts in the movement. A letter signed by Johann P. Klassen, sculptor, noted that he had heard that the emigration committee (Study Commission) had collapsed and that the Americans were unwilling to help potential emigrants. A.A. Friesen, he felt, must resign his position. In a letter referring to a meeting scheduled for 5 February, Klassen stated that they planned to take the emigration into their own hands and elect two delegates to go abroad to find suitable land. "We are determined and will never give up."[24]

When Klassen presented his report to thirty-eight delegates gathered in Rosental, Khortytsia colony, on 5 February 1923 he not only advocated that a new delegation be sent abroad, but also urged the organization of an independent agency "to lead emigration matters locally." The resolution that was subsequently adopted stipulated that this group elect a representative who would work alongside the Union delegate in negotiations with the government. Naturally, the instigator of the movement, Klassen, was elected. He was to "immediately" travel to see B.B. Janz and go with him to Moscow to confer with A.R. Owen – the representative of the Canadian Pacific Railway in Moscow – to determine if he would negotiate directly with the Mennonite emigrants regarding settlements on CPR land.[25] Another motion proposed that Owen be invited to come south and confer directly with the group.[26] Ironically, many of the dissidents soon left for Canada during June and July 1923.

In April 1923, Janz wrote, "Brother Friesen can we allow these people to go to Mexico with a good conscience?" He was referring to both the Khortytsia dissidents as well as the potential emigrants barred from entering Canada because of medical problems. Janz then specifically addressed the Khortytsia situation:

> The Khortytsia emigrants have become very active. The movement is stalled. Now they take the initiative into their own hands. They call for an independent meeting of all emigrants after Easter, establish [their own] treasury and select a delegation of at least two [persons]. They are not ministers or businesspersons. ... They declare that there are possibilities abroad that in one way or another have to be discovered even without the help of the North American Mennonites.[27]

The movement was headed "by the former theologian and later artist Johann P. Klassen."[28] Janz expressed concern that "such anarchistic tendencies" threatened the entire emigration structure. One either has to deal and work with the [current] delegation (Study Commission) and decide whether the new one will be subordinate or work alongside it. Or do we have to start all over again?"[29] Would it mean the election of another delegate in addition to A.A. Friesen, "who [now] knows the land, the people, and the [prevailing] circumstances, and whom we know and work with."[30]

Meanwhile, Janz's associate Philip Cornies dialogued with the Americans P.H. Unruh and David Hofer, who were currently in Ukraine. Unruh also had lengthy discussions with Johann P. Klassen. These may have formed the background for the Union executive committee meeting in Schönwiese, Molochna on 26–7 April. In a subsequent letter, Janz reported that:

> The presence of the Americans Unruh and Hofer prevented serious misunderstandings with regard to the emigration question. A broad- based discussion and illumination of the issues calmed restless and dissatisfied elements. P.H. Unruh's official authorization to deal with emigration matters acted as a lightning rod deflecting [criticism] and preventing a serious split. This was the only way to deal with the problem.[31]

Janz's cursory summary of events belied a much more serious situation: the Union had appointed P.H. Unruh as its representative abroad in a hasty, ill-conceived action. It was an attempt to avoid a split in the emigration movement coupled with the rather naive hope that the presence of an American would generate emigration support in that country. The failure of the 1922 emigration raised the spectre of the collapse of the movement. Though no malice was intended, the action resulted in grave consequences.

The Union did not define Unruh's mandate nor did it delineate his relationship to A.A. Friesen, who already had years of knowledge and experience working with the Canadian Mennonite Board of Colonization. How would the American fit in with an emigration movement that was becoming exclusively Canadian? Furthermore, Unruh was an advocate of Russian Mennonite settlement in Mexico, not the United States. There was another issue that possibly complicated matters. In the United States, conflicts had erupted between church-related colleges and some of the leaders of the Mennonite Church. It involved the so-called "modernism" of some professors at Bethel College, an institution within P.H. Unruh's larger Mennonite constituency. While theological in part, the issue involved the cultural pressures exerted upon Mennonite communities throughout the United States. These forces, possibly accelerated by the First World War, involved the varied manifestations of fundamentalism, language transition, and clothing styles, as well as the role of advanced education. What was sometimes seen as theological heresy often related to the Mennonite communities' concern with rapid cultural shifts. It was perhaps easier to shout "modernism" than to deal with the painful reality of a shifting social order. As a Mennonite elder, Unruh may have confused social modernization with theological modernism.[32] Perhaps this was why A.A. Friesen became suspect in the eyes of Unruh. Friesen was by nature an academic. He was a very private individual, somewhat retiring and withdrawn. He was first and foremost an emigrant molded by a Russian and European environment seeking to understand his new world. In his North American travels he encountered a multitude of Mennonite peoplehoods that had little historical connection with his own roots. Even the Russian Mennonite emigrants of the 1870s and 1880s, buffeted by assimilation pressures, were not always comprehensible to Friesen. Now, thanks to the impulsive action of the Union, he was to work alongside a confident American church elder possibly concerned with "modernism." From Unruh's standpoint, might not this withdrawn Friesen be a foreign version of American Mennonite College teachers already under suspicion? P.H. Unruh, in a private conversation with David Toews early in 1923, called Friesen an unbeliever.[33]

In the end, Janz's assertion that this was "the only way to deal with the problem" raised more problems than it solved. Ironically, many of the malcontents left with the first Khortytsia group of 726 emigrants on 22 June. A second followed on 2 July, a third on 13 July, and the last group for 1923 on 24 July. Few of the Khortytsia emigrants ever realized what long-term damage their rebellion had caused. Viewed with the benefit of hindsight, the wrong person had been elected and the right person rejected. A.A. Friesen was explicit about his feelings when he wrote to B.B. Janz in Russia:

> I must say I had not expected this from the Molochna constituency. After all, they knew me well and knew what to expect from me. It never crossed my mind to leave my position. The results of my work may not be extraordinary but I can say with good conscience that I did what I could.[34]

His letter suggested that conversations with several of the newly arrived emigrants confirmed to him that he was no longer desired as a delegate. He wished he could have resigned under different circumstances. At this point, tensions within the CMBC apparently played no role in his 1923 departure. Friesen praised David Toews "who fearlessly defended me against all the opposition."[35] Friesen did not define the nature of that opposition. In all likelihood, it stemmed from opposition to the proposed emigration from some leaders of Russian Mennonite descent in the United States. At the moment, there was no hint of any tensions between him and David Toews. "I stayed on the board as a personal service to the man I learned to appreciate during difficult times."[36]

In a letter addressed to B.B. Janz, David Toews paid Friesen an extraordinary compliment:

> Now an issue of a more personal nature. Brother A.A. Friesen, the delegate from Russia, regards the new system of representation as a putdown on the part of the Russian Mennonites whom he has faithfully and sacrificially tried to serve. I want to refrain from judging the action of the Union but I believe that the interest of our Russian brothers with regards to the emigration could hardly be better served than by Friesen. Whatever [positive] has happened with regards to the emigration until now is mainly his accomplishment, both with regards to relief and emigration. The difficulties that confronted him in his work caused him great stress, yet he did not complain or stoop to the level of his opponents who tried to blacken his name. Those of us who have worked with him for a period of time have observed his dedication, faithfulness and capability. We are grieved that the people whom he served so faithfully no longer have confidence in him.[37]

In an effort to ease the tensions, B.B. Janz requested that H.B. Janz, a recent Canadian immigrant from Halbstadt, meet with Friesen in an effort to defuse any misunderstandings related to the action of the Union in appointing P.H. Unruh. Writing to Friesen, Janz indicated that the most significant differences had been clarified, yet he also felt there were personal issues that still needed to be resolved. In his dialogue with H.B. Janz, Friesen apparently held B.B. Janz personally responsible for some aspects of the Union fiasco. Janz wrote that, in thinking back, he could not recall any occasion where he held any personal grudges against Friesen. How he wished they could talk personally. Would the opportunity present itself in the new continent? Janz, who was now under constant surveillance by the secret police, wrote, "I'm not reluctant to speak openly today for I may not have a tomorrow."[38] Could they not reconcile their differences?

In Germany, B.H. Unruh was incensed at the news of P.H. Unruh's appointment as another union representative abroad. He felt it was a mistake to capitulate to Khortytsia's emigrant pressure. Apparently the terms for P.H. Unruh's mandate were not fixed and B.H. Unruh felt he had been granted authority equal to that of other Study Commission members. When B.H. Unruh and A.J. Fast met with P.H. Unruh in London, where they attempted to inform him about the current emigration structure, B.H. Unruh wondered whether his namesake would help or hinder the cause. "We had not elected him and could not un-elect him. We had to try and win him for our cause."[39] In the course of the consultation, B.H. Unruh felt constrained to defend Friesen against accusations emerging from American Mennonite circles that he was an unbeliever. Following the meeting, B.H. Unruh concluded that P.H. Unruh somehow felt restricted by his equal partnership with A.A. Friesen.

Following Friesen's resignation, Unruh in Germany urged continued cooperatione with P.H. Unruh. He was, after all, a very influential person in his American constituency. Should not the Union in Soviet Ukraine make cooperation with the Study Commission mandatory for Unruh and provide him with specific instructions?[40] B.H. Unruh observed that the copies of the correspondence sent by Friesen to P.H. Unruh revealed cordiality and no polemic of any kind. The situation in North America was, as Friesen informed Janz, somewhat different. "I have maintained a very superficial contact with P.H. Unruh. Any actual co-operation would not have been possible for the very reason that I was never convinced that Unruh would seriously support any emigration."[41] Speaking as a private person in 1924, he observed that, "the real opposition was more against the [emigration] cause than against me personally."[42]

There is little reason to doubt the sincerity of both Toews' and Friesen's reflections on the resignation. Friesen blamed it on the lack of confidence demonstrated by the Molochna constituency, but staunchly defended Toews as a friend in difficult times.[43] Toews, for his part, lauded Friesen's talent and dedication.[44] B.H. Unruh was not aware of any tension between them.

Following his resignation from the Study Commission, Friesen continued to work as the manager of the CMBC. Even though he no longer officially represented his constituency in the USSR he was still very much a contact person for the flow of immigrants now entering Canada. There were ongoing policy decisions related to emigrant settlement as well as the day to day crises associated with mass immigrant arrivals. All seemed to be well until Friesen, rather unexpectedly it would appear, submitted his resignation from the CMBC on 6 May 1926. In his brief letter of resignation, Friesen cited, "the necessity for providing better for my family" as the basic reason for his action.[45] As the weeks passed it became evident that there were other issues. He did not agree with David Toews on "general policies" nor on "methods of conducting the work" in the Rosthern office.[46] Others apparently agreed with him. B.H. Unruh observed that "strict organization and discipline" was essential in an operation the size of the emigration movement.[47] A letter addressed to Unruh some two months later was more direct. It lauded David Toews for his initiative and generosity but noted that he "lacks a practical business sense."[48]

It is possible that Friesen offered his resignation too hastily. In early June he had already been reflecting on how deeply he had been involved in the immigration work and mused whether "I should have had more patience."[49] Less than a month later he commented, "It is unfortunate that public spirited men devoting their time and energy for a good cause have to meet with so many unpleasant things."[50] Almost nine months after his resignation he reflected how most of the persons associated with the early emigration movement had been eliminated, how "certain persons" had too much influence, and that he still personally felt "acute bitterness."[51] Perhaps the letter was symptomatic of a drawn-out process that began with his resignation in the wake of his mounting frustration with CMBC administrative policies. He had experienced a deep personal hurt. Memory must have often taken him back to the painful events that separated him from his colleagues and in a broader sense from his sense of peoplehood; however exhausting and difficult his role in the Study Commission, the assignment brought with it the sense of being indispensable, which indeed he was. Then came the tension-laden success of the immigration to Canada where, associated with CMBC, he again played a crucial role. When he resigned, he became obsolete and soon forgotten. Perhaps he found it difficult to extinguish the lingering anger of being rejected at home in Canada and abroad in Soviet Ukraine. Mention of the CMBC seemed to trigger a litany of unresolved issues. Perhaps that is what happened in 1934 when *Der Bote* published what was in hindsight a frivolous article. The Mennonite newspaper, perhaps a bit short of reliable news, identified Rabbit Lake as the source of a ridiculous rumour.[52] Apparently, the Mennonite Brethren in the United States had given David Toews $60,000 to distribute among Brethren ministers in Canada. Even though Friesen requested clarification from Toews, public gossip as well as indiscreet CMBC members soon targeted Friesen as the source of the fabrication. Apparently, it was even recorded in board minutes. Friesen felt that David Toews made no serious effort to discredit the hearsay. In a long and bitter letter, he reiterated many painful memories and experiences, and reviewed, as he called it, "the history of our relationship."[53]

Friesen recounted his early role in the emigration movement. He visited American Mennonite congregations from Pennsylvania to California. Then, as a member of the Study Commission, he had helped to galvanize and centralize earlier relief efforts in the formation of the Mennonite Central Committee. In his attempt to arouse support for immigration in Canada he worked with H.H. Ewert of Gretna, Manitoba and the Mennonite Brethren representative H.H. Neufeld of Herbert, Saskatchewan. Friesen candidly pointed out that Toews, for whatever reason, did not participate in the preliminary work of the board. Yet when Toews, as the chairperson of the Canadian Mennonite Conference, finally joined the board, Friesen gave him the highest marks. He had confronted opponents of the movement, taken an enormous business risk, and used his public position to win support for the project. "I admired your courage. You were an instrument in the hand of God. I have always given you full credit for all of your efforts."[54]

Friesen then pointed out Toews's deficits: he had no sense for business and no practical experience in the field. Why then did he keep interfering? Where were all the funds he controlled distributed? Toews did not work systematically, was incapable of objectivity, and never listened to the opinions of others. He was ambitious, overbearing, and egotistical. But Friesen, too, admitted his faults. He was too impatient, sensitive, and exacting. Added to this was the fact that he was never very healthy. He was highly disciplined, thanks to his many years in school and the ten years he spent in a regular job. "You were the product of the schools of your day and I of the schools of my day."[55] In spite of that fact, Friesen felt they could have bridged their differences if Toews had been willing.

Though divergent personalities played a role in their dispute, Friesen pointed to major policy issues on which they had disagreed. One was the so-called B-bond affair, which involved the sale of first and second mortgages on lands, purchased from Sommerfeld and Khortytsia Mennonites in Manitoba for Russian Mennonite immigrants. In the end, thanks to a variety of factors, the second mortgage holders (B-bonds), most of whom were Amish and Mennonites in the United States and Ontario, lost their investment.[56] The promotion of the bonds involved H.H. Rogers of the Intercontinental Land Company, who in Friesen's judgment was "simply out for profit"[57] from gullible Mennonites. Friesen's verdict was straightforward: "You simply did not see through Rogers."[58] He reminded Toews that "I alone protested against the plan. You were not happy with me."[59] At the time of Friesen's letter, the B-bond issue had still not been entirely resolved.

Friesen had another policy disagreement with the chairperson of the CMBC. It related to the collection of the *Reiseschuld* (travel debt) owed to the CPR. Friesen had argued for the creation of a reserve fund for those unable or unwilling to pay their travel costs. From the very onset, Toews had been too generous with the *Reiseschuld* payments. He had returned the promissory notes to people when they paid their private debts without taking into account that it was a collective debt. Because no reserve fund existed and people felt they had paid their debt, the *Reiseschuld* crisis had intensified.

There were other policy questions. For a number of years the accounts of the board were never properly audited and in the end had to be audited by a special commission.[60] Friesen also felt that the board had dealt too leniently with immigrants. They had not behaved well: they arrived in Canada and avoided contact with their Canadian neighbours. The board should have assisted them in assimilating before public opinion moved against them.[61] It also failed to decisively intervene when it came to finding settlement sites for the newcomers who refused to settle on virgin land and demanded farms already under cultivation. That, Friesen felt, had been a grave error.[62] Throughout his tenure on the board, Toews all too often confused opposition against the cause with opposition against himself, and so accused his opponents of being agitators and naggers.[63]

The lengthy letter also dealt with the issue of Friesen's resignation. In the letters of late 1923 and 1924, he had cited the Russian-Mennonite constituency's loss of confidence in him as the main reason for his departure from the Study Commission. Thinking back as to why he left the CMBC in 1926, he became more personal and perhaps more honest. He had been unable to find a common working basis with Toews and so quietly resigned. He should have publicized his reasons. It "would have been a big fight but it would have clarified the issues."[64] Friesen then reviewed some bitter memories of his attempt to be reinstated. He had, after all, been secretary and general manager of the CMBC for a number of years. Toews could at least have been open with him by stating that there was no position for him. Instead, he pretended to look for a possible position for Friesen, who all the while was without employment. Why the board resisted rehiring a somewhat impetuous brother in dire straits is difficult to determine. Was it typical of Mennonite ecclesial politics to punish criticism by closing ranks and maintaining a code of silence? Yet, both before and after his resignation, Friesen did not publicly criticise Toews or the board. No other members of the board came to his aid because, as he saw it, "no one on the board dared to oppose you."[65] In 1927, Friesen became deathly ill with pneumonia. None of his former colleagues came to see him or cared about him, and "in the end a total stranger came to our aid."[66]

What was intended as an objective review becomes less so as the letter progresses. It does not appear to be a question of outright anger but rather a sense of a deep hurt distorting objectivity. On the surface, the lengthy letter details the causes of a broken relationship. On another level, it possibly reflects the agony of a man excluded from the community he once loved and served. Was it, in Mennonite terms, the case of a brother pushed out of the fold and subsequently shunned and forgotten? There is poignancy in the statement that an outsider came to his rescue at a time of crisis and illness.

David Toews responded to Friesen's letter at length. He reviewed some of the major issues related to immigration and addressed a number of fiscal matters raised by Friesen. The tone of the letter was defensive and personal and sought to address accusations that Toews deemed false. He rightfully saw his person under attack and responded vigorously. Reading the letter it appears that a decade had done little to heal old wounds, correct wrong perceptions, offer forgiveness, and seek reconciliation. No archival evidence seems to exist that suggests the differences were ever resolved. The contributions of both men were indispensable to the success of the Russian Mennonite emigration of the 1920s, yet they spent their last years in the same province alienated from one another.[67]

Some Reflections

A.A. Friesen was certainly accorded prominence in the Russian-Mennonite world of his day. His intellectual achievements placed him on the faculty of the Halbstadt College while his analytical and practical skills brought him to the notice of the 1917–18 German and Mennonite Congress movements in the Molochna. His election as chairperson of the Study Commission was certainly a vote of confidence by his Mennonite constituency. Unfortunately, few of his many talents had much significance in the North American setting. The Mennonite cultures he encountered were varied as to origin and traditions. Even his fellow Russian Mennonites who had emigrated in earlier years portrayed no uniformity. Friesen faced all of the disadvantages of an immigrant in a new land. There was much to process: the difficulty of understanding Mennonite diversity; the sense of being a stranger lacking definable status; and the varied internal politics within the diverse communities that he engaged, almost all of which challenged him to rethink what it meant to be Mennonite.

Above all, Friesen found himself promoting a cause that perilously divided the entire constituency. Battle-hardened veterans like David Toews, B.B. Janz, and B.H. Unruh seemed immune to the abundant criticism emerging from their constituencies. Friesen, the newcomer, fought what must have seemed a lonely battle. In all likelihood his inclusion in the CMBC provided a sense of security in a new land and a much needed income and operational base. He was not only a day-to-day participant in board activities, but also the lifeline for both the Russian and Ukrainian Unions. It was assumed that he would understand the various crises encountered by both groups and interpret these to the board. Simply put, he was central to the emigration drama, as anyone paging through the A.A. Friesen papers in the Mennonite Library and Archives quickly realizes. The CMBC files in the Mennonite Heritage Centre are equally convincing. He was always the objective analyst capable of providing the broader picture.

Friesen knew his own strengths and weaknesses. He acknowledged his shortcomings: his impatience, his preciseness, his over-concern with good organization, his capacity for anger, his sensitivity. The scientist in him demanded straightforwardness and honesty. As one of his daughters commented: "[W]hen we weighed a pound of shingle nails in the Rabbit Lake lumber yard it meant adding the very last shingle nail." This exacting A.A. Friesen probably spoke his mind in the board meetings. Maybe he did not fit well into a Canadian Mennonite diplomatic world, which at times was given to possible duplicity and para-messages.

Available documentation offers no conclusive insight into Friesen's resignation from the Study Commission. In his letters he cited the actions of his colleagues in faraway Russia as the primary reason for his decision. Subsequently, his conversations with recent emigrants confirmed his worst fears. Both B.B. Janz and B.H. Unruh found the move difficult to understand and for a time Unruh refused to publicize the resignation. In all likelihood, the resignation was the action of a man deeply hurt after he had given so much to his constituency. With regard to his resignation from the CMBC, Friesen himself later acknowledged that his decision was too hasty. In his lengthy letter to Toews he implied that he finally came to his senses and asked to be reinstated. That did not happen. Whether, as Friesen asserted, the issue related to the politics of one individual and a board intimidated by its chairperson is difficult to determine. It seems that he never again heard from his former colleagues until the 1930s episode. In this instance, as in the past, he had to defend his integrity and suppress false rumours. The true story of what happened within the board between Toews and Friesen may never be known. Apparently they never reconciled. Should the greater have come to the lesser?

The attitude of Mennonite newspapers in the United States must have puzzled Friesen. They publicized the plight of the Russian Mennonites even before the Study Commission had arrived in America. They were ardent in their appeals for relief funds, regularly carried reports of aid workers, and praised the generosity of their readers. Why, after David Toews signed his contract with the CPR, did an editor decide to criticise the plan without examining its content or determining the motives of the people involved? Why, as in the case of *Vorwärts*, were people like A.A. Friesen specifically targeted and exposed as incompetent to thousands of readers? There are no satisfactory answers to such questions.

In retrospect, it is obvious that Friesen's early efforts on behalf of emigration to North America set the stage for the ultimate success of the movement. Thanks to his travels in the United States, he became a primary catalyst in bringing together North American relief agencies. When Russian Mennonites wrote to "Dear Brother Friesen," they acknowledged their dependence and confidence in him. As Russian and Ukrainian Mennonite leaders plotted complex emigration strategies amid constantly shifting variables, Friesen supplied them with key information about developments in the United States and Canada. Apparently undaunted by the stress of his daily schedule, he wrote reports and letters which, when read today, reflect his extraordinary giftedness. The tragic news from his homeland, especially the letters of B.B. Janz, must have profoundly affected his innermost feelings. Yet personal feelings – whether they related to his homeland, job or private life – rarely interfered with his ability to remain objective and identify key issues during his tenure with the board. Ironically, when he abruptly resigned in 1923, he had virtually fulfilled the mandate granted him in 1919 by his Russian Mennonite constituency.

If Russian Mennonite emigrants of the 1920s had been asked to cite the men most responsible for their presence in Canada, David Toews and B.B. Janz would likely be named. Fewer would have mentioned B.H. Unruh in Germany or A.A. Friesen in Canada. Subsequently, Unruh's long service to the Mennonite constituency during the flight to Moscow in 1929, as well as his concern for refugees in the wake of the Second World War guaranteed him a well-deserved place among Russian Mennonite heroes of the twentieth century. By contrast, Friesen's appearance on the Mennonite landscape was brief and, for some, enigmatic. From the outset he challenged Russian Mennonites to rethink who they had been and who they now wanted to be as they entered a new land. His observations of co-religionists in both North America and the former Russian Empire raised important issues of faith and religious identity amidst fierce pressures to accommodate. And his determination to urge disparate Mennonite organizations to unite for a common cause helped to found the Mennonite Central Committee, whose legacy would long outlast his own life.

There are two monuments erected to the emigration leaders of the 1920s in Rosthern, Saskatchewan and Coaldale, Alberta. Perhaps a third is needed in the cemetery at Rabbit Lake.[68]

NOTES

1 The Canadian Mennonite Board of Colonization was founded in 1922 as in inter-Mennonite organization dedicated to the immigration and resettlement of Mennonites fleeing the Bolshevik Revolution.

In 1960, the board merged with the Mennonite Central Relief Committee, founded in 1940 in response to relief need in Europe. The new organization was called the Canadian Mennonite Relief and Immigration Council. The CMBC records are housed at the Mennonite Heritage Centre in Winnipeg, Canada.

The A.A. Friesen Collection, thanks to the efforts of that indefatigable collector, Cornelius Krahn, was given to the Mennonite Library and Archives in North Newton, Kansas. Duplicate letters may exist in the collections. The ones cited are the ones available to me. All references will use the abbreviations CMBC and AAF. There is a rich extant literature on Mennonite emigration from the Soviet Union and resettlement in North America, including Frank H. Epp, *Mennonite Exodus: The Rescue and Resettlement of the Russian Mennonites since the Communist Revolution* (Altona: D.W. Friesen, 1962); Frank H. Epp, *Mennonites in Canada, 1920–1940: A People's Struggle for Survival* (Toronto: Macmillan, 1982); Paul Toews, *Mennonites in American Society, 1930–1970: Modernity and the Persistence of Religious Community* (Scottdale: Herald Press, 1966); Helmut Harder, *David Toews Was Here: 1870–1947* (Winnipeg: CMBC Publications, 2002); Esther Epp-Thiessen, *J.J. Thiessen: A Leader for His Time* (Winnipeg: CMBC Publications, 2001; and John B. Toews, *Lost Fatherland: The Story of the Mennonite Emigration from South Russia* (Scottdale: Herald Press, 1967).

2 Autobiographical material in possession of his daughter, Helene Wieler, Kelowna, B.C.

3 "Congress of Representatives of the German settlements of Katerynoslav Province and the Three Northern Districts of Tavrida province held in Prischib on May, 14, 1918" (Peter F. Braun Russian Mennonite Archive. Microfilm copy in the archives of the Mennonite Historical Society of B.C., Abbotsford, B.C., file 3606). The minutes of the Second All-Mennonite Congress can also be found in the Braun Archive, file 3607. A.A. Friesen kept a diary of the Study Commission's rather perilous journey out of Ukraine. Thanks to the rapid inflation of the ruble, its members often lacked funds for travel and accommodation. A copy of the diary is in the possession of Helene Wieler, Kelowna, BC.

4 Ibid. The Friesen files in North Newton, Kansas, contain a number of letters detailing locations visited and contacts made by Unruh and Friesen. In a letter dated 7 July 1920, the two write: "it would be advisable, in our opinion, if all the groups of Mennonites would join hands in the work and engage in this relief work unitedly." A few weeks later Friesen figured prominently at the Joint Meeting of Mennonite Relief Committees held in Elkhart, Indiana, on 27–8 July 1920. His presentations on both the questions of relief and emigration constituted the central agenda of what now emerged as the Mennonite Central Committee. Additional information on the activity of the Study Commission can be found in: A. Friesen to B.H. Unruh, Hillsboro, Kansas, 30 July 1920; A. Friesen to Dr S.K. Mosiman, 21 July 1920. In the Friesen collection there is also an undated document detailing his many travels in Canada, Mexico, and the USA. The total: 27,747 miles (44,654 kilometres).

5 A.A. Friesen to "Liebe Maria," 6 August 1920 (Letter in possession of Helene Wieler, Kelowna, BC).

6 Ibid.

7 A.A. Friesen to "Liebe Maria," 8 October 1921 (Letter in possession of Helene Wieler, Kelowna, BC).

8 Elva Krehbiel Leisy, "Henry Peter Krehbiel (1862–1946)," *Mennonite Life*, 1X, no. 4 (1954): 162–6.

9 A.A. Friesen, "Alt-Mexico als Siedlungsgebiet fuer Mennoniten," *Vorwärts*, X1X, no. 7 (18 February 1921): 9. See also AAF, A.A. Friesen to Johann Willms (Halbstadt, Taurida), Hillsboro, Kansas, 22 February 1921. He noted that if Mennonites went to Mexico, they had the option of living in a closed or open culture, each with its consequences. In a later, rather personal letter to B.H. Unruh, Friesen rightly credits the Study Commission with obtaining relief supplies for starving Mennonites but is discouraged by the disunity among North American Mennonites. Amid the broad-ranging report a poignant sentence: "I am concerned about my daily bread and have difficulty obtaining it." AAF, A.A. Friesen to B.H. Unruh, Bluffton, Ohio, 15 December 1921.

10 AAF, A.A. Friesen, "Betrachtungen ueber die gegenwaertige Lage der Mennoniten in Russland und die Aussichten fuer eine Auswanderung." All subsequent quotations are from this document.

11 See, for example, some of the documents preserved in the A.A. Friesen Collection. K. Wiens, "Zur Auswanderungsfrage der Mennoniten," 20 June 1922; P.B., "Einige Gedanken zur Auswanderungsfrage," 21 June 1922; H. Janz, "Warum ich auswandere," 21 June 1922; J. Janzen,"Meine principelle Stellung zur Auswanderungsfrage," 22 June 1922.

12 On the founding of the CMBC, see Frank H. Epp's excellent coverage in his *Mennonite Exodus* (Altona, MB: D.W. Friesen and Sons, 1962), 72–6.
13 AAF, "Bundesrat … to Studienkomission," undated (April or May, 1921?).
14 AAF, A.A. Friesen "An den Mennonitschen Bundesrat des noerdlichen Kaukaus des Stawropoler Gouv und des Don-Gebietes," (Philadelphia, PA: 19 August 1921).
15 CMBC, Jacob J. Hildebrand to A.A. Friesen, Novo-Omsk, 22 December 1922; 19 January 1923; 13 March 1923. P. Toews to A.A. Friesen, Moskalenko, Siberia, 27 January 1923. Jacob J. Hildebrand and Peter Toews were sent to Moscow to explore emigration possibilities. In short order, two lists containing 707 and 426 names were prepared for possible emigration to Paraguay. They had heard of the Paraguayan Congress decree no. 514 guaranteeing Mennonite rights and privileges and sent their lists to the Paraguayan consulate in Berlin. What information could Friesen provide? In his reply Friesen cited his concerns about Paraguay, even anticipating the possibility of a future border conflict with Bolivia. He dismissed as hopeless Hildebrand's suggestion that perhaps a neutral Mennonite state could be established somewhere. As he repeatedly stated in his reports and correspondence, modern states were assimilationist. CMBC, A.A. Friesen to J. J. Hildebrand, 29 January 1923; 6 April 1923; 17 April 1923.
16 CMBC, A.A. Friesen to H. H. Schroeder, 31 May 1921; 27 June 1921; 19 August 1921; 30 December 1921.
17 *Vorwärts* 20, no. 37 (15 September 1922): 4.
18 Epp, *Mennonite Exodus*, 119–36.
19 *Der Zionsbote*, XXXIX (18 October 1922): 5.
20 "Ein Wort zur Aufklaerung," *Vorwärts* 20, no. 49 (8 December 1922). Toews' defense was reprinted in *Vorwärts*, 20, no. 46 (17 November 1922).
21 A.L. Schellenberg, "Ein Wort ueber die Kolonisationsarbeit in Canada," *Vorwärts* 21, no. 1 (5 January 1923): 1.
22 For example, see the personalized account of B. Schellenberg, "Khortytsia, August, 1919," *Friedensstimme* XV11, no. 32 (7 September 1919): 3–4; "Report from Kitschkas "*Friedensstimme* XV11, no. 34 (14 September 1919): 2–4; Roland, "During the Civil War in the Old Colony 1918–1920," (manuscript in possession of the Mennonitsche Forschungstelle, Weierhof, Germany). A report submitted to American Mennonite Relief representative Alvin Miller by a Heinrich J. Braun contains some sobering statistics especially with regard to the typhus epidemic (Levi Mumaw Papers, IX–1-1–9, Mennonite Historical Library, Goshen, Indiana).
23 AAF, B.B. Janz to the Mennonite Colonization Association of North America and the Mennonite Executive Committee of Colonization, 22/23 January 1923.

24 AAF, Johann Klassen to Mr. Neufeld, 1 February 1923.
25 AAF, "Protokoll der Vertreter-Versammlung saemtlicher Auswanderer der alten Kolonie in Rosental am 5ten February, 1923."
26 Ibid. In April, the same group elected its own delegation to America as well as their own representatives for Ukraine. B.B. Janz papers (Centre for Mennonite Brethren Studies, Winnipeg, Manitoba), "Memoirs," Protokoll der Sitzung der Vertreter der Emigranten des Chortitzer Rayons in Rosental am 10 April 1923.
27 AAF, B.B. Janz to the MCA and MECC, 16 April 1923.
28 Ibid.
29 Ibid.
30 Ibid.
31 AAF, B.B. Janz to the *Studienkomission*, 24 May 1923. The April 1923 minutes of the Union executive council noted that "the [emigration] problem currently lies in America not Russia. It is rooted in the disputes surrounding this question in America. This necessitates that the administration undertakes new steps in order to facilitate a quick and satisfactory solution to the problem. In the opinion of the administration Mr. Unruh of Newton, Kansas, should be encouraged to use his influence on his home churches to facilitate this matter. For this purpose the administration grants him a mandate [to act on behalf of the Union.] The council also instructs the chairperson (B.B. Janz) to contact A.A. Friesen in order to clarify and regulate the question of representation in America." Minutes of the Executive Council Meeting of the Union of Citizens of Dutch Lineage in Ukraine held at Schönwiese, 26–7 April 1923 (State Archive of the Russian Federation, A-123, I-1, F 2).
32 Helpful references on this subject include James C. Juhnke, *A People of Two Kingdoms: The Political Acculturation of the Kansas Mennonites* (Newton, KS; Faith and Life Press, 1975). Paul Toews, "Fundamentalist Conflict in Mennonite Colleges: A Response to Cultural transitions?" *Mennonite Quarterly Review* LV11, no. 3 (July 1983): 241–56.
33 CMBC, David Toews, "Memoirs," 19. When Friesen's daughter Neti wrote to her father regarding her personal crises prior to baptism, he responded with what might be the only faith declaration he ever committed to paper. She apparently wondered about unanswered questions left by her studies in science and philosophy. His response:

> In my younger years I more or less walked the same pathway you did but I had no one who had walked that way ahead of me, who could provide some direction, I have long since come to the conclusion, as have

> many before me, that no conflict exists between knowledge and religion. The two disciplines stand along side one another. The one touches the realm of the mind while faith is intuition, that innermost ability to discern realities hidden to the senses and to logical thought. The basis of religion is a personal encounter with God, the constant communication with God through prayer and the application of insights so derived in everyday life. In the final analysis, the accumulation of dogmas and various church practices are the products of human effort and not of crucial importance. I have never been an advocate of any specific denomination, but I see no particular reason why I should prefer another denomination above my own. … I am sending you, as my eldest daughter, the Bible your mother gave to me. Honour it in memory of her.

A.A. Friesen to "Liebe Neti," Rabbit Lake, Saskatchewan, 20 January 1942 (A.A. Friesen Duplicate letter Collection Mennonite Historical Society of British Columbia).

34 CMBC, A.A. Friesen to B.B. Janz, 11 April 1924. As late as October 1923, the Union executive noted that A.A. Friesen was "... looked upon as the representative of the Union in emigration matters," and that they desired "that all issues related to emigration be regulated ... with Union representatives A.A. Friesen and B.H. Unruh." Minutes of the Council Meeting of the Union of Citizens of Dutch Lineage in Ukraine held in Schoenwiese on 3 October 1923 (General Archive of the Russian Federation, A-423, J-1, F2).

35 CMBC, A.A. Friesen to B.B. Janz, 11 April 1924.

36 Ibid.

37 CMBC, David Toews to B.B. Janz, 22 September 1923.

38 CMBC, B.B. Janz to A.A. Friesen, 17 November 1924.

39 AAF, B.H. Unruh, "Zur Orientierung," 6 February 1924, 5.

40 Ibid., 6–7.

41 CMBC, A.A. Friesen to B.B. Janz, 11 April 1924. In the correspondence there are muted references to P.H. Unruh's opposition to Russian Mennonite emigration to the United States as well as his relationship with A.A. Friesen. One letter explains the American reluctance this way: "I think that the U.S. Mennonites should help the immigrants in Canada some[what] for a start but you know how hard it is to arouse sympathy when it touches the pocket book." AAF, G.G. Hiebert to A.A. Friesen, Long Beach, California, 19 March 1925.

42 CMBC, A.A. Friesen to B.B. Janz, 11 April 1924.

43 Ibid.

44 CMBC, David Toews to B.B. Janz, 22 September 1923. On David Toews, see Harder, *David Toews Was Here.* In this detailed study Harder portrays the many complexities facing the emigration movement in Canada as well as the enormous personal burdens it imposed on Toews.
45 AAF, A.A. Friesen to David Toews, 6 May 1926.
46 AAF, A.A. Friesen to Col. J.S. Dennis, 28 May 1926.
47 AAF, B.H. Unruh, "Fuer mein Privatearchiv," 9 June 1926.
48 AAF, C.H. Warkentin to B.H. Unruh, 16 August 1926.
49 AAF, A.A. Friesen to J.J. Klassen, 9 June 1926.
50 AAF, A.A. Friesen to G.G. Hiebert, 5 July 1926.
51 AAF, A.A. Friesen to Gerhard Ens, 16 February 1927.
52 D.H. Epp, "Sitzung der Canadian Mennonite Board of Colonization," *Der Bote* 11, no. 32 (8 August 1934), 1. The article spoke of rumours "which bring discredit to the Board" and then noted, "it was mentioned that this rumor spread from Rabbit Lake and the surrounding region." Friesen was the only person in Rabbit Lake that had an obvious connection with the Board. Somewhat unwisely, David Toews again raised the issue when he reported to *Der Bote* that he had investigated the rumour while at a church dedication in Mayfair and found that very few settlers in the region were associated with it. Others denied being connected with it. David Toews, "Eine Erklaerung," *Der Bote* 11, no. 36 (5 September 1934), 3. Toews stated that the slander (Klatscherei) was "directed against me personally." Readers familiar with the situation would have thought of A.A. Friesen. Little wonder he lashed out in his lengthy letter.
53 A.A. Friesen to David Toews, Rabbit Lake, Saskatchewan, April 1935 (manuscript in possession of Helene Wieler, Kelowna, BC).
54 Ibid., 7.
55 Ibid., 12.
56 Epp, *Mennonite Exodus*, 301–4.
57 Friesen to Toews, April 1935, 15.
58 Ibid.
59 Ibid., 16.
60 Ibid., 22–3.
61 Ibid., 24.
62 Ibid., 25.
63 Ibid., 28–9.
64 Ibid., 18.
65 Ibid., 23.
66 Ibid., 21. Harder's study of David Toews finds it difficult to explain the tension between the two men. He cites minor irritants: smoking in the

office; Toews' apparent disregard of a requested salary increase; Friesen's occasional overbearing manner when dealing with clients; finally, his reluctance to clarify his resignation. Harder, *David Toews Was Here*, 150–1.

67 AAF, D. Toews to A.A. Friesen, 29 April 1935.

68 There was naturally a lengthy sequel to Friesen's resignation from the CMBC and his move to Rabbit Lake, Saskatchewan. The relocation removed him from most issues related to immigration and resettlement and to a degree from the larger Mennonite world. Yet long hours of work in the lumberyard did not deter him from broad reading, letter writing, and activity in the local community. At times he reflected on the dilemma of the educated Mennonite living amid an uneducated congregation, the possibility of dairying in the Rabbit Lake district, recent political trends in Germany, or a brother-in-law in Winnipeg attracted by the promises of National Socialism. (See the letters in the AAF collection dated 13 April 1939; 16 April 1939; 6 October 1939; 7 December 1927; 10 June 1939.) His last letter to friend B.H. Unruh noted "in the business I am manager, clerk, accountant, correspondent etc. – all in one person." He continued, "I am treasurer in the congregation, head of the School Board, president of the local Chamber of Commerce, the local representative of the Federal Meteorological Service, president of the local Liberal Party etc." AAF, A.A. Friesen to B.H. Unruh, 2 September 1948. He observed wryly that these were all honorary positions with no remuneration.

PART FOUR

Mennonite Identities in the Soviet Cauldron

7 Collectivizing the *Mutter Ansiedlungen*: The Role of Mennonites in Organizing Kolkhozy in the Khortytsia and Molochansk German National Districts in Ukraine in the Late 1920s and Early 1930s

COLIN P. NEUFELDT[1]

Introduction

The opening of former Soviet archives has significantly broadened our understanding of Soviet collectivization and dekulakization in the late 1920s and early 1930s, but the collectivization experiences of many ethno-religious minority groups have not yet been investigated to any great extent. A case in point is the collectivization experience of the Soviet Mennonite community, which few historians have examined using Soviet archival resources.[2] As a result, little is known about how Mennonite communities were collectivized, what role Mennonites played in the collectivization of their villages, or how Mennonites participated in the administration of newly established kolkhozy (collective farms; *kolhospy* in Ukrainian).[3] This chapter will address some of these questions by examining the collectivization of the two Mennonite *Mutter Ansiedlungen* (mother settlements) in Ukraine: Khortytsia in the German national *raion* (district) of Khortytsia (near Zaporizhzhia along the Dnipro River) and Molochna in the German national raion of Molochansk (along the Molochna River northeast of Melitopol').[4] More specifically, this chapter will focus on how these communities responded to the government's collectivization campaign in the late 1920s and early 1930s. It was in this chaotic environment that the Stalinist regime forced Mennonites in Ukraine to abandon many of their economic, political, religious, and social institutions and traditions, and to redefine themselves as Soviet kolkhozniki (kolkhoz members).

Collectivizing the Soviet Countryside

The collectivization of Khortytsia and Molochna did not occur in a vacuum, but on the heels of a Soviet government decision in the late 1920s to forcibly collectivize the major grain-producing regions of the USSR. In 1927–8 the Soviet leadership was on the brink of embarking on an ambitious program to industrialize the country. It intended to finance industrialization by exporting peasant grain sold to the state at below-market prices. Few peasants, however, were interested in making this kind of sacrifice. The Soviet peasantry was still reeling from the devastation and destruction of the First World War, the 1917 revolutions, the Russian civil war, war communism, and the disastrous famine of 1921–2. The Bolshevik introduction of the New Economic Policy (NEP) in 1921–2 helped to facilitate the recovery of the Russian economy and agriculture, but it was not until 1926 that agricultural production reached pre–First World War levels. When rumours began to circulate in late 1926 that capitalist countries were planning to invade the USSR, the peasants feared the return of food requisitioning and began hoarding grain. Although many of the rumours were unfounded, the Stalinist faction in the Soviet leadership characterized the war scare and the sharp decline in peasant grain sales as a national crisis. At the Fifteenth Party Congress in December 1927, Stalin claimed that the grain crisis had become so dire that repressive administrative measures in the Soviet countryside were required to ensure the regular delivery of peasant grain to the state and safeguard the country's long-term industrialization.[5]

The Soviet leadership introduced the first administrative measures in early 1928 when it implemented *chrezvychaishchina* – extraordinary measures that included new taxes and forced grain procurements to extract money and grain from the countryside. Initially, chrezvychaishchina targeted enemies of the regime, such as kulaks (i.e., more industrious peasants, who were sometimes called *ekspertniki* [experts] in Ukraine) and *byvshie liudi* (former people, such as former members of the landowning classes, factory owners, industrialists, clergy, tsarist police officers, and White Army participants). It did not take long, however, before the repressive measures of chrezvychaishchina began to affect *seredniaki* (middle peasants) and even the traditional allies of the Bolsheviks – the *bedniaki* (poor peasants) and the *batraki* (landless agricultural workers). At the same time, the government ordered the OGPU (a branch of the state political police that operated from 1923 to 1934) to arrest private grain traders and kulaks, heightening the terror in the countryside; by April 1928, nearly 16,000 individuals were in police custody in the USSR.[6] Although some Bolshevik leaders complained that Stalin's approach was too extreme and reckless, his will prevailed; by the end of 1928, administrative measures and force, not the marketplace, were dictatating the economy of the Soviet countryside.[7]

Government repression against the kulaks intensified in 1929. In late spring the government initiated the Ural-Siberian Method (USM), which required bedniaki and seredniaki in each village to assign grain procurement quotas to each village household, with kulak households required to supply the lion's share of grain deliveries to the state. The USM pitted poorer peasants against richer peasants, and quickly incited class antagonism and divisions in the villages. Kulaks who did not meet their quotas were penalized with the *piatkratka*, a fine five times the monetary value of the grain assessment. Those who failed to pay the piatkratka had their property confiscated and were sentenced to forced labour under article 61 of the Criminal Code.[8]

In late December 1929, Stalin announced that the nation's kulaks must be "liquidated as a class."[9] A month later the politburo issued a secret decree entitled *Concerning Measures for the Liquidation of Kulak Farms in Raions of Wholesale Collectivization* (hereafter "the Politburo Decree"). Issued on 30 January 1930, the Politburo Decree stipulated that 3 to 5 per cent of the peasantry were kulaks, who either had to be resettled or executed. Stalin's announcement and the Politburo Decree gave local officials carte blanche to "dekulakize" the Soviet peasantry en masse. By March 1930, thousands of kulak households had been disenfranchised, dispossessed of their property, arrested, and transported to newly established special settlements in the northern and eastern territories of the USSR. The special settlements were organized by the OGPU and ultimately became the foundation for Stalin's GUITLTP (later renamed GULAG), the administrative department that oversaw the country's vast network of forced labour camps. By the end of 1931, more than 1.8 million kulaks and state enemies had been exiled.[10]

The attack against the kulaks was vital to the government's efforts to collectivize Soviet agriculture and create the first socialist state in history. Soviet leaders were convinced that collectivizing individual peasant farms into sovkhozy (state farms) and kolkhozy would not only solve the country's perennial grain crisis, but also provide secure, predictable, and increasing amounts of food for the urban populations, agricultural materials for industry, and agricultural goods for export, all of which would subsidize and ensure the success of the nation's industrialization program. But collectivization held little appeal for the peasantry, and sovkhozy and kolkhozy contributed a mere 2.2 per cent of the gross farm production of the USSR in the mid-1920s.[11] It was only after dekulakization was initiated in the late 1920s and widespread terror pervaded the countryside that bedniaki, batraki, and seredniaki joined kolkhozy en masse. In 1929 the Soviet leadership predicted that 85 per cent of peasant households would be collectivized by 1934. In time, Soviet leaders reasoned, the peasants would be grateful that they had joined the kolkhozy, especially when the government increased the flow of industrial goods, tractors, and agricultural equipment to the kolkhozy.[12]

As 1929 drew to a close, Stalin announced that 1929 had proven to be "the year of the great turn" in the country's labour productivity, industrialization efforts, and agricultural development. He boasted that the peasants were flocking to kolkhozy "by whole villages, volosts and districts," and that the remarkable growth in the sovkhoz and kolkhoz movement had enabled the country to emerge from the grain crisis. At the Central Committee Plenum held in November 1929, the Soviet leadership demanded that entire villages and raiony in grain-producing regions be collectivized within "an historically minimum period," preferably by the spring of 1930.[13] On 5 January 1930, the Central Committee issued a decree calling on supporters to "replace large-scale kulak production with large-scale collective-farm production" and to complete the collectivization of major grain producing areas by 1930–1. To speed up the collectivization process, the Central Committee dispatched OGPU officials and the "25,000ers" (more than 27,000 factory workers, party members, Red Army soldiers and Komsomol members) to infiltrate the countryside and compel bedniaki, batraki, and seredniaki to join the kolkhozy and participate in large-scale socialist production.[14]

All of these efforts resulted in spectacular collectivization statistics: in the last three months of 1929, 3 million peasant households joined kolkhozy; nearly 10 million had joined by February 1930 and in the one-month period between 20 January and 20 February 1930, the percentage of collectivized households in the USSR climbed from 21.6 to 52.7 per cent. In Ukraine, 60.8 per cent of peasants were in kolkhozy by 1 March 1930.[15] These impressive percentages, however, belied the disorganization and chaos that pervaded most newly established kolkhozy. In addition to their failure to provide adequate resources, direction, and leadership to newly established kolkhozy, Soviet leaders were also unclear about the size, supervision, and organizational structure of the kolkhozy during the initial formation phase, with some leaders still demanding that kolkhozy operate as "giant, fully socialized enterprises" modelled on state-owned factories that employed wage labour and were led by chairmen who served as "plant managers."[16]

In an effort to resolve these issues, the government established Narkomzem (People's Commissariat of Agriculture) and Kolkhoztsentr (All-Union Centre of Agricultural Collectives) to supervise the organization and operation of kolkhozy. The government also decided that three different types of kolkhozy would be permitted in the countryside: the association for joint cultivation of land (commonly referred to as "TOZ" or "SOZ"), the artel, and the commune. The organizational structure and operation of TOZy, artels, and communes varied considerably from region to region, but what fundamentally distinguished these three types of kolkhozy from one another was the degree to which the means of production in each type of kolkhoz was socialized. The government viewed the TOZ as the lowest form of socialist production. The land in a TOZ was worked in common by all kolkhozniki and most of the larger agricultural equipment was owned collectively, but all of the animals and most of the smaller agricultural implements remained in the personal possession of the individual members. In an artel, on the other hand, each household was entitled to keep a small plot of land for personal use, but the remaining arable land was held and worked in common. The draft animals and agricultural implements were owned collectively, but each individual artel household was allowed to have a small agricultural enterprise (e.g., a few bee hives or a small egg operation) for personal use. In January 1930, the Central Committee confirmed that the artel would serve as the most common form of kolkhozy, at least for the foreseeable future. The commune, however, was regarded as the highest form of socialist production: all the land in a commune was worked collectively; all animals, machinery, and farm buildings were owned in common; and commune members often shared living quarters and ate their meals together.[17] The government published *Model Statutes* in February and March 1930 which explained how to incorporate and operate these different types of kolkhozy.

In February 1930, just as dekulakization and collectivization were proceeding at maniacal speed, the Soviet leadership began to have second thoughts about the pace of these campaigns; some leaders were especially concerned that the campaigns might have disastrous consequences for the upcoming crop year and result in a shortage of workers to complete the spring sowing, harvest, and fall fieldwork. Stalin announced his decision to suspend these campaigns in an article entitled "Dizzy with Success" published in *Pravda* on 2 March 1930.[18] Stalin acknowledged that the country had made great strides in collectivization, but he also chided local party and government officials for using excessive force in their dekulakization efforts, becoming "dizzy with success" and thereby endangering collectivization. Not surprisingly, "Dizzy with Success" aroused disbelief, anger, and frustration among lower-level officials, who were the scapegoats for the leadership's excesses. The article also resulted in celebrations and riots, as many peasants interpreted Stalin's article as permission to leave the kolkhozy. Within weeks, 8 million households had quit the kolkhozy and returned to their farms with some 7 million draft animals. By April 1930, the nation's collectivization rates had plummeted to 37.3 per cent, demonstrating that many kolkhozy were nothing more than "paper collectives" with little peasant support.[19]

"Dizzy with Success" signalled the government's retreat from, but not abandonment of, full-scale collectivization. The government made it clear at the Sixteenth Party Congress in June–July 1930 that collectivization was still on its agenda, and in the late summer of 1930 it initiated a new collectivization drive after much of the harvest was off the fields. The Soviet leadership also announced that all kolkhozy were required to deliver their tractors and farm machinery to the newly established *mashino-traktornaya stantsiya* (machine tractor stations or MTS), which would now provide tractor and other technical services to kolkhozy. The politburo also reimplemented repressive measures (including high taxes and grain quotas) in the countryside to compel peasants to move back to the kolkhozy, and predicted that 65 to 70 per cent of households in the main grain-producing areas would be collectivized by the fall of 1931.[20]

The government's collectivization efforts once again produced significant results. By the end of 1930 the total number of collectivized households reached 6.6 million, with some 113,000 kolkhozy in operation. To ensure that this latest collectivization drive lost no momentum, Kolkhoztsentr dispatched "20,000ers" into the countryside in late December 1930. Inspired by the 25,000ers, the 20,000ers were experienced collective farmers who were ordered to spur on collectivization efforts in more "backward" villages. Their efforts and those of other government bodies proved very successful. More than six million households joined kolkhozy in the first four months of 1931; by mid May, the total number of collectivized households had reached 12.5 million (50.4 per cent) – almost the same number of households that were in collective farms on the eve of the publication of "Dizzy with Success" in March 1930.[21]

This second collectivization drive continued until August 1931, when the politburo made the following announcement: "[T]he measure of the completion of collectivization in the main in a particular district or region is not the obligatory inclusion of all 100 percent of poor- and middle-peasant households, but the recruitment for the kolkhozy of at least 68–70 percent of peasant households and at least 75–80 percent of the area sown by peasant households."[22] The announcement signalled a period of consolidation for collectivization, but under no circumstances would there be any reversal in the gains that had been achieved. In fact, during the last four months of 1931 another 1.2 million peasants joined kolkhozy, increasing the total percentage of collectivized household from 57.7 to 62.5 per cent.[23] At the end of 1931, Kolkhoztsentr confidently reported that the "overwhelming majority of districts in the Soviet Union have been involved in comprehensive collectivization, and in a very large proportion of them comprehensive collectivization may be considered completed in the main."[24]

Collectivizing Khortytsia and Molochna

With settlements in some of the most fertile grain-producing regions of Ukraine, the Mennonite community experienced the full force of Soviet collectivization. Numbering just over 56,800 in 1925, the Mennonites lived in settlements scattered across southern Ukraine, but the majority lived in the former Mennonite colonies of Khortytsia and Molochna (Molotschna).[25] The Mennonite communities in Ukraine had had an uneasy relationship with the Soviet regime ever since its inception. As Bobyleva explains in her contribution to this volume, many Mennonites blamed the Bolshevik regime for the destruction of their communities during the civil war and the 1921–2 famine. In the opinion of the Bolsheviks, the Mennonite community was a German-speaking, isolationist, ethno-religious sect whose members had participated in counter-revolutionary activities: the Mennonites had enthusiastically welcomed the German Army occupation forces into their villages in the final months of the First World War, supported the counter-revolutionary White Army during the civil war, and organized *Selbstschutz* (self-defence) units to defend themselves against attacks by anarchists and the Red Army. This anti-Bolshevik behaviour was a convenient justification for the government's seizure of large tracts of Mennonite farm land in 1921 and its subsequent redistribution to landless Ukrainian and Russian peasants.[26]

In these difficult circumstances, Mennonites recognized the necessity of developing a mutually beneficial relationship with Soviet authorities. Even before the end of the civil war, an increasing number of Mennonites had sought positions within nascent Soviet institutions at the village, *volost* (small district; later referred to as raion) and *guberniia* (province; later referred to as oblast) levels. By 1920–1, for example, a large number of Mennonites in the Khortytsia settlement found employment in the following soviet institutions in their villages and the Khortytsia raion: *komnezama/kombedy* (committee of the village poor or CVP), *ispolkom* (executive committee), *otdel upravleniya* (administration department), *zemlya otdel* (land department), *prodkom* (food provisions commission), *nalog komissiya* (tax commission), *narodnye zasedateli* (peoples' assessors at the Peoples' courts), *truda otdel* (mandatory labour department), *narobraz* (commissariat for education), *revkom* (revolutionary military commission), and *voenkomat* (military commissariat). Several Khortytsia Mennonites, including Peter J. Berg, were appointed to serve in the *gubispolkom* (provincial executive committee) and *gubkomnezam* (provincial committee of the village poor) in the early 1920s where their decisions and actions affected tens of thousands of inhabitants living in the Zaporizhzhia region.[27]

During the early years of Soviet rule, Mennonite peasants from Khortytsia and Molochna also showed their support for the regime by participating in nascent government attempts to establish collective farming operations in the countryside. By 1921–2, for example, Mennonite bedniaki, batraki, and workers helped to establish and operate a number of artels in the Khortytsia raion, including the Druzhba artel in Kanzerovka, Uniya artel in Khortytsia/Kanzerovka, the Vosxhod artel in Kanzerovka, Novaya Zhizn artel in Nieder Khortytsia, Rabnik artel in Nieder-Khortytsia, and Groza artel in Pavlovka (Osterwick). Many of these artels were small (between five and twenty households), but were often populated largely by Mennonites. During the height of the famine in January/February 1922, Mennonite and non-Mennonite officials in the Khortytsia *volispolkom* (volost ispolkom) also ordered local Mennonite and non-Mennonite peasants to establish *kollektivy* (collectives) for the purpose of the 1922 spring seeding campaign. Ranging in size from four or five households to as many as forty households, these kollektivy were essentially informal associations of Mennonite peasants who worked together to plough and plant their fields. Although many of these artels and kollektivy were no longer operating by the mid 1920s, they nevertheless represented some of the first Mennonite experiences in the regime's collective farm experiment.[28]

Shortly after the civil war, Mennonites also organized the Verband der Bürger Holländischer Herkunft (Union of Citizens of Dutch Lineage or VBHH) to lobby the government for Mennonite concerns. Established in 1922 under the leadership of B.B. Janz, the VBHH received permission from Soviet Ukrainian authorities to operate as a semi-autonomous economic association to represent Mennonites communities across Ukraine.[29] The VBHH was able to secure several significant economic concessions from the Bolsheviks, including land allotments for Mennonite farmers that were substantially larger (up to 32 *desiatinas* [a desiatina equals 1.09 hectares] per farm in some settlements) than those granted to Ukrainian and Russian peasant households. The VBHH also assisted in the reconstruction of Ukraine after the civil war and the famine of 1921–2 by accessing foreign capital, participating in limited industrial enterprises, operating benevolent and cultural institutions, establishing credit agencies and agricultural associations in many Mennonite villages, and helping to create two artels (Vpered and Novaya Ukriana). These local VBHH economic organizations and artels worked to rebuild devastated seed and crop cultivation, develop livestock herds, establish dairy operations, and improve farm mechanization in Mennonite settlements. The VBHH also worked hard to safeguard the right of Mennonites to farm their lands as independently as was possible in the Soviet countryside and to continue their traditional agricultural and economic practices with the least amount of interference from Soviet authorities.[30]

In 1925, however, the VBHH came under attack when the Ukrainian government began accusing it of participating in counter-revolutionary activities and preventing the sovietization of Mennonite communities. Ukrainian authorities forced the VBHH to cease operations in 1926 and converted many VBHH operations into Soviet cooperatives. In the Khortytsia raion, for instance, the largest VBHH organizations were reorganized into Khliborob (an agricultural credit cooperative) in Khortytsia, Mennobshchestvo (an agricultural cooperative association) in Schönwiese, Mennpotreb (a consumers' cooperative association) in Schönwiese, and LAKTA (a livestock and dairy association) in Khortytsia. In the Molochna colony the most important VBHH organizations were reorganized into Mennsel'khoz (Halbstadt Mennonite agricultural credit cooperative), Mennpotreb

(Halbstadt Mennonite consumers' cooperative association; later Halbstadt Potreb consumer cooperative), Menntrud (Gnadenfeld Mennonite agricultural credit cooperative), Mennpo (Gnadenfeld Mennonite consumers' cooperative association), and the Molochnaya Cattle Association.[31] Local authorities also transferred assets from liquidated VBHH agencies to government-sanctioned committees for mutual assistance (which collected machinery, seeds, and money from wealthier peasants to help poorer peasants); peasant benefit societies (which provided grain and goods to poorer peasants, invalids and Red Army veterans); associations for common tillage (which managed thousands of hectares of land on behalf of local farmers); village agricultural credit associations (which provided financial credit to peasants); village agricultural cooperatives: *raĭzhivotnovodsoyuz* (raion animal associations); livestock associations; dairy and butter associations; machine tractor associations; as well as collective farms.[32] Mennonites who were previously employed in VBHH organizations often found employment in these newly reorganized Soviet agencies, with some attaining senior administrative postings.[33] Most of the former VBHH organizations eventually came under the supervision of government-run Koopsoyuzy (Union of Cooperative Societies) and Kolkhoztsentr, and were used to facilitate the collectivization of Mennonite communities in the late 1920s and early 1930s.

The sovietization of the VBHH marked the beginning of the end of the economic independence and entrepreneurial practices that Mennonite farmers still enjoyed in Soviet Ukraine in the 1920s. The government's reorganization of the VBHH sent a clear signal that the government would no longer recognize the authority of Mennonite organizations, that traditional Mennonite agricultural and economic practices were no longer acceptable, and that the interests of bedniak and batrak peasants now dictated the economic and agricultural agenda in the countryside. Without the VBHH or any other Mennonite organization to advocate for their concerns to senior government officials, a growing number of Mennonite farmers were under enormous pressure to join peasant-run agricultural cooperatives and to share their agricultural assets, including their land and equipment, with their non-Mennonite neighbours.

The new Soviet nationalities policy, announced in 1923, was another important factor in the collectivization of Mennonite settlements in Ukraine. Commonly referred to as *korenizatsiia*, this policy granted every soviet national group its own national territory ranging in size from republics and oblasti to raiony, national soviets, and kolkhozy. The policy also encouraged each national group to use its language in government institutions within the group's territory; celebrate acceptable forms of cultural expression; and recruit and promote members of the national group into the Communist Party and leadership positions in village soviets, collective farms, and government institutions in the national territories. Nine German national raiony were established in Ukraine in the 1920s, with several set aside for Mennonite communities. One of these was Molochansk, which was established in 1924 and included Mennonite villages from the former Molochna colony. In 1928 the government amalgamated the Molochansk and Prischib national raiony into the expanded Molochansk German national raion, which included Mennonite, German, Ukrainian, and Russian settlements. The raion consisted of twenty-six village soviets (twenty Mennonite and German, five Ukrainian, and one Russian) totalling more than 174,910 hectares (142,300 cultivated hectares). There were 136 settlements in the raion, fifty-nine of which were predominantly German-speaking Mennonite settlements; there were also more than thirty communities populated by German-speaking Lutherans, Catholics, Baptists, and Adventists. Government records state that the Molochansk raion had a population of 47,300 people in 1934, of which 30,100 (64.8 per cent) were considered German and 10,400 (22.3 per cent) Ukrainian. In early 1935, the raion was partitioned into two smaller national raiony: Molochansk, with its centre at Halbstadt/Prischib, and Rot Front, centred in Waldheim.[34]

The national raion of Khortytsia was significantly smaller than Molochansk. Officially established in 1929, the Khortytsia raion had a total of 44,700 hectares, twelve village soviets and a population of 19,750 (12,365 Mennonites and Germans, 6,569 Ukrainians, 530 Russians and 286 Jews). There were thirty-eight villages in Khortytsia, eighteen of which were predominantly Mennonite.[35]

As was the case in other national raiony, individuals living in the Molochansk and Khortytsia national raiony were categorized according to their social class (i.e., byvshie liudi kulak, seredniak, bedniak, batrak, or worker), as well as their ethnic-national background (German, Ukrainian, Russian, Jewish, etc.). This Soviet version of affirmative action gave priority to Mennonites and ethnic German residents – especially if they were bedniaki, batraki, workers, or Red Army veterans – for positions in government agencies and kolkhozy in the German national raiony.[36] Party membership was not required for many of these positions, and Mennonites began applying for employment in state agencies in increasing numbers, especially after the government's liquidation of the VBHH in 1926. By 1928–9, hundreds of Mennonites in the Khortytsia and Molochansk national raiony were employed with the Soviet state in various capacities. Most worked as chairmen, secretaries, and representatives on the village soviets; by 1929, Mennonites controlled the executive councils of eight of the twelve village soviets in the Khortytsia raion.[37] Mennonites also assumed leadership positions in the *potrebsouiza* (consumer associations), CVP, Raboche-krest'ianskaia inspektsiia (Workers' and Peasants' Inspection Committee or WPIC), MTS, People's Court, *raĭzemotdel'* (raion land division committee or RLDC), *raĭkoopzerno* (raion grain association), *raĭpocebtroiki* (raion seeding troika), *raĭcel'bank* (raion village bank), *raĭtorgotdel'* (raion market commission), *raĭkolkhospzernonosoiuz* (raion kolkhoz grain union), and *raĭmetodburo* (raion methodical office).[38]

Two of the most influential state and party organizations in which Mennonites served were the *raĭispolkom* (raion executive committee or REC)[39] and the *raĭpartkom* (raion party committee or RPC), the two institutions that largely coordinated the dekulakization and collectivization of the Khortytsia and Molochansk national raiony.[40] Mennonites dominated the REC and RPC in Khortytsia, and played major roles in interpreting and implementing government policies, especially between 1928 and 1930. Mennonites also assumed important roles in the Molochansk REC and RPC, but they often shared this responsibility with Germans from non-Mennonite settlements. There were even a few Molochansk Mennonite communists who served with the OGPU and later the NKVD (a branch of the political police operating from 1934 to 1946). While the number of Mennonites who were communist party members was relatively small when compared to the entire Mennonite population, these Mennonite communists participated in pivotal communist party meetings and decisions that determined the pace and scope of collectivization in the Khortytsia and Molochansk raiony.[41]

What motivated Khortytsia and Molochansk Mennonites to become involved in the Soviet political process in the 1920s and early 1930s? The extant archival records provide some clues. For some Mennonites the prospect of a regular income and the promise of job security were justifiable reasons to work for the state, especially for poor Mennonite bedniaki, batraki, and workers who had large families to feed and house. These reasons certainly explain why so many Mennonites sought employment in government agencies already during the civil war and 1921–2 famine, and later during dekulakization and collectivization in the late 1920s and early 1930s.

For other Mennonites it was the promise of *korenizatsiia* – the right to assume greater decision-making authority and control over the political, economic, agricultural, social, and cultural institutions in the national raiony as a whole – that motivated them to sign on with the state. This opportunity proved attractive because it resembled the political and economic leadership roles that Mennonites played in their communities prior to the revolution, during the civil war and 1921–2 famine, as well as when VBHH leaders were dealing with local Soviet officials in the early 1920s. By 1927–8, the Bolshevik regime had begun to circumscribe the decision-making authority of local officials in their national territories, and it was obvious that Mennonites would not be able to exercise the same kind of power and authority in their communities as they had previously commanded. But many Mennonites saw the urgency in taking control of local government posts as quickly as possible. With the atrocities committed in Mennonite villages during the civil war and the 1921–2 famine still fresh in their minds, Mennonites simply did not trust local non-Mennonite officials to look after the best interests of the Mennonite settlements. Their mistrust was not unfounded: non-Mennonite officials increasingly demanded that the special Mennonite landholding privileges obtained by the VBHH be revoked and Mennonite landholdings be partitioned into smaller units, thereby freeing up land for redistribution to non-Mennonite bedniaki and batraki. With the dissolution of the VBHH, Mennonites were left to their own devices; many naturally sought postings in village and raion political bodies to stop or limit attacks against and encroachments upon hard-fought Mennonite economic and agricultural interests.[42]

The radical change in Bolshevik policy towards sectarian groups such as Mennonites, Baptists, Tolstoyans, and Seventh-Day Adventists in the 1920s also provided an incentive to seek government employment. During the civil war and the first years of NEP, the Bolshevik leadership employed a bifurcated approach towards sectarian groups. On the one hand, Soviet leaders such as V.D. Bonch-Bruevich (the administrative secretary of the Council of People's Commissars) viewed sectarian groups as possible allies in government efforts to socialize the countryside.[43] Bonch-Bruevich and other Bolshevik leaders were inclined to see the sects, including the Mennonites and Baptists, as expressions of peasant social dissatisfaction with the Orthodox Church and tsarism. These Soviet leaders also identified with sectarian teachings on social and economic equality, and they believed that granting these sects a few concessions (such as exemption from military service in the Sovnarkom decree of 4 January 1919) would encourage the sectarian communists to establish kolkhozy in the Soviet countryside.[44]

The Bonch-Bruevich "utopian approach" towards sectarians, however, was not adopted by everyone in the Soviet regime. The Soviet government's police organs (the Cheka, GP.U, and OGPU) and the Commission to Establish the Separation of Churches and the State (also known as the "Antireligious Commission of the Central Committee of the Communist Party") rejected many of Bonch-Bruevich's policies towards sectarians in the early 1920s and instead treated these religious minorities as anti-Soviet, kulak-inspired movements that threatened the USSR. In 1922 and 1923, these government organizations began implementing massive repressive measures against sectarian groups, particularly, evangelical movements. They also implemented "divide-and-conquer" tactics to incite dissension and schisms among sectarian groups and wear down their resistance. The Chekists, GPU, and OGPU, for example, used the exemption of pacifist sectarians from of Soviet military service to foment disagreements within Baptist, Evangelical Christian, Seventh-Day Adventist, and Molokan groups in an effort to weaken their unity and effectiveness.[45]

By 1924, the Bolshevik leadership had abandoned Bonch-Bruevich's utopian approach to sectarians. It now viewed the sectarians as a lost cause, and accused them of exploiting Bolshevik concessions for their own counter-revolutionary purposes. This hard-line Bolshevik policy resulted in vicious attacks against Mennonite organizations such as the Kommission für Kirchenangelegenheiten (Commission for Church Affairs or KfK). At the same time, the Bolsheviks stepped up their own nation-wide antireligious efforts, many of which were directed towards sectarian organizations. In 1925, for example, the Soviet regime organized the League of the Godless (later renamed the League of the Militant Godless), a government-funded organization that sponsored nation-wide atheistic propaganda campaigns and anti-religious activities (atheistic speeches and plays) to intimidate churches and stifle religious observance. In 1927 Ukrainian authorities implemented the *Ukrainian Administrative Code*, which severely limited the activities of churches and religious groups.[46] Collectively, these Bolshevik initiatives made it abundantly clear to Mennonites that participation in Mennonite-sponsored institutions was out of the question.

The regime's increasingly restrictive emigration policy was another factor that encouraged Mennonites to consider greater participation in local soviet organs. In the mid-1920s, the VBHH facilitated the emigration of thousands of Soviet Mennonites to North America, but shortly after its dissolution the government implemented measures that made it substantially more difficult for Soviet Mennonites to leave the country. Between March 1926 and April 1927, for example, almost 5,700 Soviet Mennonites were granted exit visas, but this number dropped to fewer than 750 between April 1927 and May 1928. With the likelihood of emigrating to the West becoming more remote, a growing number of Mennonites recognized that their best chance for survival lay in working within the existing government institutions.[47]

Personal beliefs and ambitions also motivated Mennonites to seek government and party positions. There were Mennonite bedniaki, batraki, workers, and educated professionals who were wholeheartedly committed to Bolshevik ideology and dedicated their lives to creating the first socialist state. This was the motivation of Nikolai N. Boldt, the Molochansk Mennonite bedniak who became a party member in 1918 and served in the Red Army during the civil war. Boldt participated in important Molochansk party meetings that determined the pace and scope of NEP, and later dekulakization and collectivization campaigns in the raion. He also served as chairman of the kolkhoz at Hierschau, Molochansk and continued to perform important party work in the raion until he was purged from the party and his position as kolkhoz chairman in 1934.[48]

Some Mennonites were motivated by the prospect of upward social mobility that accompanied a government or party post. Mennonite bedniaki, batraki, and workers actively sought out government positions as well as party memberships to earn a higher income, secure more benefits (e.g., better housing and educational opportunities), and qualify for promotions in the government and party hierarchy. The following Molochansk Mennonites, for example, used their party memberships to secure important positions at the Waldheim MTS in the early 1930s: Peter K. Köhn, Nikolai N. Fast, Jakob J. Regier, Schellenberg, Penner, Heier, Peter J. Wedel (mechanic), Johann D. Funk (senior mechanic), Isaak F. Hilderbrandt (MTS director), and Vasilia V. Martens (MTS director). Another Mennonite, Andrei P. Goerzen, used his party membership to obtain the position of senior veterinarian technician for the Molochansk raion. There were also ambitious Molochansk Mennonite women, such as Anna K. Lepp (party candidate in 1928), Elena A. Klassen (party member in 1930), and Pavlina A. Suderman (party candidate in 1932), who saw their party membership as a ticket to a better life. In the case of Anna K. Lepp, for example, her party membership helped her to assume the position of director of a butter production facility in Hierschau (Molochansk). Elena A. Klassen, Pavlina A. Suderman, and other Mennonites enrolled at the Soviet party school in Molochansk to give them an advantage in their climb up the social mobility ladder.[49]

Finally, some Mennonites sought out government employment because of fear, intimidation, or the desire to protect their families. During the government's dekulakization and collectivization campaigns, individuals who not did demonstrate ardent support for the regime's policies were also accused of kulak or counter-revolutionary sympathies; their family members were also accused of being co-conspirators and treated as enemies of the state. Membership or employment in a local state or party organization served as a buffer to these kinds of accusations. In Molochansk, for example, fear and intimidation appear to have been factors in the spike in the number of membership applications in the RPC: in 1927 there was only one party candidate in the RPC, but this jumped to twenty-one when dekulakization and collectivization were initiated in 1928–30; in 1931–2, when collectivization was almost complete and famine conditions began to appear in a number of Molochansk settlements, the number of party candidates quickly climbed to 147.[50]

Avoiding dekulakization and hunger was perhaps one of the reasons why Vasily A. Penner, a Mennonite who worked as a school teacher in Lichtenau, Molochansk in the 1920s, sought the security of a government post and later party membership. In early 1930, when dekulakization and collectivization were reaching a frenetic pace, Penner joined the executive of the Münsterberg village soviet where he helped to administer the collectivization of Mennonite farms. In 1932, when famine conditions were beginning to ravage large areas of Molochansk, Penner was successful in his nomination as a candidate member of the party, and subsequently became chairman of the Alexandertal village soviet. These new party connections served him well: Penner was promoted to chairman of the Lichtenau village soviet in 1933, after which he obtained a highly desirable position at the Molochansk Raĭcel'bank in 1935.[51] Penner was not the only Molochansk Mennonite who saw the benefits of joining the party during the early days of the 1932–3 famine; other Molochansk Mennonites who signed on as party candidates at this time included Jakob P. Schmidt, Andrei P. Goerzen, David K. Unruh, Viktor A. Schulz, Abram A. Buller, Jakob P. Pankratz, Heinrich P. Schmidt, Emmanuel I. Lorenz, T.T. Foth, Johann J. Plett, Jakob J.

Brandt, Konstantine Prochnau, Jakob M. Hooge, F.D. Klassen, Heinrich H. Hildebrandt, Gerhard J. Friesen, David J. Braun, Franz F. Funk, and Goossen.[52]

Periodic *chistki* (cleansings or purges) of local state and party offices did not stop Khortytsia and Molochansk Mennonites from applying for government and party positions. Between August and October 1929, for instance, the Ukrainian government launched a massive investigation to identify and purge kulak and alien elements that had infiltrated government offices in the Molochansk raion. As a result of the investigation, every Mennonite community saw between 10 and 50 per cent of their employees in the village soviets denied work, expelled from their positions, or relocated to another community; in some Molochansk communities, more than 50 per cent of the Mennonite members of the local soviet apparatus were purged. Many of those removed from their posts included village soviet chairmen, village soviet executive officials, members of village CVP and cooperative societies, and local health care professionals. A similar purge was undertaken in Khortytsia in December 1929 and January 1930, when dozens of Mennonites lost their local government posts. This brutal treatment of Mennonite officials, however, appears not to have deterred other Molochansk and Khortytsia Mennonites from applying for these recently purged state and party positions.[53] In late 1929, for example, no fewer than fifty-five Molochansk Mennonites had submitted applications to the Molochansk RPC for membership as party candidates.[54]

Mennonite participation in state and party offices included a broad spectrum of service and time commitments. Most Mennonites who served in a non-executive capacity on the village soviet, the CVP or the WPIC spent a few hours per month or per week at meetings or doing committee work, while their main employment was elsewhere in the kolkhoz. By comparison, Mennonites who worked in the executive office of the village soviet, CVP, WPIC, RPC, REC, or other raion agencies often did so in a full-time capacity and worked long hours.

In carrying out their duties and responsibilities on behalf of the regime, Khortytsia and Molochansk Mennonite officials and party members were not minor actors in the collectivization dramas that unfolded in their raiony; they played leading roles in the reorganization of their communities into Soviet kolkhozy, and their decisions affected not only their own communities, but also Ukrainians, Russians, Germans, Jews, and other ethnic groups living in their raiony. In Khortytsia, for example, the leading organization that administered and supervised the regime's chrezvychaishchina, dekulakization, and collectivization campaigns was the REC. Between 1928 and 1931, Mennonites exerted a leadership presence on the REC executive. In 1930, for instance, no fewer than eleven of the twenty-five members on the REC were Mennonites; two of the seven people who qualified as candidate members for the REC were also Mennonites.[55] Some of these Mennonites assumed leading roles on the REC executive and worked at the highest levels. For example, the Mennonite communist party member Heinrich G. Rempel served as Khortytsia REC chairman between 1928 and January 1930.[56] Chairman Rempel worked closely with the local OGPU, RCP, CVP, village soviets, and other state organs to ensure that government and party policies were properly implemented in Khortytsia and that the raion met its government targets. Rempel also depended on the assistance of other members of the REC executive, which included Ukrainians, Jews, and the Mennonites Abram J. Töws (chairman of the Khortytsia raïzemotdel') and I.A. Knelsen (Khortytsia CVP chairman). In fact, Rempel often consulted only with Töws, Knelsen, and the Jewish REC member, Y.A. Friedman (chairman of the REC Finance Commission), on daily issues affecting the raion; collectively, they issued the overwhelming majority of notices and directives to village soviets, the CVP, and WPIC on matters relating to the implementation of chrezvychaishchina, dekulakization, and collectivization policies in the raion.[57]

In January 1930, the Mennonite and communist party member Johann P. Quiring replaced Rempel as Khortytsia's REC chairman. Helping Quiring with his new duties were Friedman, Töws, and two new Mennonite members of the REC: Johann J. Wilms (REC executive secretary) and Heinrich A. Dyck (technical secretary for the REC). In the first half of 1930, Quiring, Friedman, Töws, Wilms, and Dyck were the most powerful men in Khortytsia, and their names and signatures appeared on many REC dekulakization and collectivization directives. In fact, it was during the REC chairmanship of Rempel and Quiring that the vast majority of kolkhozy were organized in Mennonite settlements in the Khortytsia raion.[58]

In late June 1930, Quiring was replaced by the non-Mennonite Shefer as REC chairman, but this was not the end of Mennonite participation in the Khortytsia REC. Other Mennonites, including Ivana Penner and Friesen, continued to do the government's bidding as Khortytsia REC members in the early 1930s.[59]

Mennonites also served on the REC in Molochansk and helped to administer the government's chrezvychaishchina, dekulakization, and collectivization campaigns in the raion. In 1928, for example, the Mennonite Schmidt served as chairman of the Molochansk REC, Dück was the REC secretary, and Gerhard D. Foth was an REC member. Mennonite women also served on the Molochansk REC; the party candidate Maria Pauls, who was a member of the Waldheim village soviet and the former chairman of the Waldheim CVP, was promoted to the Molochansk REC in 1929. A Ukrainian, Baliukevich, assumed the chairmanship of the REC by late 1930, but Molochansk Mennonites and Germans continued to serve on the REC executive, including Unger, who worked as REC secretary. By late 1931, the chairmanship of the Molochansk REC was assumed by the Mennonite Penner, during whose tenure the inhabitants of the Molochansk raion were subjected to relentless and unprecedented expropriation campaigns siphoning surplus grain, meat, and agricultural produce. Although Penner only served as REC chairman until October 1932, when he was replaced by the non-Mennonite Willkel, Penner's policies and programs helped to initiate famine conditions in a number of Molochansk villages. By 1934, the chairmanship of the Molochansk REC was again in Mennonite hands when the Mennonite party member Wiebe held the post.[60]

By co-opting Mennonites to become agents of the state, the government succeeded in using Mennonites to do much of the dirty work associated with collectivizing the Mennonite communities in Khortytsia and Molochansk. These Mennonite officials were also under increasing government pressure to produce spectacular results in collectivizing their communities. In early 1929, for example, Mennonite and non-Mennonite officials in the Khortytsia REC devised an ambitious plan to collectivize half of the farms in the raion in a four-year period. These plans were soon rejected by regional officials as too modest, however, and in early 1930 they issued orders to the REC demanding that virtually all Khortytsia households be collectivized, preferably by March 1930, but failing that before the end of the year.[61] Regional authorities also expected local officials to consolidate the small kolkhozy into one large kolkhoz in each village and to substantially increase the number of hectares of arable land in each kolkhozy, even if this meant expropriating privately held land or bringing the poorest land into cultivation.

This was a herculean task that forced Khortytsia and Molochansk officials to employ a variety of strategies to meet the increasingly outlandish government collectivization targets. One common strategy was to bombard the local Mennonite population with propaganda touting the advantages of joining the local kolkhoz. In the late 1920s and early

1930s, state-sponsored German-language newspapers and periodicals such as *Das Neue Dorf*, *Deutscher Kollektivist* (Molochansk), *K. Liebnecht* (Molochansk), *Halbstädter Zeitung* (Molochansk), *Jungstorm*, and *Stürmer* (Khortytsia) routinely included articles and exhortations from the Soviet leadership and local authorities about the national urgency to collectivize; to personalize the urgency, the periodicals also included the testimonials of German and Mennonite kolkhozniki extolling the benefits of kolkhoz life.[62]

Local authorities also organized competitions and conferences to inspire and attract the poorest Mennonite households to establish or join kolkhozy. Regional and raion authorities in both the Khortytsia and Molochansk national raiony organized contests between villages to determine which settlement could collectivize the fastest and with the highest percentage of households. Officials arranged conferences in larger centres to motivate peasants to collectivize. In February 1930, for example, officials sponsored such a conference for the German-Mennonite populations in Khortytsia. Those who attended the conference had questions about collectivization, some of which stymied conference organizers. For example, if a man is a kolkhoznik but his wife refuses to join the kolkhoz, how will she be treated? Should a village of German and non-German residents be organized into one national kolkhoz or into two separate kolkhozy based on ethnicity? If a village is "half-German and half-Russian," is it permissible for the German farmers to join a German kolkhoz in a neighbouring German village? Will the government treat German kolkhozy differently than non-German kolkhozy? Which national minorities are the most resistant to the collective farm movement?[63] It is clear from their questions that Mennonite and German participants had considered some of the practical problems arising from collectivization, especially as they related to female resistance to the kolkhoz movement and the challenge of different ethnic groups working and living together in one kolkhoz.

Religious persecution, antireligious legislation, and the aggressive activities of the League of the Militant Godless undoubtedly played a role in convincing some Mennonites to join kolkhozy. Officials in both the Khortytsia and Molochansk raiony viewed Mennonite religious leaders – including ministers, elders, deacons, choir directors, youth leaders, Sunday school teachers and members of the KfK – with suspicion. These officials were convinced that collectivization could only succeed if the influence and control that Mennonite religious leaders exerted over their communities were neutralized. One of the tactics that

Khortytsia and Molochansk officials used to accomplish this objective were levies that targeted clergymen. In 1928–30, for example, Khortytsia and Molochansk authorities imposed heavy grain levies on Mennonite clergymen followed by tax levies designed to siphon whatever resources the local clergy possessed. Religious leaders who failed to pay their assessments were sometimes rescued by their congregations, which raised additional funds and grain to pay the levies, but congregations eventually found it impossible to help their religious leaders and their property was confiscated.[64]

Local Khortytsia and Molochansk authorities also relied on other recently enacted laws to bar Mennonite religious leaders from joining kolkhozy, strip them of any social security rights, and deny them access to public housing. An amendment to the 1924 *Soviet Constitution* prohibited all religious propaganda and enabled local authorities to arrest any church leaders accused of participating in evangelistic activities; in essence, this amendment confined Mennonite ministers to preaching only within their own congregations. Khortytsia and Molochansk authorities also used the *Decree on Religious Associations*, passed in April 1929, to harass Mennonite congregations and their leaders. Although the decree protected freedom of worship, it also included a series of regulations that made it virtually impossible for religious leaders to perform their functions. More specifically, these regulations prohibited churches from supplying aid to their members or charities; holding special meetings for children, youth, or women; conducting general meetings for religious instruction, study, or recreational purposes; and opening libraries or storing any books except those necessary for conducting worship services. This law also banned religious instruction to children under eighteen unless this instruction was from their parents. It was now illegal for anyone to hold a Sunday school class, lead a prayer meeting, or conduct a church youth choir.[65]

The government did not stop there with its antireligious legislation. In August 1929 it introduced *nepreryvka* (the continuous work-week) that banned Sundays and religious holidays (including Christmas and Easter) as special days of rest for workers and school children.[66] Parents who kept their children at home to observe such holidays were now given stiff fines. In October 1929 the government implemented the *Instructions of the People's Commissariat of the Interior*, a law that facilitated the closure of a number of Mennonite congregations in Khortytsia and Molochansk. The decree required all religious associations to register with local officials by 1 March 1930 or be deemed closed. Local authorities also had broad discretionary powers to grant or withhold the registration of local congregations, treat any unregistered religious service as illegal, and limit or reduce the number of religious associations in their jurisdiction. As a result, important Mennonite religious associations, such as the KfK, no longer had any legal status.[67]

The Politburo Decree of January 1930 contained some of the most repressive legislative measures against religious organizations and more specifically sectarian communities. It directed soviet officials to revise existing laws on religious associations to ensure that church councils and sectarian communities could not be converted into bases of support for kulaks, the disenfranchised, or anti-soviet elements. The decree also directed the Central Committee Organizational Bureau to issue an order concerning the closure of churches, sectarian prayer houses, and other religious structures to ensure that the wishes of the village soviets and the peasantry to facilitate their closure could be implemented quickly. As sectarian communities, Mennonite settlements were specifically targeted for these measures.[68]

Local authorities in Khortytsia and Molochansk implemented this antireligious legislation in an effort to isolate Mennonite religious leaders from their congregants. These officials also supported the League of the Militant Godless, Komsomol (Communist Youth League), CVP and WPIC, which were given the task of harassing and ridiculing religious leaders. By 1928–9, these state-supported groups established antireligious cells in Khortytsia and Molochansk settlements, inundated Mennonite communities and schools with antireligious literature, organized blasphemous protests against Mennonite churches and members, and harassed local ministers. School teachers were also required to provide antireligious instruction to students. As part of this campaign, League members engaged in public debates with Mennonite ministers in order to humiliate them and lure Mennonite youth away from the churches. While this tactic may have prompted some young people to renounce their churches and join the League, it sometimes backfired when Mennonite ministers embarrassed their atheistic debating opponents with ingenious rebuttals and arguments. By 1931, however, local officials resorted to physical threats to compel Mennonite participation in the antireligious work. In Molochansk, for instance, local authorities promised to retract the food ration cards of Mennonite kolkhozniki who refused to forsake their Christian beliefs and join the local League of the Godless circle; in some cases, they also threatened to exile those kolkhozniki who refused to join the League.[69]

To increase the pressure on Mennonite congregations, local authorities authorized and encouraged the conversion of Mennonite church buildings for non-religious use. Until 1928, most Mennonite congregations in Khortytsia and Molochansk enjoyed relatively unhindered use of their church buildings, even though the title to all religious facilities had reverted to the state in 1918. In 1928–9, however, government bodies, kolkhozy, factories, and anti-religious groups began to take possession of Mennonite churches, often by levying unreasonable assessments on the congregations and then evicting the congregations when they failed to pay the assessments. Some churches were demolished while others were converted into facilities for public use, such as government offices, orphanages, clubhouses, theatres, granaries, or livestock shelters. In 1929, for example, Khortytsia authorities permitted workers from the Engels factory to commandeer a Mennonite church and use it as a cultural hall; the authorities also signed off on the demolition of the Einlage Mennonite church so that materials from the church could be recycled to build a school. Officials in Khortytsia and Molochansk did not outlaw the use of every Mennonite church for religious purposes; in some settlements, officials permitted Mennonites limited use of their church buildings for religious services until 1932–3. This became increasingly rare, however, and by late 1933 many of the old forms of Mennonite worship – Sunday services, baptisms, prayer meetings, and Bible studies – were no longer public events; they could only be celebrated privately or covertly in small groups.[70]

The ruthless and relentless persecution of Mennonite religious institutions and leaders convinced some Mennonite households in Khortytsia and Molochansk to seek refuge in local kolkhozy and sign on as kolkhozniki, but it was the government's chrezvychaishchina and dekulakization campaigns that proved most effective in driving Mennonite households into kolkhozy en masse. In Khortytsia, for example, it was the Mennonite-dominated REC, under the leadership of Rempel and Quiring, that was responsible for dekulakizing most of the Mennonite kulaks in the raion.[71] In February 1930, for example, Quiring, Wilms, Töws, and the other members of the Khortytsia REC examined lists of kulak households prepared by village soviets in the raion. The lists explained why these particular kulak households should be dekulakized, which families should be resettled inside Ukraine or exiled to other regions of the USSR, and which members of the kulak families should be executed. After the REC executive reviewed the lists, Quiring, Wilms, and Dyck (REC technical secretary) signed their names at the bottom of the resolutions confirming the dekulakization of at least eighty-three households in the national raion. The majority of the households that were subsequently exiled outside Ukraine were Mennonite.[72]

The dekulakization work of Quiring, Wilms, and other Mennonites on the Khortytsia REC did not stop in February 1930. Quiring and Wilms prepared and signed off on another list of dekulakization candidates in April; this time the list contained the names of seventy-six expert families (76 per cent of whom were Mennonite) that were to be disenfranchised and processed for either arrest or exile.[73] In early May, Quiring, Wilms, and the Khortytsia REC prepared a secret report proposing seven possible sites for new kulak settlements in the Khortytsia raion. The idea was to use these settlements as holding areas for the least threatening kulak families in the raion; here they would live apart from the rest of the population until authorities decided what to do with them. In September, the Khortytsia REC, which now included the Mennonite Ivana Penner, passed a resolution to establish four kulak collection settlements in the raion. Often referred to as *zbornyi*, each kulak collection settlement could accommodate between seventeen and twenty-two kulak households. By early 1931, seventy-eight families had been moved onto the four sites, of which seventy-three (93.5 per cent) were Mennonite; the actual population of the settlements totalled 452 individuals, 438 (96.9 per cent) of whom were Mennonites. The Mennonite families built makeshift huts at the zborni and toiled in harsh conditions until they were exiled.[74]

That Mennonite officials were involved in the dekulakization of their communities should not come as a surprise. Their extensive involvement in the political and party institutions in the Khortytsia and Molochansk raiony made it impossible for them not to be key players in the dekulakization campaign. What is also important to note is that dekulakization in Khortytsia and Molochansk was especially severe and extensive for a number of reasons. First, Khortytsia and Molochansk Mennonites generally had larger landholdings than their non-Mennonite neighbours as a result of special concessions obtained by the VBHH in the early 1920s. Many Mennonite families not only owned between 15 and 32 desiatinas of land, but also rented an additional 5 to 10 desiatinas – an amount that was often five to twelve times larger than most surrounding Ukrainian peasant farms.[75] With more land, some Mennonites hired batraki and bedniaki to help with the sowing and harvest. Doing so, however, made these Mennonites liable to the charge of being wealthy peasants who exploited the poor, and thus obvious candidates for categorization as a kulak or an expertnik. A second reason why Mennonites were routinely included on kulak lists was because of the antisectarian attitude of the Bolshevik leadership. In the early 1930s the politburo implemented a number of decrees that identified sectarian communities, religious associations, and church councils as bases of support for kulaks, disenfranchised persons, and anti-soviet elements.[76] Such communities were the target of more severe dekulakization measures. A third factor was the past counter-revolutionary activities of Mennonite communities. They were viewed as enemies of the regime because of their opposition to the Bolshevik revolution, their support of the German occupation forces and White Army during the civil war, their Selbstschutz activities, and the VBHH demands for special concessions during the early 1920s. A fourth factor was rooted in ethnic hostility: anti-German sentiment thrived at almost every level of the government, notwithstanding the pro-nationality measures of korenizatsiia. Local officials – including Mennonite officials – accused Mennonite settlements of being nests of kulak opposition and therefore more resistant to collectivization.[77] A fifth reason for higher Mennonite dekulakization rates was the religious and ethnic cohesiveness that existed in the Mennonite villages. Authorities found this intolerable, and they dekulakized Mennonite religious leaders in the hope that this would dissolve community cohesiveness, ignite class warfare in the villages, and persuade more poor Mennonites to join the newly established kolkhozy. A sixth reason for the aggressive dekulakization campaigns in the Mennonite raiony was that Mennonite officials, especially those in the REC and RPC, were under enormous pressure to prove their loyalty to the regime; as a result, some were especially harsh in the implementation of dekulakization policies in their own communities and their national raiony in an effort to demonstrate to their political superiors that they were not favouring their own kind. Finally, dekulakization was used as a way of punishing Mennonites for their past emigration activities. Mennonite efforts to emigrate were particularly strong in the fall of 1929, when more than 9,000 Soviet Mennonites from Siberia, Orenburg, the Caucasus, Kuban, Ufa, Memrik, Samara, the Crimea, and Ukraine fled to Moscow in an attempt to obtain exit visas. Their story made international headlines and initiated a foreign-relations crisis that so embarrassed the Soviet government that it quickly issued exit visas to more than 3,880 Mennonites.[78] More than 5,200 Mennonites, however, did not receive exit visas; instead, many of the adult males were imprisoned or exiled while their families were loaded onto unheated cattle and freight cars in November and December of 1929, and transported back to their home villages without adequate food or water. The vast majority of Mennonites who survived the trip home from Moscow were dekulakized and exiled within months of arriving home.[79]

Dekulakization proved catastrophic for Khortytsia and Molochansk Mennonites. The arrest and exile of hundreds of Mennonite leaders and ministers created panic and confusion in Mennonite villages.[80] The decapitation of the Mennonite leadership quickly destabilized the communities, making it easier for local authorities to convince poorer Mennonite peasants that Soviet authority – not Mennonite kulaks and religious leaders – now controlled the political, economic, and social agenda in the Mennonite villages. Next, officials targeted some seredniak, batrak, and bedniak Mennonite households for dekulakization, often accusing them of being *podkulachniki* (kulak hirelings or agents). By early 1931, almost every Mennonite village in Khortytsia and Molochansk had witnessed the arrest and exile of Mennonite families that fell into these categories. Some Mennonite households tried to avoid this fate by destroying their property or participating in *samoraskulachivanie* (self-dekulakization measures such as liquidating personal property, partitioning landholdings, destroying livestock or equipment, or fleeing to another region of the country), but most came to the realization that trying to evade dekulakization was futile, and that life outside the kolkhoz was almost impossible. As one Mennonite grimly observed, "[O]ne can either starve at home or work in the artel."[81] In short, dekulakization triggered the disintegration of the traditional economic, religious, and social hierarchies that had governed Mennonite settlements for more than a century, thereby facilitating the accelerated conversion of Mennonite settlements into Soviet kolkhozy.[82]

Local officials were not prepared to deal with the flood of the peasantry into the kolkhozy in 1929–30; as a result, the collectivization of Khortytsia and Molochansk was neither uniform nor organized. In fact, the collectivization of these raiony could best be characterized as haphazard and devoid of planning or leadership. One of the reasons for this was that many of the directives emanating from government offices in Moscow, Kharkiv, Kyiv, and Zaporizhzhia were based on Bolshevik theory rather than sound economic policies or proven agricultural practices. The job of local authorities, however, was not to question the wisdom of these directives, but to implement them. What made this task even more exasperating was that the expectations from senior government officials often changed on a weekly or even daily basis, forcing local authorities to make decisions and revise their plans on the fly with little consideration for the long-term consequences. In this respect, the collectivization of Khortytsia and Molochansk was an ad hoc affair.

Despite these challenges, local officials were still able to collectivize Khortytsia and Molochansk in relatively short order, or at least so it appeared on paper. In 1926–7, for example, there were only two communities (Khortytsia and Kandrovka) in the Khortytsia area with a kolkhoz, but there were a growing number of *zemobschestva* (land associations; *zemel'ni hromady* in Ukrainian), many of which had Mennonite members and leadership. In 1928, however, many of these land associations were purged of their kulak families, and reconstituted with new incorporation statutes. In July 1928, for instance, Mennonites in Blumengart (Khortytsia) barred six Mennonite families from joining a reorganized all-Mennonite zemobschestvo after local officials labelled the families as *lishenetz* (disenfranchised) due to their kulak background. Khortytsia did not stop there in its collectivization efforts; by the end of 1928, the raion had established two communes, three SOZy, a workers' settlement (with socialized farmland), three kolkhozy, and eighteen zemobschestva and cooperatives, as well as eighteen machine-tractor associations.[83] One of the new cooperatives was Druzhba, which was established in Schönhorst, Khortytsia in May 1928; it was populated largely by Mennonites, and initially came under the chairmanship of Johann M. Neufeld.[84] To facilitate the success of these nascent kolkhozy, the Khliborob credit association entered into agricultural contracts with these organizations to purchase their produce at set prices and provide them with credit, agricultural machinery, and seed grain in return.[85]

When dekulakization accelerated in 1929–30, Khortytsia Mennonites began moving into kolkhozy in large numbers. By November 1929, Khortytsia had a commune, thirty-six kolkhozy, and a number of zemobschestva; together they totalled 581 farmsteads, 3,121 people, and 8,380 hectares of land.[86] By 1 January 1930, 18.3 per cent of all land in the raion was collectivized. One month later, collectivization rates had increased to 42 per cent, with more than 17,710 hectares (3 per cent belonging to the commune, 27 per cent to artels, and 70 per cent to SOZy). By the end of the year, 40,380 hectares (almost 100 per cent of the land in the raion) was collectivized. Some of the Mennonites who were recognized for playing an important role in organizing kolkhozy in early 1930 included A. Braun (Eisenfeld); Rempel, at

Internatsional SOZ (Nieder-Khortytsia); J.K. Klassen, at Rekord SOZ (Nieder-Khortytsia); P.P. Giesbrecht, at Landmann SOZ (Neuendorf); Krieger, at Progress; and J. Tiessen (Burwalde).[87]

Every Mennonite community in Khortytsia now had at least one kolkhoz, and some communities (such as Khortytsia, Neuendorf, Schöneberg, Einlage, Osterwick-Kronsthal, and Nikolaipol) had two or three kolkhozy. By the spring of 1930, there were at least thirty-four kolkhozy in Khortytsia raion – three communes, nineteen artels, and twelve SOZy. Of the 3,822 households in the raion, 2,482 (64.9 per cent) were in kolkhozy: 239 households were in the commune, 1,445 in artels, and 798 in SOZy. There were also at least thirty-four Machine-Horse Stations (MHS) – government-approved associations that supplied agricultural machinery and horses to kolkhozy. By June 1930, most of the zemobschestva had been liquidated and their lands, property, and family members had been absorbed into neighbouring kolkhozy.[88]

The collectivization of Molochansk bore similarities to what had occurred in Khortytsia. Molochansk Mennonites began organizing and leading zemobschestva in 1927, and by 1928 the raion had one state farm, three communes (with seventy-one members and 436 desiatinas of land), seven agricultural artels (with 120 members and 1,041 desiatinas of land), seventy-four societies for communal working of the land, twenty-four tractor associations, twenty-nine livestock cooperatives, four milking cooperatives, three garden cooperatives, two soil improvement cooperatives, and one poultry cooperative.[89] By August 1929, 5.3 per cent of the households in the raion had been collectivized; a month later, 28 per cent of all households and 26 per cent of all land in the raion belonged to kolkhozy. After the government launched its repressive dekulakization campaign in early 1930, Molochansk officials proudly reported that 92 per cent of the households and 93 per cent of the land in the raion had been collectivized. Although the percentage of collectivized households dropped to 58 per cent in the months following the publication of Stalin's "Dizzy with Success," the percentage of collectivized households increased significantly in the last four months of 1930.[90] By the end of the year, raion reports indicated that 90 per cent of all bedniak and seredniak households and 92 per cent of all bedniak and seredniak land were now under kolkhozy control. The raion had 127 kolkhozy, of which ninety-six were artels and thirty-one were SOZy; there was also a commune (Gigant), fourteen dairy *fermy* (farm units), seventeen swine fermy, and several cattle associations.[91]

Molochansk officials continued to post impressive collectivization results in 1931: 96 per cent of the households and 97 per cent of the land in the raion was collectivized. The raion kolkhozy also increased their landholdings by 80 per cent – from 63,470 hectares in 1930 to 116,250 hectares in 1931. The raion also had three sovkhozy, two MTS, the Skotvoda cattle association, thirty commodity milk fermy, twenty dairy breeding operations, seven cattle-breeding facilities, eighty-four swine fermy, and a large number of chicken fermy.[92]

By 1 June 1932, 99.7 per cent of Molochansk households and 99.9 per cent of Molochansk land was considered collectivized. There were now 114 kolkhozy, three sovkhozy, one commune, two MTS, two livestock breeding operations, and one seed-cleaning operation. A total of 120,700 hectares of cultivated land were in the kolkhoz sector, while the four sovkhozy controlled 22,700 hectares of cultivated land. Germans and Mennonites constituted 65 per cent of the entire kolkhoz population in the raion, Ukrainians 22.3 per cent, and Russians 6.5 per cent. While a few kolkhozy were composed exclusively of Ukrainians, most had a mix of Ukrainians, Russians, Germans, and Mennonites.[93]

Despite enormous state pressure to conform, a few Mennonite families refused to participate in the kolkhoz experiment, usually for religious or ideological reasons. The village soviet from Einlage (Khortytsia), for example, reported that 34 of the 183 farms in the area had not joined kolkhozy by the spring of 1930. By 1932–3, however, the number of non-collectivized Mennonite households had dwindled to a handful, when famine conditions, as expertly detailed in Beznosov's essay in chapter 8 in this volume, compelled many of the remaining opponents of socialism to seek kolkhoz membership.[94]

Some Final Observations

The collectivization of the former Khortytsia and Molochna colonies in the late 1920s and early 1930s was chaotic, violent, and destructive, but ultimately successful. By the fall of 1930, 92 per cent of the land in the Molochansk raion and almost 100 per cent of the land in the Khortytsia raion had been collectivized. The government's all-out attack against Mennonite economic, religious, and political institutions and traditions facilitated the rapid collectivization of these districts. The arrest, imprisonment, and exile of Mennonite families incited widespread panic and fear in Mennonite villages. The deportation of Mennonite religious leaders, kulaks, experts, and wealthier peasant households decapitated the leadership cadre in the Mennonite settlements, thus removing the most strident and influential opposition to collectivization. In short order, the traditional religious, social, economic, and political cohesiveness of the Mennonite communities began to dissolve, destabilizing many Mennonite communities and driving the vast majority of the poorer Mennonite families into the nearest kolkhozy.

Mennonites played key roles in the dekulakization and collectivization of their communities in the Khortytsia and Molochansk raiony. As members of the REC, RCP, village soviets, WPIC, CVP, MTS, and other raion organizations, Mennonites served as agents of the regime by identifying kulak households, facilitating their arrest and exile, expropriating kulak property, and then transferring it to local state institutions, kolkhozy, and sovkhozy. Mennonites supervised the collectivization of their communities, helped in the conversion of Mennonite organizations into Soviet agencies, carried out government orders that set the pace and direction of collectivization, and punished those who resisted or expressed opposition to the government's plans for the countryside. In carrying out their duties, these Mennonite officials helped to undermine the authority of traditional Mennonite religious, political, and economic institutions and the leaders at their helm. These Mennonite officials also gave legitimacy to the state-sponsored violence against Mennonite villages and worked to convince fellow Mennonites that joining a kolkhoz was the easiest way to avoid dekulakization and exile. In this respect, Mennonites were directly responsible for collectivizing the Khortytsia and Molochna Mutter Ansiedlungen.

One cannot help but feel some sympathy for these Mennonite officials, especially those who signed on with the state to protect the interests of their communities and families, and to prevent non-Mennonite officials from taking control of their villages after the VBHH was liquidated. But not long after these Mennonites assumed these influential positions they were given the heinous tasks of determining who within their communities would be dekulakized, which of their churches would be closed, and how their villages and farms would be collectivized. This was no easy task, especially when their political masters issued unrealistic demands and punished those whose undivided loyalty to the Bolshevik state was in question. And even though some of these Mennonite officials performed their jobs to the best of their abilities, a large number were summarily purged from their positions, especially in 1929–30 and in 1933–4 when the regime undertook a campaign of "national cultural construction" in Mennonite- and German-populated regions to identify and eliminate Hitlerites and Nazi sympathizers working to undermine the kolkhozy and the Soviet state.[95] Perhaps some of these purged Mennonite officials took some consolation in the fact that their work had somehow minimized the effect of the collectivization and dekulakization campaigns in their villages. But many of these Mennonites must have questioned whether their service to the state had been worth the cost.

Regardless of the motivations that Mennonites had when they assumed leadership positions in local state and party organizations or the personal sacrifices they made on behalf of their communities, there is no doubt that they played a critical role in the transformation of their communities in the late 1920s and early 1930s: they acted as a solvent in dissolving the economic, political, religious, and social institutions that had previously governed their Mutter Ansiedlungen. They also had a hand in establishing Soviet-sponsored institutions that would dominate their communities for years to come. Notwithstanding that almost everything about Soviet collectivization violated their traditional beliefs and values, these Mennonites still participated – whether voluntarily or involuntarily – in the reinvention of their communities into Soviet kolkhozy. In this respect, these Mennonites were the unlikely but important catalysts in the transformation of Mennonites into Soviet kolkhozniki.

NOTES

1 The author thanks Lynette Toews-Neufeldt, Wesley Berg, Johann Esau, Leonard Friesen, and the anonymous reviewers for their comments and suggestions in preparing this article.

2 Following the collapse of the Soviet Union in 1991, Russian and Ukrainian scholars have published an impressive number of primary source documents from former Soviet archives and libraries. Some of the most important collections of archival records focusing on collectivization in the late 1920s and early 1930s include the following: V.P. Danilov, R.T. Manning, L. Viola et al., eds., *Tragediia sovetskoĭ derevni: kollektivizatsiia i raskulachivanie: dokumenty i materialy v 5 tomakh, 1927–1939*, 5 vols. (Moscow: Rossiĭskaia polit. ėntsiklopediia, 1999–2006); Alexis Berelowitch and V.A. Danilov, eds., *Sovetskaia derevnia glazami VChK-OGPU-NKVD, 1918–1939: dokumenty i materialy v 4 tomakh* (Moscow: ROSSPĖN, 1998); Lynne Viola, Sergei Zhuravlev, Andrei Mel'nik, Tracy MacDonald, and Andrei Nikolaevich, eds., *Riazanskaia derevnia v 1929–1930 gg Khronika golovokruzheniia:*

Dokumenty i materialy (Toronto and Moscow: ROSSPĖN, 1998); Valeriĭ Vasyl'ev and Lynne Viola, eds., *Kollektivizatsiia i krest'ianskoe soprotivlenie na Ukraine: noiabr' 1929-mart 1930 gg* (Vinnytsia, Ukraine: Lohos, 1997).

Some of the largest collections of unpublished materials on the Mennonite collectivization experience in southern Ukraine, and in particular Khortytsia and Molochansk, are located in the archives *Derzhavnyi arkhiv Zaporiz'koi oblasti* and *Oblpartarkhiv Zaporiz'koho obkomu KPU* in Zaporizhzhia, Ukraine.

Collections of letters form the bulk of published accounts of the Mennonite experience during Soviet collectivization. The most extensive collections of Mennonite letters concerning collectivization are found in the following periodicals: *Die Mennonitische Rundschau* (hereafter *MR*), Winnipeg, MB; *Der Bote* (hereafter *DB*), Winnipeg, MB; and *Zionsbote* (hereafter *ZB)*, Hillsboro, KS. While these letters provide a wealth of information, it is clear that many of them were edited before they were published in *MR*, *DB*, and *ZB*. This, of course, raises questions about what information was removed from the letters before they were printed.

Unfortunately, there are few other published sources that shed light on the Soviet Mennonite collectivization experience. One source is Peter Rahn's *Among the Ashes: In the Stalinkova Kolkhoz [Kontiniusfeld] 1930–1935* (Kitchener, ON: Pandora Press, 2011); this is a collection of Mennonite letters detailing the collectivization of Kontiniusfeld, Molochansk. Other sources include: A.A. Töws, *Mennonitische Märtyrer*, 2 vols. (Winnipeg, MB and Clearbrook, BC, 1949, 1954); John B. Toews, *Czars, Soviets and Mennonites* (Newton, KS: Faith & Life Press, 1982); and Terry Martin, "The Russian Mennonite Encounter with the Soviet State, 1917–1955," *Conrad Grebel Review* 20 (2002): 23. My earlier attempts to explain the collectivization of Mennonite communities in Ukraine can be found in the following works: Colin P. Neufeldt, *The Fate of Mennonites in Soviet Ukraine and the Crimea During the Soviet Collectivization and the Famine (1928–1933)*, 2 vols. (Edmonton, 1989); Colin P. Neufeldt, "The Fate of Mennonites in Ukraine and the Crimea during Soviet Collectivization and the Famine (1930–1933)" (PhD diss., University of Alberta, 1999); Colin P. Neufeldt, "Through the Fires of Hell: The Dekulakization and Collectivization of the Soviet Mennonite Community (1928–1933)," *The Journal of Mennonite Studies* 16 (1998): 9–32.

3 The *Global Anabaptist Mennonite Encyclopedia Online* acknowledges that the term "Mennonite" is somewhat ambiguous and can include not only those individuals who entered the Mennonite religious community by an adult decision (e.g., baptism), but also those who entered the Mennonite ethnic

group by birth. Harold S. Bender and Rodney J. Sawatsky, "Mennonite (The Name)" in *Global Anabaptist Mennonite Encyclopedia Online,* 1989, accessed on 27 June 2013 at http://www.gameo.org/encyclopedia/contents/M4673ME.html. My use of the term "Mennonite" is not restricted to those who were active members of a Mennonite church; it also includes ethnic Mennonites who were born into Mennonite families and lived in Mennonite communities in Soviet Ukraine.

4 In Mennonite and German writings about their settlements in Ukraine and Russia, the phrase "Mutter Ansiedlung" is often used to describe a Mennonite settlement (e.g., Khortytsia or Molochna) that established a daughter colony (*Tochter Kolonie*) in another region of the country. David G. Rempel and Cornelia Rempel Carlson, *A Mennonite Family in Tsarist Russia and the Soviet Union* (Toronto: University of Toronto Press, 2002), 307.

5 R.W. Davies, Mark Harrison, and S.G. Wheatcroft, eds., *The Economic Transformation of the Soviet Union, 1913–1945* (Cambridge: Cambridge University Press, 1994), 62, 111; R.W. Davies, *The Soviet Economy in Turmoil* (London: Macmillan, 1989), 62–4; Lynne Viola, V.P. Danilov, N.A. Ivnitskii, and Denis Kozlov, eds., *The War against the Peasantry, 1927–1930* (New Haven, CT: Yale University Press, 2005), 17–22.

6 Danilov et al., *Tragediia sovetskoĭ derevni,* 1:111–13, 119–35, 136–7, 141–8, 231–6; Lynne Viola, *The Unknown Gulag* (Oxford: Oxford University Press, 2007), 16. "OGPU" is the acronym for *Ob"edinënnoe gosudarstvennoe politicheskoe upravlenie* (United State Political Administration) which operated between 1922 and 1934.

7 Danilov et al., *Tragediia sovetskoĭ derevni,* 1:319–55, 464–6, 473–9, 525–8; Viola et al., *The War against the Peasantry,* 67.

8 Danilov et al., *Tragediia sovetskoĭ derevni,* 1:612–17, 659–60; Y. Taniuchi, "A Note on the Ural-Siberian Method," *Soviet Studies* 33, no. 4 (1981): 518; Viola et al., *The War against the Peasantry,* 128.

9 I.V. Stalin, *Sochineniia,* 13 vols. (Moscow: Gos. izd-vo polit. lit-ry, 1946–51), 12:167.

10 Danilov et al., *Tragediia sovetskoĭ derevni,* 2:85, 126; Iu. N. Afanas'ev, V.P. Kozlov et al., eds., *Istoriia stalinskogo Gulaga: konets 1920-kh-pervaia polovina 1950-kh godov: sobranie dokumentov v semi tomakh,* 7 vols. (Moscow: ROSSPĖN, 2004–5), 1:105, 115, 127; 5:107, 136; A. Berelowitch et al., *Sovetskaia derevnia glazami VChK-OGPU-NKVD,* 3:312, 327; Viola, *The Unknown Gulag,* 151–2, 196; R.W. Davies and Stephen G. Wheatcroft, *The Years of Hunger: Soviet Agriculture, 1931–1933* (New York: Palgrave Macmillan, 2004), 24, 47. GUITLTP is the acronym for *Glavnoe upravlenie*

ispravitel'no-trudovykh lagerei i trudovykh (Main Administration of Corrective Labour Camps and Labour Settlements). GULAG is the acronym for *Glavnoe Upravlenie ispravitel'no-trudovykh LAGerei* (Main Administration of Camps).

11 R.W. Davies, *The Socialist Offensive, 1929–1930* (Cambridge: Harvard University Press, 1980), 6.

12 Viola et al., *The War against the Peasantry*, 122.

13 Danilov et al., *Tragediia sovetskoĭ derevni*, 1:740–2; 746–64; Davies, *The Socialist Offensive*, 166.

14 Danilov et al., *Tragediia sovetskoĭ derevni*, 2:61–6, 85–6; Lynne Viola, *The Best Sons of the Fatherland* (Oxford: Oxford University Press, 1987), 43; *Derzhavnyi arkhiv Zaporiz'koi oblasti* (hereafter "DaZo"), fond R-286, opis 1, sviazka 228 (hereafter DaZo: R-286/1/228).

15 Danilov et al., *Tragediia sovetskoĭ derevni*, 2:11; Davies and Wheatcroft, *The Years of Hunger*, 4; Viola et al., *The War against the Peasantry*, 216.

16 R.W. Davies, *The Soviet Collective Farm, 1929–1930* (London: Macmillan Press, 1980) 46.

17 Danilov et al., *Tragediia sovetskoĭ derevni*, 2:85–6; DaZo: R-235/4/208; Davies, *The Soviet Collective Farm*, 5, 57, 68.

18 Stalin, *Sochineniia*, 12:191.

19 Danilov et al., *Tragediia sovetskoĭ derevni*, 2:364–5; Davies, *The Soviet Collective Farm*, 106; Vasyl'ev and Viola, *Kollektivizatsiia i krest'ianskoe*, 152, 204.

20 Danilov et al., Tragediia sovetskoĭ derevni, 598–601, 613–32, 786–7.

21 Ibid., 2:725–37; 3:95–6, 130–2; Davies, *The Soviet Collective Farm*, ix, 28; Davies and Wheatcroft, *The Years of Hunger*, 1, 4.

22 Rossiski gosudarstvennyi arkhiv sotsial'no-politicheskoi istorii 17/3/840, as cited in Davies and Wheatcroft, *The Years of Hunger*, 17. See also Danilov et al., *Tragediia sovetskoĭ derevni*, 3:171–2.

23 Davies and Wheatcroft, *The Years of Hunger*, 18.

24 *Kolkhoznoe stroitel'stvo* (1931), 4–9, as cited in Davies and Wheatcroft, *The Years of Hunger*, 18.

25 V.I. Marochko, ed., *Sil's'kohospodars'kyĭ soiuz nashchadkiv hollands'kykh vykhodtsiv na Ukraïni (1921–1927): zbirnyk dokumentiv i materialiv* (Kiev: Instytut istoriï Ukraïny, Natsionalna akademiia nauk, Ukraïny, 2000), 78.

26 In 1921 the Bolsheviks undertook an equalization of land program which saw German and Mennonite settlements lose 50 per cent of their landholdings. As a result, Mennonite landholdings in Ukraine were reduced to 135,650 desiatinas by 1922. Marochko, *Sil's'kohospodars'kyĭ soiuz*, 78.

27 DaZo: R-121/1/7–9, 15, 19, 23–9, 34, 36, 44, 53, 55, 61, 63, 67, 69, 72–3, 75, 85, 87–94, 96, 98; R-236/1/1–66, 69.

28 Ibid.: R-236/1/19, 22–3, 26, 38, 53, 60–1; R-121/1/29, 53, 60, 64, 67, 87–9, 90, 96.

29 Marochko, *Sil's'kohospodars'kyĭ soiuz*, 34–47; John B. Toews, *Lost Fatherland: The Story of Mennonite Emigration from Soviet Russia* (Scottdale, PA: Herald Press, 1967), 60, 76; John B. Toews and Paul Toews, eds., *Union of Citizens of Dutch Lineage in Ukraine (1922–1927)*, trans. John B. Toews, Olga Shmakina, and Walter Regehr (Fresno, CA: Centre for Mennonite Brethren Studies, 2011). In the sixteenth century Mennonites from the Netherlands settled near Danzig and along the Vistula Delta in Poland. For some time, these Mennonites used Dutch as a literary language, but a growing number of Mennonites also began using *Plattdeutsch* (Low German) in their daily conversation. By the eighteenth century, High German had replaced Dutch in worship services and written correspondence. When Mennonites began migrating to Russia in the eighteenth and nineteenth centuries, Dutch was used infrequently. Most migrants used Low German in their day-to-day conversations and High German in worship services and literary contexts. During the First World War, when anti-German hostility was rampant throughout Russia, the Mennonites argued that they were of Dutch descent to deflect this hostility. They eventually succeeded in convincing the tsarist government to treat them as Dutch. By the mid-1920s, however, the Soviets were treating the Mennonites as "Germans." Rempel and Carlson, *A Mennonite Family in Tsarist Russia*, 161; Cornelius Krahn, "Plattdeutsch," *Global Anabaptist Mennonite Encyclopedia Online*, 1959, accessed on 28 April 2013 at http://www.gameo.org/encyclopedia/contents/plattdeutsch.

30 Marochko, *Sil's'kohospodars'kyĭ soiuz*, 78, 120; DaZo: R-235/3/28, 50; B.B. Janz, "Wie kam Prof. Alvin Miller vom Norden hier nach Moskau?" (in the author's possession); B.B. Janz, "Zweite Reise nach Moskau," in John B. Toews, ed., *The Mennonites in Russia from 1917 to 1930: Selected Documents* (Winnipeg, MB: Christian Press, 1975), 100; Martin, "The Russian Mennonite Encounter," 20; James Urry, "After the Rooster Crowed: Some Issues Concerning the Interpretation of Mennonite Bolshevik Relations during the Early Soviet Period," *Journal of Mennonite Studies* 13 (1995): 30. The Mennonite effort to negotiate special concessions from Bolshevik authorities was in keeping with a practice that dated back to the sixteenth century when Mennonite leaders began securing special religious, economic, agricultural, political, social, and military concessions from European princes in exchange for their agricultural and entrepreneurial skills. The Mennonites continued this practice when they negotiated the *Privilegium* with the Romanovs and obtained unprecedented privileges (i.e., religious freedom, control of landholdings, control of local political,

economic, and educational institutions, and freedom from military service) in Russia. In their talks with Bolshevik authorities, VBHH leaders were primarily concerned with preserving as many of the past economic, religious, social, and educational institutions as possible.

31 Marochko, *Sil's'kohospodars'kyĭ soiuz*, 252; DaZo: R-235/4/58; R-235/1/751, 753, 816; R-3452/1/1; R-286/1/396. Organizations that played leading roles in the conversion of the *VBHH* into Soviet agencies were the Ukrainian government's Chief Co-op Committee, the Zaporizhzhia Okrug Committee, the Melitopol Okrug Co-op Committee, Kherson Okrug Co-op Committee, Kryvyi Rih Okrug Co-op Committee and the Bureau of Mennonite Co-op Network (BMCN). The BMCN was a Soviet-sponsored organization located in Kharkiv; one of its objectives was to facilitate and legitimize the conversion of VBHH cooperatives into state agricultural credit cooperatives. P. Funk was a Mennonite member of the BMCN executive in 1926 and played an important role in the conversion of Khortytsia VBHH co-ops into Soviet co-ops. Marochko, *Sil's'kohospodars'kyĭ soiuz*, 194, 222–6.

32 By 1927–8, Mennonites were operating a host of government-approved associations in Khortytsia and Molochansk. In Khortytsia, for instance, the villages of Burwalde, Nieder Khortytsia, Neuhorst, Einlage, and Nikolaipol operated peasant benefit societies that collected thousands of rubles for poor families. Mennonites in Molochansk and Khortytsia also organized a number of tractor associations, including the Druzhba and Einigkeit tractor associations in Ohrloff (Molochansk), and Krasnaya Zarya tractor association near Neuendorf (Khortytsia). DaZo: R-235/1/713a, 765; R-235/4/56, 62, 75, 212; R-4031/1/1.

33 Khortytsia Mennonites dominated the executive committees of land associations in Nikolaifeld, Kronstal (Dolynsk), Osterwick (Pavlovka), Schöneberg, Rosengart (Novo-Slobidka), Franzfeld (Varvarovka), and Hochfeld (Morozovski). DaZo: R-235/1/751, 753; R-235/4/56, 62, 111, 367; R-1429/1/12.

34 Terry Martin, *The Affirmative Action Empire: Nations and Nationalism in the Soviet Union, 1923–1939* (Ithaca, NY: Cornell University Press, 2001), 12, 20; Meir Buchsweiler, *Volksdeutsche in der Ukraine am Vorabend und Beginn des Zweiten Weltkriegs- ein Fall doppelter Loyalität* (Gerlingen: Bleicher 1984), 147; *Der Bote* (hereafter *DB*), Winnipeg, 3 January 1929, 3; M.I. Panchuk, O.P. Koval'chuk, and Bohdan Volodymyrovych Chyrko, *Natsional'ni menshyny v Ukraïni, 1920–1930-ti roky: istoryko-kartohrafichnyĭ atlas* (Kiev: Chetverta khvylia, 1996), 63–81; DaZo: R-235/2/144; PR-226/1/32; R-286/1/115, 130, 166, 170, 389; R-235/4/21.

35 In 1929–30 the Khortytsia raion was one of twelve raiony in the Zaporizhzhia okrug. The Khortytsia raion was subdivided into twelve village soviets: Khortytsia; Nyzhnia Khortytsia (Nieder Khortytsia); Kitchkas (Einlage); Baburka (Burwalde); Smoliansk (Schöneberg); Pavlivka (Osterwick); Shyroke (Neuendorf); Nikolaipol (Nikolaifeld); Zeleny-Hai; Veselivske; Lukashevo; and Novo Zaporizhzhia. In 1930 the total area of the Khortytsia raion amounted to 46,832.52 hectares, of which 37,278.49 hectares were cultivated. In the fall of 1930, the Khortytsia raion was absorbed into the Zaporizhzhia city soviet. DaZo: R-235/1/757, 808; Buchsweiler, *Volksdeutsche*, 148.

36 Oblpartarkhiv Zaporiz'koho obkomu KPU (hereafter "OZoKPU"): fond 7, opis 1, sviazka 138 (hereafter OZoKPU: 7/1/128).

37 DaZo: R-235/4/36. For Mennonite chairmen of village soviets in the Khortytsia raion, see DaZo: R-235/4/53, 56, 62; R-235/1/730, 781, 811, 815, 823; R-235/2/138. For Mennonite chairmen in Molochansk village soviets, see DaZo: R-3452/1/21; R-286/1/108, 115, 123, 133. For a discussion of Mennonites in various administrative roles at the village and district levels, see Neufeldt, "The Fate of Mennonites in Ukraine," 41–9, 155–9; Colin P. Neufeldt, "Separating the Sheep from the Goats: The Role of Mennonites and Non-Mennonites in the Dekulakization of Khortitsa, Ukraine (1928–1930)," *Mennonite Quarterly Review* 83, no. 2 (2009): 232–48, 266–71, 279–84, 286–91.

38 For Mennonites who served in the village CVP, see DaZo: R-862/1/35; R-235/2/133. For Mennonites who served in the village WPIC, see DaZo: R-286/1/108–09, 111, 115–16, 123, 133. For Mennonites who served in the potrebsouiza at the raion and village levels, see DaZo: R-286/1/142. For Mennonites who served at the raion-level CVP, see DaZo: R-286/1/116, 398. For Mennonites who served in the raion-level WPIC, see DaZo: R-286/1/115–16, 406. For Mennonites who served in the MTS, the People's Court, and other raion-level organizations, see DaZo: R-286/1/114, 232, 406; R-235/4/211; R-235/2/61.

39 DaZo: R-235/1/757, 808, 811, 813; R-286/1/115–16, 229, 394; R-235/2/138.

40 Khortytsia Mennonites who were party members or candidates between 1928 and 1934 included the following: Peter Kazdorf, Aganeta K. Sawatsky, Heinrich G. Rempel, Johann P. Quiring, Vera F. Schultz, Enns, Johann J. Wilms, A. I. Wölke, Matis, and Wiebe. DaZo: R-235/1/811; OZoKPU: 1/1179/49; 7/1/132. Molochansk Mennonites who were party members or candidates between 1928 and 1934 included the following: Hiebert, D. Schellenberg, Lepp, Schulz, Heinrich H. Hildebrandt, Nikolai Boldt, Jakob J. Regier, D.K. Unruh, David J. Braun, Anna K. Lepp, Jakob

P. Pankratz, Vasilii A. Penner, L.K. Petker, Heinrich P. Schmidt, Peter K. Koehn, Abram A. Goerzen, Jakob J. Brandt, Leonid U. Petker, Johann J. Plett, Konstantin S. Prochnau, A.P. Kopp, Johann J. Fröse, G. Hiebert, Vasilia V. Martens, Johann D. Funk, Jakob M. Hooge, Penner, Franz Dietrich Klassen, Martens, Jakob P. Schmidt, Andrei P. Goerzen, Emanuel J. Lohrenz, Viktor A. Schulz, Abram A. Buhler, Elena A. Klassen, Pavlina A. Suderman, Franz F. Funk, Peter J. Wedel, Peter J. Wedel, Isaak F. Hildebrandt, Heinrich H. Hildebrandt,Theodore August Lemke, Andrei P. Schmidt, Nicolai N. Fast, Jakob P. Pankratz, Tobias T. Foth, Johann J. Plett, Viktor A. Schulz, Penner, Maria Pauls, Gossen, Peter P. Heinrichs, Jakob M. Dyck, Andrei K. Schmidt, Johann A. Klassen, Gerhard J. Friesen, Andrei P. Goerzen, V. A. Schulz, Jakob F. Willms, Johann K. Wiebe, Sergei J. Hiebert, Dmitri G. Hiebert, Abram J. Tiessen, Lydia K. Neufeld, Heinrich K. Unruh, Lorenz, and Peter P. Sawatsky. DaZo: R-286/1/107, 114–16, 120, 170, 190, 192, 207, 216, 227, 229, 232, 243, 254, 394, 397–400, 406, 408, 415. Many of these Mennonite candidates and members were later purged from the party in 1934–5.

41 NKVD is the acronym for *Narodnyĭ kommissariat vnutrennikhh del* (People's Commissariat of Internal Affairs). Mennonites who joined the NKVD included Johann A. Klassen (party member/NKVD member), Heinrichs, Fast and Schmidt. DaZo: R-286/1/271, 400.

42 DaZo: R-3452/1/2–3; Rempel and Carlson, *A Mennonite Family in Tsarist Russia*, 220; Anna Baerg, *Diary of Anna Baerg, 1916–1924*, Gerald Peters, trans. and ed. (Winnipeg, MB: CMBC Publications, 1985).

43 Andrei I. Savin, "'Divide and Rule': Religious Policies of the Soviet Government and Evangelical Churches in the 1920s," trans. Walter Sawatsky, *Religion in Eastern Europe*, 32, no. 1 (2012): 3. Bonch-Bruevich's approach toward religious sectarians was supported by Lenin, G.E. Zinoviev, M.I. Kalinin, A.I. Rykov, and A.V. Luncharskii. Alexsandr Etkind, *Khlyst: sekty, literatura i revoliutsiia* (Moscow: Kafedra slavistiki Universiteta Khel'sinki, Novoe literaturnoe obozrenie, 1998), 663–6.

44 Etkind, *Khlyst*, 651–71; Eberhard Müller, "Opportunismus oder Utopie? V.D. Bonč-Bruevič und die russischen Sekten vor und nach der Revolution," *Jahrbücher Für Geschichte Osteuropas* 35, no. 4 (1987): 509–33; Savin, "Divide and Rule," 3; Alexander Fodor, *A Quest for a Non-Violent Russia: The Partnership of Leo Tolstoy and Vladimir Cherkov* (Landman, MD: University Press of America, 1989), 168; Marite Sapiets, "Anti-religious Propaganda and Education," in *Candle in the Wind: Religion in the Soviet Union*, eds. Eugene B. Shirley Jr and Michael Rowe (Washington, DC: Ethics and Public Policy Centre, 1989), 93; Heather Coleman, *Russian*

Baptists and Spiritual Revolution, 1905–1929 (Bloomington, IN: Indiana University Press, 2005), 180–9.

45 *Partei und Kirchen im frühen Sowjetstaat: Die Protokolle der Antireligiösen Kommission beim Zentralkomitee der Russischen Kommunistischen Partei (Bol'ševiki) 1922–1929.* In Übersetzung hrsg. von Ludwig Steindorff, in Verbindung mit Günther Schulz, unter Mitarbeit von Matthias Kecke, Julia Rötterjer und Andrei Savin (Berlin: Lit Verlag, Geschichte: Forschung und Wissenschaft, 2007), vol. 11; V.S. Izmozik, *Glaza i ushi rezhima: gosudarstvennyĭ politicheskiĭ kontrol' za naseleniem Sovetskoĭ Rossii v 1918–1928 godakh.* (St Petersburg: Izd-vo Sankt-Peterburgskogo universiteta ėkonomiki i finansov, 1995), 115–16; Savin, "Divide and Rule," 4–16; Felix Corley, *Religion in the Soviet Union: An Archival Reader* (London: MacMillan Press, 1996), 15; Coleman, *Russian Baptists and Spiritual Revolution*, 190–7.

46 Toews, *Lost Fatherland*, 186; DaZo: R-235/3/23; K. Sawatzky, "Unser Zukunft in Rußland" in Toews, *Selected Documents*, 113; Daniel Peris, *Storming the Heavens: The Soviet League of the Militant Godless* (Ithaca, NY: Cornell University Press, 1998), 29–30, 43–68, 78; Albert Boiter, "Law and Religion in the Soviet Union," *The American Journal of Comparative Law* 35, no. 1 (1987): 109.

47 Yuri Felshtinsky, "The Legal Foundations of the Immigration and Emigration Policy of the USSR, 1921–27," *Soviet Studies* 34, no. 3 (July 1982): 342; John B. Toews, ed. and trans., *Letters from Susan: A Woman's View of the Russian Mennonite Experience (1928–41)* (North Newton, KS: Bethel College, 1988), 23; Martin, *The Affirmative Action Empire*, 35; Adolf Ehrt, *Das Mennonitentum in Russland von seiner Einwanderung bis zur Gegenwart* (Berlin: Julius Belz, 1932), 119.

48 DaZo: R-286/1/170. Other Molochansk Mennonites who joined the party for ideological reasons included Teodore August Lemke (1924), Andrei K. Schmidt (1925), Vasilii V. Martens (1925), Viktor A. Schulz (1928), Jakob M. Dyck (1929), and Franz D. Klassen. DaZo: R-286/1/114, 398, 406.

49 DaZo: R-286/1/114, 170, 216, 232, 242, 406. There were two MTS in the Molochansk raion in the early 1930s; the Molochansk MTS which serviced sixty-one kolkhozy; and the Stulnevskoi (Waldheim) MTS which serviced fifty-one kolkhozy. DaZo: R-286/1/170.

50 Ibid.: R-286/1/166.

51 Ibid.: R-286/1/400.

52 Ibid.: R-286/1/114, 170, 398, 406; PR-226/1/29; R-296/1/397.

53 Ibid.: R-1415/3/1. In early 1929 the Central Committee of the Communist Party and the Central Control Commission called for a chistka of those party members and candidates who had defects in their personal characters,

were deemed alien elements, were passive, were involved in criminal activity, or had violated party discipline. By 1930, approximately 11 per cent of all party members in the Soviet Union had been expelled. The 1929 chistka was carried out in party organizations in Khortytsia and Molochansk, and encouraged local authorites to conduct their own chistki in non-party organizations in Molochansk (August–October 1929) and Khortytsia (December 1929–January 1930). In the Molochansk raion, for example, local chistka commissions purged Mennonites from their positions in raion soviets, village soviets, kolkhozy, agricultural associations, local factories, *Lesenhallen* (reading rooms), *Bauernheime* (peasant clubs) and medical facilities. Some of the reasons cited for their expulsion included the following: having ties with former landowners, kulaks, or experts; participating in active resistance against the Soviet state; being a member of an alien element; having family members deemed to be counter-revolutionary; performing unacceptable public work; owning too much land; or being an "unknowledgeable" worker. A number of Mennonites were punished for their un-Soviet activities without being removed from their positions. Local officials also viewed "emigration fever" as a serious problem in the Mennonite communities, and used the party and non-party chistki as a means of punishing the Mennonite communities because of those who tried to leave the country in the fall of 1929.

Between 1929 and 1933 the party membership in the USSR rapidly increased from 1.5 million to 3.5 million. By late 1932, some party leaders were again concerned that these mass admissions had led to an influx of "alien elements" and "double dealers" in the party, and that large numbers of members were "insufficiently stable" or "politically almost illiterate." In January 1933, the Central Committee Plenum ordered the specially formed Central Purge Commission (CPC) to conduct a chistka of the swollen party ranks, and by the end of 1934 the CPC had succeeded in expelling approximately 18 per cent of the party membership. In Khortytsia and Molochansk, the chistki of local party organizations took place in late 1933 and early 1934. As was the case with the 1929 chistka, the chistki of 1933–4 were not confined to party organizations, but also targeted non-party organizations and kolkhozy in Molochansk and Khortytsia. In the spring of 1934, the Molochansk REC concluded that there were still at least twenty-three kolkhoz chairmen in the raion who were members of class-alien elements, and that the kolkhozy at Lichtfeld, Schönau, Rückenau, Münsterberg, Ohrloff, Gnadenfeld, and Alexandertal were overun with kulaks and fascists. As a result of the 1933–4 chistki, a large number of Mennonite party members and kolkhoz chairmen were purged from their positions. Emel'ian Iaroslavskiĭ, *Chistka partii: doklad na sobranii aktiva Moskovskoĭ organizat͡sii VKP(b) 29 marta 1929 g.: tezisy doklada na ob"edinennom plenume T͡SK i T͡SKK VKP(b)* (Moscow: Gos. izd-vo, 1929); J. Arch Getty, *Origins of the Great Purges: The Soviet Communist Party Reconsidered, 1933–1938* (Cambridge: Cambridge University Press, 1985), 43–57; J. Arch Getty and Oleg V. Naumov, *The Road to Terror: Stalin and the Self-destruction of the Bolsheviks, 1932–1939* (New Haven, CT: Yale University Press, 1999), 74–6, 125–8; Lynne Viola, "The Second Coming: Class Enemies in the Soviet Countryside, 1927–1935," in *Stalinist Terror: New Perspectives*, eds. J. Arch Getty and Roberta T. Manning (Cambridge: Cambridge University Press, 1993), 74–7; DaZo: R-1415/3/1; R-235/1/766, 814–15; PR/7/1/135–36a; R-235/3/40; R-286/1/170, 191, 207, 216, 406; Neufeldt, "Separating the Sheep from the Goats," 259–62.

54 Some of the Molochansk Mennonites who completed party candidate application forms in 1929 included the following: Abram P. Ediger (poor peasant); Peter J. Loewen; Johann P. Foth; Bernard B. Wiens (member of the Molochnaya dairy cattle association); Gerhard D. Foth (Molochansk REC member); Gerhard A. Enns (Petershagen medical worker); Peter I. Dyck (chairman of the Schönau village soviet); David D. Epp (chairman of the Schönau kolkhoz); Jakob J. Letkeman; Margarita H. Lepp (Molochansk control accountant); Heinrich H. Schulz (Ohrloff village soviet secretary); Johann A. Petker (Gnadental village soviet member); Johann D. Tiessen (Gnadental village soviet secretary); Isaak Bergen; Franz F. Wall (Molochansk hospital administrator); Anna H. Neufeld (Molochansk hospital nurse); Eliza N. Goerzen (Molochansk hospital worker); Isaak K. Wiens (Molochansk hospital nurse); Margarita H. Unruh (Molochansk hospital worker); Maria H. Schmidt (Molochansk hospital nurse); E.J. Willms (Molochansk hospital nurse); S.S. Klassen (hospital worker); Ekaterina J. Friesen (Molochansk hospital worker); Ekaterina J. Boldt (Molochansk hospital worker); Elena A Berg (Molochaansk hospital midwife); Heinrichs (doctor's orderly); Maria Tiessen; Ekaterina A. Fast (Molochansk hospital nurse); Anna J. Wall (Molochansk hospital midwife); Franz F. Willms (hospital worker); Elizabath F. Wall (hospital worker); P.J. Loewen (state factory worker); J.J. Friesen (brigade member in a Molochansk factory); Gerhard G. Klassen (state factory cashier); Andrei A. Penner (Molochansk state factory); Kornelius Wiens (cashier); Klara J. Enns (Molochansk hospital nurse); Sara A. Tiessen (Molochansk hospital nurse); Lidia Rempel (Molochansk hospital worker); Heinrich P. Ediger (Molochansk factory worker); Johann J. Tiessen (Molochansk factory worker); Boris B. Friesen (Molochansk factory worker); Peter D. Wiebe

(Molochansk factory worker); Anna J. Friesen; Heinrich A. Braun; Abram H. Willms (Molochansk savings bank worker); Nikolai N. Wiebe; Katerina Peters; Gerhard P. Peters (People's Court worker?); and V.K. Fast. DaZo: R-286/1/396.

55 The Mennonite members of the Khortytsia REC in 1929–30 included the following: Heinrich G. Rempel (Communist Party member from Khortytsia), Johann P. Quiring (Communist Party member from Khortytsia), Johann D. Rempel (Osterwick), Abram J. Töews (RLDC chairman), Heinrich A. Dick (Nikolaifeld), Aganeta K. Sawatsky (Communist Party candidate from Neuendorf), Vera F. Schultz (Communist Party member from Khortytsia), Comrade Kozlovsky (Einlage), Johann J. Wilms (Khortytsia), David Braun (Neuendorf), and Hepner (Khortytsia). The candidates for membership on the REC included Ekaterina H. Siemens (Nieder Khortytsia) and R. Zacharias (Schöneberg). DaZo: R-235/1/811; R-235/2/138.

56 DaZo: R-1/2/307; R-235/4/250; R-235/1/713.

57 Ibid.: R-1/2/348; R-1/2/42, 49.

58 Ibid.: R-235/1/808, 814. The kolkhozy established in the Khortytsia raion during the tenures of Rempel and Quiring included the following: Alpha (Khortytsia), Kolos also known as Rote Fahne (Kanzerovka, Khortytsia), Kommune International (Khortytsia), Dnieprostroi (Einlage), International (Nieder Khortytsia), Rekord (Blumengart/Nieder Khortytsia), Triumph (Neukronsweide), Schnitter (Burwalde), Bauer artel (Osterwick), Chubarya (Osterwick), Hoffnung artel (Dolinsk/Kronstal), Karl Marx SOZ (Rosenbach), Nadija (Schöneberg), Pachar (Rosengart), Khliborob SOZ (Maloshevka), Landmann SOZ (Neuendorf), Das Neue Dorf (Neuendorf), Druzhba (Schönhorst), Nikolaipol SOZ (Nikolaipol), Lenin SOZ (Novo Zaporizhzhia), Varvarovka SOZ (Nikolaipol), Morozovskiĭ SOZ (Morozovo), Dolinskiĭ SOZ (Dolinsk/Kronstal), X. Rokovina Zhovti (Zelenai Hai), Chervoniĭ Plugagor SOZ (Veseloe), Chervoe Maya SOZ (Novo Petrovksiĭ) Sadovo-ogorodnoe T-vo (Kichkas), Selyanin SOZ (Petronal), Dneprovskiĭ SOZ (Dneprovskii), Riĭ artel (Krasnopil 1), Chervoniĭ SOZ Boretz (Krasnopil 2), Tarasovkaya artel (Tarasovka), Ukraïnka (Chervona Ukraïnka), and Chervoniĭ shlyax (Veseliĭ Yar). DaZo: R-235/1/730–31, 823; R-235/2/144; R-235/4/21.

59 Ibid.: R-235/1/808; R-235/3/48.

60 Ibid.: R-3452/1/3, 13–14, 20; R-286/1/107, 130, 166, 394.

61 Julius Loewen, *Jasykowo: Ein mennonitisches Siedlungsschicksal am Dnjepr: Gründung – Blüte – Untergang* (Winnipeg, MB: 1967), 56; DaZo: R-235/1/809, 813.

62 DaZo: R-235/1/731; R-286/1/166.
63 Ibid.: R-235/1/731, 814; R-235/2/58.
64 Ibid.: R-1429/1/36; R-235/2/95. The Khortytsia Mennonite minister, A.P. Töws, saw his tax bill jump from a relatively small amount in 1926–7 to 250 rubles in 1928. *DB*, 5 September 1928, 3. Local authorities ordered a Mennonite farmer and preacher who had small farming operation near Halbstadt (Molochansk) to surrender 320 poods of wheat and 380 poods of additional grains in 1930, notwithstanding a poor harvest the previous year. He was also required to pay 336 rubles in property taxes and 183 rubles in other taxes, as well as purchase state obligations and insurance policies. *ZB*, 18 June 1930, 1. In 1930 in Ohrloff (Molochansk), a Mennonite preacher was ordered to pay two thousand rubles in taxes, and a Mennonite elder was taxed three thousand rubles. B. H. Unruh, "Bericht XXIII-A" in Centre for Mennonite Brethren Studies (Winnipeg, MB: 3 March 1931), 4. See also *MR*, 20 November 1929, 12; *DB*, 12 February 1930, 4; *DB*, 5 March 1930, 4; Colin Neufeldt, "The Fate of Mennonites in the Soviet Union and the Crimea on the Eve of the Second Revolution" (MA thesis, University of Alberta, 1989), 57, 64–71.
65 Kommunisticheskaia partiia Sovetskogo Soiuza, *Kommunisticheskaia partiia i Sovetskoe pravitel'stvo o religii i tserkvi* (Moscow: Gos. izd-vo polit. lit-ry, 1959), 78–93; Gerd Shtrikker, *Russkaia pravoslavnaia tserkov' v sovetskoe vremia 1917–1991: materialy i dokumenty po istorii otnosheniĭ mezhdu gosudarstvom i tserkov'iu* (Moscow: Izd-vo "PROPILEI," 1995), 1:307–10; Arto Luukkanen, *The Religious Policy of the Stalinist State* (Helsinki: Suomen Historiallinen Seura, 1997), 38, 67; Daniel Peris, "The 1929 Congress of the Godless," *Soviet Studies* 43, no. 4 (1991): 711–32; Coleman, *Russian Baptists and Spiritual Revolution*, 216–20; Sapiets, "Anti-religious Propaganda and Education," 95; Joshua Rothenberg, "The Legal Status of Religion in the Soviet Union," in Richard Marshall, ed., *Aspects of Religion in the Soviet Union, 1917–1967* (Chicago: University of Chicago Press, 1971), 72–4, 80; Philip Walters, "A Survey of Soviet Religious Policy," in Sabrina Petra Ramet ed., *Religious Policy in the Soviet Union* (Cambridge: Cambridge University Press, 1993), 13; *MR*, 2 January 1926, 6; *MR*, 27 February 1929, 7; *MR*, 19 June 1929, 12; *DB*, 20 November 1929, 4; *DB*, 20 November 1929, 4; *MR*, 28 August 1929, 6; *MR*, 18 September 1929, 12; *MR*, January 1930, 6. According to one eyewitness from Margenau (Molochansk), a number of Mennonite ministers were admitted as members in newly established kolkhozy in 1928–9; they were evicted from the kolkhozy, however, when their ministerial credentials were revealed. *DB*, 15 May 1929, 3. In December 1929, a Mennonite from Fürstenwerder (Molochansk) reported

that a number of clergymen were imprisoned after being accused of inciting peasants to emigrate from the USSR. *DB*, 22 January 1930, 4.

66 In the nepreryvka system, Sunday was no longer a fixed day of rest. Kolkhozniki worked four or five days, followed by a day of rest. This system ensured that kolkhozy were operating every day of the week. Nepreryvka was introduced to increase industrial and agricultural productivity, and was an important component in the government's attack against religion. Davies, *The Soviet Economy in Turmoil 1929–1930*, 84–6, 252–6; Hiroaki Kuromiya, *Stalin's Industrial Revolution: Politics and Workers, 1928–1932* (Cambridge: Cambridge University Press, 1988), 238.

67 Boiter, "Law and Religion in the Soviet Union," 111; *DB*, 25 September, 1929, 4; *DB*, 23 October 1929, 4; Neufeldt, "The Fate of Mennonites in Ukraine," 209–13.

68 Danilov et al., *Tragediia sovetskoĭ derevni*, 2:130.

69 *DB*, 14 March 1929, 3; *DB*, 25 December 1929, 4; *DB*, 30 October 1929, 4; *DB*, 23 December 1931, 3.

70 Ibid., 25 September 1929, 4; *DB*, 7 August 1929, 3; *DB*, 15 November 1933, 4; *DB*, 25 March 1931, 3; *DB*, 18 June 1930, 3; *DB*, 26 October 1932, 4.

71 DaZo: R-235/3/28, 47, 52; R-235/2/95; R-235/5/72, 76, 79; R-235/1/730; R-235/4/211; R-235/3/49.

72 Ibid.: R-235/3/28, 47; R-235/5/79. For an analysis of the role of Mennonites in the dekulakization of the Khortytsia *raĭon*, see Neufeldt, "Separating the Sheep from the Goats," 221.

73 DaZo: R-235/3/47.

74 Ibid.: DaZo: R-235/3/48; Colin P. Neufeldt, "The *Zborni* of Khortytsia, Ukraine: The Last Stop for Some Kulaks Enroute to Stalin's Special Settlements," in *Confronting the Past: Ukraine and its History, 882–2009: A Festschrift in Honour of John-Paul Himka on the Occasion of his 60th Birthday*, eds. Andrew Gow, Roman Senkus, and Serhy Yekelchyk, *Journal of Ukrainian Studies* 35–6 (2010–11): 207–23.

75 DaZo: R-673/4/5; Toews, ed., *Selected Documents*, 117–22; Toews, *Lost Fatherland*, 77; Martin, "The Russian Mennonite Encounter," 21.

76 Danilov et al., *Tragediia sovetskoĭ derevni*, 2:130.

77 DaZo: R-9/879/41; R-235/3/23, 40; R-235/1/756; R-235/4/110; Neufeldt, "Separating the Sheep from the Goats," 287.

78 DaZo: R-673/4/10; C. C. Peters, ed., *Vor den Toren Moskaus: oder Gottes Gnaedige Durchhilfe in Einer Schweren Zeit* (Yarrow BC: Columbia Press, 1960); Andrej Savin, *Ėtnokonfessiia v Sovetskom gosudarstve: Mennonity Sibiri v 1920–1930-e gody: ėmigratsiia i repressii: dokumenty i materialy* (Novosibirsk: POSOKH, 2009), 250; Harvey L. Dyck, "Collectivization, Depression and

Immigration, 1929–1930," in *Empire and Nations: Essays in Honour of Frederic H. Soward*, eds. Harvey L. Dyck and H. Peter Krosby (Toronto: University of Toronto Press, 1969), 158–9; P.P. Vibe, *Nemetskie kolonii v Sibiri: sotsial'no-ėkonomicheskiĭ aspekt* (Omsk: Omskiĭ gos. pedagogicheskiĭ universitet, 2007), 229; Erwin Warkentin, "The Mennonites before Moscow: The Notes of Dr. Otto Auhagen," *Journal of Mennonite Studies* 26 (2008): 212–14; Colin P. Neufeldt, "The Flight to Moscow, 1929: An Act of Mennonite Civil Disobedience," *Preservings*, 19 (December 2001): 35–47. Of the approximately 13,000 German-speaking refugees in Moscow in November of 1929, there were 95 Baptists and Evangelicals, 743 Catholics, 2,481 Lutherans, and more than 9,000 Mennonites.

79 *MR*, 18 December 1929, 1, 11; *MR*, 4 December 1929, 6; *DB*, 29 January 1930, 4; *MR*, 29 January 1930, 7; *DB*, 12 February 1930, 4.

80 For an examination of the Mennonite exile experience, see Colin Neufeldt, "Reforging Mennonite *Spetspereselentsy*: The Experience of Mennonite Exiles at Siberian Special Settlements in the Omsk, Tomsk, Novosibirsk, and Narym Regions (1930–1933)," *Journal of Mennonite Studies*, 30 (2012): 269–306; Neufeldt, "The Fate of Mennonites in Ukraine," 37–126.

81 *DB*, 29 April 1931, 4; *MR*, 2 July 1930, 8.

82 DaZo: R-235/1/766; *DB*, 20 May 1931, 5; DaZo: R-235/4/129; R-3452/1/7; R-235/2/67, 95; *DB*, 14 May 1930, 4; *ZB*, 9 April 1930, 12.

83 DaZo: R-235/1/823; R-235/2/144. Some of the Khortytsia kolkhozy included Maĭbutnist' commune near Rosental, Krasnyĭ Fakel commune near Khortytsia, Pershe Travnya commune near Khortytsia, X. Rokovina Zhovtnya SOZ near Neuhorst, Chervonii Khliborob SOZ near Khortytsia, and Vachiya SOZ in Schöneberg. DaZo: R-235/4/61; R-235/1/815.

84 The Mennonite Funk served as chairman of the Nikolaipol zemobschestvo in 1926, and David Funk served as chairman of the Malashveka–Schirochansk zemobschestvo in 1927. DaZo: R-235/4/21, 61–2, 75, 79, 187, 208, 367. In February and March 1928, for example, Mennonite peasants in Einlage and Kronsweide (Khortytsia) organized a zemobschestvo that enabled Mennonite and non-Mennonite peasants to farm their land collectively, but retain ownership of their respective homes, equipment, and livestock. The Kronsweide zemobschestvo was organized on 15 February 1928 with more than thirty Mennonite households; it had nearly 860 hectares and a Mennonite administration that included Abram Petkau, Jakob Heinrich Janzen, and F.P. Unrau. The audit committee for the association included Jakob J. Klassen, Klassen, and Peter J. Klassen. On 4 March 1928, the Einlage zemobschestvo N° 1 was established with more than seventy households, most of which were Mennonite. This association

controlled more than 2,085 hectares and had an administration that included Mennonites, such as Korni A. Martens and H. Martens. It also had an all-Mennonite audit commission (Isaak Pauls, Heinrich A. Dyck, and Peter P. Petkau). Einlage zemobschestvo N° 2 was also established at this time with more than 265 hectares. DaZo: R-235/4/75, 187.

85 In early 1929 the executive of Khliborob included the following Mennonites: Heinrich B. Hildebrandt (chairman), Gerhard H. Funk, David P. Löwen, David P. Penner, Gerhard G. Ens, and Abram P. Sawatsky. I.A. Knelsen served as chairman of the Khortytsia CVP. Comrades Ens and Johann J. Wilms served as raion inspector of the People's Education Committee. Comrade Epp served as secretary of the People's Court in the Zaporizhzhia region. DaZo: R-235/1/751, 753, 779, 814; R-235/2/56, 95; R-235/4/117.

86 DaZo: R-235/4/66, 127; R-235/1/757. According to one report, 7,880 hectares (18.8 per cent of all land in the district) in the Khortytsia raion were collectivized by October 1929, 11,017 hectares (27 percent of all land) by 10 November 1929, and 40,380 hectares (100 per cent of all land) by 1930. DaZo: R-235/4/21, 118.

87 DaZo: R-235/1/730; R-235/4/21; Colin P. Neufeldt, "The Public and Private Lives of Mennonite Kolkhoz Chairmen in the Khortytsia and Molochansk German National Raïony in Ukraine (1928–1934)," in *The Carl Beck Papers in Russian and East European Studies*, University of Pittsburgh, no. 2305 (January 2015): 1–87. Some Mennonites who served as kolkhoz chairmen in Khortytsia included the following: Johann M. Neufeld (Druzhba artel, Schönhorst, 1928); David J. Kozlovsky, (Dniprstroï artel, Einlage, 1929–30); Peter P. Redekopp (Internatsional SOZ, Nieder-Khortytsia, 1929); Isaak J. Rempel (Internatsional SOZ, Nieder-Khortytsia, 1929–30); Kasdorf (Nieder-Khortytsia, 1930); P.P. Sawatsky (Alpha artel, Khortytsia, 1930); Peter A. Hamm (Pachar artel, Rosengart, 1930); Johann J. Friesen (Schnitter, Burwalde, 1930); P. Pauls (Dniprstroï, Einlage, 1930); Isaak Thiessen (Dniprstroï, Einlage, 1930); A. A. Thiessen (Dniprstroï, Einlage, 1930); A. Sawatsky (Energia, Kronsthal, 1930); H. Neufeld (Forwerts, Neuendorf, 1930); Braun (Khliborob, Neuenberg, 1930); Neufeld (Einlage, 1930); Lepp (Einlage, 1930); A. A. Peters (1930); Dyck (1930); Hamm (Kataevich, Khortytsia, 1934); Ens (Torgler, Khortytsia, 1934); Penner (Kolos, Kanzerovka, 1934); Rempel (Dniprostroï, Einlage 1934); Thiessen (Dniprostroï, Einlage, 1934); Pätkau (Rekord, Nieder Khortytsia/ Blumengart, 1934); E. Braun (Dmitrov, Osterwick, 1934); Hamm (Hoffnung, Khronstal, 1934); Unger (Faktor, Schöneberg, 1934); Unger (Otto J. Schmidt, Schöneberg, 1934); Wiebe (Ernst Thälmann, Neuendorf,

1934); and Neufeld (Landmann, Neuendorf, 1934). Some Mennonites who served as Molochansk kolkhoz chairmen included the following: David J. Dirks (Tiege artel, 1930–1); Peter Neufeld (Landmann SOZ, 1930); Heinrich H. Goossen (Blumstein artel, 1930); Peter P. Dück (Blumstein artel, 1930); D.K. Janzen (Nadezhda artel, Ohrloff, 1931); Johann J. Harder (Rosenort artel, 1931–3); P. F. Töws (Tiege artel, 1931–2); Rogalsky (Liebenau artel, 1930–1); Adrian (Fischau artel, 1931); Gerhard D. Neufeld (Blumstein artel, 1931); Jacob Derksen (Blumstein artel, 1931); Fast (Teknik artel, 1931); Friesen (Novo-Ukraïna kolkhoz, Grossweide, 1931–2); Jakob G. Warkentin (Nadezhda artel, Ohrloff, 1931–2); Johann Klassen (Rosenort artel, 1931–2); Isaak I. Berg (Sovset artel, Blumenort, 1931–3); Abram Neufeld (Tiege artel, 1932–3); Lorenz (Rosenort artel, 1932); Johann D. Penner (Rosenort artel, 1932); John Tiessen (Blumstein artel, 1932); Heinrich H. Epp (Rosenort artel, 1932–3); Johann Klassen (Rosenort artel, 1933); Goerzen (Rudnerweide artel, 1932); Boschmann (Einsicht artel, 1932–3?); David K. Unruh (Nadezhda artel, Ohrloff, 1933–4); J. J. Regier (Gnadental kolkhoz, 1933); N.N. Klassen (Wernersdorf kolkhoz, 1933); Schmidt (Mariawohl kolkhoz, 1933); Martens (Tiegenhagen kolkhoz, 1933); W. Penner (Altonau kolkhoz, 1933–4); Derksen (Schönau artel, 1933); David J. Braun (Altonau artel, 1933?); Gossen (Blumenort kolkhoz, 1933–4); Derksen (Schönau kolkhoz, 1934); Wall (Sparrau kolkhoz, 1934); Pankratz (Gnadental kolkhoz, 1934); Kopp (Stalino kolkhoz, Reichenfeld, 1934); Harder (Trud artel, Pordenau, 1934); T. Fast (Schardau kolkhoz, 1934); F.F. Funk (Fischau artel, 1934); Jakob P. Sudermann (Rote Fahne kolkhoz, Altonau, 1933–4); Nikolai N. Boldt (Hierschau kolkhoz, 1934); Gossen (Lichtenau artel, 1934); J.J. Regier (Gnadental artel, 1934); Harder (Trud artel, Pordenau, 1934); J.J. Gossen (Blumstein artel, 1934); and J.H. Rogalsky (Blumstein artel, 1934). DaZo: R-235/4/79, 110, 123, 127; R-862/1/35; R-235/2/133, 165; R-235/1/757, 814, 816; R-235/5/72; R-3452/1/6–7, 9–10, 18, 20–1, 24, 28; R-1429/1/12, 54; R-286/1/103, 108, 115–20, 133, 146, 166, 192, 194, 251, 397, 399, 406; R-286/1/416; R-3452/1/9; R-226/1/29; OZoKPU: 286/73/251; *ST*, 4 October 1934, 2; *ST*, 2 April 1934, 2; *ST*, 28 March 1934, 1; *ST*, 28 May 1934, 2; *ST*, 4 July 1934, 1; *ST*, 15 August 1934, 2.

88 DaZo: R-235/2/144. By 1934, the names of Mennonite-populated kolkhozy in Khortytsia included the following: Alpha (Khortytsia), Rote Fahne also known as Kolos (Kanzerovka, Khortytsia), Torgler (Khortytsia), Kommune Internatsional (Khortytsia), Kataevich (Khortytsia), Dniprostroï (Einlage), Kitchkas SOZ (Einlage), Internatsional (Nieder Khortytsia), Rekord (Blumengart/Nieder Khortytsia), Triumph (Neukronsweide), Rosa Luxemburg also known as Schnitter (Burwalde), Bauer (Osterwick),

Litwinow (Osterwick), Dmitrov (Osterwick), Chubarya (Osterwick), Energia (Khronstal), Hoffnung (Khronstal), Karl Marx (Rosenbach), Faktor (Schöneberg), Nadija (Schöneberg), Otto Schmidt (Schöneberg), Pachar (Rosengart), Rote Heimat also known as Khliborob (Neuendorf), Karl Liebknecht also known as Landmann (Neuendorf), Ernst Thälmann (Neuendorf), Forwerts (Neuendorf), Das Neue Dorf (Neuendorf), Der 1 Landgemeinde (Neuendorf), Krasnaya Zarya (Neuendorf), Druzhba (Schönhorst), Nikolaipol SOZ (Nikolaipol), Unsere Zukunft (Nikolaipol), Varvarovka SOZ (Nikolaipol), and Progress. DaZo: R-235/4/21, 62, 79, 110; R-235/3/50; R-235/1/731, 814, 825; R-862/1/7; R-862/1/20; *ST*, 12 July 1934, 1; *ST*, 28 March 1934, 2; *ST*, 24 May 1934, 2; *ST*, 21 May, 1934, 2; DaZo: R-673/1/2347; R-286/1/148.

89 DaZo: R-3452/1/1, 3; R-1415/1/1; *DB*, 3 January 1929, 3.

90 Ibid.: R-286/1/109, 120. For a list of agricultural associations in Molochansk in 1930, see DaZo: R-286/1/389.

91 Ibid.: R-286/1/103. According to Otto Auhagen, the German consular official who visited Molochansk in the late 1920s, the Gigant commune arose from a union of four communes and an artel that originally began in 1924–5. Otto Auhagen, *Die Schicksalswende des Russlanddeutschen Bauerntums in den Jahren 1927–1930* (Leipzig: Verlag von S. Hirzel, 1942), 37.

92 DaZo: R-286/1/103, 109, 120; R-3452/1/7. In the early 1930s some of the Mennonite-populated kolkhozy in the Molochansk raion included the following: Novo Ukraïna (Grossweide), Trud (Pordenau), Zemlya i Trud (Muntau), Krasnyĭ Oktyabr', Stalinkova (Konteniusfeld), Einsicht, Nadezhda (Ohrloff), Leninfeld (Waldheim), "10-Jahre Oktoberrevolution" (Reichenfeld), Kanadasky, Tractorist (Lichtfeld), Kollektivist (Lichtfeld), Landmann, Kultura, Sovset (Blumenort), Sovsteppe (Blumstein), and Rote Fahne (Altonau). DaZo: R-286/1/115, 118, 170, 191, 194, 251, 393, 398, 406; R-3452/1/10, 20; PR-226/1/32. The names of sovkhozy in Molochansk in the early 1930s included Skalistiĭ, Karl Liebnecht, Karl Liebnecht No.3, Stalino No 2, Akkerman and Ulyanovka. DaZo: R-286/1/115. Some of the Mennonites managing pig fermy in Molochansk kolkhozy in 1931–2 included the following: D.D. Enns (Schönau), D.F. Kornies (Tiege), Gossen (Blumstein), Warkentin (Ohrloff), P. Regier (Altonau), Kroeker (Blumenort), Dyck (Rosenort), D. Janzen (Münsterberg), A.P. Heinrichs (?), Hildebrandt (Gnadental), D.P. Derksen (Margenau), Dyck (Konteniusfeld), Tiessen (?), M.M. Schulz (Pordenau), Bekker (Gnadenfeld), D. Isaak (Elizabethal), Kroeker (?), Loewen (?), Friesen (Liebenau), Warkentin (Gnadenheim), Braun (Wernerdorf), Dyck (Leninfeld), Wiebe (Neukirch), Hiebert (Heidelberg), B.P. Harder (Klippenfeld), and A. Derksen

(Hierschau). DaZo: R-286/1/110. By 1932, there were ninety-four poultry fermy in the Molochansk raion, many of which were operating in Mennonite-populated kolkhozy. DaZo: R-286/1/115.

93 Ibid.: R-286/1/115, 120, 170. By 1934, Molochansk raion had 112 kolkhozy, one commune (Gigant), one seed-development sovkhoz (Skalistiĭ), three plemkhozy (animal-breeding sovkhozy known as Karl Liebnecht, Karl Liebnecht No.3, and Ul'yanovka), and two MTS (Molochansk MTS and Waldheim [Stulnevoka] MTS). The raion controlled 174,918 hectares, of which 126,574 hectares were cultivated, 948 hectares constituted gardens, and 5,352 hectares were considered farmsteads. The Molochansk kolkhozy controlled 133,918 hectares (108,096 hectares of cultivated land, 558 hectares of gardens, and 1,344 hectares of farmstead land) as well as seventy-four milk-commodity fermy. The sovkhozy and plemkhozy in the raion controlled 23,778 hectares (20,014 hectares of cultivated land, 127 hectares of gardens, and 56 hectares of farmstead land). The raion also had three factories (Obozzavoda, Tel'man, and Teknik), a Pivzavod (brewery), the Fabrikerweise tile factory, a Soviet party school, and a tractor school in Prischib. There were also two dairies, a dried milk factory, two iron-foundary artels, two assembly line operations, one stone quarry, at least two white-clay operations, four brick factories, one incubator station, one fruit kiln, one mill, one industrial plant, some village economic organizations and oil-seed mills, a nursing home for invalids, a school for the deaf and dumb, an orphanage, a medical school, a veterinary school, an animal husbandry school, a regional cooperative school, and three hospitals. DaZo: R-286/1/130, 147, 166, 170–1, 214.

94 Ibid.: R-235/2/148; R-286/1/166, 170, 214.

95 Ibid.: R-286/1/120, 166, 169, 192.

8 Kulak, Christian, and German: Ukrainian Mennonite Identities in a Time of Famine, 1932–1935

ALEXANDER BEZNOSOV

The tragic events of the 1932–3 famine remain among the most complex and fiercely debated in all of Ukraine's historical past. It is no wonder that they have stayed in the scholarly field of vision for decades, and been actively discussed in broad circles of the Ukrainian public. We see one of the fruits of this larger discussion with Svetlana Bobyleva's contribution on Borozenko in this volume. Her study of a single settlement area makes plain how this terrible event dramatically transformed Mennonite identities in Ukraine, at least for those who survived it. Unfortunately, many aspects of this tragedy, including how the famine affected Ukraine's numerous national minorities, remain insufficiently studied. This applies especially to the experience of the region's Mennonites who, as documents show, went through all the terrible trials of the time alongside Ukrainians.

This chapter opens a window onto this previously neglected area of research and takes a different tack than Colin Neufeldt's excellent contribution on Mennonite involvement in the very mechanism of collectivization in these years. Neufeldt demonstrates that collectivization was possible in the Mennonite colonies of Ukraine because the Mennonites themselves were agents of change as much as they were its victims. In a sense, my paper begins where Neufeldt's leaves off. Based on a wide body of previously unknown sources to supplement the extant Mennonite memoirs and historical studies, I investigate what shape the so-called terror famine of 1932–3 took in the German and Mennonite settlements of southern Ukraine. In addition, I explore the efforts Mennonites made to fight against the famine, their relative success or failure, and briefly consider the overall socio-demographic impact of this tragic episode in Ukrainian history. I am particularly interested in how the early years of Stalinist collectivization formed and transformed Mennonite identities as these former colonists found themselves at the intersection of German, Mennonite, and Soviet national and class-based identities, all of which had profound international implications with Hitler's rise to power in 1933. Thus this brief but devastating episode provides us with an opportunity to consider who the Mennonites were, how they saw themselves, and how they were seen by others in the midst of famine-like conditions.

Robert Magocsi places responsibility for the Ukrainian famine on the Marxist-Leninist commitment to class war against the kulak, by which they desired "an all-purpose term with which to brand whomever they considered an enemy in the countryside."[1] The onslaught on this ill-defined kulak began in 1927 though it reached an apocalyptic crescendo between 1929 and 1931 as Soviet agents – the dreaded 25,000ers – brought Soviet power directly to the peasants. More recently, scholars have presented a more nuanced explanation of the famine than previous ones that alleged Moscow's deliberate desire to exterminate the Ukrainian people. Historians now stress the incompetence of both central and regional officials, and of the chaos brought about by rapid collectivization and impossibly high grain quotas.[2] I will return to this issue given the Ukrainian government's decision to politicize the famine in the aftermath of the Soviet Union's dissolution and the challenge it presents for historical objectivity.

Colin Neufeldt links the way in which Mennonites were labelled early on as kulaks in the collectivization process, and how they suffered accordingly (even as others were agents of the state's often clumsy interventions). Mennonites had particular reasons to be fearful of the kulak label and the fate that awaited them in a Siberian exile. One who had not yet been exiled wrote that:[3]

> [F]rom the German (Mennonite) colony of several villages in the district ninety kulak children had died on the journey to Siberia or on arrival there. We are afraid of being sent away as kulaks, because they might say you are a kulak for political or personal reasons. We had a letter from one of the kulaks saying that they were cutting wood far away in Siberia, that life was terribly hard, and that they did not have enough to eat.

One Mennonite from the village of Hierschau complained in 1930 that the state had taken away everything: "Our cattle herds have shrunk away, the granaries are empty and we have only rye bread; yet we are called *kulaks*."[4] Rather than replicate Neufeldt's strong analysis, I wish to make three brief observations about how Mennonites experienced collectivization. First, most Mennonites experienced NEP (national economic policy) as losers, not winners (as the term kulak suggested). After all, they had lost a great deal of their land and wealth in the aftermath of the revolution, civil war, and Soviet seizure of power. Now, with collectivization, those who had maintained a modicum of wealth through NEP lost even that. In the words of one correspondent from Kontensiusfeld on 4 January 1930: "The future is very black. Dark would be sufficient for me. Storage loft empty, money gone."[5] Second, those Mennonites who endured Stalinist collectivization perceived themselves to have lost out compared to their co-religionists, as over 20,000 immigrated to Canada alone in the 1920s. As the possibilities for emigration dried up towards the end of the decade, and ended abruptly in 1929, those who remained now had a strong sense that they had been "left behind." Those who remained now pleaded with those who had fled to the United States and Canada to assist them in their hour of need. For example, Katja Nickel wrote to her siblings on 27 July 1930, and likened their new lives in Canada to living in a rosebush. By contrast, those who remained were in utter darkness.[6] As we will see, that appeal for aid only increased as the dark night of famine drew near. Third, and paradoxically, many Mennonites who endured collectivization understood themselves to be living in an apocalyptic moment that was under God's sovereignty, appearances to the contrary. This confirms a perspective first identified by Lynne Viola in *Peasant Rebels Under Stalin*.[7] Ukrainian Mennonites peppered their correspondence to North America during these difficult years with biblical references, including many from the Apocalypse, assurances of God's sovereignty in the end, and references to Christian celebrations such as Pentecost.[8] In many ways, then, collectivization was much more about Mennonite self-understanding than livestock tallies and grain acquisitions, however pressing those matters were. At the heart of this situation Mennonites repeatedly had to confront the existential conundrum of who they were.

Regardless of the cause, Ukraine's great human and material wealth suffered unnecessary and dramatic losses from 1930 onward as the Stalinist revolution erupted. Robert Conquest has concluded that Soviet officials already knew by August of 1932 that state production quotas were utterly unrealistic.[9] Even earlier, in July of 1932, Oblast Party secretaries had informed delegates to the Third All-Ukrainian Party Congress that the spring harvest that year had been disastrous because of administrative incompetence and mismanagement.[10] The future did not bode well. Nevertheless, officials refused to lower the quotas even as peasant anger and frustration mounted in the second half of 1932. Cases of hunger and mass starvation were only evident towards the end of the year. German districts in southern Ukraine first experienced famine in December of 1932, which is consistent with the worst-hit areas in Ukraine, though Mennonites were concerned much earlier than that. For example, a letter from Molochna written in April of 1930 declared that the upcoming harvest was certain to be a very poor one. Those who had managed to plant crops were unlikely to realize much, as some had already experienced malnutrition. Correspondents lamented that, no less crippling, the process of collectivization and dekulakization had undermined the Mennonite sense of community. One lamented, "[W]e never get together any more. Neighbours right next door [to each other] go their separate ways."[11] Justine Martens later declared that no Mennonite family in their village would offer her family refuge after her father had been deemed a kulak, and their house and contents seized.[12] Ominous clouds lay ahead.

Surviving archival records for the Vysokopol'e German district make it possible to trace the great famine's origin, development, and dynamics. Land agents informed local authorities that peasants faced imminent starvation across the region as events unfolded in 1932. In particular, A. Kolbun, the inspector of the district Department of Health, promptly informed the Vysokopol'e district authorities of the emerging crisis.[13] However, Soviet authorities remained focused on implementing state grain procurements associated with the collectivization campaign and made no effort to assist the starving. For example, the protocols of the December 1932 to January 1933 meetings of the Vysokopol'e as well as the Molochansk district committees of the Communist Party (Bolshevik) of Ukraine [CP(b)U] make it clear that little to no aid would be forthcoming.[14] Moreover, regional Party administrators of the German districts concealed information about the famine from higher authorities. Even after the famine had become a mass phenomenon in the second half of January 1933, the district authorities severely suppressed the rare attempts by collective farmers to draw public attention to their desperate plight. Thus, Wiens, a collective farmer from the village of Prigor'e, addressed the "Sickle" collective farm members' meeting where he reported on the impossibility of fulfilling state grain procurements, let alone the stipulated quota of seed supplies. Instead, he lamented that collective farm workers had "not eaten bread at all for two to three months." The authorities' reaction to Wiens's speech was immediate. After the meeting ended a search was conducted in his home, out of which "flour and four *poods* of different grains" and "an ample quantity of vegetables, fat and meat" were found.[15] These foodstuffs, according to the authorities, were more than enough to feed the large Wiens family and confirmed his base treachery and baseless accusations of desperation.

Meanwhile, the Dnipropetrovsk regional party committee of the Communist Party of Ukraine (CP(b)U) received information about the famine in the Vysokopol'e area in the beginning of February thanks to reports submitted by local state security police (OGPU) officials. The regional party committee – having received information of a similar nature from many other parts of the region by this time – responded on 10 February 1933 with a special secret circular to the secretaries of the district party committees and the presiding officers of the district executive committees. According to this document, the party committee ordered local officials to take decisive measures to render food aid immediately to starving families of collective farmers who had earned 350 to 400 or more workday units. However, the local authorities were themselves charged with finding the necessary means for this aid and they were to obtain it exclusively from within the collective farms or at least within the bounds of their own regional jurisdictions. Officials were to undertake special measures, for instance to encourage starving collective farmers to search for caches of hidden bread that their more far-sighted and enterprising fellow-villagers might have managed to secure. The regional committee further charged that collective farms allocate 10 to 15 per cent of the discovered bread to those who found it. By contrast, collective farmers who had only accumulated a small number of workday units, as well as the few lone individuals (*edinolichniki*) who had not yet joined the collective farms, were entirely on their own when it came to the search for bread.[16] This threat of no food for no work drove collective farmers to extreme measures. One letter writer from the German village of Kassel (Komarivka) in Ukraine lamented in 8 June 1933:[17]

> Men and women must arise early, at 6 a.m., and before, go to the collective kitchen to eat a piece of bread and a little soup, and after that try to work – if they can. And if you don't work, you don't get paid ... Every day I think: only God knows if my husband will come home alive. Almost everyone who has worked with him is already dead.

Despite every indication of mounting calamity, I.I. Medlage, the secretary of the Vysokopol'e district committee of the CP(b)U waited until 17 February 1933 to inform the regional committee that the OGPU had verified reports of famine. In particular, Medlage acknowledged the authenticity of starvation incidents in a number of district settlements at that time. For example, he declared that five families of collective farmers in the village of Natal'ino were starving. Of these, three families – Lorentz Walz, Kukenberger, and Marklinger – were German. Eight more families were starving in the village of Ivanovka, including three that were German Mennonite: Andreas Ruff, Anna Kopp, and Andreas Kopp. Officials further reported that there were twenty-one starving collective-farm families in the village of Zagradovka.[18]

In reality, the situation in the district was significantly more catastrophic than Medlage's report suggested. In another investigation issued on 23 February 1933, Medlage observed that 1,185 individuals in the district had clear symptoms of extreme hunger, including swollen feet, hands, and face as well as more generalized signs of physical feebleness. Of this number, only approximately 120 were adults; the rest were children. Investigators observed that most of those starving were found in the Ukrainian villages of Zagradovka, Ivanovka, Nikolaevka, Voroshilovka, and Natal'ino, where a total of 780 were starving. In addition, investigators declared that 75 of the 80 homesteads in the German village of Suvorovka were starving, as were 285 of 680 homesteads in Vysokolpol'e. Finally, investigators concluded that 90 of 93 homesteads in the Mennonite settlement of Orlov were starving. The district authorities at this time also documented the large-scale flight of collective farmers to neighbouring districts and localities in search of food. Mennonites in particular set off in whole groups to the nearest state-administered hard currency (*Torgsin*) stores in Dnipropetrovsk and Kherson. Authorities had established these stores in 1931 for the purpose of allowing Soviet citizens to purchase goods in exchange for jewellery or foreign currency, hence the title: "Torgsin" was an acronym for "trade with foreigners" or "торговля с иностранцами." Terry Martin has already highlighted historian Elena Osokina's findings, which demonstrate that the Soviet state's interest in these transactions was clear. The state was cash-starved. Osokina has concluded that up to one-fifth of the total foreign currency used in the Stalinist industrial revolution came from the Torgsin stores. How much exactly? Anne Konrad has noted that the Soviets "made a profit of 6 million rubles in 1931, 49.2 million rubles in 1932, and 106.3 million rubles in 1933."[19]

The nearest such stores for most Mennonites in southern Ukraine were located in Berdiansk and Zaporizhzhia.[20] In the long run, Mennonite engagement with these stores would spell disaster, though at the onset of collectivization it was a godsend as they brought their remaining German marks, American and Canadian dollars, and gold and silver objects to be traded for urgently needed foodstuffs. Soon, however, collective farms had used up all of these resources. Gerhard Lohrenz, for example, recalled that his parents took their gold wedding rings to the local Torgsin store in 1932.[21]

In the second half of February 1933 – and by the decision of the regional committee of CP(b)U – a medical committee of three people was sent to Vysokopol'e. It included the representative of the provincial public health department named Goldenberg, the doctor Tul'chinskaia, and a nurse. Their main task was to organize required medical services for the starving. The committee soon established day nurseries in four population centers of the district and ordered that 945 starving children from the families of collective farmers be relocated there. However, officials scarcely allotted any funds for actually feeding the children. As a result, administrators could only allot 2.7 kilograms of flour per child on a monthly basis as well as 300 grams of sunflower seed oil, 400 grams of various cereals, and 80 grams of sugar. Children up to four years old received milk which, however, only came to the nurseries from the collective farms if those same farms had discharged the state's monthly food tax beforehand. The committee's final report quoted local officials who observed that they had opened twenty additional beds in a local hospital – enough for most of the adult victims – and that they had organized communal meals in several settlements.[22]

State regulators restricted such assistance to only the most successful collective farmers and members of their families. The rest, whether collective farmers or private hold-outs, had to save themselves from hunger without any external assistance. Jacob Neufeld later recalled that even otherwise hardworking collective farm workers could be denied state assistance if they remained faithful to the church.[23] No wonder countless peasants, Mennonites, and others ate weed seeds with which they baked bread, and they mixed the meat of previously deceased pigs and horses into it when desperate. Naturally, the use of such "foodstuffs" very often resulted in the death of the one already starving.

Meanwhile, the scale of the famine in the Vysokopol'e district steadily worsened. Instances of starvation had been recorded by the Dnipropetrovsk regional committee of CP(b)U at the end of February 1933 in twenty-eight districts within the region, of which seven were most affected. Authorities observed that no fewer than 1,027 hungry children received sustenance at the recently established feeding centres as of 6 March 1933. However, provisions imported into the district were catastrophically insufficient, as authorities did not factor in the sharp escalation in the number of the starving then occurring. Officials were therefore only able to allot each hungry child half of the required daily ration. Even more tragic was the situation of starving adults. Neither the regional committee nor the regional executive committee responsible for the organization of relief had anticipated the need to provide food to adults other than those who were active members of collective farms. Local authorities now began to distribute ears of corn in response to this broadened need for assistance. Unfortunately, those who were starving hastily consumed the corn raw, which led to a sharp increase in mortality. Twenty people died for this reason from 12 to 19 March alone, which prompted authorities to terminate the allocation of corn. At the same time, medical personnel recorded the first two cases of typhoid in the area in Kochubeevka and another one in Alexandrovka. As of 8 April 1933, 143 people had died from starvation in the village of Zagradovka alone.[24]

In order not to disrupt the beginning of the upcoming spring fieldwork, the district party committee on 18 March 1933 decided to organize communal meals at all collective farms. Once again, they only intended to provide meals for collective farmers who worked directly in the field. In a further twist, authorities ordered the farmers themselves to make the urgently required foods available that would be prepared for the communal meals. Of course, many collective farms were only able to generate a small portion of the produce required by the most vulnerable, which meant that only well-performing teams were allotted meat and fat. At the same time, authorities did not forget about themselves. In the same decision of March 1933, the district executive also established a private canteen for their own use, and organized a special farm (*spetsial'noe posobnoe khoziaistvo*) to supply it with products, including milk, meat, and vegetables.[25]

Mass starvation among the Germans appeared to match that of Ukrainians in Vysokopol'e, though officials also reported incidents of starvation in other areas settled by German nationals; this included both exclusively German villages as well as districts where the settlement was of mixed nationality. The former teacher I.U. Pisarev, who lived in Molochansk during that period, noted in his memoirs that the famine in the Molochansk district began immediately after the harvest. Though German farmers in Molochansk and in other German colonies were starving, he recalled that they did not die in massive numbers, due to their chubby (*pukhlii*) frames.[26] The facts at our disposal only make it possible to demonstrate the extent of the famine in Molochna on the basis of in-patient data from the local district hospital. According to this information – and for the period from 20 February to 20 July 1933 – no fewer than twenty Germans and Mennonites from two to eighty-five years of age went through treatment in the hospital with a diagnosis of complete emaciation related to malnutrition. Eight of these died, though information for the last twenty days of May has not been preserved. In the meantime, medical personnel gave fifty-five Ukrainians and Russians the same diagnosis during this same period, of whom ten died.[27] In addition to Molochansk, there were two more hospitals in the district, and no fewer than six medical zones. John Friesen accepts the work of Colin Neufeldt, who previously concluded that from 2 to 7 per cent of Mennonites died in the famine years compared to perhaps 15 to 30 per cent of Ukrainian nationals.[28] One can only conclude that countless Germans and Mennonites suffered from starvation along with Ukrainians, and were given similar treatment regimes.

Those German settlements found within mixed-population regions appeared to be especially hard hit. At the Kolobatino (Rosenheim) farmstead of the Odesa region, for instance, almost the entire population was starving, yet at the peak of the famine, the local collective farm only allotted provisions to working collective farmers. Authorities issued every qualified individual one kilogram of maize flour and a small amount of vegetable oil per day, as additional family members were simply not taken into account. Twelve people died of starvation here alone.[29]

Foreign philanthropic assistance undoubtedly played a vital lifeline for those on the edge of starvation. Mennonites had benefited from a similar reprieve during the 1921–2 famine when North American coreligionists, many of whom had no previous connection to Ukraine had come to their aid. Years later, N.J. Kroeker recalled his family's desperate search for food in the village of Khortytsia as years of devastation took their toll. He recalls walking to neighbouring villages with what household articles remained in the hopes that he might barter for food. And he recalled how vital a role was played by North American Mennonites when they opened up their first relief kitchen in May of 1922.[30] Many Germans and Mennonites again appealed for assistance to their co-religionists in Germany and North America in the early 1930s. By now, however, they were able to appeal directly to kin who had left Soviet Ukraine in the 1920s. An inhabitant of the village of Worms of the Odesa region, Amalia Mauch, wrote the following in her letter:

> Dear brothers and sisters! I am a single woman, I have five children and an old mother. Please help us. Please do not let us die of starvation. My husband was sentenced to 15 years and was exiled to the north. Here we are without a homeland, everything we had was taken away. We are persecuted everywhere. Please help us. Please save us from death.[31]

Though the need for food was desperately felt, by the fall of 1931 Mennonites had a long list of required goods. One letter from 8 October 1931 detailed:

> [P]lease send us clothing for the children and wash soap. Something that is inexpensive. Perhaps sock and warm underwear to wear. Else could use a pair of shoes; she's running around in tattered ones too big for her. I could use a warm dress, and Sascha underwear and [a] new pair of pants – he has only one suit that he wears. Soap is so important because it is so expensive here. Also flour and lard, if it's possible. Dear Geschwister, we are thankful for every little thing. We're going to have to sell our cow because one can't find feed for her and we likely will have to sell her for a song.[32]

According to the Ukrainian Republic's OGPU data, by May 1934 up to 40 per cent of the residents of German colonies in the Odesa region had sent letters of this nature abroad.[33] Yet individual correspondences abroad were only one way in which these difficult years in Soviet Ukraine entered the world stage, as the famine in the USSR coincided with the rise to power of Hitler's National Socialist Party (the so-called Nazis) in Germany. Intent on securing the support of Soviet Ukraine's German population, the Nazis actively joined in an anti-Soviet campaign that expanded rapidly as reports of famine in the USSR increased in number and scale. Many observers in Germany maintained that Soviet authorities had deliberately initiated the famine. A series of diplomatic démarches followed as authorities in Nazi Germany expressed concern to their counterparts in Moscow about the misfortunes of German colonists, especially those deemed German citizens but living in the USSR. This involvement marked the onset of a dangerous new wrinkle in the Mennonites' cognitive map: having been branded as kulaks at the end of the 1920s they now risked compounding that if Soviets deemed them Nazi sympathizers. Their challenge was to seek out much needed assistance without demonstrating an iota of anti-Soviet sentiment. For their part, Nazi officials demanded that Soviet authorities allow them to render adequate food aid to the German populations in the famine-affected districts, which most certainly would have included Mennonites. In turn, Soviet officials in Moscow denied the existence of a famine and refused to accept the proposed assistance. Officials in Germany persisted, and in March of 1933 publically accused Soviet leaders of attempting to conceal the truth about the famine.

In 1929, Russian Germans who had already immigrated to Germany launched a massive campaign in support of Soviet Germans under the newly formed leadership of the Central Committee of Black Sea Germans. It sought to attract the attention of the German public to the problem of refugees from the USSR and the ongoing plight of the "Germans abroad" (*Auslandsdeutsche*) who, so far, were unable to flee their Soviet overlords. Committee leaders of this campaign formed a dedicated sub-committee – *Brüder in Not* – which issued brochures and newspaper articles under the titles *Brothers in Need, In the Deepest Need, Struggling and in Mortal Need,* and so on. After receiving information on the mass famine among the Soviet Germans, the committee, with the assistance of the German government, organized the first exhibition in June of 1933 of letters that starving Germans in Ukraine had mailed to Berlin. More exhibitions followed. In addition, leaders organized public meetings. They published articles, brochures, and other materials that pertained to the famine among the Germans of the USSR. At the same time, Russian German émigrés Pastor Johann Bredel and Professor George Rath created and led another public organization known as the Union for Relief to the Starving Germans of the USSR. It also quickly intensified its own activities, including a petition that generated 25,000 signatures, and that asked the government of the Third Reich to permit all Soviet Germans to immigrate to Germany.[34]

These interrelated campaigns reached their apogee in July 1933 when Soviet authorities were accused of deliberately "exterminating by starvation the German minority" living in the USSR. At this time, Cardinal Dr T. Innitzer, Catholic Archbishop of Vienna, founded the Inter-confessional and International Relief Committee for the Russian Famine Areas. The secretary of the committee was Dr E. Ammende, also the former secretary general of the European Congress of Nationalities.

Representatives of many public and religious organizations, including Jewish institutions, participated in the work of the committee. For example, Rabbi Dr Feuchtwang was a full member in the committee. This organization assumed a great moral authority as it undertook an active fundraising campaign in the United States, England, and other western European countries. Organizers energetically collected the funds and subsequently handed them over to the committee *Brüder in Not*. In Germany itself, a number of organizations (including the German Red Cross, *Deutsche Evangelische Kirche, and Volksbund für das Deutschtum im Ausland*) also appealed to the population of Germany to donate financially in support of the "suffering Germans" in the USSR. A special account entitled *Brüder in Not* was opened in the country's banks, into which Reich President Paul von Hindenburg and Reich Chancellor Adolf Hitler were among the first to deposit 1,000 marks of their personal monies. Could any supporter of this organization have attracted more Soviet attention than the German chancellor? In addition, the German government itself allocated 17 million marks to help starving Germans in the USSR as all German organizations involved with Soviet Germans and Mennonites had been thoroughly Nazified by this time.[35] The Nazi leaders skilfully made use of the Soviet authorities' silence to indicate that a conspiracy was underway against the starving. They managed to win the sympathy of the masses and fuel an expanded notion of international Germanic solidarity. Nor was this the only instance of famine in the Soviet Union resulting in strained international relations: the Soviet reaction at this time to famine in Kazakhstan was harsher due to perceived Chinese and British interference.[36]

The intensity of Nazi Germany's anti-Soviet campaign was strong enough to threaten the complete rupture of diplomatic relations with the USSR, nor was this unexpected given Hitler's fascist government in Berlin and Stalin's socialist one in Moscow. However, Berlin was not yet interested in being completely estranged from Moscow. Hence, it attempted to at least formally distance itself from participation in the most extreme elements of the anti-Soviet campaign. On 5 July 1933, the Reich's Ministry of Propaganda recommended that German organizers curtail the number of publications about the plight of Germans in the Soviet Union. Nazi officials instructed agencies to avoid direct attacks on the Soviet government. Despite this plea, the activities of the committee continued. By August 1933, the organizations involved had already managed to collect about 500,000 marks. A number of private individuals and recent immigrants from the Soviet Union soon joined this cause, including noted professor and Mennonite leader Benjamin Unruh, the Baltic preacher Muller, an educator named Schilling, and a pastor named Schimke. All of them successfully worked together alongside other German philanthropic organizations to raise funds for the cause.[37] It should not surprise that Communist Party officials coincidentally rejected any sharp distinction between Mennonites, Germans, and Nazis, to the detriment of Ukraine's Mennonites (and Germans of course).

Initially, the relief organizers proposed to send its large consignments to the starving German settlements of Ukraine, which included Mennonites. However, organizers soon abandoned this plan because the Soviet government, which continued to deny the very fact of the famine, refused to give its consent. As an alternative, the German transport company Fast & Brilliant arranged the entry of food parcels to individual addresses in the Soviet Union. In addition, other western European countries, including Switzerland, Sweden, and Holland, as well as the United States, all transferred hard currency funds to private Torgsin accounts in the Soviet Union. Representatives then mailed the corresponding receipts to individual Germans in the USSR who could use these documents to obtain the necessary produce and critical commodities at any Torgsin branch. By this circuitous route, average transfers of 5 to 10 marks did make their way from Germany to Germans and Mennonites in the Soviet Union.[38]

In the German districts of Ukraine, foreign currency first began to arrive in December 1932 though, as mentioned above, individual families had been recipients of such gifts from their relations for several years now. One recipient wrote back to her unnamed benefactors: "We want to let you know that we got your gift, which saved us from certain death. We send you a loving heartfelt thank you for that … With your gift we bought the cheapest food: gruel, flour, and a little fat. It has been over a half a year since we've seen anything cooked with fat."[39] However, during the peak of the famine, from spring to early summer of 1933, comparatively little came through to desperate households.[40] The main flow of money transfers began to pour in only at the end of summer to early autumn of 1933, when more detailed information on the situation of Ukraine's Mennonites and Germans was received.

As indicated above, at first the Soviet leadership officially denied any mass starvation in the country, but it did not prohibit the arrival of money transfers from abroad. How could it when hard currency in the USSR was both scarce and highly in demand (both by individual families and by the state itself)? That said, Moscow's Central Committee Secretary L.M. Kaganovich proposed that party organizations at the local level should organize "by means of media statements" collective farmers who had rejected receiving money for their individual use. In its place, the farmers were to be seen requesting that funds be transferred to the common good via the MOPR Fund; the Soviet-based International Red Aid Fund established in 1922 as an alternative to the International Red Cross. Kaganovich advised each such person to inform Berlin of his decision "in a sufficiently polite but convincing manner." However, despite the threats and psychological pressure, only a few collective farmers found the strength to refuse the monies received. Subsequently, one party worker from the Spartakovka German district explained in his defence that "the temptation was too great. In the Torgsin the fine wheat flour had appeared so blindingly white and the Danube herrings had smelled so appetizing at a time when even corn meal in the collective farmers' homes was rare."[41]

The German consulates in the Ukraine – Kyiv (Consul Hencke), Odesa (Consul Roth) and Kharkiv – also worked actively to render relief to the starving. The consulate staff visited the German villages to assist with relief distribution, and each day received up to fifty to sixty people seeking food. In response, staff provided petitioners with addresses of charitable organizations in Germany where they could write directly.[42] International relief organizers and distributors seemed especially drawn to populous German and Mennonite settlements; this may have been because conditions there warranted the increased attention by consular staff, or perhaps because of the ability of those very settlements to launch larger appeals. Community leaders in those instances tended to come from the clergy – whether pastors and preachers – as well as from active members of church communities, teachers, and others who enjoyed the confidence of the local inhabitants. These individual advocates actively identified those collective farmers in their midst who were in dire need. They provided them with the addresses of charities and benevolent societies in Germany, and occasionally they received funds in their own names and distributed them among the destitute.[43]

Soviet officials alleged that, in the beginning, so-called kulaks within the German population and other equally dishonourable individuals were the first to receive external assistance. Soon, however, private and collective farmers in dire need began to receive packages of support. It also did not take long before German relief organizations changed tactics in light of the Soviets' persistent pressure on relief organizations to reject transfers received in the name of individual households. For example, agencies arranged to have money (usually 20 to 40 marks) sent by selected Germans to specific households in Spartakovka district. Significantly, such letters were sent from individuals in Germany, and from several different cities; they were not sent on behalf of any specified relief organization.[44]

The dire need for such aid did not decrease after collective farmers had completed the harvest of 1933. On the contrary, the need expanded as active Soviet functionaries, chairs of village councils, and collective farms – even individual communists – began to receive aid from abroad as of the spring of 1934. In the Luxembourg district, in particular, up to 30 per cent of collective farms and 10 to 20 per cent of collective farmers were recipients of German relief. International donors and organizations sent no fewer than 1,788 transfers to the district from 11 March to 21 April 1934, for a total value of approximately 20,000 marks.[45] They sent additional funds in the amount of 44,392 rubles in gold from abroad to the German population of the Vysokopol'e district from April 1933 to September 1934 inclusive.[46] In some instances, residents from neighbouring Ukrainian villages, mainly those previously repressed, also began to receive assistance. It is possible that these were funds from foreign Ukrainian relief organizations, sent to southern Ukraine through intermediaries on behalf of German and Mennonite relief organizations.

In total, international donors from April 1933 to April 1934 transferred around 400,000 rubles in gold from abroad to inhabitants of the German settlements in southern Ukraine. This included 132,321 rubles to the Odesa region, 203,000 to Dnipropetrovsk, 60,000 to Donetsk, and 2,500 rubles to the Moldavian Republic.[47] We can also see that foreign donors increased their giving as time passed and the need became undeniable. Food purchased with these funds saved the lives of thousands of starving Ukrainian Germans and Mennonites. We see it in letter after letter as Ukrainian Mennonites expressed their thanksgiving when relations in North America gave what they could. We see it in Jacob Neufeld's own assessment years later when he observed that financial help from relatives abroad "provided crucial help and should be acknowledged as having saved numerous lives during the famine."[48]

The example from Vysokopol'e district indicates how essential the help from abroad was for the hungry. As already mentioned, over 40,000 rubles were officially sent from abroad to the German and the

Mennonite populations in the district from April 1933 to September 1934. In the beginning of 1933, the price of 1 kilogram of flour in Torgsin stores was 20 kopecks in gold. Consequently, it was possible to buy 221,960 kilograms of flour with this money. Taking into account that in the beginning of 1933 no more than 11,000 Germans and Mennonites lived in the district, each of them, including infants, got more than 20 kilograms of flour. Part of the money also came informally in postal envelopes directly to specified destinations. In addition to cash transfers, food parcels were forwarded from the German firm Fast & Brilliant to Germans and Mennonites' personal addresses. Finally, some residents of the district received parcels from abroad with non-food items, which they later exchanged for food in cases of extreme need.

Thus, this foreign financial and food aid, along with the higher financial means still partly preserved from an earlier time, allowed a significant number of Germans and the Mennonites to avoid the fate of millions of Ukrainian peasants who fell victim to famine. However, Ukrainian Germans and Mennonites did contribute to this tragic martyrology. According to the data of V. Chentsov, at least 13,700 ethnic Germans died of starvation in Ukraine in 1933, 12,000 of whom were located in rural areas.[49] Available statistics make it possible to suggest that the human loss among Mennonites was relatively modest compared to the Germans. According to the German researcher Karl Stumpp, there were 323 famine victims in the Vysokopol'e district, 213 of whom were Mennonites and 110 Germans.[50] By contrast, Stump also concluded that thirty-six people died in Khortytsia district, which was populated almost exclusively by Mennonites.[51] Death rates in the German district of Odesa were dozens of times higher than in Khortytsia. Starvation also killed more than 300 people in the village Kandel of the Zel'ts district alone, and 132 people fell victim in Karlsruhe village in Karl-Liebknecht district.[52]

Even more Ukrainians died in districts with German nationals. The 323 Germans and Mennonites who died of hunger in the Vysokopol'e district comprised about 3 per cent of the total number of Germans. The number of Ukrainians in the district who died from starvation was much higher. In the village of Zagradovka alone, 143 died from starvation between 1 January and 8 April 1933. The total figure probably amounted to about 1 million people, or more than 18 per cent of the total number of Ukrainians. The fact that at the end of summer of 1933, the district authorities planned to resettle up to 120 families from other regions of Ukraine in some depopulated Ukrainian villages confirms such great human losses.

Meanwhile, the Soviet authorities' relatively tolerant attitude towards the recipients of aid from Germany changed dramatically from the end of 1933 onward. This should not be surprising, given the mounting annoyance at how the Soviet Union's image abroad had been tarnished by fundraisers who had used an explicitly anti-Soviet campaign to raise funds. For proof of this thesis, officials searched for and then manipulated essential facts. In addition, both the OGPU and independent communists from among Soviet Germans started to report to Moscow that the political situation in populous places among the German population had worsened. In particular, V. Balitskii, the chair of the Ukrainian Republic's OGPU, warned the following in an internal memorandum to the Central Committee in Moscow, that "the German Consulate through its kulak agents conducts a mass fascist cultivation of colonists and organizes special cadres of correspondents whom they direct to compose provocative letters about famine and mortality in Ukraine, which they send to specified addresses in Germany."[53] Balitski further reported that the agents of German diplomats in Soviet Ukraine had allegedly carried out "fascist cultivation of visitors, the German colonists, in the consulate premises, indicating to them that the armed intervention of Ukraine by German troops was imminent."[54] Such actions by consular staff, in the Chekists' opinion, had resulted in "the disruption of economic-political campaigns in rural areas. People had not joined collective farms, others had renounced all agricultural activity and fled the area to engage in acts of sabotage."[55] To confirm his conclusions, V. Balitskii pointed to the massive absence of workers in the collective farms of the Luxembourg district (Mar'ianovka and Sergeevka are mentioned) where similarly alarming trends had been observed after teams had received "Nazi assistance." Secret Soviet agents reported that in Molochansk, Spartakovka, and other districts a number of people who had received aid from Germany had abandoned their agricultural labour on collective farms. They now counted on a systematic system of relief to sustain them in the future. In the Molochansk district of Dnipropetrovsk region and the Staraia Karan' district of Donbass, many chairs of collective farms were alleged to have turned to Germany for "Nazi assistance." Curiously, some recipients claimed that they had done so because they believed that the supply of German currency would strengthen the financial position of the Soviet Union, which was indeed the case.[56] Thus, with the help of these specially selected and correspondingly interpreted "facts," officials created an illusion of large-scale anti-state activities which the recipients and organizers of foreign aid allegedly carried out. This gave them grounds for discrediting Soviet Germans and Mennonites and opened the door to their further repression.

A number of prominent and previously active Soviet party officials who had steadily implemented the policies of the Communist Party among the Ukrainian Germans were accused of having undergone political "corrosion" at this time. According to the report of one vigilant and exceedingly "steadfast" communist, a number of communists had reclaimed their German and Austrian citizenship, "hoping to reserve an exit for themselves [from the Soviet Union] just in case the corresponding consulate intervened." Those implicated included the communists Knorre, Gokkel (editor of the magazine *Neulander*), O. Baitinger (principal of the Pryshyb German Pedagogical Technical School), Geyer (principal of the Pryshyb Engineering College), M. Billik (principal of the Khortytsia German Pedagogical Technical School), and Golovskii. The latter had departed "temporarily" for his homeland in Austria, yet once there, he chose not to return to Soviet Ukraine.[57]

Naturally, the authorities could not ignore these allegations. As a result, they launched a campaign against any "Nazi assistance that undermined the authority of the socialist state." Recipients of parcels and cash resources from abroad who did not want to hand such mailings over to the MOPR Fund were henceforth deemed counterrevolutionaries and agents of German fascism. A directive by the Soviet Internal Security forces forbade "all kinds of visits of consulate representatives to villages for the distribution of relief and execution of provocative work." Hann, the secretary of the German Consulate in Odesa, and several representatives of the German transport company Deutsche Levante-Linie were expelled from the USSR. In August 1934, the Soviet Union refused to accept donations and parcels from the committee *Brüder in Not,* which it accused of anti-Soviet activities. Punitive organs at the local level pushed actively to expose the so-called organizers of "Nazi assistance." In May 1934, officials arrested sixty-five people – predominantly from church circles and among the kulaks – on this treasonous charge in Soviet Ukraine. At the same time they identified another sixty people for arrest. In particular, local Torgsin branch employees were alleged to have gone to the colonies and actively encouraged local Germans and Mennonites to seek foreign assistance – with the goal of increasing the revenue of their establishments. These employees were now persecuted severely. The campaign against "Nazi assistance" provoked authorities to search actively for "counter-revolutionary fascist organizations" in various German districts of Soviet Ukraine.

At the same time, state officials delivered a heavy blow against public educational institutions. The Ukrainian Republic's OGPU reported on 22 May 1934 that it had uncovered a "fascist organization" in the Khortytsia Pedagogical Technical School (the principal was the abovementioned M. Billik). It alleged that almost all pedagogical personnel belonged to the anti-Soviet bloc. All were subsequently arrested, and the OGPU brought similar charges against Geyer, the principal of the Pryshyb Engineering Technical School and Kampfhausen, a German national and his counterpart at the Pryshyb Agronomic Technical School. Several political émigrés were also arrested in the Odesa region with purported "ties with fascists," including Ganger, the principal of the Zel'ts Secondary School, a Professor Strem, and so on. The OGPU further reported that all those arrested attested to the allegedly mass propaganda of fascist ideas that had been expounded by teachers of German schools in the Luxembourg, Molochansk, and Karl-Liebknecht districts.[58]

From the autumn of 1934 onward, then, the higher Communist party leadership reconsidered the difficult situation that had developed in many of the Soviet German population centres. Hence, on 15 September 1934, the Communist Party Central Committee approved a special decree "On the work of the Molochansk district committee of the Dnipropetrovsk regional party," in which the NKVD was ordered to carry out measures "towards a decisive liberation of the district from anti-Soviet elements connected with German fascism."[59] The Central Committee sent an encrypted telegram on 5 November 1934 to Party committees that obliged them "to take repressive measures regarding active counter-revolutionary and anti-Soviet inclined elements, carry out arrests and expulsion, and sentence persistent leaders to be shot." In all German districts, local authorities were instructed "to demand from the German population a complete cessation of contact with the bourgeois-fascist organizations [including] the receipt of money [and] parcels."[60] The communists were further instructed to explain to the Ukrainian Germans that henceforth the government would not tolerate the smallest signs of disloyalty to the Soviet regime.

Well aware that it would not be possible to stabilize the situation in populous German and Mennonite districts by repressive measures and ideological suasion alone, the central party leadership also recommended that regional authorities render help to the starving German collective farmers with provisions, seeds, and feed. Authorities were ordered to write off German and Mennonite debt on government loans as available resources allowed them to do so. Regional party organizations developed similar initiatives in response to this Central Committee directive. The Dnipropetrovsk regional party committee thus prepared for the first such ameliorative decision on 21 November 1934. However, despite the measures taken, the political and economic situation continued to remain very difficult. Authorities approved additional decrees designed to ameliorate the crisis that had enveloped the German districts of the region and they managed to link many of these to specific and constructive measures. By that time, however, the severest part of the crisis seemed to have passed. Regional authorities now ascertained that "the political situation in the German districts had improved and strengthened recently," even as they were compelled to admit that "the attained ... effect is still extremely insufficient."[61] Once again, officials primarily intended to carry out actions of a repressive and propagandistic nature. They proposed, for example, that local officials permanently remove the so-called kulak elements from the German districts. This would be possible, they reasoned, if they initiated a few show trials against "leaders of fascist groups and organizers of Nazi assistance." Nor could it stop there, as Soviets urgently sought to remove twenty-six teachers in the Molochansk district as officials also called for a mass purge of medical workers and trades people from the same area. On a positive note, authorities encouraged the acquisition and organization of relevant political literature into the district to support the socialist transformation underway. A new round of mass political work by the region's communists among the collective farmers was intended to highlight as widely as possible "the processes of corruption in Nazi Germany, the plight of German workers and minor peasants, and the heroic struggle of the German communist party against the fascist regime."[62] The regional committee also passed a resolution that allotted the most affected Molochansk district collective farms for an extra 3,000 centners of food loans. However, even after receiving this grain, collective farms could increase the distribution of bread per workday only to 600 to 700 grams. For a similar purpose, authorities allocated only a few thousand tons of grain to the Luxembourg district.[63]

Authorities did pass measures designed to secure the ongoing socioeconomic development of the German districts, as in the decision to undertake a broad system of measures to strengthen and develop livestock breeding in the near future. Moscow understood that this was a vital sector of the district's economy and bedrock for any future success. These new initiatives coincided with a significant rise in the level of mechanization through the creation of new machine tractor stations in the German districts and the delivery of new technology and full-scale electrification of collective farms there. Other developments in the 1930s allowed for increased productivity in German and Mennonite collective farms. Increased wages in the post-famine years seemed to stimulate labourers to be more productive. Last, collective farmers developed increased specialization towards the end of the 1930s as authorities shifted away from a policy whereby all farmers were to learn all trades, from cattle breeding to grain cultivation and so on. Increased agricultural specialization within the collective farms thus contributed greatly to their increased productivity. In sum, the practical implementation of these tasks allowed the German collective farms to improve their socio-economic situation significantly by the second half of the 1930s. In the process, collective farms with Mennonite and German concentrations became among the most advanced agricultural enterprises not only in Soviet Ukraine but within the entirety of the Soviet Union. Ironically, Moscow now interpreted agricultural success, which earlier had been a negative marker of Mennonite and German capitalist proclivity, as henceforth a sign of Soviet success and nationalist integration. By this means a certain measure of entrepreneurial initiative highlighted by Venger had come full circle in the Soviet era, even as the "German question" first raised by Venger, Beznosova, and Cherkazianova continued to lurk.

Thus, it is possible to conclude the following. An examination of the German and Mennonite experiences in the early 1930s sheds light on our understanding of the terror famine of 1932–3. We know that the main causes of the famine were socio-economic, however, Bolshevik culture, and Bolshevik assumptions about the ability of technology to transform society and of the need to transform peasant society in particular, played a major role. Officials initiated a forced and chaotic process of collectivization at the end of the 1920s that drove the agricultural sector, and all agriculturalists into a deep crisis. The recently and rapidly created collective farms were unable to produce sufficient goods to feed themselves, much less the new socialist society that socialist planners had anticipated. Instead, grain production especially, decreased sharply and immediately. Moscow ignored existing realities and possibilities as it required a large quantity of grain both to export as well as to feed its rapidly expanding industrial sector. To meet that need, officials first seized grain from the newly formed collective farms. They then undertook the large-scale confiscation of provisions from so-called former kulaks regardless of nationality. Since the quantity of seized grain was insufficient to realize their overambitious plans, authorities soon transferred a system of confiscation to other social groups of the population (including members of the new collective farms), also regardless of nationality. Officials accompanied all of these actions with acts of mass terror and violence against the population as a whole. Is it any wonder that famine-like conditions were not far off, even before considering an unusually harsh climactic cycle?

Our ongoing investigation allows us to comment on similarities and differences among Soviet Germans and Mennonites during this difficult period. By the time of the 1932–3 famine, Soviet authorities had already deemed both groupings to comprise a single whole. Therefore, the strength of the authorities' pressure on each of these groups of the German population was the same. At the same time, however, the scale of deaths from hunger during the famine years differed between the Mennonites and the Germans, let alone the Ukrainians, as there were considerably fewer Mennonite deaths from hunger throughout this period.

I have argued that Mennonite identities experienced dramatic shifts in this period. The onset of collectivization reinforced their great sense of loss and vulnerability. Their correspondence with those who had departed for North America in the 1920s reinforced their sense of having erred in their decision to remain in the Soviet Union. Their language increasingly became the language of a faithful remnant alive in the age of the anti-Christ. They also sensed that their own internal Ukrainian community had become more splintered, in part because of the reality that some Mennonites chose to be agents of the new state (as Neufeldt has demonstrated), and in part because of the way in which dekulakization played itself out. Yet, almost miraculously, most Mennonites did survive the terror-famine of 1932–3. This may have been because, first, Mennonites remained relatively prosperous despite the turmoil of the NEP years. Second, the assistance offered by co-religionists abroad was undoubtedly a key reason. Jacob Neufeld is one of many Mennonite memoirists and correspondents who point to the vital role that the "flow of material assistance" from "relatives, friends, and churches abroad" played. The Soviet state's desperate need for hard currency made it an ironic partner in this survival strategy, as Mennonites were able to obtain foreign currency in exchange for foodstuffs in state-run Torgsin stores.[64] In time, the state introduced measures across the countryside to alleviate some of the worst conditions that had provoked the famine, and I have argued that in time the state was also concerned about the agricultural health of Ukraine's Mennonites and Germans.

Of course, Moscow's concerns about agricultural productivity could never trump its concerns for the protection of the Soviet state from its enemies. If Mennonites were deemed "enemies" at the onset of NEP, it was because the vast majority had acquired the wealth of kulaks despite the revolutionary losses after 1917. At the same time, their Christian faith may have had relatively little effect on Soviet thinking during NEP, but that changed dramatically with the Stalinist commitment to a socio-cultural revolution after 1928 as well as an economic one. No wonder the ranks of the Mennonite clergy were decimated during the first two Five Year Plans. Even that paled in comparison to the manner in which the abrupt rise of Nazi Germany in 1933 transformed Moscow's relationship with its own Germans, at a time when the state barely distinguished between Mennonites and Germans. It did not help that Mennonites themselves appealed directly to Nazi-supported relief organizations in Germany in the face of the Ukrainian famine. As Terry Martin has previously argued, Mennonites were doomed once their perceived Germanized identity was linked in any way to Nazi Germany. As but one example of how Moscow saw that tie, it is enough to say that German funds from relief agencies after 1934 were stigmatized as "Hitler help"; the implication for Ukraine's Mennonites, as recipients of this vital aid, was an ominous one.[65] In one of many contradictions associated with the period known as High Stalinism, then, the Soviet attempt to undergird its fragile collectivized agricultural economy, Mennonite and otherwise, coincided with fierce repression. Peter Letkemann has argued that fully 10,000 Mennonites were arrested from 1933 to 1941, more than ten times the national average. When Jacob Neufeld was arrested in 1933 he was charged with German espionage precisely because of his link to the German relief organization *Brüder in Not*. Neufeld later observed that the mass arrest of Germans and Mennonites culminated in the mass arrests of 1937 and 1938, by which time Moscow had linked all of its Germans (including Mennonites) with Hitler's Germany.[66] For Mennonites, it was the worst possible association that the Soviet state could make.

One more comment is in order. The Ukrainian state has clearly politicized the memorialisation of the "Holodomor" across this fledgling state. Recent studies have not necessarily advanced our understanding of these difficult years, though they have reinforced the degree to which we have politicized this debate.[67] Other countries have entered a debate that has occasionally seemed more focused on the Russia of today than on the Ukrainian lands of the early 1930s.[68] Even the notion of Holodomor tends to have an ethnically Ukrainian focus to it alongside a desire to lift up a notion of the Ukrainian nation that was not necessarily Ukrainian by nationality. The recent published work by historians Marples, Baidaus, and Melentyeva is welcome, therefore, as a sign of what is still possible if historians do their work without a political gaze on them. I have suggested here that a study of the Mennonite experience of famine can also provide an important piece of the famine puzzle. Though Mennonites have largely disappeared from the Ukrainian present, their crumbling villages and stone fence-lines still point to a time when they were a significant part of "our" story. Perhaps it is time to place them more squarely within it, starting with the famine years and the price they paid to survive.

NOTES

1 Paul Robert Magocsi, *A History of Ukraine: The Land and Its Peoples*, 2nd ed. (Toronto: University of Toronto Press, 2010), 594.

2 David R. Marples, Eduard Baidaus, and Mariya Melentyeva, "Causes of the 1932 Famine in Soviet Ukraine: Debates at the Third All-Ukrainian Party Conference," in *Canadian Slavonic Papers* 56 (2014), 291–312. See esp. 298, 300–1.

3 Ray Gamache, *Gareth Jones: Eyewitness to the Holodomor* (Cardiff: Welsh Academic Press, 2013), 68, n. 55.

4 Helmut T. Huebert, *Hierschau: An Example of Russian Mennonite Life* (Winnipeg: Springfield Publishers, 1986), 304, n. 10. This confirms the process outlined by Marples, Baidaus, and Melentyeva, "Causes of the 1932 Famine," 300–1. See also Gerhard Lohrenz, *The Lost Generation and Other Stories* (Winnipeg: J. Lohrenz, 1982), 16.

5 Peter J. Rahn, ed., *Among the Ashes: In the Stalinkova Kolkhoz (Kontinusfeld) 1930–1935* (Kitchener, ON: Pandora Press, 2011), 77.

6 "Letters from the Past," unpub. (Conrad Grebel University Library, 1995), 36.

7 Lynne Viola, *Peasant Rebels under Stalin: Collectivization and the Culture of Peasant Resistance* (Oxford: Oxford University Press, 1996), ch. 2.

8 See, for example, various letters in Rahn, *Among the Ashes*, 81, 93, 143, 210 and 213; and Ruth Derksen Siemens, *Remember Us: Letters from Stalin's Gulag (1930–37)*, Volume One: The Regehr Family (Kitchener, ON: Pandora Press, 2007), 49.
9 Robert Conquest, *The Harvest of Sorrow: Soviet Collectivization and the Terror-Famine* (Edmonton: University of Alberta Press, 1986), 228. Conquest argues that Stalin fundamentally wanted a dramatic crisis in the countryside. For a fundamentally different perspective on Stalin's role in the terror-famine, see R.W. Davies and Stephen G. Wheatcroft. *The Years of Hunger: Soviet Agriculture, 1931–33* (New York: Palgrave Macmillan, 2004).
10 Marples, Baidaus, and Melentyeva, "Causes of the 1932 Famine," 298–9.
11 The lament comes from a letter dated 3 May 1930 and is found in Rahn, *Among the Ashes*, 81–2. On the 1930 harvest as certain to be poor, see Rahn, *Among the Ashes*, 83–5.
12 "Memoirs of Justina Martens" in *Journeys: Mennonite Stories of Faith and Survival in Stalin's Russia*, ed. John B. Toews (Winnipeg: Kindred Publications, 1998), 53.
13 Gosudarstvennyi arkhiv Dnepropetrovskoi oblasti (GADO), f.R-2240, op.1, d.76, ll.1–2.
14 Ibid., f.P-19, op.1, d.277.
15 Ibid., f.R-2240, op.1, d.38, l.31.
16 Ibid., f.P-19, op.1, d.755, l.3.
17 "Unsigned Letter," dated 8 June 1933, in Bohdan Klid and Alexander J. Motyl, eds., *The Holodomor Reader: A Sourcebook on the Famine of 1932–1933 in Ukraine* (Edmonton: Canadian Institute of Ukrainian Studies Press, 2012), 187.
18 GADO, f.R-2240, op.1, d.76, l.3–5.
19 Terry Martin, "The Russian Mennonite Encounter with the Soviet State, 1917–1955" in *Conrad Grebel Review*, 20, no. 1 (2002): 38; Elena A. Osokina, *Zoloto dlia Industrializatsii: "TORGSIN"* (Moscow: Rosspen, 2009); and Anne Konrad, *Red Quarter Moon: A Search for Family in the Shadow of Stalin* (Toronto: University of Toronto Press, 2012), 129.
20 Rahn, *Among the Ashes*, 199.
21 GADO, f.P-19, op.1, d.755, l.3; f.P-2240, op.1, d.75, ll.5, 8ob, 25; and Lohrenz (1982), 20.
22 Ibid., f.R-2240, op.1, d.38, l.3; d.79, l.25.
23 Jacob A. Neufeld, *Path of Thorns: Soviet Mennonite Life under Communist and Nazi Rule*, edited with an introduction and analysis by Harvey L. Dyck (Toronto: University of Toronto Press, 2014), 184–5.
24 GADO, f.R-2240, op.1, d.76, ll.18, 30.

25 Ibid., f.P-19, op.1, d.754, ll.41, 49.
26 Peter Kardash, *Zlochyn* (Melbourne-Australia-Kyiv: Fortuna, 2003), 128.
27 GADO, f.R-2240, op.1, d.86, l.65.
28 John Friesen, *Against the Wind: The Story of Four Mennonite Villages (Gnadental, Gruenfeld, Neu-chortitza, and Steinfeld) in the Southern Ukraine, 1872–1943* (Winnipeg: Henderson Books, 1994), 94. Friesen cites Colin P. Neufeldt, "The Fate of Mennonites in Soviet Ukraine and in the Crimea during the Soviet Collectivization and the Famine (1928–1933)," (unpublished manuscript, 1989).
29 J. Philipps J. Die, "Dorfgeschichte von Rosenheim," *Heimatbuch der Deutschen aus Russland* (Stuttgart: Verlag Landsmannschaft der Deutschen aus Russland, 1989), 146.
30 Peter C. Hiebert and Orie O. Miller, *Feeding the Hungry: Russia Famine, 1919–1925: American Mennonite Relief Operations Under the Auspices of Mennonite Central Committee* (Scottdale, PA: Mennonite Central Committee, 1929); and N.J. Kroeker, *First Mennonite Villages in Russia 1789–1943: Khortitsa – Rosental* (Vancouver: N.J. Kroeker, 1981), 220–2.
31 *Nimtsi v Ukraïni. 1920–1930s: zbirnyk dokumentiv derzhavnykh arkhiviv Ukraïny* (Instytut istoriï Ukraïny NAN Ukraïny, Tsentral'nyi derzhavnyi arkhiv vyshchykh orhaniv vlady i upravlinnia Ukraïny (Kyiv: Instytut istoriï Ukraïny NAN Ukraïny, 1994), 181.
32 "Letters from the Past," letter dated 8 October 1931, 37.
33 V.V. Chentsov, *Tragicheskie sud'by: Politicheskie repressii protiv nemetskogo naseleniia Ukrainy v 1920–1930s* (Moscow: Gotika, 1998), 72.
34 A. German, "Bor'ba s fashistami i ikh posobnikami" in *Nemtsy Rossii: ėntsiklopediia*: vol. 1 (Moscow, 1999), 231.
35 *Nimtsi v Ukraïni. 1920–1930s* (1994), 72; and Martin, "The Russian Mennonite Encounter," 38.
36 Sarah Cameron, "Violence, Flight, and Hunger: The Sino-Kazakh Border and the Kazakh Famine," in Timothy Snyder and Ray Brandon, eds., *Stalin and Europe: Imitation and Domination, 1928–1953* (Oxford: Oxford University Press, 2014), 62–5.
37 Ibid.
38 *Nimtsi v Ukraïni. 1920 – 1930s*, 176.
39 "Unsigned Letter," dated 8 June 1933, in Klid and Motyl, *The Holodomor Reader*, 188–9.
40 GADO, f.P-19, op.1, d.756, l.13.
41 Ibid., 176.
42 *Nimtsi v Ukraïni. 1920–1930s* (1994), 176.
43 Ibid., 179.

44 Ibid., 176.
45 GADO, f.P-19, op.1, Special folder, l.73.
46 A.I. Beznosov, "Mennonity Iuga Ukrainy v gody 'velikogo pereloma' (1928–1933)," in *Voprosy germanskoi istorii: Sbornik nauchnykh trudov* (Dnepropetrovsk, 2001), 85.
47 *Nimtsi v Ukraïni. 1920–1930s* (1994), 180.
48 Neufeld, *Path of Thorns*, 157; and "Letters from the Past," 40.
49 V.V. Chentsov, *Politychni represiï v Radians'kii Ukraïni v 20s* (Ternopil', 2000), 58.
50 K. Stumpp, "Die deutschen Siedlungen des Kronau-Orloffer Gebietes," in *Heimatbuch der Deutschen aus Russland 1958* (Stuttgart, 1958), 58.
51 Stumpp, *Bericht über das Gebiet Chortitza im Generalbezirk Dnjepropetrowsk* (Berlin, 1943), 10 S., 11 Taf.
52 A. Bosch and J. Lingor, *Entstehung, Entwicklung und Auflösung der deutschen Kolonien am Schwarzen Meer am Beispiel von Kandel von 1808 bis 1944* (Stuttgart, 1990), 393.
53 *Nimtsi v Ukraïni. 1920–1930* (1994), 180.
54 Ibid, 181.
55 Ibid.
56 Ibid.
57 GADO, f.P-19, op.1, Special folder, l.23.
58 *Nimtsi v Ukraïni. 1920–1930s* (1994), 183–4.
59 GADO, f.P-19, op.1, Special folder, l.10.
60 Chentsov (1998), 76.
61 GADO, f.P-19, op.1, Special folder, ll.5–6.
62 Ibid., l.7.
63 Ibid., l.10.
64 Neufeld, *Path of Thorns*, 156–7.
65 Martin, "The Russian Mennonite Encounter," 38.
66 Konrad, *Red Quarter Moon*, 106; and Neufeld, *Path of Thorns*, 63–4; 157–8. For one strong attempt to record the names of those Mennonites who were sent into the GULAG, see Helmut T. Huebert, *1937: Stalin's Year of Terror* (Winnipeg: Springfield Publishers, 2009).
67 For an excellent discussion on this matter in English, see John-Paul Himka, "Encumbered Memory: the Ukrainian Famine of 1932–33," *Kritika* 14, no. 2 (2013): 411–36.
68 http://laws-lois.justice.gc.ca/eng/acts/U-0.4/page-1.html. Accessed on 10 June 2015.

9 Caught between Two Poles: Ukrainian Mennonites and the Trauma of the Second World War

VIKTOR K. KLETS

Anna Ivanovna Schmidt found herself in the middle of a pitched battle in early October of 1941 as the thirteen-year-old waited along with her brother and mother to be deported by Soviet forces far into the east of that vast country. They had been ordered to gather at the Stulnevo train station along with all remaining Mennonites from the Molochna colony. Had the timing been otherwise, Anna Schmidt would have ended her days in Siberia, where her father Johann had been imprisoned barely months after Anna had been born in 1929. He died there within two years of his exile. But Anna's fate would be different. Decades later she still recalled the scene vividly as it unfolded:

> They gathered us together in large numbers and made us sit just so in the open fields with our backs to the station. We waited for the trains which would take us away to Siberia. Suddenly we saw German soldiers come up the road to our right on motorcycles. They stopped, jumped off their motorcycles and into the ditch that ran along the road. Meanwhile the Russians who had been overseeing us fled across the field in the opposite direction, away from the German soldiers. We were horrified when they began to fire at each other, and we found ourselves in the middle of a terrible battle. We thought that we would all be killed. Then some Russians came and told us to run straight ahead out of the field and away from the station, which we did. I don't know how it was that no one was killed. We ran until we came to a German village where we stayed until we were able to return home to Margenau. We didn't go back to the train station which was now in the possession of the German army.[1]

Without knowing it at the time, Anna Schmidt had found herself in the middle of the largest military invasion in world history. Almost four million soldiers crossed into the Soviet Union in the early morning hours of 22 June 1941 as part of a vast Hitlerite front that stretched from the Black Sea in the south to the Baltic in the north. The Nazis advanced quickly as Soviet forces were ill-prepared and in largely indefensible positions.[2] Countless other Mennonites over the years have substantiated Anna's memories of that remarkable episode. For example, Jacob Neufeld recalled airplanes locked overhead in a deadly struggle, the sudden flight of Soviet tanks and artillery eastward, and the way in which their Soviet NKVD overseers melted away as the Nazi army arrived in full force.[3] Kyiv, the capital of Soviet Ukraine, was in German hands by 19 September 1941, though the fascists continued to steam eastward. Within two weeks an advanced battalion had reached the Stulnevo rail station and all of Mennonite Ukraine was soon in German hands.

Anna Schmidt's ordeal at the Stulnevo rail station speaks to the heart of what I want to argue about Ukraine's Mennonites in the Second World War: they were a people who were caught in the middle. One of the serious problems associated with this terrible war is that neither the Soviets nor the Nazis deemed Mennonites to be a distinct confessional sect, in contrast to the status they had enjoyed for much of the nineteenth century. The Soviet Union stressed social criteria, by which Mennonites were considered representatives of a particular social group (they were mostly deemed to be peasant kulaks). When it came to an ethnic designation, Moscow deemed Mennonites to be German, which was hardly in their favour after Hitler's rise to power. For their part, Nazi authorities prized national designations above all others, and in that respect concluded early on that Mennonites were German, pure and simple. As with Soviets, Hitler's Nazi vanguard in Ukraine disregarded ethnic nuances or religious sub-designations as unworthy of mention. They ignored the historical reality, as this volume demonstrates, that Mennonites' identities had been a complex work in progress over time, and had shifted dramatically in the twentieth century. Thus, Mennonites had identified themselves as Dutch as recently as the First World War and its aftermath, though Soviet documentation (including in Mennonite passports and military identification cards) identified them as exclusively German.[4] In this chapter I want to tease out the development and implications of these designations and demonstrate how the complex nature and diverse manifestations of Mennonite identities actually left them constantly caught between two poles, and ultimately outsiders to Nazis and Soviets alike. As part of my argument I will outline the steps by which Soviet authorities attempted to deport all of Ukraine's Mennonites eastward out of the republic.

Of course, time will not permit me to cover all topics associated with the Ukrainian Mennonite experience in the Second World War. In particular, I will not address the role of Ukrainian Mennonites in the Holocaust. A recent article published in the *Mennonite Quarterly Review* by the late historian Gerhard Rempel has brought fresh attention to this important topic. In it, Rempel divides his attention between the Stutthof concentration camp in Poland and the extermination of Jews in the vicinity of Zaporizhzhia after October of 1941.[5] I do, however, wish to make several comments on this vital topic: first, there is no question that many Mennonites welcomed the Hitlerite forces when they arrived in the fall of 1941. However, to put that in context, we also need to observe that many ethnic Ukrainians also greeted German troops when they arrived. In the words of historian Karel Berkhoff, "In certain streets [of Kyiv] the mood was openly upbeat, with dancing, embracing, and drinking." Other reports indicate that "hundreds of draft-age males came out of hiding" in Kyiv to show their support for a regime that was certain to be an improvement over the preceding Stalinist one. More recently, Serhii Plokhy has concluded: "Many in Ukraine welcomed the German advance in the summer of 1941, hoping for the end of the terror unleashed by the Soviet occupation authorities in the years leading up to the war."[6] How would we expect otherwise from Mennonites? To take but one memoir: "We [Mennonites] received and perceived the German army troops not as enemies but as our liberators."[7] Others recalled the kindnesses shown to them by the German occupation forces, who were happy to encounter German-speaking settlers in the heart of Soviet Ukraine.[8]

Second, there is no question that some Mennonites participated in murderous acts against Ukraine's Jews. The vital question is: how many is "some"? In Rempel's own judicious words, "individuals of Mennonite background were part of Himmler's machinery of death." Though he later concludes that "Mennonites participated in significant ways in the massacre" of Jews, his own painstaking research only discusses a handful of such Mennonites.[9] Another scholar, Wendy Lower, has identified Mennonites at the heart of the "ethnic German minority in Zhytomyr" during the brutal period of Nazi occupation there, but at no point does she critically engage that very German minority. Mennonites in particular are never discussed, which makes Lower's initial assertion of Mennonite involvement puzzling at best. Another scholar, Eric Steinhart, has similarly identified the Mennonite Jack Reimer as a key player in the attempted Nazi extermination of Jews.[10] But is Jack Reimer, or the handful identified by Rempel, a sufficient base from which to conclude that many or most or all Mennonites were complicit in the Holocaust? I believe it is not, though it does not make the involvement of even one Mennonite any less disturbing or more justifiable. Rempel, especially, is careful to refer to my own research on this important issue, though my own findings come closest to the conclusions reached by Hans Gerlach and Karel Berkhoff. I agree with Gerlach that Mennonites were active in all aspects of local administration, including self-defence, but not in a manner that included combat assignments. And I agree with Berkhoff's insight that people in conflict and crisis primarily want to live their lives, find work, fall in love, and raise their children; most do not seek to engage with the "grand sociopolitical developments" of their age.[11] So too with Mennonites.

I wish to make one more observation from Rempel's article on Mennonites and the Holocaust, because it points to the heart of this chapter. Although Rempel has a section titled "Soviets, Mennonites and German Identity,"[12] it provides little more than an overview of Soviet Mennonite history before the Second World War. But surely the pressing question is: what can be said about Soviet Mennonite identity in the crucible of war and German occupation? That is what I wish to address in the pages that follow.

Nazi officials immediately began to implement a new political order in all of the lands occupied by the Third Reich during the Second World War.[13] From the start, they treated Mennonites as an integral part of the German population in the conquered Black Sea steppe. Berlin desired a new regime that would allow for the efficient economic exploitation of newly acquired territories alongside exterminating undesirable ethnic groups. To reach these goals, officials preferred to work with local peoples who were already on the ground. Ethnic Germans were, naturally, highly desirable as agents of Berlin, even though Nazi officials soon realized that most of these now liberated Ukrainian Germans lacked the requisite skills.[14] More immediately, however, Nazi Germany truly counted on a distinctive "fifth column" in the conquered lands, and there is evidence to suggest that such underground organizational structures had already been established on the eve of the Second World War in Romania, Poland, Yugoslavia, Hungary, and Czechoslovakia.

The Russian scholar M.I. Semiriagi has concluded that by the close of 1934 more than 600 pro-Reich cells of the German National Socialists (Nazis) had been established in practically all countries with German minorities.[15] As a measure of their importance, Deputy Führer Rudolf Hess oversaw these organizations after 17 February 1934 as he worked to bring them fully under Berlin's control.

No wonder that after Hitler's rise to power in 1934, Moscow viewed all Soviet Germans as potential collaborators with the German state. Alexander Beznosov has already demonstrated how Soviet concern about Nazi connections worked against Ukraine's Mennonites trying to overcome famine-like conditions. Moscow's suspicion of them only intensified thereafter, and culminated in the attempted deportation of all Soviet Germans to the east of the country shortly after Hitler's forces invaded the Soviet Union.[16]

Soviet officials began to lay the legal basis for the forced resettlement of "socially dangerous" minorities on the first day of the war, 22 June 1941. On that day a decree issued by the Presidium of the Supreme Soviet of the USSR gave officials the right to forcibly remove any potential fifth column in districts where military authorities had invoked martial law. Ethnic Germans were immediately included in this category of potential saboteurs as they were deemed to be German nationals first, and only after citizens of the Soviet state. Mennonites and Germans experienced this as the continuation of hostile policies that had been issued against them since Hitler's rise to power in 1933.[17] Of course such threats were more imagined than real. Colin Neufeldt has demonstrated how many Mennonites were unfailingly loyal to the socialist state. Many now left their home villages before they were compelled to do so so they could assist in the process of mass relocation itself. These included Party members, Soviet activists, and those Mennonites who agreed to assist in the transshipment of livestock, implements, and other inventory to points deemed safe from the Nazi advance. Although their involvement cannot be regarded as a forced relocation in the full sense of the word, the fate of these first labourers paralleled those who were later forcibly relocated. In all cases they found themselves enmeshed sooner or later in the vast Soviet "labour army" (*Trudarmii*), as with Mennonites who were sent to dig defence trenches so as to obstruct the Nazi advance.[18]

Crimea's Germans and Mennonites were the first to be forcibly deported, even though officials initially declared that they wished to evacuate Germans only temporarily, for their own safety. The Military

Council of the Southern Front ordered that evacuation to commence when it issued decree number 75 on 15 August 1941.[19] Hurriedly deported Germans later confirmed that they had been told such a move would only be temporary. For example, E.P. Papc, a former resident of Simferopol, later wrote "'come to us,' they said, 'without explaining the reasons that we were being evicted from the city. We were told it would be for three months, until the end of hostilities, and that our apartment would be sealed off to safeguard it.'"[20] Countless others recorded the same scenario, and one researcher on this forced migration, P.M. Polyan, later acknowledged the inconsistency that a "purely legal deportation, which was framed as an evacuation, yet proceeded entirely along narrow ethnic lines could hardly be deemed an evacuation" of the general population."[21] I agree with this evaluation, though it must be said that Germans were not alone in having been marked for compulsory deportation at this time. The Directive No. 00931 of the Supreme Commander "On the formation and objectives of the 51st Army," issued on 14 August 1941, ordered that "all local Germans and other anti-Soviet elements be immediately and decisively removed from the peninsula." In other words, we are not talking about any mass rescue of Crimea's civilian population as much as we are a removal of "anti-Soviet elements."[22] Official assurances to the contrary, evidence suggests that Crimea's Germans and Mennonites were not easily deceived. NKVD documents reported on cries of dissatisfaction and protest from many prospective deportees, and occasional cries of revenge. One report observed that "the initial news of the evacuation greatly agitated the peninsula's German population. Some rejected the order outright, others panicked and still others engaged in provocative conversations."[23]

The evacuation of Crimea's Germans, which began on 15 August 1941, ended a week later on the 22nd, included Tchongrav, a Mennonite village that had been founded in 1912. Villagers departed by wagon on 16 August to nearby Bijuk, then north by train via Melitopol to Zaporizhzhia, where German shelling from across the Dnipro soon forced them to abandon the train and proceed eastward on foot.[24] Crimean deportees were initially placed in Ordzhonikidze district, north of the Sea of Azov, still within Soviet Ukraine. Unexpectedly swift Nazi advances compelled Moscow to issue one more deportation decree, and in September 1941, Crimea's Germans were deported much further east to the Kazakh Soviet Socialist Republic. The number evicted from the peninsula was approximately 50,000 to 53,000, of whom the majority were Crimean Germans and Mennonites.[25]

Soviet officials next focused their attention on the Volga Germans as candidates for deportation. This was confirmed by a resolution from the Central Committee of the CPSU(b) on 26 August 1941, and two days later by a similar decree from the Presidium of the Supreme Soviet. Despite the fact that these declarations concerned only one region, their introduction sealed the fate of the entire German population of the Soviet Union. Almost immediately thereafter, on 31 August 1941, the politburo of the CPSU(b) examined the issue of "the Germans living in the territory of the Ukrainian SSR." They concluded with a resolution that ordered the arrest of all "anti-Soviet elements" among the Germans of nine Ukrainian districts (Dnipropetrovsk, Voroshilovgrad, Zaporizhzhia, Kyiv, Poltava, Stalin, Sumy, Kharkiv, and Chernihiv). All German men between the ages of sixteen and sixty who were not arrested were mobilized into construction battalions. Before long, officials had formed thirteen construction battalions with a total of 18,600 labourers, for which they commandeered NKVD facilities in the Soviet east, including those of Ivdellage, Solikambumstroe, Bogoslovstroe, and Kimpersaylage.[26] We know from the lists of labourers (*trudarmeytsev*) found in camps such as Bogoslovlag and ITL Bakalstroy-Chelyabmetallurgstroy that many of them were Mennonites who had been deported from Ukraine.[27]

We gain an important perspective on these events from two tragic recollections, first, the famed Soviet athlete-weightlifter Rudolf Plyukfelder, who later reminisced that he was fourteen years old when "at the beginning of September 1941 my father was taken straight from the stables where he was working. And not only him, but others were also seized as their names had been put on a special list. Those rounded up were placed on an open lorry that was standing near the kolkhoz office, beside the corn field. Several days later they came one evening and seized my brother Vladimir straight from the field where he was working. He was only eighteen years old. I never sa[w] my father or my brother again."[28]

A second recollection of forced resettlement in September of 1941 from the Memrik Mennonite settlement has been recorded in Anne Konrad's powerful *Red Quarter Moon*: "In the morning enough ladder wagons from the surrounding Russian collective farms were brought out and we were taken to the railway junction Yasikavataia … loaded onto coal cars, with locked doors … On 23 September we were unloaded in Kraso-Tuurinsk and put into a third camp consisting of barracks, one new, built of wet wood … All of this in heavy frost, whereas everyone had been rounded up in the great heat of September, totally unprepared for winter ... People were wearing sandals and light pants and no gloves. With frostbitten limbs, the work norms could not be met, and subsequently food rations got smaller every month. A great dying took place ... By January 1942 more than half who had arrived in September 1941 had died."[29]

The Soviet deportation process had acquired a mass character by September of 1941. The Soviet State Defence Committee (GKO) resolved on the 6th of that month to resettle "Germans from Moscow and the Moscow Region and the Rostov Region." Within two weeks the GKO further ordered the "resettlement of Germans from the Krasnodar, Ordzhonikidze territory, Tula districts, Kabardino-Balkarskoy and North Ossetian ASSR" as of 21 September 1941. Crimean Germans who had previously been relocated to these districts were now deported further east. Less than forty-eight hours later, officials issued GKO decree number 720, which called for "the resettlement of Germans from the Zaporizhzhia, Stalin, and Voroshilovgrad territories."[30] We can assume that this document opened the door for the removal of all Germans from Soviet Ukraine, and we can further assume that in Soviet eyes Mennonites were indistinguishable from other Germans.

Officials who oversaw the deportation initiative on behalf of the NKVD reported on 25 December 1941 that 32,032 people had been resettled from Zaporizhzhia territory (of 53,566 who had been considered for resettlement); 9,858 of 13,000 from Voroshilovgrad district; and 35,477 of 36,380 from Stalin district. Another 3,250 had been deported from Dnipropetrovsk district.[31] Ingeborg Fleishhauer believes that the resettlement was carried out based on the lists that the Central Committee of the CPSU(b) had ordered undertaken as early as the autumn of 1934, which raises an immediate question as to their accuracy for 1941.[32] One can also conclude that even more would have been deported had the rapid Nazi advance not proceeded with seemingly irresistible force.

Under the circumstances, it is not surprising that only left-bank (Dnipro) Germans and Mennonites were deported by Moscow in the fall of 1941 as all of right-bank Ukraine was under Nazi control by late September. As a result, thousands of Mennonites and Germans soon found themselves still in Ukraine, but now under the control of Nazi Germany. For example, there were about 30,000 Germans in Mykolaiv district during the period of the Nazi occupation, approximately as many as had lived there before the war.[33] In many cases Mennonites and Germans who had gone into hiding in 1941 for fear of Soviet deportation returned once the Hitlerlite forces had seized control. Thus, seventeen people joined the village of Kolono-Nikolaevka (formerly Ettingerfeld) by the beginning of 1942, of whom eleven had been born in that very village.[34] One of these returnees later became headman of the village.

Approximately one-quarter of nearly 400,000 Germans (including Mennonites) who had lived in Soviet Ukraine during the 1937 disappeared from the ranks before the end of 1941.[35] At the same time, the German Reich Commissariat "Ukraine" reported to Berlin that there were 163,000 Germans (including Mennonites) in the entire region, including 42,000 in Zhytomyr General Commissariat, 70,000 in Dnipropetrovsk, and another 7,000 in Melitopol.[36] In addition, more than 130,000 ethnic Germans lived in the territory of Transnistria, which included Odesa, Mykolayiv, and part of the Vinnytsia region of Ukraine.[37] At the same time the Germany army had assumed that almost 50,000 Germans lived on the Crimean peninsula alone, only to find barely a handful. Even those "pure" Germans who had served faithfully as members of the Communist Party had not been spared deportation.[38]

Deportation was a major reason for the Mennonites' demise in Ukraine but it was not the only one; many former Mennonite villages had been radically transformed in the years earlier. For example, in 19 February 1942 the famed German ethnographer and Nazi official Karl Stumpp assessed the state of German and Mennonite communities located in the vicinity of Dnipropetrovsk. "Kronsgarten," he observed, "had previously been a purely Mennonite colony. Yet today various remnants from scattered German villages in Ukraine live there, mostly from Josefstal. Many Mennonites had emigrated to America in 1921, and still others were expelled by the Bolsheviks in 1930."[39] Stumpp further identified more than 26,000 Germans in the Halbstadt district in October of 1942, including significant concentrations of Mennonites.[40]

How, then, did Ukrainian Mennonites relate to the new Nazi regime of occupation, and what was the Nazi expectation of the role that Mennonites would now play within it? This question is understandably of great interest. Any cogent answer will shed light on one of the truly unknown episodes in the history of wartime Soviet Ukraine. As V.V. Karpov has observed, "although much has been written about this war, it is still really 'unknown'... not to mention the direct bias and falsification that is everywhere. We still do not know many aspects and details of the war, because there are vast extant sources which few people have bothered to investigate."[41] Studying this problem can also highlight the nature of German occupation policy towards Ukraine, elucidating the relationship between Ukraine's Germans and Mennonites on the one hand, and between both groupings and the ethnic Ukrainian population on the other. Accounting for how those relations changed from the onset of the Second World War to its conclusion will need to be carefully considered.

Nazi Germany counted on the support of Mennonites alongside "other" Germans as it began its assault on Soviet Ukraine in 1941. To that end, the first point of the program of the NSDAP declared: "We demand the unification of all Germans in Greater Germany on the principle of the right of peoples to self-determination."[42] Berlin assumed that all Germans abroad (the so-called *Volksdeutsche*) would eventually become citizens of this "Greater Germany." In the same program, the NSDAP stated that "only German people will be permitted to become citizens of this 'Greater Germany'. Germany citizenship will be solely reserved for those who have German blood flowing in their veins, regardless of their religion."[43] In addition, the operational headquarters of Germany's southern army was ordered at the outset of the Soviet invasion: "Military organizations are obliged to support *Volksdeutsche* in their disputes with local peoples."[44]

All Mennonites were included in the national list as ethnic Germans with attendant rights and responsibilities. The questionnaires used to determine these lists required that all respondents confirm their national origins. In particular, each individual was asked to confirm: "I certify that neither of my parents nor my four grandparents (both the father's and mother's side) belong, and never have belonged to the Jewish race, or the Jewish faith"; "I acknowledge that I belong to the German ethnicity (*narodnosti*)"; and "I have always acknowledged, even before 21 June 1941, that I have belonged to the German ethnicity." The incentive to claim German ethnicity was obvious as Nazi officials allotted their co-nationals special food and ration cards, and higher (by as much as 50 per cent) salaries than other ethnic groups in the performance of the same work. For example, the Dnipropetrovsk regional council was instructed to pay higher salaries to the 50 per cent of the elementary school teachers who had registered as ethnic Germans.[45] Germans were also permitted to open churches that had previously been closed by order of the Soviet state. B.V. Sokolova has researched the effect that extra rations had on Ukraine's declared ethnic Germans. In particular, a special order of the Central German Army Logistics Command ordered that all *Volksdeutsche* in the Ukrainian cities receive supplemental rations to those given their peers, including additional weekly allowances of 100 grams of meat and 60 grams of fat. Ukrainian Germans who formed the newly created self-defence military units (*gruppy samozashchiti*) were allotted an additional 1,500 grams of flour, 1,800 grams of bread, 7 kilograms of potatoes, and 250 grams of cereals, vegetables, and fish to the extent that these were available.[46] No wonder Karel Berkhoff has concluded that countless Ukrainians and Russians attempted to register as ethnic Germans, along with Ukrainian Finns, Georgians, anyone really. A bribe of 5,000 roubles was deemed sufficient.[47]

M.I. Semiryaga speaks of the creation in southern Ukraine of the Dnipropetrovsk SS Cavalry Regiment, consisting of local *Volksdeutsche*,[48] even though not all of his conclusions are accurate. More helpful is the work of A. Eisfeld, who has investigated the formation of three cavalry squadrons in the environs of Halbstadt, all of which were later converted into self-defence units.[49] Even stronger is the work of Horst Gerlach, who has documented the establishment in October 1942 of the 1st Cavalry Regiment of ethnic Germans in Molochna (again, Halbstadt), though it was active across Prishib-Molochna. Seven hundred and fifty to right hundred persons served in four separate squadrons within the Regiment, and were situated in Prishib, Halbstadt, Waldheim, and Gnadenfeld respectively. Lutherans and Catholics comprised the first of these squadrons, and Mennonites almost exclusively the other three. This cavalry regiment helped evacuate Ukrainian *Volksdeutsche* to Germany in 1943 and fought against local partisan movements before officials folded it into the 8th SS Cavalry Division "Florian Geyer."[50]

According to M.I. Semiryagi, Nazi officials relied on Ukraine's *Volksdeutsche* to fill postings as city mayors, village elders, translators, police agents, and the Gestapo.[51] In turn, the German state claimed the right to regulate all aspects of life for ethnic Germans and Mennonites. For example, Ukrainian Germans under the Nazi regime were not permitted to register their marriages, births, and deaths through the Soviet-era Registry Office (ZAGS). All such registrations were to be undertaken through the newly established offices of *Gebietskommissar*. In addition, the *Volksdeutsche* were no longer permitted to wed non-Germans.

By way of clarification, the Dnipropetrovsk *Gebietskommissar* issued the following on 11 May 1943 concerning Ukrainian German marriage practices: "The marriage of the local population shall be based on the order of 11 May 1942 ... Once again, I point out that Ukrainian officials in the ZAGS cannot register *Volksdeutsche* marital unions. Even *Volksdeutsche* officials working in the ZAGS cannot do. Such unions can only be declared by the German head of the Registry Office overseen by the *Gebietskommissar* or his deputy."[52] This order was supplemented by the order of the deputy chairman of the Apostolovo district council within the Dnipropetrovsk *Gebeitskomissariat*, which clarified the following on 5 May 1943: "The *Gebietskommissar* has ordered that it is strictly prohibited to register *Volksdeutsche* marriages in the ZAGS offices. *Volksdeutsche* marriage registrations can be undertaken in the Office of the Kryvyi Rih *Gebietskommissar* and the region's *Volksdeutsche* have been clearly informed of such."[53] New restrictions on marriages were also clearly spelled out. For example, the Pokrovskii district *Gebietskommissar* of Dnipropetrovsk region declared on 26 September 1942 that: "The marriage of local (*mestnii*) Germans with those of other ethnicities (*s drugimi natsiami*) or that as of 22 June 1941 had only Soviet citizenship as well as those who did not have even that, and since then have not acquired any other citizenship rights is prohibited."[54]

Nazi legislative overseers regulated the names of local Germans even as they oversaw new marriage prohibitions. Thus, in a letter to the Kamenskii district head on 25 May 1943, the rural council said: "The *Gebietskommissar* in a letter dated 17 May 1943 has indicated that the names such as David and Sarah, which are still found among the Germans (I should add that these were also still quite common among Mennonites – VK) have a Jewish (Yid) origin and do not meet the criteria of a German name. Tell all the Germans in your Council that those who have such names must immediately file a petition to them through the district *Gebietskommissar*."[55]

Officials of the Reich also introduced new measures in the occupied territories of Ukraine aimed at attracting local Germans into the ranks of the German army. A 20 June 1942 letter from the chair of the Vasil'kovskii district council of Dnipropetrovsk province to village elders (*starostam sel'skikh uprav*) urged them to: "make the Germans in your area aware of Field Commander Sinelnikov's announcement of 13 June 1942, that 'local Germans who prove their unwavering desire to belong to the German nation will be taken into the German army.' Let them know, further, that applications to enter the army are being accepted by the military and civil administrations."[56]

Occupation authorities also quickly reorganized primary school education offered to Germans and Mennonites. In particular, they formed separate schools exclusively for Ukraine's *Volksdeutsche*. For example, Field Commander's circular N° 679, sent on 16 October 1941 to district council chairs, stated in part:

6) new schools in communities where Germans reside are exclusively for those Germans. Non-German householders in those communities who want their children to attend those schools must receive a special permit in advance from the Field or the local Commandant's Office. Such permission will only be granted in highly unusual cases and for extreme need ...
7) When opening a new German community school is not possible in a given village because of the lack of a German teacher or only a few German children are on hand, those children are to be sent to a school in the nearest German school community to them. Only in rare instances (for example, when the distance to German school is too vast or when German children lack adequate clothing or shoes to cover the distance) can German children be sent to an existing Ukrainian school within their community.[57]

The same document also set severe limitations on the pedagogical options for Jewish children, declaring that "Jewish children will not be allowed to attend any schools."[58] As early as 15 November 1941, authorities in Apostolovo district of Dnipropetrovsk province opened two German schools to complement the 44 schools existing in the area.[59] Another German school was added by the end of the year.[60] Three of the thirty-nine elementary schools under the occupation in Zaporizhzhia were German,[61] as the local newspaper *New Zaporizhzhia* boasted that "Ukraine will only have either Ukrainian or German Schools."[62]

By 10 March 1942, there were twenty working German schools in Khortytsia and Nikolaifeld colonies (six of them offered seven-year programs), with a total enrolment of 2,401 students.[63] With 375 pupils, Khortytsia village had the largest number of students in 1942, a year in which the village also celebrated the centennial of its secondary school (Khortytsia *Zentralschule*).[64] In nearby Einlage, 232 pupils attended school whereas another 178 attended in Nikolaifeld of Zaporizhzhia region, in addition to those who attended in Neuendorf (Shirokoe: 220), Schönhorst (Ruchaevka: 261), Neu-Osterwick (294), Halbstadt (415), and Josefstal (from Dnipropetrovsk region, 250 students).[65]

Village authorities employed a wide range of strategies to find a sufficient number of German teachers. They were especially eager to attract those who had previously been banned from teaching by Soviet authorities. One extant archival file contains brief autobiographies of teachers in Khortytsia and Nikolaifeld who were able to return to teaching during the occupation. Thus we learn about Heinrich Schellenberg, the returning school director in Neu Ostervick, along with Gerhard Neufeld of that same school. Anna Lehn returned to the classroom in Khortytsia village again, as did Margarita Penner in Einlage; Johann Rempel, Margarita Unger, and Wilhelm Dick in Rosengart, and Daniel Loewen in Adelsheim; Johann Penner to Hochfeld, Cornelius Epp to Franzfeld; Helena Boer to Neuenburg; Berta Rekling and Evgenii Platz to Neuendorf; Katya Wittenberg to Schönhorst; Elizabet Savatzky to Kronstal, and so on.[66] Many of those recalled had completed teacher training institutes or technical schools before the revolution and then taught before they were removed by Soviet authorities. They now eagerly returned to teaching. Typical in this respect is Alma Schatz who had completed her courses in teaching training in Dnipropetrovsk before the German occupation. She now petitioned authorities: "I work in an office but I want to teach."[67] Alma soon had a position as a German language instructor at the Sursko-Pokrovskaya Middle School.[68] Waldemar Janzen recalled his mother coming home from a meeting to announce that she had been elected teacher of the Khortytsia elementary school. At the same time, those who had taught under the Soviet system were banned from doing so by the occupied German forces.[69]

Another strategy employed was to increase the compensation offered to teachers, though the main method was to extensively train or retrain teachers. To that end authorities established special teachers' camps (*lager*) as well as new teacher training schools. They sought not only to train a new cadre of teachers but also to nurture the strong allegiance of this new cohort to National Socialist policies.[70] We know of such new initiatives across Nazi-occupied Ukraine, including in Zhitomir, Dnipropetrovsk, Khortytsia, Kronau, Zeltse, and Prishib. Karl Stumpp's investigative unit observed the widespread establishment of German libraries at this time. Occupation authorities also distributed more than 10,000 calendars and 100,000 German paintings to *Volksdeutsche* families. They distributed German magazines for women, German fairy tale collections for schools and kindergartens, and pedagogical materials for institutes in Khortytsia, Kronau, and Dnipropetrovsk.[71]

Historians have previously investigated the restoration of church life during the Nazi occupation, including within the Mennonite settlements. In this regard, the plans of the Nazi occupiers were one and the same for Ukraine's German and Mennonite settlements. Nor was this a mere act of German goodwill. Many, including R.H. Valta, maintained that Soviet Germans all possessed a strong if latent link between their ecclesial and their Germanic identities.[72] Nazi authorities at the highest levels expected that this linkage was a strong one regardless of Lutheran, Catholic, or Mennonite affiliation, and quickly nurtured it after the war began. For example, the Reich Security Main Office issued a circular on 16 August 1941 entitled: "On the church issue in the occupied regions of the Soviet Union," identifying three main objectives: first, to support the development of religious movements given their hostility to Bolshevism; second, to keep the religious revival of the occupied territories divided lest it serve as a galvanizing movement for underground movements hostile to Germany; and third, to create the circumstances that would allow the newly established churchly organizations to assist in Germany's civil oversight of the conquered territories.[73] If the second objective was primarily concerned with the threat that Orthodoxy's revival might entail for Nazi officials, the first and third were clearly focused on how best to engage Ukraine's Germans (and, it can be assumed, Mennonites).

Not all went smoothly in this process of engineered religious renewal. For one, priests and other religious leaders were in short supply after the Stalinist devastation of the 1930s. Soviet officials had also converted many church buildings into village clubs, or for agricultural use to house livestock or store grains. Such spaces were often difficult, if not impossible, to reclaim. For example, Mennonites from the village of Nieder Khortytsia in Zaporizhzhia region later recalled this from the Nazi occupation: "Authorities reopened the church, though we had no preacher at the time. Our church building had been used to store grain before the war and it again served that purpose after war's end. Our last minister, Preacher Dick, had been repressed in 1937."[74] But villagers managed to solve all of these problems during the occupation. Practically all Mennonites were familiar with sacred scripture, and several of them were highly respected and familiar with the main canons of the Mennonite faith. Though many men had been exiled or executed during the 1930s, some remained, and eventually the village did find its sought-after spiritual leadership.

Church life among Mennonites and Germans did improve across Nazi-occupied Ukraine. Thus the newly restored Lutheran church was opened in Dnipropetrovsk in December of 1941. A local reporter said this about the event: "This and countless other churches were closed in our city under Bolshevism, and the buildings themselves were occupied by Jewish artisans. Yet on 24 December 1941, and on the very eve of Christmas, worshippers were able to attend the first service here after the restoration. The community has spent a lot of energy and effort on the restoration of God's house."[75] Old-timers later reported that a similar church opening was experienced at this time in the large Lutheran village of Josefstal, on the Dnipro River south of Dnipropetrovsk.[76] Incidentally, in the autumn of 1941 a new Faculty of Theology was also opened up in the University of Dnipropetrovsk.[77]

Religious institutions were also opened in other German population centres. For example, Horst Gerlach has noted the creation of Mennonite churches in the villages of Khortytsia, Rosental (Kantserovka), Rosengart (Novoslobodka), Kronsweide (Vladimirovskaya), Neuendorf (Shirokoe), Kronstal (Dolinskoe), Neu Osterwick (Pavlovka), Schöneberg (Smolianova), Burvalde (Baburka), Nieder Khortytsia, and Blumengart (Kapustyanka). Services for Nikolaipol were performed in Franzfeld (Varvarovka), Nikolaifeld (Nikolaypole), and Hochfeld (Morozov). German soldiers participated in the opening services of many of these churches.[78] In places where church buildings had been destroyed, officials commandeered the use of clubs, theatres, or other suitable premises. At the same time, occupation authorities did not hesitate to close buildings that they deemed contrary to the interests of the Reich. For example, old-timers from the former Mennonite village of Blumengart (Kapustyanka) in Zaporizhzhia district observed that although a Mennonite church was restored, officials closed a club and library that they deemed ideologically harmful.[79] A similar situation unfolded in the nearby village of Schönhorst (Ruchaevka).[80] Churches, once opened, attracted Ukrainians and the surrounding population in addition to the Germans and Mennonites that they were intended for, and the mood was generally a buoyant one in these settings. Old-timers from the village of Nieder Khortytsia later recalled: "During the war, the church was opened in the village. It was a fine one with a broad sanctuary lined with benches, and a separate place reserved for the preachers. Those who attended sang well, everyone had their own little songbook."[81]

The son of Heinrich Winter, the last elected Ältester of Khortytsia (he was elected in the church elections of 1943) recorded the jubilation felt by those who celebrated Christmas in 1941. Children prepared special bible verses to recite and church choirs were begun again. Even German soldiers joined in. Catechism classes were also begun as church leaders sought to overturn a generation of atheistic teaching. Everyone was encouraged to attend, young and old, married and single, baptised and non-baptised. Ninety-nine were baptized in Khortytsia in 1942 and more than a hundred the next year in Neuendorf. Years later, the son recalled his own baptism at the hands of his father, and the verse he was blessed with that day: "Commit your ways to the Lord; trust in Him and He will do this" (Psalm 37:5).[82]

Nazi occupiers assumed that they would be able to exploit deep animosities between Ukraine's *Volksdeutsche* and ethnic Ukrainians, spelling out their basic assumptions in a document entitled: "On the relationship between the *Volksdeutsche* and Ukrainians." It offered the following advice: "I ask when discussing relations between *Volksdeutsche* and Ukrainians that the former will be encouraged to separate themselves out as much as possible. *Volksdeutsche* should be especially vigilant lest they find themselves in an inferior position to Ukrainians. One must never forget that Ukraine's *Volksdeutsche* are Germans and that our credibility in the country will be damaged if respect for the *Volksdeutsche* is compromised. Thus, for example, the *Volkdeutsche* should avoid entering into a competition with the Ukrainians in business or agriculture if there is a possibility that the Germans will lose. Germans should also avoid participating with Ukrainians in theater productions or other public spectacles. If this happens, Germans should always be in the foreground."[83]

How did Ukraine's Germans, with Mennonites among them, respond to the introduction of a new political and socio-cultural regime during the period of Nazi occupation? In general, three main lines of conduct can be ascertained, which apply not only to Soviet Germans and Mennonites, but to the population as a whole in the occupied lands. Here I agree completely with I.A. Shakhraichuk and N.A. Slobodianiuk, who have concluded that some of Ukraine's Mennonites joyfully embraced the Nazi occupiers and were filled with hopes for the future. Another group was hostile to the invaders. But for the most part, Ukrainians of all ethnic stripes remained only passively engaged with the German army, and their expectations were minimal. This ambiguity is due to the fact that a significant part of the population was subjected to various repressions and harassment by the Soviet authorities and was so dissatisfied with the existing order, that many hoped that the German occupation would lead to positive change.[84] To some extent this also explained the difficult financial situation of the Germans and Mennonites before and during the war. Busse's report of the colonies near Halbstadt declared that "The position of the Ukrainian Germans here and everywhere is catastrophic. They lack sufficient clothing, undergarments, and shoes. I am convinced that if we manage to get out of the German empire clothes and shoes and then distribute them among the

Germans, they would be relieved of their greatest concerns. I believe that they will then have more strength to overcome suffering caused by past and recent events. Like almost everywhere in the area on the left side of the Dnipro River, almost all the men were deported from their villages, so that field work must be done by women and children. "[85]

Some Mennonites began to collaborate with the occupiers, especially as they sought positions within the occupation administration. This was most evident in the activities of Khortytsia district chief (*shef*) Joseph Epp, whom reports indicate had been repressed before the war. Horst Gerlach suggests that Epp was given the position of overseer because he was deemed essential to the strength of the community. He worked hard to reopen churches, village schools, and other faith-based institutions. He cooperated with other officials to prevent looting, to clean up the streets, and so on.[86] On occasion he became involved in totally personal matters. For example, one of the archive files contains a letter signed by the Khortytsia district council chair (Epp) which states: "To all citizens! A citizen named Janzen from the working village of Kichkas has lost his light coloured cow with a short tail. Anyone who finds this cow in the territory of the council is requested to return it to Janzen right way, and to immediately inform the Council of such. "[87]

Mennonites served in penal organs (*v karatel'nykh organakh*) as well as in administrative ones. Information about those who worked in the occupation zone's police and security forces is often deeply clouded. Little appears as it was. For example, reports mention an Ivan Franzevich Janzen who served in the Dnipropetrovsk gendarmerie,[88] a Peter Yajovlovich Penner (a resident of Novo-Vitebsk) who served similarly, first in Friesendorf (Stalindorf) and thereafter in the gendarmerie at Piatikhatki.[89] Petr Franzevich Dyck served in the German gendarmerie in Orlova of Mykolaiv region. The latter, according to one witness, occasionally "beat Soviet citizens to the point of killing them."[90] One other protocol is preserved of the interrogation of a Jakov Friedrich Vel'terlich of Aleksandrovka village in Dnipropetrovsk region, which records that he was arrested by the Gestapo during the war and placed in a Dnipropetrovsk-area concentration camp. The protocol itself refers to a witness from Khortytsia village named Ziss (name and patronymic unknown) who was born in 1898 and had previously served as the head of the school of mayoralty police that guarded the concentration camp.[91]

Many Mennonites also served in the German army during the war. Generally, this occurred after they had fled to Germany. Some served in non-combatant units while other Mennonites fought and still others served in the SS.[92] There is considerable interest in Henry Aronovich Suderman, originally from Starozavodskoe village, Nikopol district, in Dnipropetrovsk region. Suderman served in the German army from September 1944 until his capture in Krakow in January 1945. When asked whether he had served in the Red Army, Suderman replied: "I did not serve in the Red Army for religious reasons, as Mennonites were not permitted to do so."[93] It follows that the Soviet regime may have been more tolerant about military exemptions for religious reasons than Nazi Germany, though the desperate position of the German army by the end of the war was doubtless also a factor. Of course, Mennonites did not join the German army only towards the end of the war. According to A.D. Kampen, a resident of Khortytsia village, Mennonites began to volunteer for the German army from the onset of the occupation.[94]

German authorities also sought to expand the activities of the Hitler Youth in the occupied territories, and they were determined to enlist the *Volksdeutsche* to that end. The Hitler Youth were deemed to be the means by which Soviet Germans and Mennonites would be reeducated, and it is not surprising that Hitler Youth units were found in almost every population centre of Mennonites and Germans in occupied Ukraine. *Volksdeutsche* were in the leading governing bodies of this organization, and included many Mennonites. For example, the head of one of the detachments of the Hitler Youth camp in the village of Shirokoe, Kryvyi Rih region of Dnipropetrovsk province was Heinz Kamp. Annie Kampen was the chair of the Association of German Girls in this same camp,[95] and Anna Neufeld, who was leader of the *Volkdeutsche* in Grodno district, was group leader of the Association of German Girls there.[96]

Mennonites were also active within Nazi Germany itself. Conrad Heydens, one of Hitler's associates in the first half of the 1920s, published several books about Nazism and the Nazi Party in the 1930s. He referred to a German National Party activist with a fairly common Mennonite surname, Ernst Penner. In 1923, during the Beer Hall Putsch, Penner was "appointed" minister-president of Bavaria. Heydens calls Penner an ally of Hitler "who stood closest to him."[97] But in 1925 Ernst Penner died in a car accident shortly after his release from Landsberg prison.

In June 1942, the Dnipropetrovsk General Commissioner visited A. Rosenberg, the Reich Minister for the Eastern Occupied Territories, and

Reichskommissar Ukraine Koch. This meeting was widely covered in the press. In particular, the newspapers told of their visit to the village of Khortytsia to celebrate the 150th anniversary of the founding of the colony, and they observed how these Nazi dignitaries were greeted enthusiastically by local residents. For example, "the Dnipropetrovsk newspaper" reported that Rosenberg and Koch met with the Germans in the German colony of Khortytsia where they observed a demonstration of support by the villagers.[98] The Kryvyi Rih newspaper *Zvon* carried additional details, noting that "it was an exhilarating experience to travel the roads through the territory of the German settlement near Khortytsia. According to the District Commissioner there were 15,000 farmers in Khortytsia who belonged to the German people ... Today, they waited as, so soon after their liberation by the German army, they received a first visit from a Minister of the Führer. Reich Minister and Reichskommissar Koch was welcomed everywhere with shouts of "Heil." Joy shone in the eyes of the German peasant men and women, who again could admit their affiliation to the German people after decades of great terror. The visit to these Khortytsia Germans who had settled on the edge of the Dnipro was the culmination of this official visit."[99]

Old-timers in Ukraine still recall similar sentiments that were expressed at the time by occupied Ukraine's Germans. O.V. Shkrebitko, a resident of Nieder Khortytsia, recalls: "When the war began, the relationship between us and the Germans in our region changed. Fascists among us became enlivened and the youth most of all. Though we did not have the firing squads that other regions did, we did have local Germans who became police officers and who scoffed at us. They made fun of our komsomols (Soviet youth organizations), but they did not close them down ... The police were three local Germans, of whom Thiessen was particularly harmful. I remember one time when I was sent to the store to buy some honey after several cases had arrived. But Thiessen blocked my way and said 'none of this honey will go to the Russians, as Hitler has given it for our use (as Germans)."[100] U. Ia. Belaya, a resident of Neu Osterwick (Dolinskoe) recalled: "I sometimes think that our Germans knew that soon there would be war, but they did not talk about it. On the surface they were good to us, in appearance they were good to us, but they were always ready to lash out at us."[101]

Older residents of the former Mennonite villages mention cases where local Mennonites became hostile not only neighbouring Ukrainians, but also to some Mennonites. The following excerpts are representative.

A.D. Kampen, a resident of Khortytsia village: "As far as I know, the Germans shot an Epp who lived in the center of the village. He was not a Party member, but it is said that he was a Soviet informant in the 1930s."[102]

N.T. Poltorak, also a resident of Khortytsia village: "Graf (Raff), our Collective Farm chair was a rigorous, demanding person. He was a member of the Party. Together with a Wiebe he was active during the war in underground work (this last statement seems implausible – VK). Some of the local Germans denounced them. They were arrested and executed."[103]

B.D. Letkeman, a resident of Nieder Khortytsia: "The occupation authorities, having imposed a 'new order', shot collective farm chair Sidorenko, along with two Mennonites from Khortytsia named Wiebe (the chair of the village Soviet) and Gafor."[104]

Such recollections are consistent with information gathered after the war by Abram Isakovich Dyck (Dik), who had been born in Khortytsia district and lived before the war in the village of Kichkas. He had been a civil judge, and chair of the village Soviet deputies. Dyck described the events that unfolded after the German army entered his village: "I was arrested by the Germans after 3 or 4 days and held in custody for 24 hours. From there, and despite the early frost and bitter winds I was carted by motorcycle to a gathering point 25 kilometers away, dressed only in my underwear. There the Nazis demanded to know whom I worked for and with, and what my exact responsibilities had been. I did not confess to anything other than that I was a simple collective farmer. They arrested others with me, including Henry Davidovich Rempel – chair of the kolkhoz, and the German Abram Petrovich Braun, who had served as the chair of the village court as well as its Soviet. The Germans shot them both in the village of Shirokoe. But I managed to run away from them and go into hiding."[105] Ironically, Dyck later joined other refugees who fled the Soviet Union as the Nazis retreated. He served in the Waffen SS and participated in battles in France until he was captured by American troops.

Many Mennonites clearly supported the occupying army because of their dissatisfaction, if not outright hatred, of Soviet power. Such a response was understandable given their losses since 1917, most especially since the Stalinist revolution after 1929. Clearly the years of collectivization, famine, and repression had taken their toll. Under the circumstances, it is perhaps surprising that there were Mennonites who opposed the Nazi occupation. They aided their Ukrainian neighbours where possible and spoke harshly against the German army and the state. For example, the old-timers mention that many residents in the Mennonite village of Marinopol in Nikopol district of Dnipropetrovsk province spoke negatively about Hitler and did not want to be evacuated to Germany after 1943.[106] One of them recalled: "There was a German among the police whose name was Wiliamin Robertovich. I no longer recall his family name. But people say that he saved a lot of our (Ukrainian) people from being made slave labourers in Germany" (I.T. Troyno, resident in Baburka village)[107]; "In general, we can say that the local Germans who served as police during the occupation treated us decently" (F.A. Komissarenko, a resident of the same village)[108]; "During the war ... the relationship between village Germans and Ukrainians did not change. Basically we lived together and helped each other where we could. Of course there were villains among us, but these could not be identified by nationality." (L.D.Timoshenko, resident of Nieder Khortytsia).[109] My own research suggests that many Mennonites regarded themselves as citizens of this Soviet Russo-Ukrainian landscape after long generations of settlement here, and despite the worst hardships of the Stalinist years. In addition, a new generation of Mennonites had come of age during the Soviet era who saw themselves as unequivocally Soviet.

At the same time, there is no indication that Mennonites joined the partisan movement, even though many Soviet Germans did. For example, two heroes of the Soviet Union were German, one of whom was a native of Poltava region (Major General S.S. Volkenshtein), and the second – R.A. Klein –was from the village of Kovpak in the Volgograd region and participated in partisan intelligence during the war. Thus, Mennonite resistance to the Nazi invaders must be understood as largely a passive opposition. The extant documents do suggest, however, that Mennonites served in the Red Army during the war though numbers are difficult to substantiate as many came to the Red Army ranks via the Soviet "labour army."[110] Even here there are exceptions. For example, V.A. Pyndych, a resident of Ruchaevka village, said this about his father, A. Dyck: "My father graduated from the Saratov Flying School just before the war began ... He enlisted soon after and first saw battle over Kryvyii Rih where he served as a navigator in Bomber Command. He fought until early 1943 and was twice awarded with medals. Then he was transferred from the regular to the auxiliary army because of his German ethnicity. He could not believe that this had happened to him. After that my father was involved in road construction beyond the Volga in Saratov province. He was removed from even this position after the war's end and stripped of all his medals. After that he was only able to preserve his status as a war participant. But times change. In the 1960s my father received his first commemorative medal as a veteran. It overwhelmed my father, whom I saw drunk for the first time. The medal represented for him joy and sorrow intertwined."[111]

One can easily understand why the majority of Mennonites reacted neutrally if not passively to the new regime. The war was still going on and the outcome uncertain. On the one hand, they did not want to cooperate with the occupiers, but on the other, to actively oppose it would have been fatal. Hence, passive acceptance was the best assurance of survival. In addition, it is important to take into account the degree to which Soviet German and Mennonite thinking had been transformed by the events of the past half century before the war began. By the time the war began, surely most Germans had come to see themselves as "Russian Germans" or "Soviet Germans," or an amalgam of both. They had been born, raised, and educated in the Soviet period, and they would have been influenced by the Soviet school system and other public organizations. And they themselves would have identified not only at an ethnic level but also at a political one as citizens of the Soviet Union.

Thus, at the outset of the war and despite the repression and other hardships of the pre-war period, a host of Soviet ethnicities and social groupings "maintained the momentum created by the October revolution."[112] In other words, they identified with the popularized Soviet ideals of equality, internationalism, and social justice that had all been linked to socialism.

If so, one can ask: why were the Nazi occupiers unable to win the loyalty of most Ukrainian Germans and Mennonites? The reason is that they tried, as they say, "to do everything at once." They had the conviction of all victors that they were strong enough to secure in the villages and farms the sovereignty that they had forced on the battlefield. In other words, pure hubris. The American psychologist Charles Kiesler explains it this way: "When you attack you become convinced of your own power and unable to see its limitations. Even worse, you provoke in those you defeat a more extreme behavior which will only buttress their former views. In a sense, you reinforce their previously held convictions and in time they will begin to act out their most deeply held beliefs against you."[113] One gains a similar perspective from Dr K. Stumpp's semi-annual report directed to the Ministry for the Occupied

Eastern Territories on 10 August 1942, which stated: "The Germans, having been exposed for twenty years to Bolshevik propaganda, are unable to think like Germans of the Fatherland."[114]

Waldemar Janzen provocatively suggested that Mennonites turned against the Nazi occupation force when they began to see the disregard that the Hitlerite forces showed to the Mennonites' neighbours. In his words: "When it became evident that the occupation authorities treated [our Ukrainian neighbours] as inferior and began to exploit them, [Mennonite] sympathies with the Germany occupiers changed. The forcible conscription of younger people as factory workers in Germany was one of the most disturbing measures." He goes on to give specific examples where Ukrainians were mistreated in the presence of his mother and beloved aunt, and how distressed both were by it.[115] The fact that Janzen also suggests that Ukrainian Mennonites would certainly have known about the Holocaust – again with specific examples – adds further credence for Janzen's nuanced picture of this time.[116]

The subsequent history of the Soviet Ukrainian Mennonites is marked by two great resettlement processes. In 1943–4 they, like almost all Ukrainian Germans, were evacuated to the West as the German troops retreated – a reality that Mennonites experienced firsthand as Nazi officials converted Mennonite schools into military hospitals where German wounded were cared for, and the war dead taken away every morning. Anna Schmidt, whose ordeal at the Stulnevo train station began this chaper, left her village of Margenau on 11 September 1943. She travelled initially by cart and wagon, with her mother and brother, alongside the rest of their village. Katie Friesen recalled that German troops were everywhere in her village as her family departed; they wanted to plant landmines there before themselves fleeing westward.[117] Initially Anna's family, along with the bulk of these refugees, were settled on Polish territory though they later shifted to Germany. Even though these now formerly Soviet Mennonites deemed themselves Germans, Germany did not regard them as its own. Instead they were viewed as strangers and outsiders, a burden at a time when Germany was spiralling towards absolute defeat. For example, Joseph Goebbels wrote on his return to the capital on 8 March 1945 that "The trip to Berlin shocks me ... Along the way we meet baggage carts with refugees, mainly Germans from the Black Sea lands. The mood sours immediately: what kind of people are moving to the German Reich under the brand of so-called Germans?!"[118]

After the war's end in 1945–6, many of these were repatriated to the Soviet Union, but not to their places of residence.[119] The Soviets, who had deemed these refugees to be traitors during the period of the war, now forcibly relocated them to the eastern regions of the country, including Siberia, Altai, Kazakhstan, and the Urals. Soviet Germans and Mennonites were only rehabilitated and granted the right to return to Ukraine in 1957, though few took advantage of that possibility.

We can conclude that Soviet Mennonites were not a fifth column, as Berlin had hoped and as Moscow had feared. For Mennonites themselves this was a difficult time, though the same must be said for all peoples of the occupied territories. But unlike, say, Soviet Ukrainians or Soviet Germans, Mennonites found themselves to be strangers everywhere. So it was in Germany, so it was thereafter in the Soviet Union where they were deemed "enemies of the people" during their repatriation, thus sealing their fate.

NOTES

1 Interview with Anna (Schmidt) Friesen, 18 April 2016. I thank Anna's son, Leonard Friesen, for notes from this interview.

2 Serhii Plokhy, *The Gates of Europe: A History of Ukraine* (New York: Basic Books, 2015), 263–5.

3 Cf. Jacob A. Neufeld, *Path of Thorns: Soviet Mennonite Life under Communist and Nazi Rule*, edited with an introduction and analysis by Harvey L. Dyck, trans. Harvey L. Dyck and Sarah Dyck (Toronto: University of Toronto Press, 2014), 214–15; and Agatha Loewen Schmidt, *Gnadenfeld, Molotschna, 1835–1943* (Kitchener, ON: A.L. Schmidt, 1997), 32–3. Schmidt suggests that some 6,000 Mennonites had assembled at Stulnevo from the Molochna colony.

4 Consider for example the questionnaires completed in the Mennonite villages of Frizendorf (Stalindorf) district, Dnipropetrovskoi territory in 1943. GADO, f.3388, op.1, d.8–12, 22–5.

5 Gerhard Rempel, "Mennonites and the Holocaust: from collaboration to perpetuation," *Mennonite Quarterly Review* 84, no. 4 (2010): 507–49.

6 Karel C. Berkhoff, *Harvest of Despair: Life and Death in Ukraine under Soviet Rule* (Cambridge, MA: The Belknap Press of Harvard University Press, 2004), 28–9; and Plokhy, *Gates of Europe*, 265.

7 Waldemar Janzen, *Growing up in Turbulent Times: Memoirs of Soviet Oppression, Refugee Life in Germany, and Immigrant Adjustment to Canada* (Winnipeg: CMU Press, 2007), 45.

8 Katie Friesen, *Into the Unknown* (Steinbach, MB?: John and Katie Friesen, 1986), 43–4.
9 Rempel, "Mennonites and the Holocaust," 525.
10 Wendy Lower, *Nazi Empire-Building and the Holocaust in Ukraine* (Chapel Hill: The University of North Carolina Press, 2005). Her explicit reference to Mennonites is found on p. 15. An example of Lower's engagement with "ethnic Germans" and the Holocaust is found on pp. 90–7; Eric C. Steinhart, "The Chameleon of Trawniki: Jack Reimer, Soviet Volksdeutsche, and the Holocaust," *Holocaust and Genocide Studies* 23, no. 2 (2009): 239–62. For a nuanced reflection on how difficult it is to link ethnic Germans with complicity in Ukraine's holocaust, see Eric Conrad Steinhart, "Creating Killers: The Nazification of the Black Sea Germans and the Holocaust in Southern Ukraine" (PhD diss, University of North Carolina 2010), 128–30.
11 Horst Gerlach, "Mennonites, the Molotschna, and the *Volksdeutsche Mittelstelle* in the Second World War, *Mennonite Life*, 41, no. 3 (1986): 6; and Berkhoff, *Harvest of Despair*, 5.
12 Rempel, "Mennonites and the Holocaust," 508–12.
13 The literature on this is impressive and extensive. See Berkhoff, *Harvest of Despair*; Lower, *Nazi Empire-Building and the Holocaust in Ukraine*; Valdis O. Lumans, *Himmler's Auxiliaries: The Volksdeutsche Mittelstelle and the German National Minorities of Europe, 1933–1945* (Chapel Hill: The University of North Carolina Press, 1993); and Martin Dean, *Collaboration in the Holocaust: Crimes of the Local Police in Belorussia and Ukraine, 1941–44* (New York: St Martin's Press, 2000). Cf. Mary Fulbrook, *A Small Town Near Auschwitz: Ordinary Nazis and the Holocaust* (Oxford: Oxford University Press, 2013).
14 Lower, *Nazi Empire-Building and the Holocaust in Ukraine*, 41.
15 M.I. Semiriaga, *Kollaboratsionizm: Priroda, tipologiia I proiavlenie v gody Vtoroi mirovoi voiny* (Moscow, 2000), 390.
16 This was, of course, set within a much larger Soviet strategy of wartime deportation. See Lewis H. Siegelbaum and Leslie Page Moch, *Broad is My Native Land: Repertoires and Regimes of Migration in Russia's Twentieth Century* (Ithaca, NY: Cornell University Press, 2014), 310–25.
17 A. Eisfeld and V. Brul', "Deportatsiia," in *Nemtsy Rossii: Entsiklopediia* v 3 t. (Moscow, 1999), t. 1, 698; and John Friesen, *Against the Wind: The Story of Four Mennonite Villages* (Winnipeg: Windflower Books, 1994), 95.
18 Gerhard Lohrenz, *The Lost Generation and Other Stories* (Winnipeg: Gerhard Lohrenz, 1982), 38.
19 Ibid.

20 V. Broshevan and V. Renpening, *Bol' i pamiat Krymskikh Nemtsev (1941–2001 gg.). Istoriko-dokumental'naia kniga* (Simferopol, 2002), 123.
21 P.M. Polian, *Ne po svoei vole: Istoriia i geografiia prenuditel'nykh migratsii v SSSR* (Moscow, 2001), 111.
22 Direktiva Stavki VGK No. 00931. *Glavnokomandyiushchemu voiskami IUgo-zapadnogo napravleniia. Komanduiushchemu voiskami IUzhnogo fronta. Narodnomu komissaru Voenno-Morskogo flota, Komanduiushchemu 51-i otdel'noi armii, komandiru 9-go Otdel'nogo strelkovogo korpusa "O formirovanii i zadachakh 51-i Otdel'noi armii"*; and Broshevan and Renpening, *Bol' i pamiat Krymskikh Nemtsev*, 116.
23 Sekretariu Krymskogo obkoma BKP(b) tov. Bulatovu, *Dokladnaia zapiska ob evakuatsii nemetskogo naseleniia iz Krymskoi ACCR, 1 sentiabria 1941g.*; and *Reabilitirovannye istoriei. Avtonomnaia respublika Krym*, ed. V.P. Antipenko et. al. (Simferopol, 2006), 48, 49, 51.
24 Helmut Huebert, *Hierschau: An Example of Russian Mennonite Life* (Winnipeg: Springfield Publishers, 1986), 324; and Helmut Huebert, *Crimea: The Story of Crimea and the Mennonites Who Lived There* (Winnipeg: Springfield Publishers, 2013), 101.
25 Ingeborg Fleischhauer, "'Operation Barbarossa' and the Deportation," in *The Soviet Germans Past and Present* by Ingeborg Fleischhauer and Benjamin Pinkus, ed. Edith Frankel (London: C. Hurst & Company, 1986), 88.
26 A.A. German, T.S. Ilarionova, and I.R. Pleve, *Istoriia nemtsev Rossii: Uchebnoe posobie* (Moscow, 2005), 423; and A.A. German, *"Esli ostanus zhiv ..." Zhizn i udivitel'nye izlomy sud'by rossiiskogo nemtsa Edvina Griba* (Moscow, 2007), 16–18.
27 See *Gedenkenbuch: Kniga pamiati nemtsev-trudarmeitsev ITL Bakalstroi-Cheliabmetallurgstroi 1942–1946 gg.* v 2 t. (Moscow, 2011), vol. 1, *Kniga pamiati nemtsev-trudarmeitsev ITL Bakalstroi-Cheliabmetallurgstroi, 1942–1946 gg.*; and vol. 2, *Avtory-sosaviteli kniga pamiati nemtsev-trudarmeitsev Bogoslovlaga, 1941–1946 gg.*
28 R.V. Pliukfel'der, *Chuzhoi sredi svoikh* (Moscow, 2008), 33–4.
29 Anne Konrad, *Red Quarter Moon: A Search for Family in the Shadow of Stalin* (Toronto: University of Toronto Press, 2012), 147.
30 *Istoriia rossiiskikh nemtsev v dokumentakh (1763–1992 gg.)*, ed. V.A. Ayman and V.G. Chebotareva (Moscow, 1993), 165; and "Mobilizovats nemtsev v rabochie kolonny ... I. Stalin," in *Sbornik dokumentov (1940–e gody)*, ed. N.F. Bugaia, 2nd ed. (Moscow, 2000), 32–3.
31 A.A. German, T.S. Ilarionova, and I.R. Pleve, *Istoriia nemtsev Rossii: Khrestomatiia* (Moscow, 2005), 269, 271.

32 I. Fleschauer, *Das Dritte Reich und die Deutsche in der Sowjetunion* (Stuttgart, 1983), 104.
33 M.M. Shitiuk et al., *Nimtsi Pivdnia Ukraini: Istgoriia I suchasnist'* (Mikolaiv, 2009), 373, 375.
34 GADO, f.2311, op.1, d.24, l.52.
35 *Vsesoiuznaia perepis naseleniia 1937 goda: Obshchie itogi: Sbornik dokumentov I materialov* (Moscow, 2007), 87. Germans (according to the 1937 census: 401,880 people; according to the 1939 census: 392,458 persons). Cf. *Istoriia rossiiskikh nemtsev* (1993), 156; "Mobilizovats nemtsev" (2000), 17; *Deportatsii narodov SSSR (1930-e– 1950-e gody)*, ed. O.L. Milov (Moscow, 1995), Part 2. *Departatsiia nemtsev (sentiabr 1941–fevral' 1942 gg.). (Materialy k serii "Narody i kul'tury")*, 22.
36 A. Eisfeld', "Velikaia Otechestvennaia voina 1941–1945," in *Nemtsy Rossii: entsiklopediia*, vol. 1 (1999), 338.
37 Shitiuk et al., *Nimtsi Pivdnia Ukraini*, 375.
38 Fleischhauer, "'Operation Barbarossa' and the Deportation," 76–7.
39 Tsentral'nyi gosudarstvennyi arkhiv vyschikh organov vlasti I upravleniia Ukrainy (hereafter TsGAVOVU), f.3676, op.4, d.4, l.81.
40 Ibid., f.3676, op.4, d.4, l.116.
41 V.V. Karpov, "Marshal Zhukov, ego soratniki I protivniki v gody voiny I mira (Literatura mosaika)," *Roman-gazeta* no. 11 (1991), 6, 7.
42 K. Heiden, *NSDAP: Fiurer I ego partiia* (Moscow, 2004), 29.
43 Ibid.
44 TsGAVOVU, f.3206, op.2, d.131, l.71.
45 GADO, f.2443, op.1, d.2, l.14.
46 B.V. Sokolov, *Pravda i mify* (Moscow, 2002), 322.
47 Berkhoff, *Harvest of Despair*, 212.
48 M.I. Semiriaga, *Tiurmnaia imperiia natsizma i ee krakh* (Moscow, 1991), 99.
49 Eisfeld', "Velikaia Otechestvennaia voina," 339.
50 H. Gerlach, *Die Russlandmennoniten: Ein Volk Unterwegs*, 3rd ed., (Kirchheimbolanden, 1998), 94, 96; and Gerlach, "Mennonites, the Molotschna, and the *Volksdeutsche Mittelstelle*," 6.
51 Semiriaga, *Tiurmnaia imperiia*, 98–9.
52 GADO, f.2311, op.1, d.1, l.44.
53 Ibid., f.2311, op.1, d.1, l.60.
54 Ibid., f.2311, op.1, d.91, l.12.
55 Ibid., f.1, op.2, d.25, l.53.
56 Ibid., f.1, op.1, d.23, l.279.
57 Ibid., f.1, op.1, d.29, l.279.
58 Ibid.

59 Ibid., f.2443, op.1, d.60, l.41.
60 Ibid., f.2443, op.1, d.60, 1.47.
61 Kozachok, *Robota nochatkovikh ta serednikh shkil m. Zaporizhzhia* (10 grudnia, Nove Zaporizhzhia, 1941), no. 9.
62 *Pro robotu v shkolakh* (12 listopada, Nove Zaporizhzhia, 1941), no. 1.
63 TsGAVOVU, f.3676, op.4, d.3, l.31.
64 GADO, f.2281, op.1, d.10, l.61–4, 67.
65 Ibid., f.2281, op.1, d.10, l.58–63.
66 Ibid., f.2276, op.1c, d.1896c, l.2–4, 6, 8–9, 12.
67 Ibid., f.2276, op.1c, d.1896c, l.1.
68 Ibid., f.2443, op.1, d.32, l.165a-166.
69 Janzen, *Growing up in Turbulent Times*, 44–5.
70 TsGAVOVU, f.3676, op.4, d.3, l.39.
71 Ibid., f.3676, op.4, d.4, l.89.
72 R. Kh. Val't, *Oblomki vsemirnoi istorii. Rossiiskie nemtsy mezhdu Stalinym i Gitlerom*, 2nd ed. (Essen, 1996), 251.
73 B.N. Kovalen, *Povsednevnaia zhizn' naseleniia Rossii v period natsistskoi okkupatsii* (Moscow, 2011), 472–3.
74 "Vospominaniia F. D. Polivody (Letkeman) c. Nizhnaia Khortitsa Zaporozhskogo raiona Zaporozhskoi oblasti," in *Zhivi i pomni: Istoriia Mennonitskikh kolonii Ekaterinoslavshchiny*, ed. S.I. Bobyleva et al. (Dnipropetrovsk, 2006), 155.
75 *Dnipropetrovs'ka gazeta* (1941), 28 listopada.
76 *Tsentr ukrainsko-nemetskikh istoricheskikh issledovanii Dnipropetrovskogo natsional'nogo universiteta im. Olesia Gonchara*. Tekushchii arkhiv (hereafter TsUNII DNU) *Materialy istoriko-etnograficheskoi ekspeditsii 1998g*.
77 *Dnipropetrovs'ka gazeta* (1941), 28 listopada.
78 Gerlach, *Die Russlandmennoniten*, 86–7.
79 Bobyleva, *Zhivi i pomni*, 134.
80 Ibid., 221.
81 "Vospominaniia L.D. Timoshenko (s. Nizhniaia Khortitsa Zaporozhskogo raiona Zaporozhskoi oblasti)," in Bobyleva, *Zhivi i pomni*, 166.
82 Henry H. Winter, *A Shepherd of the Oppressed: Heinrich Winter: Last Ältester of Chortitza* (Wheatley, ON: Henry H. Winter, 1990), 75–7.
83 GADO, f.2567, op.1, d.7, l.126.
84 See M.A. Slobodianiuk and I.A. Shakhraichuk, *Rukh Oporu na Dniprpetrovshchini v roki Velikoi Vitchisnianoi viini (1941–1945)* (Dnipropetrovsk, 1998), 10.
85 TsGIAVOVU, f.3676, op.4, d.4, l.117.
86 Gerlach, *Die Russlandmennoniten*, 83.

87 Gosudarstvennyi arkhiv Zaporozhskoi oblasti, f.1636, op.1, d.2, l.116.
88 GADO, f.6478, op.1, d.8528, l.4.
89 Ibid., f.6478, op.1, d.13372, ll.1–2.
90 Ibid., d.22278, l.2.
91 Ibid., d.43107, l.16.
92 Ibid., f.6478, op.1, d.38413, l.1; d.50381, l.1, d.50387, l.1; d.33104, l.1; d.33106, l.1; d.83208, l.1; d.82554, l.1–3; d.82924, l.1–3; d.93002, l.1, d.34831, l.1; d.34832, l.1; d.36620, l.3; d.92045, l.1; d.111129, l.1; d.93255, l.1; d.38642, l.1; d.41308, l.1; d.93004, l.1; d.100508, l.1; d.33996, l.1; d.91336, l.1; d.118733, l.1; d.34132, l.1; d.40703, l.1; d.33358, l.1; d.46646, l.1; d.46653, l.1; d.100656, l.2, 3; d.34205, l.1, 4; d.48772, l.1, 3; d.51011, l.2; d.13372, l.2; d.122289, l.1; d.122620, l.1; d.120967, l.1; d.26287, l.1; d.35161, l.4; d.35164, l.1; d.35166, l.1; d.100644, l.4; d.33270, l.1; d.33271, l.1; d.33272, l.1; d.33295, l.1; d.33730, l.1; d.75946, l.3.
93 GADO, f.6478, op.1, l.4.
94 TsUNII DNU, Materialy istoriko-etnograficheskoi ekspeditsii 2002 g.
95 O.V. Soloviov, "Diial'nist' Gitleriugendu sered ukrainskikh fol'ksdoiche" in *Voprosy germanskoi istorii* (2002), 125.
96 Ibid., 129.
97 Heiden, *NSDAP*, 228.
98 *Dnipropetrovs'ka gazeta* (28 Chervnia 1942 g.).
99 *Devin* (Krivii Rig) (1942), 11 lipniia.
100 TsUNII DNU, Materialy istoriko-etnograficheskoi ekspeditsii 2002 g.
101 Ibid.
102 Ibid.
103 Ibid.
104 Ibid.
105 GADO, f.6478, op.1, d.75946, l.2.
106 See TsUNII DNU, Materialy istoriko-etnograficheskoi ekspeditsii 2003 g.
107 Ibid., 2002 g.
108 Ibid.
109 Ibid.
110 GADO, f.6478, op.1, d.40196, l.1; d.34832, l.1
111 TsUNII DNU, Materialy istoriko-etnograficheskoi ekspeditsii 2001 g
112 E.F. Iaz'kov, *Istoriia stran Evropy I Ameriki v noveishee vremia (1918-1945gg.): Kurs lektsii* (Moscow, 1998), 232.
113 D. Maier, *Sotsial'naia psikhologiia* (St Petersburg, 1999), 349.
114 TsGAVOVU, f.3676, op.4, d.4, l.128.
115 Janzen, *Growing up in Turbulent Times*, 46.

116 Ibid., 47. For more on the negative impact of forced labour deportation to Germany see Dean, *Collaboration in the Holocaust*, 112–18; and Plokhy, *Gates of Europe*, 273–4.

117 Anni Schmidt, *My Life on the Road, 1943–1951* (Waterloo, ON: 2006); and Friesen, *Into the Unknown*, 52. Cf. Harry Loewen, ed., *Road to Freedom: Mennonites Escape the Land of Suffering* (Kitchener, ON: Pandora Press, 2000); Pamela E. Klassen, *Going by the Moon and the Stars: Stories of Two Mennonite Women* (Waterloo, ON: Wilfrid Laurier University Press, 1994); and Neufeld, *Path of Thorns*, section 3.

118 I. Gebbels (J. Goebbels), *Poslednie zapisi*, ed. A.A. Galkin (Smolensk, 1998), 219.

119 Konrad, *Red Quarter Moon*, 170–5.

Appendix

Dnipropetrovsk State University, *Khortitsa '99*, and the Renaissance of Public (Mennonite) History in Ukraine

LEONARD G. FRIESEN

The contributions found in this volume make it plain that new sources and approaches over the past several decades have dramatically transformed the field of Imperial Russian and Soviet Mennonite history. That this happened in the first place is remarkable. But how it happened that a cohort of Russian and Ukrainian scholars became passionately engaged with Mennonite history is itself a story that needs to be told. Central to this story is the remarkable Institute of Ukrainian-German Historical Research at Dnipropetrovsk State University (DSU) and one moment in 1997 when a DSU graduate student encountered a senior Canadian historian at the Zaporizhzhia regional archive. Their collaboration led to a resurgence of public and Mennonite history in southern Ukraine and culminated in the academic conference known as *Khortitsa '99*, from which would be sown the seeds for this volume. It is a story that needs to be told if this volume is to make any sense.

Nataliya Venger (then Ostasheva) was the DSU graduate student. She had graduated from the university in 1989 and proceeded to teach school for two years. In 1990 she returned to DSU for further historical study.[1] Venger was informed by the university that Serhii Plokhy, the young charismatic chair of the World History Department, had one slot available for a graduate student. When approached, he agreed to take her on as his student and even suggested that she investigate a Mennonite subject. Mennonite? To connect the dots between Plokhy and the Mennonite question will require us to take a step back. DSU had been founded in 1918 by the government of Hetman Pavlo Skoropadksy, and was initially known as the University of Ekaterinoslav in honour of the city's pre-revolutionary name.[2] This had also been the name of the Imperial Russian province in which the city was located, in which the

Khortitsa mother colony was itself situated. It was renamed Dnipropetrovsk in the mid-1920s. The city had been a closed city to foreigners from the 1950s onwards, in large part because of military armaments that were constructed there during the Cold War.

The city's closed status meant that it received special funding from Moscow, though it also limited the international connections possible for DSU, even after détente had begun. Contact with North American scholars was impossible before Gorbachev though it was possible at least to make inroads into Eastern Europe. Svetlana Bobyleva, a professor at DSU – whose important micro-study of the Borozenko settlements is part of this volume – credits Anatoly S. Zavialov, who founded a laboratory dedicated to the study of German history in 1987, which was transformed into an Institute in 1997,[3] a time when the university created a number of research institutes. Zavialov's institute was the only one attached to the World History Department. Bobyleva describes Zavialov as "a talented organizer, an energetic individual, someone able to create a productive atmosphere in the department."[4] Zavialov initially focused on the German Democratic Republic (DDR), which coincided with his own research interest.[5] Zavialov sought to create a center for Germanic studies focused on the two Germanys, not on the investigation of Germans within the Soviet Union. Thus, colleagues of the institute investigated themes as diverse as the development of the DDR, German militarism, revanchism, German workers' movements, Imperial Germany, and western European themes more generally. Many of their findings were subsequently published in the Institute's flagship journal, *Questions of Germany History* (*Voprosy Germanskoi Istorii*), which was first published in 1973.

An important shift occurred in July 1989 when Serhii Plokhy became the chair of the World History Department. Officials had appointed him director of the institute by the end of the year. The larger world had begun to change dramatically with Gorbachev's vaunted *perestroika*. It was soon apparent that the centre – Moscow – might not hold. If so, what would come after? Ukrainian scholars anticipated that dramatic change was underfoot. They began to energetically probe questions about Ukrainian national identity, which itself raised the question of non-Slavic minorities and their "Ukrainian" identity within the region. How integral, scholars now asked, had these minorities been to the region's history? Importantly, officials removed some of the more onerous travel restrictions on foreigners. As part of this, Dnipropetrovsk ceased to be a closed city by 1989. I was fortunate to be able to travel to Dnipropetrovsk in that year as a tourist, and to return to the city the next year when I became the first western scholar to visit Plokhy at DSU. It was clear that something very special was underway. German scholars, including German scholars of the Germanic populations of southern Ukraine, were among the first to make their way to Dnipropetrovsk a few years after my visit. When they arrived in the mid-1990s they encountered a thriving institute that bore Plokhy's mark even after his departure.

Plokhy's own engagement in this story is itself remarkable, as this volume's introduction has already suggested. By 1989 he was already widely published in Cossack and Ukrainian history, with a particular interest in religion. As a child he had heard stories about the region's Mennonites from his grandmother. He was able to make a further connection after he read Ipatov's short book about Mennonites.[6] Ipatov's stress on Mennonites as an ethno-confessional grouping had jelled with his own interests at the time, but he knew little more. A watershed moment in his own life came in 1986 when Plokhy was invited to Columbia and Harvard universities on academic exchanges. There he encountered western sources for the first time that actually described the "true" history of Mennonites and Germans in Ukraine. Plokhy describes what happens next:[7]

> Upon my return to Dnipropetrovsk in the summer of 1987 I went to the local archives and forced them to show me documents from the fond of *Kontora instrannykh poselentsev* (I saw references to that fond in the works I read in the United States). So, the interest was there, and now I knew that the sources were available right here at home. Then, in 1989, when I became chair, I had an opportunity to do something about that: to match ideas with people and resources. While I was more interested in the Mennonites than other groups (primarily because of my interest in religion), the project I inherited dealt with German history, so in the spirit of continuity, the emphases in the official pronouncements, correspondence, reports, etc. were on the German aspect of the research – after all we were the Department of the World History.

Bobyleva, the institute's current director, argues that Plokhy transformed the institute as a whole to focus on ethnic Germans within Ukraine. His goal, she wrote, was to liquidate the "blank pages" in the region's history.[8] Up until then, the subject of Germanic peoples in Ukraine had been taboo, a situation that authorities exacerbated when they refused Germans and Mennonites the right to resettle to Soviet Ukraine after Khrushchev had issued his amnesties in the mid-1950s – by which he effectively obliterated the Soviet GULAG. No wonder the leading Soviet scholar of southern Ukraine, Elena Druzhinina, barely mentioned Mennonites in her multi-volume study.[9] A revamped institute under Plokhy's direction was suddenly hard at work to complete the picture. Plokhy's own research on Mennonite-related topics, though modest, bore fruit in one article that pertained to their intermarriage with non-Mennonites.[10] The article was published in 1995, though his affiliation with the university had ended three years earlier in March of 1992.[11] An impressive career first at the University of Alberta and, thereafter, at Harvard University, awaited him. No wonder he was still held in awe years later by his colleagues at Dnipropetrovsk. Plokhy's time at the helm of Dnipropetrovsk's nascent institute had been short though his influence was long-standing. He ushered an entire generation of younger scholars into the ranks, including Nataliya Venger, whom we encountered earlier.

Venger defended her dissertation on Mennonite entrepreneurs in 1996 and was on the edge of her own strong career by the end of the millennium, one that would see her rise to become chair of the World History Department by February of 2013.[12] That lay in the future. Back in 1996 she had already published her first article. Venger was back in the Zaporizhzhia Archive in 1997 when Aleksander Tedeev – then an assistant in the regional Archive – suggested that she meet a senior historian, Harvey Dyck, who was undertaking research there at the same time, describing Dyck as a serious professor from Canada.[13] Venger recalls that she gave Dyck a portion of her dissertation when they first met. His interest in it had been immediate. Dyck read it quickly, and then offered insightful comments and suggestions (though he deemed it an important work). Venger also told him about the Dnipropetrovsk Institute, and invited him to Dnipropetrovsk. Dyck told her of his own plans for a major international conference on Mennonite history in Ukraine, an idea that he had raised with Tedeev on their very first meeting in 1994.[14]

Towards *Khortitsa '99*

Aleksandr Tedeev recalls that Harvey Dyck had been calling for a major international scholarly conference on Mennonite history since at least 1996.[15] He wanted it placed in Zaporizhzhia, that great Stalinist city, which in the course of the twentieth century had absorbed the original Mennonite settlement of Khortitsa, and he wanted Tedeev to play a pivotal role as a co-organizer. Tedeev boldly agreed. This project – which would come to fruition in the event known as *Khortitsa '99* – would itself have marked a significant accomplishment. And yet it was only a portion of the activity undertaken by Dyck in a stretch that may have marked the most productive period of his career. Dyck moved quickly on a number of fronts to engage in acts of public history as well as narrowly academic pursuits. He firmly believed that the "base" of the academic conference required a multifaceted superstructure that included a new Mennonite library in Ukraine; a massive reproduction effort of Mennonite sources and a corresponding user's guide to the Zaporizhzhia Regional Archive; a museum exhibition; and finally, the memorialization of the Mennonite experience. He maintained that it all had to come together as one piece if any of it was to be successful.

A Mennonite Library

It was immediately clear to Dyck that the emerging Mennonite scholarly community in Ukraine had been working in the dark, academically speaking. With almost no access to English- or German-language primary or secondary materials, they did not know how their own research fit into the larger scholarship. As a result, they did not realize how important their own contributions were in bringing a Ukrainian voice to Mennonite identity formation, let alone a Mennonite voice to the formation of a Ukrainian state. A library was needed, and Dyck worked energetically to bring it about. He developed key partnerships, including with Paul Toews, the American historian and director of the Center for Mennonite Brethren Studies in Fresno, California; and Lawrence Klippenstein, at the Mennonite Heritage Centre, Winnipeg. In time, they were able to amass a collection of materials – everything from Mennonite newspapers from the imperial era to back issues of the *Mennonite Quarterly Review* along with important secondary works – in part by systematically appealing to Mennonite libraries and archives across North America and Germany. A solution was also found to the issue of how most effectively to transport these materials to Ukraine, thanks to Dyck's close personal contact with Walter and Marina Unger.

The Ungers created the annual Mennonite Heritage Cruise to Ukraine in 1994,[16] of which the first of these immensely popular treks took place in 1995. Many Mennonites who participated in these tours had either been born in Ukraine, or had forebears born there, and every tour included several days based in Zaporizhzhia. From the start, thanks to the enthusiastic support of the Ungers, participants became vital to the success of a number of initiatives, from fundraising to an important audience for public events (more on this below) to, in this instance, an informal courier service that brought library materials to Zaporizhzhia. In addition, Paul Toews brought along a suitcase or two of library materials going back many years, to the 1990s and beyond. In time these various deliveries resulted in the establishment of a library at the regional Archive in Zaporizhzhia. Somewhat later there were enough materials to create a second Mennonite library; this one attached to the Research Institute at DSU.[17]

Museum Exhibition

There were a number of important museums in Zaporizhzhia at this time whereby the city was able to celebrate everything from its Cossack past to its industrial present. On one occasion in the mid-1990s, Dyck toured the city's local history museum (*Zaporozhskii kraevedcheskii muzei*) with Maria De Jager, one of the few Mennonites who had managed to live in the city even after Mennonites had been banned from doing so. Dyck had initially sought De Jager out because their fathers had been close friends. Her very existence had become known to him through a mutual acquaintance, Nicholas Dyck. In time, that connection with De Jager would yield yet another major monograph for Dyck,[18] but that was not in the works when the two met at the local museum on a lovely Sunday afternoon. Harvey Dyck made two important observations during their visit: first, that Mennonites were almost entirely absent from the displayed history of the region even though they had been there from the time the Cossacks had been removed in the late eighteenth century until the Stalinist 1940s; and second, that the museum had a hall dedicated to temporary exhibitions. Could there be an exhibition at the Museum on Mennonite history which could coincide with the anticipated *Khortitsa '99* academic conference, he wondered?[19]

In time, Dyck's efforts bore fruit in an unprecedented museum exhibition, one that coincided with the conference itself. Nor was this a mean feat, as it was the first time that a religious group had been featured at a Zaporizhzhia museum. This was clearly a new Ukraine with new identities in formation, including religious ones. With significant obstacles before him, such an exhibition might not have happened had Dyck not managed to enlist the support of regional officials in the Zaporizhzhia municipal government, in this instance Iurii Shapovalov. Even here, fate had intervened as Dyck relied on local translators such as Olga Shmakina to assist him with the technical matters related to formal agreements. Shmakina, who herself would develop a sterling reputation among Mennonite visitors to Ukraine, had a close personal connection with Shapovalov, who later became director of the museum itself.[20]

Boris Letkeman, who would also feature prominently in the events leading up to *Khortitsa '99*, believes that Harvey L. Dyck developed a close, almost symbiotic, relationship with his translators which made eventual success possible. On the one hand, they were often able to persuade Dyck of an alternate approach when post-Soviet proprieties demanded it. Often, Letkeman recalled, he would suggest to Dyck that it needed to happen a certain way and not as Dyck had first imagined. It was a measure of the Canadian professor's strength of character that Dyck often pondered the matter overnight and then agreed in favour of the suggested changetack.[21] Dyck sought out specialists in Toronto at the Royal Ontario Museum, who gave him sage advice on mounting an exhibition. He also had the expertise and experience of Ontario College of Art designer Paul Epp as well as museum specialists in Winnipeg and Steinbach, Manitoba.

Nataliya Venger suggested that part of Dyck's success may have been the pronounced inclination of many Ukrainians to respect the role and moral authority of their leaders (*rukovoditeli*), and that Harvey Dyck, a senior professor from a world-renowned university, filled the bill nicely.[22] Paul Toews concurred, though he added three other factors that may have contributed to Dyck's success: first, there was a long-standing Soviet deference to authorities, especially academics; second, it may well be that Ukrainians were more inclined to remember and to memorialize and so were sympathetic to Dyck's efforts from the outset; and third, the local *Inturist* office in Zaporizhzhia had, under the lead of Larissa Goriacheva, developed its own strong institutional ties over the years, which gave Harvey Dyck a vital platform when he arrived on stage.[23] Dyck himself later credited Michael Siderenko, chair of the Monuments Commission for the province of Zaporizhzhia for his unfailing assistance in this area. Sidorenko, a stalwart progressive during Soviet days and a key figure in the acceptance process, met Dyck, heard his proposals, and said "[Y]our plan is noble. For the first time in our province the victims of repression and not the perpetrators will be remembered. I give you complete support in your efforts to memorialize the Mennonite story in Ukraine." Unfortunately, Siderenko's grave illness prevented him from appearing at the important last dedication of the monument in Zaporizhzhia in 2009.

Another key figure in the museum exhibition was Uri Shapovalov, director of the Zaporizhzhia regional museum, mentioned above. For the museum exhibition, Shapovalov authorized a purchasing mission to buy up old Mennonite furniture in local villages where Mennonites had lived and from which they had been evicted, exiled, or had fled in 1943 (to German-occupied Poland and beyond). Shapovalov told the anecdote of his mother working for Mennonites on the island of Khortitsa. She had been well paid, treated kindly, and taught to read, and with her earnings had purchased a wooden sleeping sofa (*Schlop Bank*). "I know the *Schlop Bank*. I grew up with one. My mother had one." From his childhood he had a fondness for Mennonites and their memorabilia.

Last, Harvey Dyck's own tenacity must be mentioned, his refusal to accept concerns at the outset that he had set the bar too high. In his eyes all was attainable if the collective will and energy were equal to the challenges. In the words of one of the *Inturist* translators who often accompanied him, "Harvey started smoothly; then when it looked that they would refuse him he added metal to his voice."[24] Another recalled that he worked endlessly with drafts of various correspondences that would need to be sent out. Once, when tired, he simply lay down on the floor in Goriacheva's office for a few minutes. He awoke shortly after and in true Stakhanovite fashion he was soon back at it. So it was that the museum project was soon up and running, a task for which Dyck engaged the major Mennonite museums of North America to lend some of their own collections.[25]

The Zaporizhzhia Museum exhibit lasted a year and then went to Dnipropetrovsk for another six months. It reached out to the public to tell the story of Mennonites in Ukraine as countless school groups viewed the exhibition, which was also commented on by the local media. Thus, it fulfilled a key goal of *Khortitsa '99* – to return the Mennonite history of the area to the Ukrainian population – not only to those in Zaporizhzhia but to the entire Ukraine.

The Memorialization of the Mennonite Experience

In many ways, Dyck's engagement with the larger Ukrainian community in the lead-up to *Khortitsa '99* transformed him into a truly public historian, as his passion for a museum exhibition had already demonstrated. But well beyond temporary exhibitions, Dyck sought a way to erect a permanent memorial to the Mennonite experience in Ukraine. In a paper written in 2007 entitled "A Memorializing of the Mennonite Historical Experience in Tsarist Russia and the Soviet Union," Dyck reflected on his motivation for memorialization in the first place. He stresses the multifaceted ways in which Mennonites had been part of the Russian Empire for generations, such that their villages and estates stretched out by 1900 from the "homeland" (what Dyck calls "a Mennoland of mother settlements and daughter colonies") to "the Crimea, the pre-Caucasus, the Transvolga and western Siberia." The Mennonites' geographic expansiveness across the empire mirrored their broader socio-political engagement; one in which they "played a complex, generally dynamic role in the settlement and transformation of southern Ukraine." Then, Dyck continues, they experienced fierce persecution and terror which left them devastated. Perhaps a third perished, others fled, so that those Mennonites who did return to Ukraine in Stalin's time did so "often now in handcuffs, under guard, humiliated, and fearing for their lives."[26] In Dyck's telling, the Soviet terrors and devastation always threaten to overwhelm a remembrance of the Mennonites' imperial dynamism.

For that reason alone it is significant that two markers were soon on the planning books, and were intended to be unveiled during *Khortitsa '99*. The first was to be a modest plaque – in English and Ukrainian – to be placed at the entry-way to a building that once housed the Khortitsa mother Mennonite church in the founding Mennonite colony of Khortitsa. The building, which in 1999 served as the local cultural centre (*Dom Kultura*) for the Khortitsa suburb of Zaporizhzhia was also pegged as the site of the grand opening for the academic conference.[27] The planning committee intended that that particular historical marker would affirm the foundational role that Mennonites had played in the earliest settlement history of the region. In Dyck's words, "It is intended to recognize the ethno-religious character of the original Mennonite settlers in Khortitsa."[28] Organizers soon planned a second monument, to be placed in the former village of Nieder Khortitsa. Unlike the first one, though, this monument was intended to recognize villagers who had lived and died in similar village settings across Ukraine, in particular those who had perished during the years of repression and civil war. The Nieder Khortitsa monument was also to serve as an important linkage to the Mennonite past and present in Ukraine. On the one hand, it marked the village where the noted Mennonite historian David G. Rempel had been born, along with his forebears.[29] On the other, the village remained the beloved *Stammort* (home village) of Boris Letkeman, who had lived there all his life, and whose world was dramatically reshaped by the events of *Khortitsa '99*.[30]

Khortitsa '99: The Conference

The museum, the memorials, and even the archival work all served as a rich backdrop for the academic conference that began on 26 May 1999. For the next four days, a Mennonite voice that had long been silent was heard again in Zaporizhzhia. It soon became obvious that these events were of more than mere sectarian interest to those Mennonite descendants who participated. Ukrainians gathered in large numbers at all public events associated with the conference, though even the public's reaction was nothing compared with the enthusiastic engagement by scholars from the Ukrainian-German Institute at DSU. Indeed, their presence was all the remarkable given the efforts by German scholars in the 1990s to use the institute as a base for the historical investigation of Ukraine's German Lutherans and Catholics.[31]

But the Mennonite story had clearly captivated the DSU Institute, and nothing quite matched the energy of those days. Ukrainian scholars deeply appreciated how Dyck nurtured what had been only recently an isolated scholarly outpost. Now, suddenly, the stage was theirs as much as anyone's. Years later, the memory of the conference was clearly etched on the hearts and minds of the Dnipropetrovsk scholars: "It was four days of joy," the Institute's current director Bobyleva reflected in 2011. Others, including Alexander Beznosov, Oksana Beznosova, and Nataliya Venger, had similar reflections: "[T]he very form of the conference was different, and taught us a great deal about how academic conference were conducted in the west"; "we loved the subject matter, and the chance to meet with western colleagues for the first time."[32] In the words of a Ukrainian graduate student immediately after the conference: "It's like there is a whole new world! At your conference people argued and debated – you didn't just bow down to your seniors and accept their version of events. It was like we were all colleagues!"[33]

The conference included ten sessions spread out over four days, as well as the more public events, which included the unveiling of the Khortitsa Church plaque and the Nieder Khortitsa memorial. Dyck's recent graduate student and budding scholar, John Staples, was active throughout as Conference Secretary. A guest lecture by Professor Orest Subtelny, York University, Ontario, at the Zaporizhzhia State University attracted many Ukrainian students and academics. More than thirty scholars from Russia, Canada, Germany, the United States, Paraguay, and – of course – Ukraine were actively involved, and scores of others had also made their way to Ukraine from across the globe for the public events. Most panels were deliberately multinational and multilingual, though translation was available (the formal language of the conference was Ukrainian; the working languages were Russian and English).

Papers dealt with both the imperial and Soviet eras, from three perspectives: those that directly engaged sources that were previously unused; second, those that approached Mennonite history from new disciplinary approaches (as in women's or environmental history); and, third, those that sought to engage Mennonite history within the larger prism of Imperial, Soviet, or even European history. There were daily press releases of the conference, Ukrainian television reports, and newspaper photos and articles as dignitaries, foreign and local, participated in events. Perhaps no one was more affected by the events of these days than Boris Letkeman of Zaporizhzhia, a retired Soviet engineer whom Dyck described as a man with a great heart. Letkeman was moved to tears by the suddenly public recognition of his people after years of repression and silence. He said, "Now I and my fellow Mennonites can walk on the street of Zaporizhzhia with our heads held high."

Within the conference itself, as one might expect, scholars disagreed about the relative role that Mennonites played in Ukrainian history and about the role that the famed Mennonite "Privilegium" had played in Mennonite economic success, among other topics. They conversed in Russian, German, and English, and occasionally in a mixture of all three. They wandered through village cemeteries graced by new monuments, along dusty side streets; they sat in vast public squares adjacent to broad tree lined avenues that marked both Stalinist modernism and post-Stalinist decline. They toured a museum filled with Canadian Mennonite artefacts that had originally come from the very lands that they were now displayed on. They walked to the Dnipro River and imagined how it must have looked in 1789. It is safe to say that there had never been an academic conference like it in "Russian" Mennonite studies, nor has there been since. In the end, this publication owes its very existence to the scholarly interactions and collegiality fostered by *Khortitsa '99*. Of no less significance, the public memorialization of the Mennonite experience in Ukraine – perhaps the greatest legacy of that first encounter between Dyck and Venger in the Zaporozhe archive – was only possible because of the public and political attention to Ukraine's Mennonites occasioned by that same conference.

A final comment: My meetings with Aleksander Tedeev in Zaporizhzhia, and in Dnipropetrovsk with members of the institute in the summer of 2011 about this particular publication project, were ones of great and mixed emotion. On the one hand, Ukrainian colleagues were delighted to know that their voices would finally be heard in the English speaking world; that the legacy of *Khortitsa '99* would continue. But on the other, they were worried that the foundation laid by Dyck and others would not be adequately built upon. In a sense, having lived through the isolation that came with being a closed city in Soviet times, they now feared that their own research and writing would similarly be shut out by scholars and a readership that was unable to read their works, or to appreciate the depth of their analysis.

May this volume be a positive step, then, in drawing attention to the work of the tireless scholars and archivists, in Ukraine especially, those who daily work in very difficult circumstances to tell a story of regional identity formation that has utterly captivated them. It is thanks to all of them that the opportunity to understand Imperial Russian, Ukrainian, and Soviet Mennonite history has never been better than it is now. With such a past of rich and compelling complexity, one can only hope that the future of Mennonite studies is a bright one. May this volume stand as a contribution to that worthy aspiration.

NOTES

1 Email from Nataliya Venger to author, 30 July 2013. Though the university is now known as Oles Honchar Dnipropetrovsk National University, it was named after the 300th anniversary of the reunification of Ukraine with Russia during the Soviet era. Email from Serhii Plokhy to author, 26 July 2013.

2 Email from Serhii Plokhy to author, 26 July 2013.

3 S.I. Bobyleva, "Izuchenie problem istorii I kul'tury Nemetsko-Mennonitstkovo Issledovanii Dnipropetrovskogo Natsional'nogo Universitata," in *Voprosy Germanskoi Istorii* (2007), 12; email from Serhii Plokhy to author, 26 July 2013; and email from Nataliya Venger to author, 30 July 2013.

4 Bobyleva, "Izuchenie problem istorii," 12.

5 Email from Serhii Plokhy to author, 12 July 2013.
6 I.N. Ipatov, *Kto takie Mennonity* (Kazakhstan, 1978).
7 Email from Serhii Plokhy to author, 12 July 2013.
8 Bobyleva, "Izuchenie problem istorii I kul'tury," 19.
9 Cf. E.I. Druzhinina, *Severnoe prichernomore v 1775–1800 gg.* (Moscow, 1970); E. I. Druzhinina, *Iuzhnaia Ukraina v 1800–1825 gg.* (Moscow, 1970); and E.I. Druzhinina, *Iuzhnaia Ukraina v period krizisa feodalizma 1825–1860 gg.* (Moscow, 1981).
10 Serhii Plokhy, "Mezhdu Liuterom i Menno: smena konfessii v koloniiakh Iuga Ukraina (pervaia tret 19 veka)," in *Voprosy germanskoi istorii: Ukrainskie i nemetskie sviezi v novoe i noveishee vremia* (Dnipropetrovsk, 1995), 42–57.
11 Email from Serhii Plokhy to author, 12 July 2013.
12 Email from Nataliya Venger to author, 30 July 2013.
13 Notes from interview with Nataliya Venger, Dnipropetrovsk, 12 June 2011.
14 Notes from interview with Aleksandr Tedeev, Zaporizhzhia, 15 June 2011.
15 Ibid.
16 Walter Unger, "About the Mennonite Heritage Cruise," http://home.ica.net/~walterunger/About-Us.html.
17 Notes from a phone interview with Paul Toews, 27 June 2011.
18 Jacob A. Neufeld, *Path of Thorns: Soviet Mennonite Life under Communist and Nazi Rule*, ed. Harvey L. Dyck, trans. Harvey L. Dyck and Sarah Dyck (Toronto: University of Toronto Press, 2014).
19 Notes from interview with Harvey L. Dyck, Toronto, 4 August 2011.
20 Ibid.
21 Notes from interview with Boris Letkeman, Zaporizhzhia, 16 June 2013.
22 Notes from interview with Nataliya Venger, Dnipropetrovsk, 12 June 2011. By contrast, some have suggested that a very different ethos within the western scholarly community may explain why Dyck's relations there were often more contentious, and his legacy more uneven.
23 Notes from phone interview with Paul Toews, 27 June 2011.
24 Notes from interview with Ludmilla Kariaka and Larissa Goriacheva, Zaporizhzhia, 15 June 2011.
25 See correspondence, for example, between Harvey Dyck and the Mennonite Heritage Village, Steinbach, Manitoba, in possession of author.
26 Harvey L. Dyck, "Memorializing the Mennonite Historical Experience in Tsarist Russia and the Soviet Union," attached to email, 17 September 2007, 1–2.
27 Correspondence, Harvey Dyck to Paul Toews, April 1999, in possession of author.

28 Ibid.
29 Harvey L. Dyck, "Introduction," in David G. Rempel and Cornelia Rempel Carlson, *A Mennonite Family in Tsarist Russia and the Soviet Union, 1789–1923* (Toronto: University of Toronto Press, 2002), xxxv.
30 Notes from my interview with Boris Letkeman, Zaporizhzhia, 16 June 2011.
31 I was the only western scholar to visit Dnipropetrovsk in Plokhy's time there, though others came in the years immediately following his departure. German historians Alfred Eisfeld (Göttingen) and Detleff Brandes (Düsseldorf) were among the first German scholars to visit, and to take advantage of these new scholarly possibilities. Both were senior scholars, both had established research centers at their respective institutions on the Germans of Eastern Europe, and both had entered into partnerships with the institute. As a sign of this new change of direction, the Dnipropetrovsk-based Institute hosted a history conference on the Germans of Ukraine prior to 1999.
32 Notes from my meeting with the Institute members at DSU, 14 June 2011.
33 Email from John Staples to author, 20 July 2013.

Contributors

Alexander Beznosov is a graduate of Dnipropetrovsk State University where he defended his doctoral dissertation in 2010, entitled "The Social-Political Life of the German and Mennonite Population of South Ukraine (1917–29)." He was previously senior instructor in world history at Dnipropetrovsk State University. He now works as a historian in the Department of History and Culture at the Institute of Ethno-Cultural Education in Moscow.

Oksana Beznosova is a graduate of Dnipropetrovsk State University where she completed her dissertation on "Late Protestant Sectarianism in Southern Ukraine (1850–1905)." She has worked previously as a senior investigator at the university, and is now project manager of the Local History Department at the International Union of German Culture in Moscow.

Svetlana Bobyleva is a professor of history in the World History Department at Dnipropetrovsk National University, Ukraine, and director of the University's Institute of Ukrainian-German Historical Research. Her extensive publications on Mennonites in southern Ukraine include *Zhivi i pomni: Istoriia Mennonitskikh kolonii Ekaterinoslavshchiny.*

Irina (Janzen) Cherkazianova received her doctorate in history at the St Petersburg Institute of History in 2009 with a thesis entitled "School Education among Russia's Germans: Problems of Church, State, and Societal Relations (1830–1917)." Cherkazianova lives in St Petersburg, Russia, and is the editor of the journal *Ezhegodnik Mezhdunarodnoi assotsiatsii issledovatelei istorii i kul'tury rossiiskikh nemtsev.*

Leonard G. Friesen is a professor of history at Wilfrid Laurier University, Canada. His previous books include *Rural Revolutions in Southern Ukraine: Peasants, Nobles, and Colonists, 1774–1905*; and *Transcendent Love: Dostoevsky and the Search for a Global Ethic*.

Viktor K. Klets is an associate professor of world history at Dnipropetrovsk State University, Ukraine, and a specialist in the history of the Second World War. He has published a number of works on Ukraine's Germans and Mennonites during the Nazi occupation.

Colin P. Neufeldt is an associate professor of history at Concordia University of Edmonton, Canada, where his research focus is the history of Mennonites in Soviet Ukraine in the 1920s and 1930s. His most recent publications include *The Public and Private Lives of Mennonite Kolkhoz Chairmen in the Khortytsia and Molochansk German National Raĭony in Ukraine (1928–1934)*. Colin and his family live in Edmonton, Alberta, where Colin also practices law.

John R. Staples is a professor of history at State University of New York, Fredonia. His publications include *Cross-Cultural Encounters on the Ukrainian Steppes: Settling the Molochna Basin, 1784–1861* and joint editorship of *Transformation on the Southern Ukrainian Steppe: Letters and Papers of Johann Cornies*, Volume 1: *1812–1835*.

John B. Toews enjoyed a forty-year teaching career in Medieval European history at the University of Calgary, Canada, and Reformation church history at Regent College, a graduate school in Vancouver, Canada. His many books include *Lost Fatherland: The Story of the Mennonite Emigration from Soviet Russia, 1921–1927*; *Czars, Soviets and Mennonites*; *Perilous Journey: The Mennonite Brethren in Russia, 1860–1910*; and *Journeys: Mennonite Stories of Faith and Survival in Stalin's Russia*.

Nataliya Venger is a professor of history and chair of the World History Department at Dnipropetrovsk National University, Ukraine. Her publications include *Ocherki istorii nemtsev i Mennonitov iuga Ukrainy*, *Na perelome epoch … Mennonitskoe Soobshchestvo Ukrainy v 1914–1931 gg.*; and *Mennonitskoe Predprinimatel'stvo v Usloviiakh Modernizatsii iuga Rossii*.

Index

Akulev, Mikhail, 39, 43, 58
Alexander I, 68–9, 112, 170
Alexander II, 79, 149
Alexander III, 39, 148, 150, 168
Alexandertal, 226, 250
Alexanderwohl, 157
Alexandrovsk, 158, 159, 163, 165
Anabaptist, 40, 115, 242, 243, 245

Baptist(s), 15, 18, 21, 40, 99, 111, 135, 141, 221, 224, 249, 253, 255
Berdiansk, 90–5 97, 108, 149, 266
Bergmann, Herman Abramovich, 98–9, 158, 160
Bessarabia, 9, 19, 91–2, 94, 102, 121, 124, 173, 176
Black Sea, 3–4, 9–12, 17, 25, 33, 49, 149, 182, 270, 288, 290, 310, 312
Brandes, Detlef, 9, 19, 332
Brezhnev, 4
Bulgarian(s) 75, 87, 94, 140, 142, 147

Catherine II, 32, 170–1
Catholic(s), 10, 25, 63, 88, 91–2, 98, 115, 161, 221, 255, 270, 297, 301, 328
Caucasus, 12, 20, 61, 63, 176, 187, 235, 327
Cold War, 4, 6, 13, 320
Coleman, Heather, 6, 18, 111, 131, 135, 141, 248, 249, 253
Colonist legislation of 1871, 94, 113, 117, 122, 124, 128, 131, 147, 173
Cossack(s), 7, 11, 19, 32, 35, 39, 321, 324
Crews, Robert, 110, 113, 126, 135, 137, 140
Crimea (Krym), 7, 9, 56, 63, 102, 176, 178, 183, 234, 242, 254, 285, 291–2, 294–5, 313, 327
Crimean War, 122, 133

Danzig, 10, 101, 245
Dnieper/Dnipro xi, 3, 33, 34, 211
Dnipropetrovsk National University (DNU) (Dnepropetrovsk State University) (Dnipropetrovsk State University), viii, 8, 11, 14, 21, 27, 56, 57, 315–16, 319, 330, 333–4
Doukhobor, 63, 78, 187
Duma(s), 98–9, 154, 161, 162, 165

Dutch, 86, 101, 105 160, 163, 183, 206, 219, 234–5, 288
Dyck, Harvey L, ix, 13, 21, 27, 76, 137–8, 172, 174, 255, 284, 311, 322, 324–6, 331–2

Einlage, 117, 138, 233, 238–9, 246–7, 252, 255, 256–8, 299–300
Eisfeld, Alfred, 27, 175, 297, 312, 314, 332

Friesen, Aileen, 12, 21, 129, 141
Friesen, Peter M., 56, 77, 138, 152, 173, 292

"German question," 147, 149, 150–1, 153, 157, 162, 166–7, 174, 280
Gnadenfeld, 69, 79, 95, 98, 148, 220, 250, 258, 297, 311
Greek(s), 7, 65, 75, 142, 150, 182
Guardianship Committee for Foreign Colonists, 72, 75, 79, 90, 111–14, 118–20, 122–3, 127, 136–7, 144, 170

Halbstadt, 71, 77, 90, 94–6, 103, 107–9, 138, 148, 157, 182, 193, 199, 203, 219–20, 253, 295, 297, 299, 303
Hierschau, 225, 226, 257, 259, 261, 283, 313
Hillis, Faith, 10, 20, 26, 56, 134, 141
historiography, 13, 14, 19, 28, 43, 62, 76, 120, 124, 137
Hitler, Adolf, 16, 54, 261, 269, 271, 282, 288, 291, 305–6, 308
Hitlerite, 241, 288, 295, 310
Hutterite(s), 112, 136, 137, 140, 187

International Red Cross, 49, 271, 273
Iushanle, 64, 68, 71–3, 79, 84

Janz, B.B., 187, 190, 193–4, 199–201, 204–7, 219, 245
Jew(s)(ish), 7, 11, 20, 50, 75, 108, 141, 221, 227, 228, 271, 289–90, 296, 298–99, 301

Kazakh Soviet Socialist Republic (Kazakhstan), 109, 271, 292, 311, 331
Keppen, Petr, 71, 80, 93
Kharkiv (Kharkov), 102, 138, 187, 236, 246, 273, 293
Kherson, 9, 33, 57, 92, 94, 96, 99, 152, 155, 170, 173, 175, 246, 265
Khortytsia (Khortitsa) church, 118, 137, 327, 328
Khortytsia (Khortitsa) island, 325
Khortytsia (Khortitsa) school, 90, 96, 277–8, 299, 300
Khortytsia (Khortitsa) village, 153, 158, 165, 204, 211, 218, 219, 237, 238, 247, 252, 255–7, 268, 285, 299, 300, 302, 304–7, 323, 327
Khrushchev, 4, 322
Kichkas, 158, 252, 304, 307
Klaus, Alexander, 116, 139–40, 170–1
Kleine Gemeinde, 31, 36, 58, 73, 80, 114, 118, 138, 140
Komsomol(s), 53, 214, 232, 306
Konrad, Anne, 265, 284, 286, 293, 313, 317
Kryvyi Rih, 246, 289, 305–6, 308
Kuban, 61, 121, 235
Kyiv (Kiev), 18, 59, 102, 134, 136, 170, 173, 176, 236, 244, 246, 273, 285, 288–90, 293

Letkeman, Boris, 307, 315, 325, 328–9, 331–2
Lichtenau, 118, 138, 226, 257

Liquidation Legislation (World War I), 154–60, 162–4, 168–9
Loewen, Royden, 20, 35, 58, 104, 109, 140
Lutheran(s), 10, 25, 63, 88, 91–2, 97, 101, 115, 118, 120–1, 127, 161, 255, 297, 301, 302, 328

Magocsi, Paul Robert, 7, 19, 261, 283
Makhno, Nestor, 14, 26, 39, 41–2, 44, 58, 59, 183, 189
Makhnovists, 37, 39, 45, 58
Margenau, 138, 253, 258, 287, 310
Martin, Terry, 13, 14, 19, 28, 43, 62, 76, 120, 124, 137
Mennonite Brethren, 31, 72, 77, 116–17, 121–2, 127, 129–30, 132, 136, 138–39, 188, 196, 205, 245, 253, 323, 334
Mennonite Central Committee, 19, 184, 196, 201, 203, 285
Ministry of Internal Affairs, 68, 89–90, 99–100, 118, 129, 138, 155, 163, 176
Ministry of National Education, 93–5, 97, 99–100
Ministry of State Domains, 68, 71, 90–1, 93, 111–12, 118–19, 125, 170
Mongol, 4, 7
Myeshkov, Dmytro, 9, 19

Netherlands (Holland), 10, 101, 183, 245, 273
Neuendorf, 238, 246–7, 252, 256–8, 299–300, 302
Neufeld, Jacob, 21, 266, 274, 281–2, 284, 288, 311, 331
New Economic Policy (NEP), 19, 50, 52, 53, 212, 223, 225, 262, 281
Nicholas I, 90–1, 170
Nicholas II, 135, 157–8, 160, 163
Nizhnaia Khortytsia (Nieder Khortitsa, Nieder Khortytsia), 158, 218, 238, 246–7, 252, 256–7, 301–2, 306–8, 315, 327–8
NKVD, 54, 222, 241, 243, 248, 278, 288, 292–4

Odesa (Odessa), 9, 35, 76, 81, 90, 95–6, 98, 102–03, 109, 136, 171, 172, 174, 182, 268–9, 273–5, 277–8, 295
OGPU, 212–14, 222, 224, 228, 241, 243, 264–65, 276, 278
Omsk, 9, 20, 100–02, 109, 174, 188, 255
Orenburg, 9, 20, 235
Orlov (Orloff), 94, 138, 286, 265
Osterwick, 165, 218, 238, 246–7, 252, 257–8, 299, 302, 306

Patterson, Sean David, 39, 58
Paul I, 112, 113, 146
Petershagen, 96, 118, 138, 251
pietism (pietists, piety, pietistic), 11, 14, 62–5, 74–7, 92, 107, 122, 130, 138
Plokhy, Serhii, ix, 6–8, 11, 17, 42, 135, 141, 166, 178, 289, 311, 317, 319–22, 330–2
Politburo, 213, 216–17, 232, 235, 293
Prussia(n), 10, 61, 63, 75, 87, 90, 112–13, 124, 131

Rempel, Gerhard, 289–90, 311–12
Riga, 95, 102
Romania(ns), 7, 290
Rosental, 255, 285, 302, 191, 205
Russification, 36, 89–90, 104–5, 122, 140, 150

Stalin, 19, 211–14, 216, 251, 284–5, 294
Saratov, 88, 92, 94, 97, 136, 173, 308–9

Saskatchewan, 16, 181, 185, 188, 196, 201, 206–08
Schmidt, Anna (Anni), 287–88, 310–11, 317
Schönhorst, 237, 252, 256, 258, 299–300, 302
Schönwiese, 191, 205, 206, 219
Selbstschutz, 36, 217, 235
Siberia, 9, 10, 13, 20, 21, 26, 51, 99, 204, 213, 243, 255, 261, 287, 311, 327
Simons, Menno, 10
Stalin, 19, 211–14, 216, 251, 284–5, 294
Stumpp, Karl, 54, 57, 275, 286, 295, 300, 309

Tatar(s), 6, 7, 12, 33, 63, 64, 66, 75, 78, 93, 95
Tavrida, 92–7, 102–3, 116, 148, 155, 157, 160, 165, 170, 176, 202
Tiege, 90, 157, 257, 258
Tiegenhagen, 114, 257
Toews, Paul, 20, 27, 31, 202, 205, 245, 323–5, 331

Unruh, Benjamin H., 183–4, 187, 194–5, 199–201, 203, 206–8, 272
Urry, James, 14, 18, 21, 62, 76, 79, 87, 106, 110, 116, 135, 137, 138, 141, 245

Waldheim, 221, 225, 229, 249, 258–9, 297
Wardin Jr, Albert, 15, 21, 111, 121, 134, 135, 139, 141
Werth, Paul, 11, 20, 86, 98, 110, 113, 131, 135, 146

Zagradovka, 265, 267, 275
Zaporozhe *Sech*, 32
Zemstvo, 31, 103, 157, 158
Zhuk, Sergei, 5, 11, 18, 20, 98, 108, 117, 314

www.ingramcontent.com/pod-product-compliance
Lightning Source LLC
LaVergne TN
LVHW090149080826
844660LV00013B/731/J

* 9 7 8 1 4 8 7 5 0 1 9 4 5 *